Mass Communication Chronology

1961 Key's Public Opinion and American Democracy

Kennedy makes nation's first live TV presidential press conference

Berelson's "Great Debate on Cultural Democracy"

Schramm team's Television in the Lives of Our Children *published*

1962 *Festinger's cognitive dissonance article appears*

Kraus's Great Debates

1963 *JFK assasinated*

Bandura's aggressive modeling experiments first appear

Networks begin one half-hour newscasts

1964 McLuhan's Understanding Media

1965 *Color comes to all three commercial TV networks*

Comsat satellite launched

1966 Mendelsohn's Mass Entertainment

Berger and Luckmann's Social Construction of Reality

1967 Merton's On Theoretical Sociology

Stephenson's Play Theory

1969 *Blumer coins "symbolic interaction"*

1971 Bandura's Psychological Modeling

1972 *Surgeon General's Report on Television and Social Behavior released*

McCombs and Shaw introduce "agenda-setting"

Gerbner's Violence Profile initiated

FCC requires cable companies to provide "local access"

1973 *Watergate Hearings broadcast live*

1974 *Blumler and Katz's* Uses of Mass Communication

Noelle-Neumann introduces "spiral of silence"

Goffman pioneers frame analysis

Home use of VCR introduced

1975 *ASNE's Statement of Principles replaces Canons*

1983 Journal of Communication *devotes entire issue to "Ferment in the Field"*

1985 Meyrowitz's No Sense of Place

1987 *Chaffee and Berger formalize "communication science"*

1990 Signorielli and Morgan's Cultivation Analysis

1991 Boyz N the Hood *banned from many theaters*

Kremlin coup against Premier Gorbachev

Gulf War explodes, CNN emerges as important news source

1992 *ACT disbands, says work is complete*

1993 *Ten years after "Ferment," Journal of Communication tries again with special issue, "The Future of the Field"*

Mass Communication Theory
Foundations, Ferment, and Future

Mass Communication Theory

Foundations, Ferment, and Future

Stanley J. Baran, Ph.D.
San Jose State University

Dennis K. Davis, Ph.D.
University of North Dakota

Wadsworth Publishing Company
Belmont, California
A Division of Wadsworth, Inc.

Communications Editor: Todd R. Armstrong
Editorial Assistant: Joshua King
Production Services Coordinator: Debby Kramer
Production: Forbes Mill Press
Print Buyer: Karen Hunt
Permissions Editor: Bob Kauser
Designer: Robin Gold
Copy Editor: Robin Gold
Illustrator: Patty Arnold
Cover: Ark Stein, The Visual Group
Compositor: Forbes Mill Press
Printer: Malloy Lithographing, Inc.

 This book is printed on acid-free recycled paper.

International Thomson Publishing
The trademark ITP is used under license.

Printed in the United States of America.

1 2 3 4 5 6 7 8 9 10—99 98 97 96 95

Library of Congress Cataloging-in-Publication Data

Baran, Stanley J.
    Mass communication theory : foundations, ferment, and future /
Stanley J. Baran, Dennis K. Davis.
       p.   cm.
    Includes bibliographical references.
    ISBN 0-534-17670-4
    1. Mass media—Philosophy.   I. Davis, Dennis K.   II. Title.
P90.B285   1994
302.23'01—dc20   94-16637

Dedicated to Sidney Kraus
Friend, mentor, and colleague

Contents

Era 2

Era 3

Era 4

List of Lists

Preface

This book is written at a time of considerable turmoil within the media industries, the field of communication theory and research, and the nation at large. In many ways, this ferment parallels similar eras over the past two centuries — times when rapid technological change outpaced our ability to predict or understand what was taking place. The stakes are high; the price to be paid for our failure to understand media is dear. Just look at this morning's newspaper: The impact of television violence is in the news again, so are banning rap lyrics, the information super-highway, questions about alterations in how election campaigns are run and how democracy is practiced, free press versus fair trial, and on and on. How are we supposed to take it all in and make sense of it?

Today, we enjoy two important advantages over earlier eras in understanding the very complex media/individual, media/society, and media/culture interactions. We can look back at the way media industries have developed and we can use existing theories to help interpret what is happening now. This book is written to help you do this.

A Unique Approach. One unique feature of this book is the way it provides balanced, comprehensive introductions to the two major bodies of theory that currently dominate the field: the social/behavioral theories, which some have labeled communication science, and the cultural/critical theories. We need to know the strengths and the limitations of these two bodies of theory. We need to know how they developed in the past and are developing in the present because not only are these two schools of thought the mass communication theory of today, they promise to dominate our understanding of mass communication for some time to come.

Many texts emphasize social/behavioral theories and either ignore or denigrate cultural/critical theories. Instructors and students are then forced to supplement their texts with books that introduce critical/cultural theories—books that often express open hostility toward social/behavioral theories. To solve this problem (and hopefully advance understanding of all mass communication theory) this book systematically explains the legitimate differences that exist between researchers who use the different theories. We also consider possibilities for accommodation or collaboration between them.

The use of history. This book assumes that it is important for those who study mass communication theory to have a strong grounding in the historical development of media theory. Therefore, in the pages that follow we trace the history of theory in a clear, straightforward manner. We include discussions of historical events and people that students will find inherently interesting, especially if instructors use widely available videotapes and other materials to illustrate them (such as political propaganda, the War of the Worlds broadcast, Hitler, and so on).

The use of topics. It is important, too, that students realize that theories have been developed to address important questions about the role of media—enduring questions that will again become quite important as new media are introduced. We must be aware of how the radical changes in media that took place in the past are related to the changes taking place now. Examples can be found in discussion questions at the end of chapters.

This book attempts this "engagement" with mass communication theory in several ways: discussion questions; reading lists; boxes that explain or illustrate important ideas, events, or theorists; chapter summaries; and an extensive bibliography.

The big picture. This textbook provides a comprehensive, historically based, authoritative introduction to mass communication theory. We have provided clearly written examples, graphics, and other materials to illustrate key theories. We trace the emergence of two main bodies of mass communication theory—social/behavioral and critical/cultural. There are many examples of each and an in-depth discussion of their strengths and limitations. We emphasize that media theories are human creations that typically are intended to address specific problems or issues. We believe that it is easier to learn theories when they are examined with contextual information about the motives of theorists and the problems and issues they addressed.

In the next few years, as mass media industries undergo rapid change, it is quite likely that understanding media theory will become even more necessary and universal. All of the old questions about the role of media in society and in people's lives will resurface with renewed relevance. This book traces how these questions have been addressed in the past and it provides insights into how they might be addressed in the future.

The supporting philosophy of this book. The philosophy of this book is relatively straightforward: Though today's media technologies may be new, their impact on daily life may not be so different from past influences. Changes in media have always posed challenges but have also opened up opportunities. We can use media to improve the quality of our lives or we can permit our lives to be seriously disrupted. As a society, we can use media wisely or foolishly. To make these choices, we need theories — theories that explain the role of media for us as individuals and guide the development of media industries for our society at large. This book should help us develop our understanding of theory so we can make better use of media and play a role in the development of new media industries.

Acknowledgments

In writing this book, we have had the assistance of many people. Most important, we have drawn upon the scholarly work of several generations of social theorists. Their ideas have inspired and guided contemporary work. It's an exciting time to be a communication scholar.

We work within a research community that may be in ferment but that is also both vibrant and supportive. In these pages, we acknowledge and explain the contributions that our many colleagues across the United States and around the world have made to mass communication theory. We regret the inevitable errors or omissions and we take responsibility for them. We are grateful to our reviewers: Samuel Becker, University of Iowa; Sandra Braman, University of Illinois; Ken Hadwiger, Eastern Illinois University; Khosrow Jahandarie, Eastern Connecticut State; Timothy Meyer, University of Wisconsin-Green Bay; Michael Salwen, University of Miami; Milton J. Schatzer, Pepperdine University; Ardith Sohn, University of Colorado; Glen Sparks, Purdue University; Mary Trapp, California State University at Hayward; Charles Whitney, University of California, Santa Barbara; and John Windhauser, Louisiana State University. They helped us avoid some errors and omissions but they bear no responsibility for those which remain. We also wish to thank Kris Clerkin, Robin Gold, Josh King, and Todd Armstrong, our Wadsworth friends, whose encouragement and advice sustained us. Their task was made less difficult than it might otherwise have been by our first Wadsworth editor, Becky Hayden. This accomplished professional taught us how to avoid many of the sins usually committed by novice textbook authors. She made us better writers, and in knowing her, better people.

Production work on the manuscript was handled in San Jose. The staff there did much of the mechanical work that is a necessary part of preparing any manuscript but for which little recognition ever comes. Special thanks to Sarah Clark.

We must also thank our families. We admit that this has become something of a cliche. The truth, however, is that it is the families of authors who must endure their detachment, bad moods, and absences as the book is crafted. In Grand Forks, the Davis family — Nancy, Jeni, Kerry, Andy, Mike — and in San Jose, the Baran family — Kim, Simmony and Chan — indeed suffered our detachment, bad moods, and absences. All did so with charm and love.

Finally, this book is the product of a collaboration that has gone on for more than twenty years. We started our professional careers at Cleveland State University in 1973 in a communication department headed by Sidney Kraus. Sid inspired us, along with most other junior faculty, to become active, productive researchers. Today, a disproportionate number of active communication scholars have direct or indirect links to the Cleveland State program. Sid demonstrates the many ways that a single person can have a powerful impact upon a discipline. Though his scholarship, his mentorship, and his friendship he has left a truly indelible mark.

SECTION *One*

Introduction to Mass Communication Theory

Chapter 1

Introduction

On Tuesday August 20, 1991, the Kremlin coup against the Gorbachev regime was in its second day when the world was treated to a fascinating display of the power of new communication media. Deep within the walls of the heavily defended Russian Parliament Building, a fax machine fed press releases from Russian President Boris Yeltsin to another fax machine in the United States. From there, the releases were transferred to Voice of America and Radio Liberty stations operating in Western Europe. These stations broadcast the releases back into the Soviet Union where they were heard by crowds of people standing outside the barricaded Parliament Building. This information was received even at the dacha in the Crimea where Gorbachev was under house arrest. To reach people standing within sight of the building from which the messages originated as well as reaching the deposed leader of the nation, messages literally traveled not only halfway around the world and back, but back and forth, 26,000 miles into space where they were bounced off a geostationary communication satellite. George Kennan, an architect of the U.S. Cold War and Soviet containment policy, was asked at the time by television journalist Jim Lehrer why the Soviet Union had undergone such a radical transformation. His response was immediate, the "communications revolution."

This example illustrates the tremendous ambiguity and flexibility of a whole range of new media that are transforming social orders and cultures around the world. Each new technological device expands the possible uses of existing technologies. New media can be combined to create media systems that span great distances but that can also serve a broad range of highly specific purposes. In retrospect, we might now regard the first century of mass communication as one dominated by expensive, clumsy technologies that provided very limited services to gigantic audiences. We were forced to accommodate our needs to what the old media technologies could provide. Highly centralized media systems were established and controlled by large corporations located in the largest cities. For most of us the term "mass media" still is synonymous with these "big media." Now, although we are caught up in a communications revolution, our attention is still riveted on the media dinosaurs. We are only beginning to understand the potential of alternative media to serve needs we didn't know we had.

As this revolution in electronic media gains momentum, each month brings significant innovations. Each year, important new technologies appear—digital audio tape recorders, compact discs, personal computers, video tape recorders, direct broadcast satellites, video disks. For many Americans the immediate consequences of this revolution have been both pleasant and benign. Sheltered within a stable social order, the new media have largely expanded our options for entertainment and information content. Instead of choosing from a handful of movies at local theaters or on three network television stations, we can select from hundreds of titles available on cable channels, videotapes, and video discs. By exchanging copies of records, tapes, and discs with friends, we can create large home music libraries. At any given moment we can tune to several different newscasts on television and radio. Using personal computers we can access remote data bases and scan endless reams of information on diverse, specialized topics. An array of print media are available—many edited to suit the tastes of relatively small audiences. The old marketplace of ideas has become a gigantic supermarket. If you want it, you can probably get it somewhere.

But the Russian example should remind us that there is more to modern media than glitzy entertainment or up-to-the-moment facts. There are good reasons why every competent military coup targets media for seizure. And it is not a coincidence that the spread of new forms of media technology is often associated with increased social instability. The old Soviet KGB's power was based on its control of communications technology. In the old USSR, you needed a license to own even a typewriter. The KGB yielded power when it lost control over newer forms of media when books, for example, could circulate in the form of audio cassette recordings. Media are the means by which modern social orders are created and sustained. But new technologies permit and in some cases require experimentation. Powerful new media industries can be created almost overnight and these industries can have the ability to reshape social orders and transform cultures. But the results of this change are often quite unpredictable. Therefore, we must develop theories that can give us greater insight into media's role in relation to social change.

In this textbook we will examine how media scholars have conceptualized the role of media during the past century. Our purpose is to provide you with a broad and historically grounded perspective on what media can do *for* you and *to* you. We have reviewed some of the best (and worst) thinking concerning the role and potential of media. We ask that you join us in looking back to the origins of media and the early efforts to understand their influence and role. We will trace the challenge of new technology and the rise of various media industries and focus on the theories that were developed to make sense of them. Finally, we will conclude with a review of current theory and assist you in developing a personally relevant perspective on media.

Keep in mind, though, that this is not a book about new media technology, although we will often use examples of new technology to illustrate our points and to demonstrate the relevance of various theories. Our purpose is to help you place new technology into historical and theoretical perspective. The challenges we face today as we move into the information age are similar in certain respects to those faced during the era of the penny press or the Golden Age of Radio. We can learn much from examining how people have tried to understand media technology and anticipate its consequences for their lives. The theories of past generations can assist us as we face the challenges of today's new media.

This book is structured chronologically. This organizational scheme represents, in part, our support of Rogers, Dearing. and Bergman's (1993, p. 69) belief that

> the most common means of investigating intellectual histories is the historical method, which seeks to understand paradigmatic change by identifying key instances of personal and impersonal influence, which are then interpreted as determining the parameters and directions of a particular field of study. A social scientific understanding of such histories, while acknowledging the importance of key instances of intellectual influence, must seek to identify patterns that represent influence over time.

Our chronological structuring also reflects our view that most social theories, including media theory, are never completely innovative and are always the products of the particular era in which they are constructed. Present-day theories are for the most part updated versions of old ideas, even when they provide seemingly radical revisions or sophisticated syntheses of earlier notions. To understand contemporary theories, it's important to understand the theories on which they are based. This does not mean, however, that mass communication theory developed in an orderly, chronologically stable way, with new, improved ideas supplanting older, disproved notions. Theories about media and violence, for example, have been around as long as there have been media (Wartella and Reeves, 1985). Concern about harmful media effects were voiced in this country as early as 1900 and were strongly articulated in the 1930s and again in the 1950s. The U.S. Congress reopened its consideration of the issue once again in the spring of 1993. The 1960s were the heyday of mass communication scholars' theoretical attention to the problem of media and subsequent viewer, listener, or reader aggression.

This book is also based on the assumption that <u>all social theory is a human construction</u> — *an active effort on the part of communities of scholars to make sense of their social world*. Individual theories often have many different objectives. Some forms of theory mainly guide the decision-making of political and social elites. These theories tend to focus on the *structure* of society and attempt to explain how it can best be preserved. Other forms seek transformation of the status quo. They explore the *dynamic processes* that underlie social change. Their purpose is to guide useful social change. Scholarly communities differ in what they want to accomplish with the theories they create. From one decade to the next, there are important, qualitative shifts in theory construction as new groups of scholars emerge with new objectives and new ways of organizing older ideas. For example, during times of social turmoil or external threat, scholarly communities often become allied with powerful elites and work to preserve the status quo. At other times, scholarly communities spring up that are critical of the existing social order and work to reform or transform it. Still other communities have long-term, humanistic goals that include liberal education and cultural enlightenment.

This book gives priority to one particular form of theory that we will refer to as *scientific theory*. In Chapter 2, this type of theory is described in some detail. Scientific theories <u>try to describe and explain</u> events objectively. Scholarly communities that develop scientific theory <u>use *empirical research* methods</u> to continually evaluate the utility and validity of theory. Empirical research <u>is conducted by making structured, systematic observations of events</u>. Based on these observations, erroneous ideas can be identified (and discarded) and valid notions can be developed. Empirical research permits increasingly useful theory to be developed and enables useless theories to be rejected. Throughout this book, we will describe the difficulties and limitations of scientific research. It is easy to speculate about the potential or problems of media but often hard to do empirical research to evaluate that speculation.

Many of the older theories reviewed in this book have been rejected after scientific research. They are no longer taken seriously by scientific researchers even though some of them are still widely accepted outside of scientific communities. As far as scientists are concerned, these are unscientific. They can't be verified by the research methods used within the scientific community. At any given point in time, there is considerable controversy over which theories have been validated or rejected by research. Sometimes, research communities are split because some believe that a particular theory has been rejected while others continue to support it. Proponents believe that better or more innovative research will eventually establish the validity of the theory.

We will consider <u>four distinctive eras</u> in the development of <u>mass communication theories</u>, beginning with the origin of media theory in the nineteenth century and ending with the emergence of an array of contemporary perspectives. As we explore each, we will describe the various types of mass communication theories that were constructed, consider their objectives, and illustrate both their strengths and their limitations. We will point out the purposes that these theories served and the reasons why they were replaced or ignored by later scholars. In most cases, these theories couldn't be validated by scientific research. Evidence was found that directly contradicted key notions. Eventually, proponents gave up trying to find evidence to support them and interest in them faded.

We will tell the story of mass communication theory development. This story should help you better understand how past theories evolved and why current theories are considered important. Although many of the older theories have been rejected as unscientific and are no longer used to guide research, they remain important as milestones (Lowery and DeFleur, 1988), and some continue to enjoy contemporary acceptance by segments of the public and some media practitioners. Most important, though, you can't adequately appreciate existing theories without some knowledge of earlier perspectives.

In recent decades, the number and variety of mass communication theories have steadily increased. Media theory has emerged as a more or less independent body of thought in the social science literature. This book is intended as a guide to this diverse and sometimes contradictory literature. You will find ideas developed by scholars in every area of the social sciences, from history and anthropology to sociology and psychology. Ideas have also been drawn from the humanities, especially from philosophy and literary analysis. The resulting ferment of ideas is both challenging and heuristic. These theories provide the raw materials for constructing even more useful and powerful theoretical perspectives.

If you are looking for a concise, consistent definition of theory, you won't find it in this book. We have avoided narrow definitions of theory in favor of an inclusive approach that finds value in most systematic, scholarly efforts to make sense of media and their role in society. We have included recent theories that some contemporary researchers consider unscientific. Some of the theories reviewed are "grand," they try to explain entire media systems and their effects on society. Others are very small and provide narrower insight into the use or role of media. Our selection of theories for inclusion in this book has been based partly on their enduring, historical importance and partly on their potential to contribute to future scholarship. This process is necessarily subjective and is based upon our own understanding of mass communication. Our consideration of contemporary perspectives has been limited to those that illustrate enduring or innovative conceptualizations.

Three Questions about Media

Throughout this book we weave a discussion of three issues or questions provoked by mass media that have driven and continue to drive the development of mass communication theory:

- What potential is offered and what threats are posed by *new forms of media technology*?
- What sort of media bureaucracies or industries should be created to *control or regulate media technologies* so that their potential is realized and their threats minimized?
- How can media serve *democratic and culturally pluralistic societies*?

These issues have provoked ongoing debate and controversy over the past century. Most theories in this book address one or more of these questions. With the development of new forms of media technology, old questions have resurfaced and new answers have been sought. Recently, video games and videocassette recorders inspired some of the same controversies sparked in earlier eras by the penny press, dime novels, and nickel movies. Cable television did the same, as did television before it and radio before that. These controversies are not new. They recur routinely in a predictable fashion whenever new media appear.

In every era, proponents argued that new media technology had the potential to interconnect people in powerful new ways, that technology could aid the formation of new communities by bridging cultural differences and dissolving barriers posed by space and time. New media advocates offered novel ways of structuring media industries to use this potential. Advocates looked forward to the creation of ideal social orders in which media would serve as a bulwark for democracy, cultural pluralism, and dynamic yet stable social change. Inevitably, media proponents were and are opposed by critics who charge that new technologies are inherently dangerous, that they will inevitably undermine the existing social orders and precipitate widespread unrest and disorder. These critics support preservation of existing media industries and the status quo. For them, the risks associated with media experimentation are unwarranted. They regard the media proponents as idealistic dreamers and themselves as practical realists.

Media proponents also believe that media can be used to fundamentally alter our personal lives in useful, meaningful ways. They argue that new technology can expand each person's cultural and experiential horizons. They envision newly energized, *active audiences* in which people find ways of making media serve them so that their lives are more interesting and purposeful. Media opponents fear that average people will be overwhelmed by new technologies, paralyzed by the mesmerizing power of new media, and ultimately transformed into gigantic, *passive audiences*—a world of couch potatoes. Proponents foresee the rise of a responsible citizenry who use media to construct increasingly democratic forms of government while opponents see instead the rise of demagogues whose power is based upon the cynical manipulation of the public. Proponents envision ideal social orders in which new technology fosters cultural understanding so that people practicing many different cultures can live in harmony. Opponents argue that the same technology will sharpen and deepen cultural stereotypes and spread fears about other cultures. Thus, instead of creating harmony, new media will incite conflict or even open warfare.

It is impossible, for example, to discuss any aspect of the Rodney King beating in Los Angeles, the Simi Valley jurors' decision, the turmoil that verdict sparked, or the rage that fueled the disorder without talking about the media. For many of the citizens of South Central Los Angeles, the hovering television news helicopters symbolized intrusive media power. "As tension rose, and the skies of Los Angeles filled with smoke, the journalist's camera came to be seen by the rioters as another enemy rather than a witness to their anger," wrote *Columbia Journalism Review* (O'Neill, 1992, p. 23). Should we say that TV journalists caused this problem? Did they simply reinforce an existing condition? Would there have eventually been a riot no matter what news media did? To address such questions we need to look at theory and the research based on it.

Within academia, many scholarly communities developed to investigate the role of media. Sometimes these scholars worked in close association with either proponents or opponents of media. Funding for their work came from groups, foundations, or corporations that lauded or feared media. These communities created a broad range of media theories—from the media paranoia found in some mass society notions to the Global Village community envisioned by Marshall McLuhan in the 1960s. Often theories began as little more than listings of media hopes or fears written by media proponents or critics. As theories evolved, research was conducted based on these ideas and both the ideas and the research were critically evaluated. Occasionally, theories excited widespread public interest, as when Marshall McLuhan declared that the "medium is the message (and massage)." But more often, interest in media theory has been limited to universities, government agencies, media industry researchers, and special interest groups like Fairness and Accuracy in Media (FAIR) and the now-disbanded Action for Children's Television (ACT).

For example, the various theories of television violence inspired great controversy within the media industries and in academia by pitting industry researchers against university researchers and ACT (Rowland, 1983). But these disputes tend to receive little attention from the general public even when they are reported by the news media. Senator John Pastore became infamous among television network executives for his scathing criticisms of televised violence and inferior children's programming. But his name never became widely known.

Throughout of this book, you will find boxes that feature the three questions about media. Some boxes focus attention on specific events that highlight or illustrate an issue. Others deal with debates between different groups over an issue. Some discuss how a theorist addressed an issue and tried to resolve it. And still others highlight and criticize important, issue-related examples of bad media theory. We hope that you will find these useful in developing your own thinking about these issues. You will be asked to try to relate material in these boxes to contemporary controversies, events, and theories.

Most of the older controversies and theories featured in these sections had few long-term consequences. If we have learned anything about media over the past century, it is that media are not demonic forces that inevitably precipitate societal or personal disasters. Media alone don't create couch potatoes or foster massive political demonstrations. But neither are they benign agents of a New Order ushering in the Age of Aquarius. People using media have the power to create either division or community. Media technology alone is powerless to initiate useful change. But technology can augment and amplify the actions of individuals and groups and in so doing facilitate rapid and widespread social change on a massive scale.

Media technology does have certain inherent biases—it amplifies and encourages some ways of conceptualizing the social world and some forms of action more than others. We must develop theories that explain these biases if we are to use media wisely. Rather than simply provoking fear or inspiring optimism, media theory should serve as a tool that guides our understanding and use of new technology. Media theory should enable us to shape media industries that serve our needs and minimize unplanned disruption to our personal lives and the society around us.

Four Eras of Media Theory

This book is divided into five sections. In the first section (which you are now reading), we introduce you to this book, to mass communication theory, to the three media related issues and to media research (Chapter 2). In the remaining four sections (Chapters 3 to 14), we trace specific eras in the development of media theory. Each section surveys key events, theorists, and theories. Individual chapters give in-depth consideration to the most important theories. In each section, we discuss how world events influenced thinking about media and show a timeline to help you relate important events in the development of media to the appearance of various theories and theorists. Recommended class exercises encourage you to imagine how you might have regarded media had you lived in these eras. Chapters feature important theorists and their work, giving you insight into their concerns and motivations. Special attention is given to the three recurring media issues and to dominant perspectives on media in each era.

Each era was characterized by one or two dominant perspectives on media. When two perspectives were prevalent, they often were diametrically opposed. We will trace the rise and decline of these perspectives. In each era, claims about essential understanding of media's role were undermined by conflicting arguments, new research findings, or the appearance of a cogent new theory. With the decline of dominant notions, new perspectives gained adherents and the role of media was reconceptualized. In each era, the three issues we listed earlier were addressed in new ways, with new controversies and new theories resulting.

Within each era, the emergence of important conflicting perspectives can best be seen as the accomplishment of a research community working within the constraints imposed by its own values, pre-existing ideas, and research standards. Each research community was also constrained by competing theories, limited financial resources, externally imposed political restrictions, and social values held in the larger society. Although isolated theorists can produce innovative conceptualizations, research communities give recognition to, develop, and then popularize these notions. We will consider how such communities have grown and functioned as we describe the theories they fostered or rejected.

As we move through the various eras of media theory, you will gain an understanding of how current thinking about media has evolved. You will learn why certain forms of theory are now considered obsolete even though they may still appear interesting and potentially useful. Sometimes you will find that ideas that contemporary media scholars consider outdated are still discussed as valid in *TV Guide* or *Parent's Magazine*. You will learn why specific theories appeal to present day researchers as well as something about the research communities in which they work. You will learn about the discoveries that researchers hope to make as they work with current theories. In the last two chapters, you will be brought up-to-date on the two perspectives on media that dominate current media research and offered an overview of some of the most interesting work being done today within these perspectives. The advantages and limitations of these perspectives will be outlined. You will be encouraged to use ideas from both perspectives to think about your own use of media and the way that new technologies might affect your life and your social world. We hope that some of you will seriously consider a career in media research. We hope that all of you will become more active users of media, individuals who can take a leading role in shaping media to serve your needs and those of your community, nation, and world.

Now, we'll briefly summarize the four major eras in mass communication theory. This summary should help you anticipate topics that will be covered in much greater detail in later chapters.

The Era of Mass Society and Mass Culture

Our description of mass communication theory begins with a review of some of the earliest notions about media. These ideas were initially developed in the latter half of the nineteenth century as new media technologies were invented and popularized. Although some theorists were optimistic about new technology, most were extremely pessimistic (Brantlinger, 1983). They blamed new industrial technology for disrupting peaceful, rural communities and forcing people to live in urban areas merely so they could serve as a convenient work force in large factories, mines, or bureaucracies. Theorists were fearful of cities because of their crime, cultural diversity, and unstable political systems.

For many social thinkers, mass media symbolized everything that was wrong with nineteenth century urban life. Media were singled out for virulent criticism and charged with pandering to lower class tastes, fomenting political unrest, or violating important cultural norms. Most theorists were educated members of dominant elites who feared what they couldn't understand. The old social order based on a landed aristocracy was crumbling and so was its culture and politics. Were media responsible for this, or did they simply accelerate these changes?

The dominant perspective that emerged during this period is referred to as *mass society theory*. It began as a collection of contradictory notions — some quite radical, others quite reactionary. Interpreting mass society notions is difficult because they come from both ends of the political spectrum. They were developed by monarchists who wanted to restore the old political order and by revolutionaries who wanted to impose radical changes. The same basic criticisms of media were therefore advanced by ideological foes. In general, mass society ideas held strong appeal for any social elites whose power was threatened by change. Media industries, such as the penny press, were a convenient target for their criticisms. These industries catered to socially inferior audiences using simple, often sensational content. They were easily attacked as symptomatic of a sick society — one which either needed to return to old values (monarchism) or be forced to adopt a set of totally new values (revolution). During this period, many intense political conflicts strongly affected thinking about the mass media.

The essential argument of mass society theory is that media undermine the traditional social order. To cope with this disruption, steps must be taken to either restore the old order or institute a new order. But who should do this? Should established authorities be trusted to take control of media? Should media entrepreneurs be allowed to operate freely? Should revolutionary groups be given access to media? At the end of the nineteenth century and the beginning of the twentieth, fierce debate erupted over these questions. This conflict often pitted a landed aristocracy whose power was based on tradition against urban elites whose power was based on the industrial revolution.

In time, the leaders of the industrial revolution gained enormous influence over social change. They strongly favored all forms of technological development, including mass media. In their view, technology was inherently good since it facilitated control over the physical environment, expanded human productivity, and generated new forms of material wealth. New technology would bring an end to social problems and lead to the development of an ideal social world. But in the short-term, industrialization brought with it enormous problems—exploitation of workers, pollution, and social unrest.

Today, the fallacies of both the technology critics and advocates are quite apparent. Mass society notions greatly exaggerated the ability of media to quickly undermine social order. The theory failed to consider that media's power ultimately lies in the freely chosen uses that audiences make of it. Mass society thinkers were unduly paternalistic and elitist in their criticism of average people and in their fear that media's corruption of the masses would inevitably bring social and cultural ruin. But technology advocates were also misguided and failed to acknowledge the many unnecessary, damaging consequences that resulted from applying technology without adequate consideration for its impact.

Emergence of a Scientific Perspective on Mass Communication

Mass society notions were especially dominant among media theorists during the 1930s and into the 1940s. They have enjoyed intermittent popularity since then whenever new technology poses a threat to the status quo. During the 1930s world events seemed to continually confirm the truth of mass society ideas. In Europe, reactionary and revolutionary political movements used media in their struggles for political power. German Nazis introduced propaganda techniques that ruthlessly exploited the power of new media technology. These practices seemed to permit political leaders to easily manipulate public attitudes and beliefs. All across Europe, totalitarian leaders like Hitler, Stalin, and Mussolini rose to political power and were able to exercise seemingly total control over vast populations.

Private ownership of media, especially broadcast media, was replaced by direct government control in most European nations. An important exception occurred in Great Britain where an independent public corporation, The British Broadcasting Corporation (BBC), was established to operate broadcast media. The explicit purpose of all these efforts was to maximize the usefulness of media in the service of society. But the unintended outcome in most cases was to place enormous power in the hands of ruthless leaders who were convinced that they personally embodied what was best for all their citizens.

At the very peak of their popularity during the 1930s, mass society notions came under attack from a most unlikely source—an Austrian immigrant trained in psychological measurement who fled Nazi Germany on a Ford Foundation fellowship (Lazarsfeld, 1969). That immigrant was Paul Lazarsfeld, and for the field of mass communication research he proved to be the right person in the right place at the right time. Like many of his academic colleagues, Lazarsfeld was interested in exploring the potential of newly developed social science methods, such as surveys and field experiments, to understand and solve social problems. He combined academic training with a high level of entrepreneurial skill. Within a few years after arriving in the United States, he had established a very active and successful social research center, the Bureau for Applied Social Research at Columbia University. Despite the generic name, the bureau conducted considerable media-related research throughout its early years.

Lazarsfeld provides a classic example of a transitional figure in theory development—someone well grounded in past theory but also innovative enough to consider other ideas and methods for evaluating theory. Though quite familiar with and very sympathetic to mass society notions (Lazarsfeld, 1941), Lazarsfeld was above all an empiricist. He argued that it wasn't enough to merely speculate about the influence of media on society. Instead, he proposed to conduct carefully designed, elaborate field experiments in which he would be able to observe media influence and measure its magnitude. It was not enough to assume that political propaganda is powerful—you needed hard evidence to prove the existence of such effects (Lazarsfeld, et. al., 1944). His most famous efforts, the Voter Studies, actually began as an attempt to demonstrate the media's power, yet proved, at least to him and his colleagues, just the opposite.

By the early 1950s, Lazarsfeld's work had generated an enormous amount of data (by pre-computer standards). Interpretation of this data led him to conclude that media were not nearly as powerful as previously imagined. Instead, he found that people had numerous ways of resisting media influence and were influenced by many competing factors. Rather than serving as a disruptive social force, media seemed to reinforce existing social trends and strengthen rather than threaten the status quo. He found little evidence to support the worst fears of mass society theorists. Though Lazarsfeld never labeled his theory, it is now referred to as the limited effects perspective.

Today, the limited effects perspective encompasses a large number of smaller media theories. These view media as playing a very limited role in the lives of individuals and the larger society. Many of these theories are widely used in guiding research even though their shortcomings are recognized. They are especially useful in explaining the short-term influence of routine media usage by various types of audiences. A number of these theories are referred to as *administrative* theories because they are used to guide administrative decisions. For example, they might guide television advertisers as they develop and evaluate campaign strategies to boost sales.

The Limited Effects Paradigm Emerges

During the 1950s limited effects notions about media continued to gain acceptance within academia. Several important clashes occurred between its adherents and those who supported mass society ideas (Bauer and Bauer, 1960). In 1960, several classic studies of media effects (Klapper, 1960; Campbell, Converse, Miller, and Stokes, 1960; Deutschmann and Danielson, 1960) were published that provided apparently definitive support for the limited effects notions. By 1961, V.O. Key had published *Public Opinion and American Democracy*, a theoretical and methodological *tour de force* that integrated limited effects notions with social and political theory to create a perspective that is now known as *Elite Pluralism*. Advocates of mass society notions came under increasing attack as "unscientific" or "irrational" because they questioned "hard scientific findings." They were further discredited within academia because they became associated with the anti-communist "Red Scare" promoted by Senator Joseph McCarthy in the early 1950s. McCarthy and his allies focused considerable attention on purging alleged Communists from the media. These purges were justified using mass society arguments—average people needed to be protected from media manipulation.

By the mid-1960s, the debate between mass society and limited effects notions appeared to be over—at least within the mass communication research community. The body of empirical research findings continued to grow and almost all of these findings were consistent with the latter view. Little or no empirical research supported mass society theory. This was not surprising since most empirical researchers trained at this time were warned against its fallacies. For example, in the 1960s, a time of growing concern about violence in America and the dissolution of respect for authority, researchers and theorists from psychology, not mass communication, were most active and prominent in examining television's contribution to these societal ills (we will examine their efforts in Chapter 9).

Many communication scientists stopped looking for powerful media effects and concentrated instead on documenting modest, limited effects. Some of the original media researchers had become bored with media research and returned to work in political science or sociology. In a controversial essay, Bernard Berelson, one of the men who worked closely with Paul Lazarsfeld, declared the field of communication research to be dead (Berelson, 1959). There simply was nothing left to study. Berelson argued that it was time to move on to more important work. Ironically, he wrote his essay just before the field of media research underwent explosive growth. Throughout the late 1960s and the 1970s, students flooded into journalism schools and communication departments. As these grew, so did their faculty. As the number of faculty increased, so did the volume of research. But was there anything left to study?

Cultural Criticism: A Challenge to the Limited Effects Paradigm

Though most American social researchers found limited effects notions and the empirical research findings on which they were based persuasive, researchers in other parts of the world were less convinced. Mass society notions continued to flourish in Europe where both left-wing and right-wing concern about the power of media was deeply rooted in World War II experiences with propaganda. Europeans were also skeptical about the power of quantitative social research methods to verify and develop social theory. These methods were widely viewed as a distinctly American fetish. Some European academics were resentful of the influence enjoyed by Americans after World War II. They argued that American empiricism was both simplistic and intellectually sterile. Although some European academics welcomed and championed American ideas, others strongly resisted them and argued for maintaining approaches considered to be less biased or more traditionally European.

One group of European social theorists who vehemently resisted post-war U.S. influence are the neomarxists (Hall, 1982). These left-wing social theorists believe that media enable dominant social elites to maintain their power. Media provide the elite with a convenient, subtle, yet highly effective means of promoting world views favorable to their interests. Mass media can be viewed, they argue, as a public arena in which cultural battles are fought and a dominant or hegemonic culture is forged. Elites dominate these struggles because they start with important advantages. Opposition is marginalized and the status quo is presented as the only logical, rational way of structuring society. Within neomarxist theory, efforts to examine media institutions and interpret media content came to have high priority.

During the 1960s, neomarxists in Britain developed a school of social theory widely referred to as British cultural studies. It focused heavily on mass media and their role in promoting a hegemonic world view and a dominant culture among various subgroups in the society. Researchers studied how members of those groups used media and demonstrated how this use led groups to develop ideas that supported dominant elites. Researchers were surprised to discover that groups often resisted the hegemonic ideas and propagated alternative interpretations of the social world (Mosco and Herman, 1981). Although British cultural studies notions can be criticized for making easy assumptions about the influence of media, they revived important questions about the potential power of media in certain types of situations—questions that 1960s American media scholars ignored because they were skeptical about the power of media.

During the 1970s, questions about the possibility of powerful media effects were again raised within U.S. universities. Initially, these questions were often advanced by scholars in the humanities who were unschooled in the limited effects perspective and untrained in the scientific method. Their arguments were routinely ignored and marginalized by social scientists because they were unsupported by "scientific evidence." Some of these scholars were attracted to European-style cultural criticism. Others attempted to create an "authentic" American school of cultural studies—though they drew heavily on Canadian scholars like Harold Innis and Marshall McLuhan (Carey, 1977). This cultural criticism, although initially greeted with considerable skepticism by "mainstream" effects researchers, gradually established itself as a credible alternative to minimal effects notions.

Effects Researchers Strike Back: Emergence of Moderate Effects

Minimal or limited effects notions have recently undergone important transformations, partially due to pressures from cultural studies but also due to changes in social research methods. A new perspective has emerged which we will refer to as the *moderate effects perspective*. Several factors have forced a reexamination of old research questions concerning the power of media. New evidence specifies occasions when media influence can be strong (for example, Noelle-Neumann, 1973; Iyengar and Kinder, 1986). This evidence is being collected using innovative research methods that make it easier to study long-term media effects. These methods also enable researchers to probe short-term effects in greater depth, assisting them in locating some forms of influence that eluded earlier studies (Berger and Chaffee, 1987).

Which methods?

At the heart of the moderate effects perspective are notions about an *active audience that uses media content to create meaningful experiences* (Bryant and Street, 1988). The moderate effects perspective acknowledges that important media effects can occur over longer periods of time as a direct consequence of viewer or reader intent. People can make media serve certain purposes, such as using media to learn information and induce meaningful experiences.

This "meaning making perspective" asserts that when people use media to make meaning—when they are able to intentionally induce desired experiences—there are significant results. Sometimes these consequences are intended by consumers, but sometimes results are not anticipated and are not wanted. Factors that intrude into and disrupt this making of meaning may have quite unpredictable consequences. The perspective implies that future research should focus on people's success or failure in their efforts to make meaning using media. Both intended and unintended consequences of media use should be studied.

Theorists who develop moderate effects ideas have struggled with a critical deficiency in older limited effects notions. The limited effects perspective was unable to understand or make predictions about media's role in cultural change. By flatly rejecting the possibility that media will play an important role in such change, theorists were unable to make sense of striking instances where the power of media appears to be obvious. For example, limited effects theorists are forced to deny that media could have played a significant role in the Civil Rights, Anti-Vietnam War, Women's, and the 1960s counter-culture movements. Yet leaders of these movements made significant use of media, both to recruit and communicate with members and as a vehicle to express their views to the public. Moreover, a little common sense and a touch of historical reflection would argue that these movements were quite successful in their media use. One possible cause of the limited effects perspective's failure to account for these obvious examples of large-scale media influence rests in the notion of *levels of analysis*.

Social research problems can be studied at a number of levels, from the *macroscopic* to the *microscopic*. Researchers, for example, can study media impact on cultures, societies or nations, organizations or groups, small groups, and individuals. It should be possible to approach the issue of media effects at any of these levels and discover comparable results. But the limited effects researchers tended to focus their attention on the microscopic level, especially on individuals, from whom they could easily and efficiently collect data. When they had difficulty consistently demonstrating effects at the micro level, they tended to dismiss the possibility of effects at the cultural, or macroscopic, level.

For example, the limited effects perspective denied that advertising imagery could cause significant cultural changes. Instead, it argued that advertising merely reinforces existing social trends. At best (or worst), advertisers or politicians merely take advantage of these trends to serve their purposes. Thus, political candidates may be successful in seizing upon patriotism and racial backlash to promote their candidacies in much the same way that product advertisers exploit what they think are attitude trends among Yuppies or the Baby Boom generation.

These reinforcement arguments may be valid, but in their early forms they were unnecessarily limited in scope. Moderate effects theorists developed reinforcement notions into a broader theory that identifies important new categories of media influence. These theorists argue that at any point in time, there will be many conflicting or opposing social trends. Some will be easier to reinforce using the marketing techniques available to advertisers. Potentially useful trends may be undermined as public attention is drawn toward opposing ones. From among the trends that can be easily reinforced by existing marketing techniques, advertisers and political consultants are free to base their promotional communication on those that are likely to best serve their short-term self interests rather than the long-term public good. Thus, many potentially constructive social trends may fail to develop because existing techniques can't easily reinforce them or because opposing trends are reinforced by advertisers seeking immediate profits. The very same Saturday morning cartoons that promote the sale of sugared cereals might just as effectively encourage child viewers to consume healthier food.

Ongoing Debate over Issues

The popularity of cultural studies and the rise of moderate effects notions have intensified discussion of the three media related issues. No doubt you've been involved in arguments over violence and sexism on MTV, media coverage of the 1991 Gulf Crisis, and any of a number of media effects issues. But though this debate could stimulate increased research and the development of better theories, it could also generate more heat than light. We must better understand why it has been so hard to come to a clear understanding of media influence and why it has been so easy to promote fallacious ideas about media.

The closing chapters of this book will look at the two emerging perspectives on media, how they address the three media related issues, and how they are translated into contemporary research efforts. You will be encouraged to use these theories to develop your own positions on the issues and to defend your views against alternate arguments. The theories in this book will remain abstract ideas until you incorporate them into your own views about media and their importance in your life. Ultimately, you are responsible for making media work for you and for guarding against negative consequences.

We are entering a period in history not unlike the close of the nineteenth century—an era in which an array of innovative media technologies might be shaped into powerful new media institutions. Have we learned enough from the past to face this challenging and uncertain future? Will we merely watch as media entrepreneurs shape new media institutions to fill gaps created by the collapse of existing institutions? Or will we be part of an effort to shape new institutions that better serve our own needs and the long-term needs of the communities in which we live? We invite you to address these questions as you read this book, and we will pose them as a final challenge.

Significant Readings

Delia, Jesse (1987). "Communication Research: A History." In C. Berger and S. Chaffee, eds., *Handbook of Communication Science.* Beverly Hills, CA: Sage.

Lazarsfeld, Paul F. (1969). "An Episode in the History of Social Research: A Memoir." In D. Flemming and B. Bailyn, eds., *The Intellectual Migration: Europe and America, 1930–1960.* Cambridge, MA: Belknap Press of Havard University.

Lowery, Shearon and DeFleur, Melvin (1988). *Milestones in Mass Communication Research.* White Plains, NY: Longman.

Rogers, Everett M. (1986). "History of Communication Science." In E.M. Rogers, ed., *Communication Technology: The New Media in Society.* New York: Free Press.

Wartella, Ellen and Reeves, Byron (1985). "Historical Trends in Research on Children and the Media 1900–1960." *Journal of Communication,* 35: 118–133.

Chapter 2

Mass Communication Theory

We can't see quarks. We don't even have pictures of them. Yet we believe they exist. Why? Because scientists, ever since the mid 1960s, have theorized that these subatomic particles exist inside protons and neutrons. The existence of quarks was supposedly proven in 1990 when scientists at the Stanford Linear Accelerator Center in California shot some electrons down a two-mile-long tube into some hydrogen and then used two magnetic spectrometers (one weighing 880 tons, the other 650) to detect what happened when the speeding electrons banged into the hydrogen's protons and neutrons.

Too confusing? Richard Taylor, the scientist who received the Nobel Prize for science in 1990, tried to explain it as comparable to shooting at a pillow that has a rock in it. The pillow is the proton and the rock is the quark. "Sooner or later, you'd make one shot that hits the rock, and the bullet would bounce sideways," he explained. "It was analyzing those patterns that led to the conclusion that we were actually looking at small things inside the proton" (Gottlieb, 1990, p. 7A). The Swedish Academy of Sciences, when they awarded the Nobel to Taylor, called it "one of the most dramatic events in the history of physics."

But no one has ever seen a quark, just the spectrometer's measure of an electron's bad hop after hitting something like a stone in a pillow. Still, we're convinced that the quark exists and that science has actually discovered what has been theorized for 30 years to exist, the nucleus of the atom.

Ours is certainly a society that respects and believes its scientists. Science has given us an admirable standard of living and a deep understanding of the world around us.

So why does our society have so much difficulty accepting the theories and findings of *social scientists*, those who apply logic and observation — that is, science — to the understanding of the social, as opposed to the physical world?

Overview

That's what we will look at in this chapter, questions about social science and the theories it spawns — specifically mass communication theories. We'll examine the difficulties faced by those who attempt to scientifically study human behavior and the particular problems encountered when the issue is human behavior *and* the mass media. We'll define theory and offer several classifications of mass communication theory, but most important, we will try to convince you that the problems that seem to surround the development and study of mass communication theory aren't really problems at all, but rather they are challenges that make the study of mass communication theory interesting and exciting.

Science and Human Behavior

At the center of our society's occasional reluctance to accept the theories of the social scientists is the *logic of causality*. We understand this logic. We'll use boiling water as a simple example. If we (or our representatives, the scientists) can manipulate an independent variable (heat) and produce the same effect (boiling at 100 degrees) under the same conditions (sea level) every time, then a *causal relationship* has been established. Heating water at sea level to 100 degrees will cause water to boil. No matter how many times you heat beakers of water at sea level, they will all boil at 100 degrees. Lower the heat, the water does not boil. Heat it at the top of Mount Everest, it boils at lower temperatures. Go back to sea level (or alter the atmospheric pressure in a laboratory test), it boils at 100 degrees. Repeated observation under controlled conditions. We even have a name for this, the *scientific method,* and there are many definitions for it. Here is a small sample:

1 "A means whereby insight into an undiscovered truth is sought by (1) identifying the problem that defines the goal of the quest, (2) gathering data with the hope of resolving the problem, (3) positing a tentative hypothesis both as a logical means of locating the data and as an aid to resolving the problem, then (4) empirically testing the hypothesis by processing and interpreting the data to see if the interpretation of such data will resolve the primary question that initiated the research" (Leedy, 1985, p. 82)

2 "A search for truth through accurate observation and interpretation of fact" (Leedy, 1981, p. 10)

3 "A special systematized form of all reflective thinking and inquiry" (Kerlinger, 1964, p. 13)

4 "A method . . . by which our beliefs may be determined by nothing human, but by some external permanency — by something upon which our thinking has no effect . . . The method must be such that the ultimate conclusion of every man shall be the same. Such is the method of science. Its fundamental hypothesis . . . is this: There are real things whose characters are entirely independent of our opinions about them" (Peirce, 1955, p. 18)

5 "A simplified version of the logic of scientific method can be summarized as follows: Scientists begin the encounter with nature by making observations. Somehow through a kind of creativity mill, a *hypothesis* is generated about how some process of nature works. On the basis of this hypothesis, a test or experiment is logically *deduced* that will result in a set of particular observations that should occur, under particular conditions, if the hypothesis is true" (Pine, 1989, p. 42).

Throughout this century, some social researchers have tried to apply the scientific method to the study of human behavior and society. As we noted in Chapter 1, Paul Lazarsfeld was one of the first to advocate applying social research methods to the study of mass media. There were a number of other important pioneers whose work we will consider in later chapters — Carl Hovland, Bernard Berelson and Elihu Katz to name only a few. Although the essential logic of the scientific method is quite simple, its application in the social sciences can be quite complicated. Frequently, the research situation faced by social researchers resembles that of the people who theorized and then tried to gather evidence about quarks. Social scientists conceptualize things that can't be seen and then measure their influence *indirectly* by watching for their presumed influence on things that can be observed. Do quarks exist? Do attitudes exist?

Take, as another example, the much discussed issue of press coverage of political campaigns and its impact on voter turnout. We know that more media attention is paid to elections than ever before. Today, television permits continual, eyewitness coverage of candidate activity. Mobile vans trail candidates and beam stories off satellites so that local television stations can air their own coverage. Yet, despite advances in media technology and innovations in campaign coverage, U.S. voter participation, even with the increase that occurred in the 1992 presidential election, remains woefully low. The United States has one of the lowest rates of participation of all the democracies in the world. Can we assume that television campaign coverage has caused voting to decline? This is an assertion that mass society theorists would have been quick to make. Would they be right? How could or should we verify whether this assertion is valid?

As we shall see, this was the situation that the pioneers of mass communication research faced during the 1930s. There were precious few scientific studies of but many bold assertions about the bad effects of mass media. Individuals like Lazarsfeld and Hovland, though, were reluctant to accept these claims without making observations that could either support them or permit them to be rejected.

They faced many problems, however, in applying the scientific method to the study of mass communication. How can there be repeated observations? No two audiences, never mind any two individuals, who see political coverage are the same. No two elections are the same. Even if a scientist conducted the same experiment on the same people repeatedly (showing them, for example, the same excerpts of coverage and then asking them if and how they might vote), these people would now be different each additional time because they would have had a new set of experiences (participation in the study).

How can there be control over conditions that might influence observed effects? Who can control what people watch, read, or listen to, or to whom they talk, not to mention what they have learned about voting and civic responsibility in school, family, and church? One solution is to put them in a laboratory and limit what they watch and learn. But people don't grow up in laboratories or watch television with the types of strangers that they meet in a laboratory experiment. They don't consume media messages hooked to galvanic skin response devices or scanned by machines that track their eye movements. And unlike atoms under study, people can and sometimes do change their behaviors as a result of the social scientists findings, which further confounds claims of causality.

Four reasons make implementation of the scientific method a difficult task for social researchers:

1   **Most of the significant and interesting forms of human behavior are quite difficult to measure.** We can easily measure the temperature at which water boils. With ingenious and complex technology, we can even measure the weight of an atom or the direction of a deflecting quark. But how do we measure something like civic duty? Should we count the incidence of voting? Maybe a person's decision not to vote is her personal expression of that duty. Try something a little easier, like measuring aggression in a television violence study. Can aggression be measured by counting how many times a child hits a rubber doll? Is gossiping about a neighbor an aggressive act? How do we measure an attitude (a predisposition to do something rather than an observable action)? What is three pounds of tendency to hold conservative political views or sixteen point seven millimeters of patriotism?

2   **Human behavior is exceedingly complex.** Human behavior does not easily lend itself to causal description. It is easy to identify a single factor that causes water to boil. But it has proved impossible to isolate single factors that serve as the exclusive cause of important actions of human behavior. Human behavior may simply be too complex to allow scientists to ever fully untangle the different factors that

Box 2a Curiosity — Evidence — Knowledge: The Communication Scientist as Social Detective

by Dr. John A. Courtright, along with John Bowers, author of Communication Research Methods *and Professor of Communication at the University of Delaware.*

As you read the various chapters of this book, you will be exposed to (and hopefully learn) a good deal of information about mass communication and its widespread impact on our daily lives. Some of this knowledge will be straightforward and correspond to your common sense, while other parts of this knowledge base will be quite complex, highly theoretical, and may even run counter to your intuition.

Whether simple or complex, you may be surprised to learn that every bit of knowledge in this book represents the answer to one of several simple questions that scholars of communication routinely ask: Why? How come? What would happen if . . . ? Communication scientists are constantly displaying their endless curiosity by asking these basic questions and then systematically seeking their answers.

What makes the curiosity of the communication scientist — actually, *any* scientist — different from yours or some other nonscientist is not found in their superior intellect or charming personality. What is different is the approach that communication scientists employ to satisfy their curiosity. What distinguishes this scientific approach to asking and answering questions is a never-ending emphasis on *systematically* seeking the answers. This "system," in turn, consists of the numerous procedures, techniques, approaches, and analytic devices that communication scientists learn during their formal university training. Just as a carpenter must learn to use

skillfully a hammer, saw, and level, the communication scientist is trained to use the tools of his or her trade.

Putting aside the idea of formal training for a moment, the best way to think about a communication scientist is not as a carpenter, but rather to imagine her or him a detective who is constantly obtaining evidence to prove a case. A detective may *know* that a person committed a crime, but unless he or she can obtain the evidence, a gut-instinct isn't good enough. Similarly, a communication scientist may "feel in her bones" that television has a certain impact on a particular group of people (say, children under the age of twelve), but unless systematic and scientifically accepted procedures can produce convincing evidence of that impact, this scientist cannot persuade a jury of her peers (other trained communication scientists) of its existence.

clear analogy

Consequently, as you read the various sections in this book, remind yourself that what you are learning is the result of curiosity, followed by the systematic gathering of evidence. Even if a finding or theoretical assertion strikes you as nonsense ("I never behave like that!"), recall that the evidence has convinced knowledgeable scientists that the average person *does* behave like that (Maybe you're not average?). Finally, if you like the idea of being a social detective, you might consider pursuing a career as a communication scientist and scholar.

combine to cause observable actions. We can easily control the heat and atmospheric pressure in our boiling experiment. We can relatively easily control the elements in the quark experiment. But if we want to develop a theory of the influence of the press on political campaigns, how do we control which forms of news coverage people choose to use? How do we control the amount of attention they pay to specific types of news? How do we measure how well or poorly they comprehend what they consume? How do we take into account factors that influenced people long before we started our research? For example, how do we measure the type and amount of political socialization done by parents, schools, or peers? All of these things (not to mention countless others) will influence the relationship between people's use of the media and their behavior in an election. How can we be sure what *caused* what? Voting might have declined even more precipitously without television coverage. Remember the very same factors that led one person to vote may lead another to stay home.

3 **Humans have goals and are self-reflexive**. We do not always behave in response to something that has happened, but very often we act in response to something we hope or expect will happen. Moreover, we constantly revise our goals and make highly subjective determinations about their potential for success or failure. Water boils *after* the application of heat. It doesn't think about boiling. It doesn't begin to experience boiling and then decide that it doesn't like the experience. We think about our actions and inactions, we reflect on our values, beliefs, and attitudes. Water doesn't develop attitudes against boiling that lead it to misperceive the amount of heat it is experiencing. It stops boiling when the heat is removed. It doesn't think about stopping or have trouble making up its mind. It doesn't have friends who tell it that boiling is fun and should be continued even when there is insufficient heat. But people do think about their actions and they frequently make these actions contingent upon their expectations that something will happen. Do you generally go to a particular film only because you saw a single ad for it (simple causal relationship) or because, although never having seen any promotional material for it, you anticipate a good time — you go to the movie to make meaning, to create a specific kind of experience for yourself. For example, in one famous television violence study we'll discuss later (Chapter 9), young boys behaved aggressively, not because they had seen violent television shows, but because they *wanted* to see those programs. They were frustrated when experimenters denied them the ability to watch programs that they liked.

4 **The simple notion of causality is sometimes troubling when it is applied to ourselves**. We have no trouble accepting that the speeding electron knocked loose a quark; we relish such causal statements in the physical world. We want to know how things work, what makes things happen. As much as we may like to be thrilled by horror movies or science fiction films where physical laws are continually violated, we trust the operation of these laws in our daily lives. But we often resent causal statements when they are applied to ourselves. We can't see the quark or the breakup of the water molecule, so we readily accept the next best thing, the word of an objective expert, that is, a scientist. But we can see ourselves reading the paper and not voting and going to a movie and choosing a brand-name pair of slacks and learning about people from lands we've never visited. We don't need experts telling us about ourselves or explaining to us why we do things. We're not so easily influenced by media, we say. But most of us are convinced that other people are much more likely to be influenced by media (the so-called *third-person effect*). So although we don't need to be protected from media, they might. We are our own men and women, independent, free-thinking individuals. We weren't effected by those McDonald's ads, we simply bought that Big Mac, fries, and a large Coke because, darn it, we deserved a break today. And after all, we did need to eat something and the McDonald's did happen to be right on the way back to the dorm.

Schizophrenic Social Science

Another reason that social scientists often don't get the respect accorded their hard science colleagues relates to the schizophrenic nature of social science itself. Kenneth Bailey (1982, p. 5) wrote, "To this day you will find within social science both those who think of themselves as scientists in the strictest sense of the word and those with a more subjective approach to the study of society, who see themselves more as humanists than as scientists." In other words, not all social science adheres to the same standards for conducting research or accepting evidence.

This book is about mass communication theory, so let's take an expressly mass communication example: televised violence. Do you believe that televised violence can lead viewers to increased levels of aggression? Surely this must be an easier thing to demonstrate than the existence of unseeable quarks. This link has been theorized ever since the first silent movie hero slugged the first silent movie villain. This link has been scientifically demonstrated in countless studies and has been articulated before the U.S. Congress by the government's top scientist, the Surgeon General. But you know very well that every viewer does not go out and hit his or her neighbor after watching *Rocky XIV.* In fact, most viewers don't. In fact, some scientific evidence refutes the media and aggression link. But other survey, experimental, observational, and humanistic evidence argues that the connection does exist. On the other hand, there is observational, humanistic, and experimental evidence that it does not. So, the question remains: What is the most useful way to conceptualize the complex relationship that exists between specific forms of media content and individuals who use this content to induce experiences and to make meaning for themselves? To address such complex questions about the role of media, we must develop theories.

Defining Theory

Scientists, physical or social, deal in theory. Theory has numerous definitions. Bowers and Courtright (1984, p. 13) offered a traditionally scientific definition: "Theories . . . are sets of statements asserting relationships among classes of variables." Bailey's (1982, p. 39) conception of theory accepts a wider array of ways to understand the social world: "explanations and predictions of social phenomena . . . relating the subject of interest . . . to some other phenomena."

Our definition, though, will be drawn from a synthesis of two, more generous views of theory. Assuming that there are a number of different ways to understand how communication functions in our complex world, Steven Littlejohn (1989, p. 15) defined theory as "any conceptual representation or explanation of a phenomenon." Denis McQuail (1987, p. 4) also took this broader view, calling theories "sets of ideas of varying status and origin which may explain or interpret some phenomenon." These latter two writers are acknowledging an important reality of communication (Littlejohn) and mass communication (McQuail) theories: there are a lot of them, the hypotheses they produce are testable to varying degrees, and they are situationally based.

McQuail (1987, p. 4–5) even described "four kinds" of mass communication theory:

1 **Social scientific theory.** These theories are based upon and guide empirical research. They permit statements about the nature, workings, and effects of mass communication. These statements or *hypotheses* are tested by making systematic and objective observations regarding mass media, media use, and media influence. For example, theories of explaining the television and aggression link are typically social-scientifically based.

2 **Normative theory.** This form of theory explains how ideal media ought to operate within a specific system of social values. Theories of the press' role in a democracy would most likely fit here as would theories of media in an Islamic republic or an authoritarian state.

3 **Working theory.** This type of theory is normative, but with a practical bent. It involves not only how media *should* ideally operate, but how they *can* operate to meet specific ends. Theories of advertising and consumer behavior might fit here.

4 **Common-sense theory.** This refers to the knowledge and ideas (theories) that all of us have by simple virtue of being media consumers. Each of us has our own theory about why the quality of contemporary television is as it is.

No doubt other commentators on mass communication have suggested other means of understanding (theories) about mass media. Many argue, for example, that the best way to theorize about the media is through *critical theory*, defined as ranging "between, at one pole, spastic polemics against the status quo through 'criticism,' new or otherwise, of literature, drama, or art, from a liberal or even anarchistic individualist point of view, to sharp critical analysis of communications phenomena in their *systemic* context" (Smythe and Dinh, 1983, p. 123). But another author, writing in the same issue of *The Journal of Communication* (an edition devoted to "Ferment in the Field"), quoted sociologist and media observer Kurt Lang: "In the interest of gaining valid and meaningful knowledge, which is not the monopoly of any single tradition or school, we are all critical, with or without a capital 'C'" (1979, p. 83). What we see now is that much of our understanding of the mass media, and therefore many of our most useful theories, come, not only from social scientists, but also from social critics and social observers as well. Still, a good, useable theory should contain a *set* of statements that defines key concepts; specify the *relationships* between those concepts; *describe* some phenomenon through the use of those concepts; offer *predictions* about the phenomenon; and suggest *explanations* for the phenomenon's occurrence.

Mass Communication and Theory

But if we can agree on a very general definition of theory—something akin to Littlejohn's or McQuail's, not even demanding scientific proof, only reasonableness of our observations or explanations—why is there so little agreement about what constitutes a generally accepted theory of mass communication? Englishman and keen observer of American media and American media theory, Jeremy Tunstall, gave this answer: "'Communication' itself carries many problems. Either the 'mass media' or 'communication' would cover a dozen disciplines and raise a thousand problems. When we put the two together, the problems are confounded. Even if the field is narrowed to 'mass media,' it gets split into many separate media, many separate disciplines, many separate stages in the flow, and quickly you have several hundred subfields" (1983, p. 92–93). Or to put it another way, several hundred theories.

Now it should be clear that mass communication theory is really mass communication *theories*, each more or less relevant to a given medium, audience, time, condition, and theorist. But this shouldn't be viewed as a problem. Mass communication theory can be personalized, it is ever-evolving, it is dynamic. What we hope to do in the following pages is provide you with the basics: the traditions that have given us what we now view as classic theories of mass communication, some idea of the contexts in which they were developed and in which they flourished (if they did), the knowledge to decide for yourself what does and does not make sense, and some definite clues as to where mass communication theory stands today.

Box 2b   Questions, Questions . . .

by Joe Waterhouse, Associate Professor of Philosophy, San Jose State University

Thinking is asking questions. Thinking well is asking good questions.

Good questions aren't accidents; they occur only after the appropriate preparation. Preparation involves complete immersion in a field, immersion that can last several years and in some cases a lifetime. Preparation requires understanding what may be called the problem-situation; the array of background information for the problem, including the theories that offer competing solutions to the problem; and, the pros and cons of these theories. Typically every problem has several main theories that have been proposed as solutions. Understanding a problem means understanding why each of these proposed theories is both attractive and unattractive. These attractive and unattractive features are the pros and cons of the theories.

But preparation is not, by itself, sufficient for asking good questions. Progress is made in science when someone with the appropriate preparation has the creative imagination to ask a new question. This new question does not have to be complicated. In fact, frequently it is viewed later as an utterly simple one. Nonetheless, when first proposed, the question is new, provocative and fundamental—one that changes the field irreversibly.

And good questions produce an avalanche of questions.

You are a scientist. You ask questions, formulate various hypotheses as answers, evaluate these answers for yourself, and are led by this process to ask newer and deeper questions.

How are you going to be a good scientist? Ask questions! As you read a page ask one hundred questions. For each of those questions propose one hundred answers. For each answer ask one hundred new questions. Don't stop! Ever!

Texts are more than material to be learned: texts are resources for asking questions. If a text says that something is true, ask if it is always true, or only true in some circumstances. If it is only true in some circumstances, ask what these circumstances are. And ask why these circumstances make a difference. Ask what the evidence is for the hypothesis, and why that evidence is regarded as relevant. Ask if other hypotheses can explain the evidence. If some hypothesis will not work, ask why not. And, above all, always ask why! Ask why about every part of an hypothesis! Ask why about everything!

Suppose, for example, you start with the question—what is responsible for the recent political transformation in the Soviet Union? Many hypotheses could be proposed to answer this query; the one by George Kennan reported in Chapter 1 is that the communications revolution is the primary factor. But multiple questions now arise:

- How did the communications revolution produce the transformation?

- What produced the communications revolution?

- Is that which produced the communications revolutions in some way responsible in itself for the transformation in the Soviet Union?

- What is being referred to as a "transformation" in the Soviet Union?

- Is there a transformation throughout the republics of the old Soviet Union or only in some areas?

- If there is a transformation in some areas but not others, why?

- If the communications revolution has reached some areas and not others, why?

Box 2b Continued

- What is the evidence that the communications revolution is primarily responsible for the transformation?
- Are alternative hypotheses possible?
- Why is each alternative hypotheses rejected?
- Have there been transformations in countries not reached by the communications revolution?
- What produced the transformation in these other countries?
- Why didn't the forces that produced transformation in other countries work in the Soviet Union?

There is no end, no place to stop. Some answers to questions are better than others, but no answer is final. Not only does each question generate another question, but it is closer to the truth to say that each question generates innumerable additional questions.

Or does it?

Summary

Social science is often controversial because it suggests causal relationships between things in the environment and people's attitudes, values, and behaviors. In the physical sciences, these relationships are often easily visible and measurable. In the study of human behavior, however, they rarely are. Human behavior is quite difficult to quantify, often very complex, and often goal-oriented. Social science and human behavior make a problematic fit. The situation is even further complicated because social science itself is somewhat schizophrenic . . . it is many different things to many different people.

Nonetheless, social science develops theories—conceptual representations or explanations of phenomena—and tests the hypotheses those theories generate. Mass communication theory can be divided into four categories: social scientific, normative, working, and common-sense theories. The explanatory power of mass communication theory, however, is constantly challenged by the presence of many media, their many facets and characteristics, their constant change, an always-developing audience, and the ever-evolving nature of the societies that use them.

Discussion Questions

1 Can you think of any examples of social science evidence from any field that you accept? Any that you reject? Can you think of any evidence of media influence that you have either accepted or rejected?

2 Can you develop your own definitions of the scientific method and theory that are more useful to you than what we've suggested?

3 Do you believe what social science has told us about television violence and viewer aggression? Why or why not?

4 Think about the issue of the effects of media stereotypes of racial and cultural minorities. Do you believe that they can influence your attitudes towards members of those groups? Why or why not? What role did the media play in forming your attitudes about the Rodney King situation and the riots that followed the jury decision acquitting the four police officers?

Significant Names

Paul Lazarsfeld   *Denis McQuail*

Jeremy Tunstall

Significant Readings

Bowers, John W. and Courtright, John A. (1984). *Communication Research Methods*. Glenview, Il.: Scott, Foresman.

"Ferment in the Field: Communication Scholars Address Critical Issues and Research Tasks of the Discipline." *Journal of Communication*, 33, Summer, 1983, entire issue.

Littlejohn, Steven W. (1989). *Theories of Human Communication*. Belmont, CA: Wadsworth.

Pine, Ronald C. (1989). *Science and the Human Prospect*. Belmont, CA: Wadsworth.

Important Terms

Causality   *Causal Relationship*

Scientific Method   *Theory*

Third-Person Effect   *Hypothesis*

SECTION *TWO*

Era of Mass Society and Mass Culture

1926   NBC begins network broadcasting
Talking pictures introduced

1927   Radio Act of 1927 creates FRC

1933   Payne Fund's Movies, Delinquency and Crime

1934   Communications Act passes, creates FCC

1938   War of the Worlds broadcast

1939   First public broadcast of television
World War II erupts in Europe

1940   Lazarsfeld's voter studies begin in Erie County

1941   US enters WWII

1942   Hovland conducts first war propaganda research

1945   WWII ends
Allport and Postman's rumor study published

1947   Hutchins Commission issues report on press freedom
Hollywood 10 called before HUAC

Chapter 3

The Rise of Media Industries and Mass Society Theory

Reporters dependent solely on official accounts delivered at approved press conferences where more questions are ignored than answered. Government officials censoring reports before they are transmitted to the public. Tight control over the granting of press credentials, limiting them to "friendly" reporters. Physical fitness tests for journalists. Government agents removing reporters from the scene of a story at gunpoint. A military officer opening a press briefing with the welcome, "Let me say up front that I don't like the press, your presence here can't possibly do me any good, and it can hurt me and my people."

This can't happen in a democracy; maybe in Hitler's Germany or Stalin's Russia. It surely did happen as Chinese students protested in Tiananmen Square. But here in America we would never have accepted such a threat to our right to know.

But we did. All of these restrictions and limitations were imposed on the press during the 1991 Gulf War in Saudi Arabia, Iraq, and Kuwait. Public opinion polls at the time showed that more than 80 percent of the public approved of *all* military restrictions on reporting the war. Yet respected CBS journalist Walter Cronkite wrote in *Newsweek* magazine at the height of the war (February 25),

An American citizen is entitled to ask: "What are they trying to hide?" The answer might be casualties from shelling, collapsing morale, disaffection, insurrection, incompetent officers, poorly trained troops, malfunctioning equipment, widespread illness—who knows? But the fact that we don't know, the fact that the military apparently feels there is *something* it must hide, can only lead eventually to a breakdown in home-front confidence and the very echoes from Vietnam that the Pentagon fears most."

During the Gulf War, American journalists were thrust into a very troublesome position. Their professional values and standards demanded that they provide independent, objective coverage of events. But the military was determined to curtail coverage and channel it in ways that would build support for the war effort. Many of the commanding officers had learned about news media during the Vietnam War. They were determined to contain and control media coverage during what was designed to be a brief and limited war. Their plans were based on a knowledge that when wars begin, public opinion almost always favors "our boys." They recognized and exploited this advantage. Journalists were frustrated but there was little they could do. Their complaints went unheeded and, when voiced publicly, were seen as evidence of media arrogance or overaggressiveness.

For over a century now, the role of media has been debated. At times there has been strong public support for independent and aggressive media institutions. But at other times public support erodes amid charges of media irresponsibility or greed. Just how much can we trust independent media industries? Just how free should a free press be? Can social order be maintained if media aggressively pursue profits and ignore their responsibility to society? Should any action be taken if it becomes clear that media are doing things that undermine order and exacerbate social problems? And if action is deemed necessary, who should take it—government officials, the local police, community groups?

Overview

Clearly, a lot is at stake when we debate the role of media. Controversy over media influence can have far-reaching consequences for society and for media institutions. In this chapter we will trace the rise and fall of *mass society theory*. Mass society theory is an all-encompassing perspective on Western, industrial society that attributes an influential but often quite negative role to media. Media are viewed as having the power to profoundly shape our perceptions of the social world and to manipulate our actions in subtle but highly effective ways. This theory assumes that media influence must be controlled. The strategies for control, however, are as varied as the theorists who offer them.

As we review the rise of mass society theory, we will highlight central assumptions and arguments, many of which have failed the test of time or of scientific research. We must be careful not to brand all forms of media criticism as necessarily naive forms of mass society theory. Some of the arguments first raised by mass society theorists still deserve attention. We will return to these arguments in later chapters and see how they have been used by contemporary media critics.

The debate over media that we trace in this chapter is in many respects a critical battleground in a larger "culture war"—a continuing struggle to define the cultural foundation of the broader social order in which we all live. The participants in this war are drawn from all segments of society. Central to the conflict are media entrepreneurs—the people who risk capital for the right to earn profits by producing and distributing media content. These individuals are inevitably opposed by other social elites who object to their actions and distrust the power that they wield. The moral high ground in this struggle is claimed by all sides. Media entrepreneurs inevitably embrace the press freedom granted in the First Amendment to the Constitution. They argue, with considerable justification, that this freedom is fundamental to democracy. But critics charge that when press freedom is abused, when what they consider to be higher values are violated, then media must be restrained. But just who determines which values are higher and who determines when they have been violated? These are issues for the Great Debate over media.

The Beginnings

In 1896 William Randolph Hearst, a prominent newspaper publisher, sent a photographer to Cuba to cover the possible outbreak of war against Spain. Historian Luther Mott (1941, pp. 527–537) reported that the cameraman replied with this telegram:

> HEARST, JOURNAL, NEW YORK
>
> EVERYTHING IS QUIET. THERE IS NO TROUBLE HERE.
>
> THERE WILL BE NO WAR. WISH TO RETURN.

The publisher's reply was quick and to the point:

> PLEASE REMAIN. YOU FURNISH THE PICTURES AND
>
> I'LL FURNISH THE WAR. HEARST.

At the time, Hearst was publisher of one of the largest newspapers in New York City as well as head of a chain of papers that stretched as far west as San Francisco. He was a leader in the dominant medium of his era—the mass newspaper. Every city on the U.S. East Coast had several large, highly competitive papers, as did major cities across the continent. Competition, unfortunately, encouraged irresponsibility. Most urban newspapers resembled weekly scandal sheets like the *National Enquirer* that we find at today's supermarket checkout counters.

Hearst may well have sent a photographer to Havana because he intended to make up war stories that would sell papers, and his irresponsibility triggered harsh critical response. The first theories of mass media developed as a reaction against practices such as this—in other words, against the excesses of a maturing, highly competitive media industry.

This was a turbulent period in world history, one characterized by enormous social change. Industrialization and urbanization reshaped both Europe and the United States, initiating what is now referred to as the *modern age*. Most of this change was made possible by the invention and then rapid dissemination of new forms of technology. But technological change occurred with little consideration for its environmental, social, or psychological impact.

As with every instance of rapid social change, new social elites emerged and the power of old elites was challenged. In the late 1900s, increasing social control was wielded by a handful of industrial entrepreneurs—men who created vast monopolies based on factories, railroads, and the exploitation of natural resources. These men became known as the Robber Barons. The social change they wrought can be rationalized as progress, but a high price was paid—workers were brutalized, vast urban slums were created, and huge tracts of wilderness were ravaged.

Media were among the many technologies that shaped that modern era. An industrial social order had great need for fast and efficient distribution of information. The advantages of new media like the telegraph and telephone were soon recognized and each new innovation in media was quickly adopted—first by businesses and then by the public. During the 1860s, the telegraph was to the Civil War what CNN was to the 1991 Gulf War: It helped provoke and then satisfy widespread public interest in fast-breaking new coverage of the conflict. By the time the Civil War ended, the telegraph had spawned a number of "wire services" that supplied news to affiliated papers spread across the nation—the first electronically based media networks had been created.

In the mid and late nineteenth century, popular demand for cheap media content drove the development of several new media—the penny press, the nickel magazine, and the dime novel. High-speed printing presses and Linotype machines made it practical to mass produce the printed word at very low cost. Urban newspapers boomed all along the East Coast and in major trading centers across America. Newspaper circulation wars broke out and led to development of "yellow journalism," the irresponsible side of the penny press.

Intense competition swept aside many small circulation and more specialized print media. By increasing accessibility through lower prices, however, the new mass newspapers were able to serve people who had never before had easy access to print. Many papers succeeded because they attracted large numbers of readers in urban slums—first generation immigrants, barely literate in English, who wanted their piece of the American dream.

The Rise of Yellow Journalism

At the beginning of the twentieth century, every industry had its barons, and the most notorious — if not the greatest of the press lords — was William Randolph Hearst. Hearst specialized in buying up failing newspapers and transforming them into profitable enterprises. He demonstrated that the news business could be as profitable as railroads, steel, or oil. One secret to his success was devising better strategies for luring low-income readers. His newspapers combined a low-selling price with innovative new forms of content that included lots of pictures, serialized stories, and comic strips. Some experts even say that yellow journalism got its name from one of the first comic strips — The Yellow Kid.

Like most yellow journalists, Hearst had little respect for reporting accuracy. Events were routinely overdramatized. Along with other New York newspaper publishers, Hearst was blamed for initiating the Spanish-American War in 1898 through inflammatory coverage that goaded Congress to declare war over an unexplained explosion on the battleship Maine. Hearst's telegram to his photographer capsulized much of what was wrong with yellow journalism. Reporters typically gathered only sketchy details about events and turned them over to editors who wrote exaggerated and largely fictitious accounts. Not surprisingly, during this period the public status of reporters was among the lowest for any profession or trade. By contrast, the printers who operated high-speed presses enjoyed greater respect as skilled technicians.

Cycles of Mass Media Development and Decline

The rise of mass media in the 1900s followed a pattern of industrial development that has been duplicated following every subsequent "revolution" in media technology. Whenever important new media technologies appear, they destabilize existing media industries — forcing large-scale and often very rapid restructuring. Large corporations based on old technologies go into precipitous decline while a handful of the upstart companies reap enormous profits. To survive, the large corporations are forced into cutthroat competition to gain control of new technology. Sometimes they succeed and sometimes they fail.

This process is called *functional displacement*. For example, we are currently witnessing the decline of network television brought about by the growing popularity of cable television and of VCRs. At the same time we are seeing the rise of Turner Enterprises with its highly successful CNN cable channel. The movie industry is experiencing a strong resurgence fueled by videocassette profits and suburban theater revenues. If network television is to survive amid all this change, it must find functions that it can serve better than any of the newer media. Most corporations that control network television have already diversified their holdings and purchased companies that operate the new media.

The success of new media often brings a strong critical reaction—especially when they adopt questionable, competitive strategies to produce content or attract consumers. During the era of the penny press mass newspapers quickly displaced small circulation, specialized papers, and many did so using highly suspect formulas for creating content. These strategies became even more questionable as competition increased for the attention of readers. In contrast to yellow journalism, current day "Trash TV" programs like "Cops," "Hard Copy," "Geraldo," and "Inside Edition," are as tame as kittens. But yellow journalists justified their practices by arguing that "everyone else is doing it" and "the public likes it or else they wouldn't buy it."

New media industries often specialize in giving people what they want—even if the long term consequences might be negative. Unlike the "established" older media, new media lack the ties to other traditional social institutions that encourage or compel social responsibility. As each of the new media technologies developed and as industries grew up around them to assure stable supplies of attractive (if questionable) content, they necessarily displaced earlier industries and forms of communication. Often social roles and relationships were seriously disrupted as people adjusted to new media and their content. Most of these problems were impossible to anticipate. For example, during the 1950s one of the first serious sociological studies of the impact of television on American life found little evidence of disruption. The study noted that one of the most important changes brought about by television was that people spent less time playing cards with extended family members or friends. On the other hand, nuclear families actually spent more time together—mesmerized in front of the ghostly shadows on tiny television screens. Research by Schramm, Lyle, and Parker (1961) reported optimistically that towns with television actually had higher levels of library use and lower comic book sales than those with only radio. Given widespread public distrust of comic books in the 1950s, these findings implied that television could be a positive force.

As media industries mature, they often become more socially responsible—more willing to stop engaging in unethical tactics and more concerned about serving long-term public needs rather than pandering to short-term popular passions. Cynics say that responsibility is achieved only when it will enhance rather then impede profit making; that is, responsibility is possible only when cutthroat competition gives way to oligopoly—a handful of surviving companies stop competing and agree to carve up the market and the profits. In this situation, companies can turn their attention to public relations and eliminate the most offensive content production practices.

During the 1920s, two of the most powerful yellow journalists did just that, reforming so much that they succeeded in making their names synonymous with public service rather than bad journalism. The Pulitzer Prize and the work of the Hearst Foundation are widely (and properly) credited with advancing the professionalization of journalism and raising the ethical standards of the industry. Also during this decade, the American Society of Newspaper Editors was formed and pledged to "tell the truth about the news" in its famous "Canons of Journalism." A fledgling media industry had come of age.

The history of mass media in the United States has been one of ebb and flow between periods dominated by mature, socially responsible media industries and competitive eras characterized by innovative and sometimes irresponsible practices. About the time that competition among mass newspapers was finally brought under control, publishers faced challenges from powerful new entertainment media—records, movies, and radio.

As these newer industries grew, they also experienced periods of intense competition that tested or crossed moral and ethical boundaries. Censorship of the movie industry was hotly debated throughout the 1930s. Government control of radio was widely and frequently advocated. In time, each industry matured and carved out a particular niche in the overall market for media content. Each developed codes of ethics and means of applying these codes. In almost every case, new industries chose to engage in self-censorship rather than accept external controls. The rapid spread of television in the 1950s brought another major restructuring of media. Today, yet again another set of powerful communications technologies are transforming media. Personal computers are already delivering ever-increasing amounts of information into our homes. At some point, they will pose a threat to the survival of newspapers and broadcast media.

Within the American media system, the most powerful forces influencing industry restructuring are *technological change*, *content innovation*, and *consumer demand*. None of these operates independently. During eras of rapid change such as we are now experiencing, innovations in media technology force (or permit) rapid alterations in both the form and type of media content that we receive. Our demand for this content is also changing. Old media-use habits break down and new ones form as emerging media provide new choices in content. Some of us rent more and more videos while others prefer cable television offerings or home computer services.

Mass Society Critics and the Great Debate over Media

With every change in the media industries, media critics have emerged to raise questions about unethical practices and to voice concern about long-term negative consequences. They raise important and appropriate questions. During the early stages of development or restructuring, media industries are especially susceptible to criticism. Although this criticism is often warranted, it is important to recognize that many of the critics are not neutral observers with only the best interest of the public in mind. Most are not objective scientists or dispassionate humanists who rely upon systematic observation or well-developed theory for their positions. Rather, their criticisms are to some extent rooted in their own self-interest.

Even when individual critics are selfless, they are increasingly likely to be paid by special interests for their work. Often their ideas would go unnoticed without promotion by special interests. For example, when television began to compete with newspapers, newspapers were filled with stories reporting the complaints of television critics. During the 1970s much of the research critical of children's television would have gone unnoticed by the general public had it not been for the promotional work of Action for Children's Television.

Changes in media industries typically increase the pressure on other social institutions to change. Instability in the way we routinely communicate has unsettling consequences for all other institutions. Typically, the leaders of these institutions resent external pressures and are reluctant to change their way of doing things. In our society, the rise of the media industries has been interpreted by critics as threatening every other social institution including political, religious, business, military, and educational institutions. The constant calls for overhauling political campaign financing are only one example. Media are even seen to have profoundly affected families—the most basic social institution of all.

It's hardly surprising then that leaders of these social institutions, and the special interest groups they sponsor, have raised a constant stream of concern about the power and harmful impact of media. As new media develop, critics fight to prevent their growth or to control their structure. For example, the development of television and later cable television were frozen for several years while the Federal Communications Commission listened to the arguments of industry critics. Although it is unfair to place all of this criticism into a single category, many of the views expressed are consistent with mass society theory. This venerable theory has a long and checkered history. Mass society theory is actually many different theories that share some common assumptions about the role of media and society.

Mass Society Theory Assumptions

Mass society theories first appeared late in the nineteenth century as various social elites struggled to make sense of the disruptive consequences of modernization. Some (that is, the monarchy, the clergy, upper class politicians) lost

Box 3a Fearful Reactions to New Media

The introduction of each new mass medium of this century has been greeted with derision, skepticism, fear, and sometimes silliness. Here is a collection of the thought of the time that welcomed movies, talkies, radio and television.

Movies and Talkies

When you first reflect that in New York City alone, on a Sunday, 500,000 people go to moving picture shows, a majority of them perhaps children, and that in the poorer quarters of town every teacher testifies that the children now save their pennies for picture shows instead of candy, you cannot dismiss canned drama with a shrug of contempt. It is a big factor in the lives of the masses, to be reckoned with, if possible to be made better, if used for good ends. Eighty percent of present day theatrical audiences in this country are canned drama audiences. Ten million people attended professional baseball games in America in 1908. Four million people attend moving pictures theaters, it is said, every day. $50,000,000 are invested in the industry. Chicago has over 300 theaters, New York 300, St. Louis 205, Philadelphia 186, even conservative Boston boasts more than 30. Almost 190 miles of film are unrolled on the screens of America's canned drama theaters every day in the year. Here is an industry to be controlled, an influence to be reckoned with.

American Magazine, September, 1909, p. 498

And if the speech recorded in the dialogue (of talking pictures) is vulgar or ugly, its potentialities for lowering the speech standard of the country are almost incalculable. The fact that it is likely to be heard by the less discriminating portion of the public operates to increase its evil effects; for among the regular attendants at moving picture theaters there are to be found large groups from among our foreign-born population, to whom it is really vitally important that they hear only the best speech.

Commonweal, April 10, 1929, p. 653

The version of life presented to him in the majority of moving pictures is false in fact, sickly in sentiment, and utterly foreign to the Anglo-Saxon ideals of our nation. In them we usually find this formula for a hero: He must commit a crime, repent of it, and be exonerated on the ground that he "never had a mother" or "never had a chance"—or perhaps that he was born poor. The heroine is in most cases the familiar, passive, persecuted heroine of the melodrama.

Outlook, July 26, 1916, p. 695

Radio

In general one criterion must be kept in mind: the radio should do what the teacher cannot do; it ought not to do what the teacher can do better. However radio may develop, I cannot conceive of the time when a good teacher will not continue to be the most important object in any classroom.

Education, December, 1936, p. 217

Is radio to become a chief arm of education? Will the classroom be abolished, and the child of the future stuffed with facts as he sits at home or even as he walks about the streets with his portable receiving set in his pocket?

Century, June, 1924, p. 149

Television

Seeing constant brutality, viciousness and unsocial acts results in hardness, intense selfishness, even in mercilessness, proportionate to the amount of exposure and its play on the native temperament of the child. Some cease to show resentment to insults, to indignities, and even cruelty toward helpless old people, to women and other children.

New Republic, November 1, 1954, p. 12

Box 3a continued

Here, in concept at least, was the most magnificent all forms of communication. Here was the supreme triumph of invention, the dream of the ages—something that could bring directly into the home a moving image fused with sound—reproducing action, language, and thought without the loss of measurable time. Here was the magic eye that could bring the wonders of entertainment, information and education in to the living room. Here was a tool for the making of a more enlightened democracy than the world had ever seen. Yet out of the wizardry of the television tube has come such an assault against the human mind, such a mobilized attack on the imagination, such an invasion against good taste as no other communications medium has known, not excepting the motion picture or radio itself.

Saturday Review, December 24, 1949, p. 20

power or were overwhelmed in their efforts to deal with social problems. For them, the mass media were symbolic of all that was wrong with modern society. Mass newspapers of the yellow journalism era were viewed as gigantic, monopolistic enterprises that employed unethical practices to pander to semi-literate mass audiences. Leaders in education and religion resented media's power to attract readers using content they considered highly objectionable, sinful, and Philistine (Brantlinger, 1983).

The rise of the mass press after 1840 posed a direct threat to the political and business establishment. Political newspapers were swept aside by the penny press in the 1840s and 1850s and then buried by the yellow journalism of the 1880s and 1890s. The political ambitions of the leading yellow journalist, William Randolph Hearst, posed a very real threat to established politicians and businessmen. Hearst was a populist of his own devising—a man likely to pursue whatever cause would increase his personal popularity, even at the expense of the professional politicians around him. Hearst papers joined with other mass newspapers and magazines in producing sensational news stories that savagely attacked opponents in business and government. These accounts had strong reader appeal and came to be more feared by their targets than is the crew of "60 Minutes" today.

Envy, discontent, and outright fear were often at the roots of mass society theory. This theory makes several basic assumptions about individuals, the role of media, and the nature of social change. These assumptions are listed below and then each is discussed in some detail.

1   The media are a malignant, cancerous force within society and must be purged or totally restructured.

2   Media have the power to reach out and directly influence the minds of average people.

3   Once people's minds are corrupted by media, all sorts of bad, long-term consequences result—bringing ruin not only to individual lives but also creating social problems on a vast scale.

4   Average people are vulnerable to media because they have been cut off and isolated from traditional social institutions that previously protected them from manipulation.

5   The social chaos initiated by media will inevitably be resolved by establishment of a totalitarian social order.

6   Mass media inevitably debase higher forms of culture, bringing about a general decline in Civilization

The first assumption is that *the media are a malignant, cancerous force within society and must be purged or totally restructured* (Marcuse, 1969, 1978). Although only the most extreme critics proposed dismantling media industries, some opponents of the new media proposed turning control of them over to other elites. In Europe this argument won out during the 1920s and broadcast media were placed under the control of government agencies. Ironically, these efforts had disastrous consequences when the Nazis came to power in Germany. In the United States, many schemes that would have turned control of new media over to churches, schools, or government agencies were considered. Ultimately, a compromise was reached and a free enterprise broadcasting industry was created under the more-or-less watchful eye of a government agency—the Federal Radio Commission, which later evolved into the Federal Communications Commission (FCC).

But why are the media so dangerous to society? What makes them cancerous? A second assumption is that *media have the power to reach out and directly influence the minds of average people* (Davis, 1976). This is also known as the "direct effects assumption" and has been hotly debated since the 1940s. Although each version of mass society theory has its own notions about the type of direct influence different media may have, all versions stress how negative this influence is and the extreme vulnerability of average people to immediate, media-induced changes. Average citizens are portrayed as being helpless before the manipulative power of media content. For several generations now, critics have envisioned innocent audiences of teenagers succumbing to gangster movies or heavy metal music, naive grade school children victimized by comic books or Teenage Mutant Ninja Turtles, unsuspecting adults transformed magically into couch potatoes by the power of "I Love Lucy" or "Twin Peaks," and gullible old people handing over their last dime to televised insurance hucksters or greedy televangelists.

Although it is not hard to locate isolated examples that illustrate every one of these conditions, it is misleading to regard any one of them as universal. When empirical researchers tried to measure the pervasiveness of such effects in the 1940s and 1950s, they were surprised to discover how difficult it was to develop conclusive evidence. People simply were not as vulnerable to direct manipulation as critics wanted to assume. Often, other factors block direct influence or severely limit it.

3   The third assumption is that *once people's minds are corrupted by media, all sorts of bad, long-term consequences result—bringing ruin not only to individual lives but also creating social problems on a vast scale* (Marcuse, 1941). Over the years, virtually every major social problem we confront has been linked in some way to media—from prostitution and delinquency to urban violence and drug usage to the defeat in Vietnam and our loss of national pride. Tramps in the gutter have had their work ethic destroyed by reading trashy novels. Teenage delinquents have seen too many gangster movies. Disaffected housewives have seen too many soap operas and drug addicts have taken too seriously the underlying message in most advertising—the good life is achieved through consumption of a product, not by hard work. There is some truth in these criticisms but they are also highly misleading. Media are only one kind of institution that has shaped and continues to shape modern life. For such criticisms to be constructive, they must go beyond sweeping assertions. Unfortunately, most early mass society theories failed to do this.

4   Mass society theory's fourth assumption is that *average people are vulnerable to media because they have been cut off and isolated from traditional social institutions that previously protected them from manipulation* (Kreiling, 1984). The early conservative mass society theorists idealized the past and had romantic visions of what life must have been like in medieval villages of Europe. Older social orders were thought to have nurtured and protected people from external manipulation. Although these views have some validity (every social order has some redeeming qualities), they neglect to consider the severe limitations of all previous social orders—including Greek democracy. Most pre-modern social orders found it necessary to limit individual development and creativity. People were routinely compelled to do the jobs their parents and grandparents had done. They had to learn specific social roles based upon the accident of being born in a certain place at a certain time. The personal freedom we value was unknown and unimportant. Folk communities were closed systems in which traditional culture structured social life from generation to generation. Even now we hear people speak longingly of the traditional values of pre-television America. But the America of the 1930s, 1940s, and 1950s afforded few opportunities to minorities, confined most

women to homemaker roles, limited higher education access to a small elite, and imposed a host of other conditions that would cause rebellion today.

Yet the arguments that mass society theorists make about the vulnerability to manipulation of isolated individuals are compelling. These arguments have been restated in endless variations. They assert that when people are stripped of the protective cocoon provided by the traditional community, they necessarily believe everything that media communicate to them. Media are charged with gradually replacing many of the social institutions in a folk community. Media become the most trusted and valued source of messages about politics, entertainment, religion, education, and on and on. Thus, in the urban slums of nineteenth century America as in twentieth century suburbia, news media compete to be friendly neighbors. It's like hearing it from a friend.

The disintegration of traditional communities has unquestionably provided many opportunities for media entrepreneurs. For example, story telling was an important form of entertainment in many folk communities. As these communities declined, a market opened up for different forms of mediated entertainment such as movies, television, and videos. Should mass media be blamed for luring people away from folk communities by offering more powerful forms of entertainment? Or were media simply providing people with attractive content at a time when folk communities had lost their ability to control their members?

It is also useful to recognize that the influence of media may fluctuate sharply in relatively short periods of time. Certain media may indeed play more important roles during times of social instability or national crisis. But this doesn't mean that they are routinely or consistently dominant in comparison to other institutions or organizations.

5　　The fifth assumption is that *the social chaos initiated by media will inevitably be resolved by establishment of a totalitarian social order* (Davis, 1976). This assumption was developed during the 1930s and reached its peak of popularity during the Red Scare of the 1950s. Mass society is envisioned as a chaotic, highly unstable form of social order that will inevitably collapse and then be replaced by totalitarianism. Mass society, with its teeming hordes of isolated individuals, must give way to an even worse form of society—highly regimented, centrally controlled, totalitarian society. Thus, to the extent that media promote the rise of mass society, they increase the likelihood of totalitarianism.

From 1930 to 1960, mass society theorists outlined a classic scenario for degeneration of mass society into totalitarianism. This describes rather accurately the rise of Hitler in Germany. In times of rapid and chaotic social change, demagogues arise who promise average people that important social problems can be solved by joining extremist political movements. These demagogues use media very effectively to manipulate average people and attract their support. As their movements gain strength they place heavy political pressure on the traditional

Box 3b Quotes from *1984*

. . . He was alone. The past was dead, the future was unimaginable. What certainty had he that a single human creature now living was on his side? And what way of knowing that the dominion of the Party would not endure *for ever*? Like an answer, the three slogans on the white face of the Ministry of Truth came back at him:

WAR IS PEACE

FREEDOM IS SLAVERY

IGNORANCE IS STRENGTH

He took a twenty-five-cent piece out of his pocket. There, too, in tiny clear lettering, the same slogans were inscribed, and on the face of the coin the head of Big Brother. Even from the coin the eyes pursued you. On coins, on stamps, on the covers of books, on banners, on posters, and on the wrapping of a cigarette packet—everywhere. Always the eyes watching you and the voice enveloping you. Asleep or awake, working or eating, indoors or out of doors, in the bath or in bed—no escape. Nothing was your own except the few cubic centimeters inside your skull (Orwell, 1948, pp. 25–26).

. . . He gazed up at the enormous face. Forty years it had taken him to learn what kind of smile was hidden beneath the dark mustache. . . . But it was all right, everything was all right, the struggle was finished. He had won the victory over himself. He loved Big Brother (Orwell, 1948, p. 245).

elites. Compromises place increasing power in the hands of demagogues. This power is exercised irresponsibly—political opposition is suppressed and democratic political institutions are undermined. Gradually, power is consolidated in the hands of the most ruthless demagogue and this person establishes a totalitarian state.

Fear of totalitarianism is a modern fear—a fear that only people who value individualism and democracy can experience. For such people, totalitarianism is a nightmare society—one in which everything they value most has low priority. All expression of individualism is outlawed. All forms of communication are severely limited and monitored by government.

A novelist, George Orwell, constructed a most enduring vision of this nightmare world in 1948. His novel, *1984*, effectively articulates the view of media inherent in mass society theory. In Orwell's world, Big Brother watches everyone through an eye on the top of their television. Televised propaganda is used to foment hatred against external enemies and promote love of Big Brother. The hero of the novel, Winston Smith, works at a job in which he literally rewrites history. He disposes of old newspaper stories, photographs, and other documents that are inconsistent with current propaganda. All records of dissidents and traitors are wiped out. Government engages in doublespeak—language whose meaning is so corrupted that it has become useless as a medium of expression. Peace means war. Freedom means enslavement. Justice means inequity and prejudice. Anyone who deviates from the dictates of the regime is imprisoned and "re-educated." Orwell describes the struggles and ultimate conversion of Winston Smith. At the conclusion of the novel, proof of Smith's loyalty to the Party is demonstrated by his spontaneous, emotional response to Big Brother on the telescreen.

Throughout the first half of this century awareness of the spread of totalitarianism grew. For many, it symbolized everything that was loathsome and evil but others saw it as the "wave of the future." They dismissed democracy as impossible because average people could never effectively govern themselves. Democracies were perceived as inherently weak, unable to resist the rise of strong, determined leaders. Across Europe, in Latin America, and in Asia fledgling democracies faltered and collapsed as the economic Depression deepened. The United States was not immune. Radical political movements arose and their influence spread rapidly. In several states, right-wing extremists were elected to political office. Pro-Fascist groups held gigantic public rallies to demonstrate their support for Hitler. Radicals fought for control of labor unions. The thousand-year Reich envisioned by Hitler seemed more likely to endure than did democracy.

But why was totalitarianism so successful? Why was it sweeping the world just as the new mass media of radio and movies were becoming increasingly prominent? Was there a connection? Were radio and movies to blame? Many mass society theorists believed that they were. Without these media, they thought, dictators couldn't have gained popularity or consolidated their power. Broadcast media were said to be ideally suited to directly persuading average people and welding vast numbers of people into regimented, cohesive societies. Movies communicated powerful images that instilled the positive and negative associations desired by dictators. What these critics failed to note is that when the Nazis or Communists were most successful, average people had strong reasons for wanting to believe the promises about jobs and personal security made by these extremists. Personal freedom has little value when you are starving and even a wheelbarrow full of money won't buy a loaf of bread.

One of the profound ironies of the efforts to oppose the rise of totalitarianism is that these efforts often threatened to produce the very form of government they were intended to prevent. In the United States, an important example of this was provided by Joseph McCarthy, an obscure U.S. Senator from Wisconsin who came to national prominence in the 1950s by claiming to oppose the spread of communism within the U.S. government. Just how far should one go in the defense of democracy? Are there times when you have to indefinitely suspend basic democratic principles in order to "save" it? McCarthy argued that communists were so close to gaining control in the United States that it was necessary to purge many people from government and the media. He claimed that if the rules of democracy were followed, these evil people would escape discovery and bring down our political system. McCarthy claimed to have a long list of names of communists that he dramatically displayed to journalists and newsreel cameras. Journalists cooperated by publishing his charges in front-page stories under banner headlines.

Media criticism of McCarthy was muted. Many journalists feared being labeled communists if they opposed him. Indeed, McCarthy followers were very successful in getting media practitioners fired from their jobs. Black lists were circulated and threats were made against media organizations that hired those named on them. Edward R. Murrow, the most prominent broadcast journalist of the 1950s, is credited with stopping the rise of McCarthy with news reports and documentaries that questioned his tactics and the substance of his charges. Should media be blamed for causing the rise of McCarthy — or credited with stopping him?

Although totalitarianism was the biggest fear aroused by mass society theorists, they also focused attention on a more subtle form of societal corruption — mass culture. The sixth and final assumption of mass society theory, then, is that *mass media inevitably debase higher forms of culture, bringing about a general decline in Civilization* (Davis, 1976).

To understand this criticism, you must understand the perspective held by Western cultural and educational elites during the past two centuries. In the decades following the Enlightenment (an eighteenth century European social and philosophical movement that stressed rational thought), these elites saw themselves as responsible for nurturing and promulgating higher forms of culture, not only within their own societies but also around the world. In retrospect, their perspective suffers from some serious limitations. The literary Canon promoted by these elites consisted mostly of white, male, Western, Anglo-Saxon, and Protestant literature. Too often they believed that it was the white man's burden to bring civilization and high culture to uncivilized parts of the world — even if this meant suppressing indigenous cultures and annihilating the people who practiced them. As we saw in 1992, the five-hundred-year anniversary of Christopher Columbus's arrival on the American continent, this event was no longer universally hailed as giant step in the march of Civilization. Questions were openly asked about his and other explorers' brutality and destruction of otherwise competent cultures.

For defenders of high culture, mass media represented an insidious, corrosive force within society — one that threatened their influence by popularizing ideas and activities that they considered trivial or demeaning. Rather than glorify gangsters (as movies did in the 1930s), why not praise great educators or religious leaders? Why pander to popular taste — why not seek to raise it to higher levels? Why give people what they want instead of giving them what they need? Why trivialize great art by turning it into cartoons (as Disney did in the 1930s)? These questions were raised by mass society theorists—and they had long and overly abstract answers for them.

In Europe, these concerns justified government supervision of media through direct control or indirectly through public corporations like the British Broadcasting Corporation. Government there assumed responsibility for using media to advance high culture. Broadcasts of symphony concerts and Shakespearean drama were intended to enlighten the masses. Media were supposed to give people what they needed *not* what they wanted. This earned the BBC the nickname "Auntie Beebe."

Rise of the Great Debate Over Media

The confrontation between mass society theorists and apologists for the media industries has been going on throughout this century. We will trace its various forms in subsequent chapters. The debate continues today in renewed and increasingly interesting variations. Recall Vice President Dan Quayle's attacks in 1992 on Hollywood's "cultural elite" and his much publicized war of words with fictional television character Murphy Brown. Dan Quayle probably had not read much mass society theory but his views echoed its assumptions. If asked, he would probably deny that he meant to imply that media have widespread direct effects. He did not expect that the childbirth rate among unwed mothers would suddenly skyrocket just because the unwed Murphy Brown had a baby. His main concerns appear to have been cultural in nature. He accused the fictional Murphy Brown of "glamorizing" the role of unwed mother—a role that he apparently disdained.

In 1961, Bernard Berelson wrote an insightful summary of the Great Debate over Media that he entitled, "The Great Debate on Cultural Democracy." According to Berelson, the participants in this debate were *Practicus* (that is, media industry apologists), *Academicus* (that is, Mass Society Theorists), and the emerging *Empiricus* (that is, mass communication researchers who used social science methods). For Berelson, resolution of the debate was simple—just listen to mass communication researchers like himself as they develop useful answers to the issues raised by the others. Berelson argued that both Practicus and Academicus had clear biases, but not so Empiricus. The Empiricus position was even more persuasive because it seemed to represent a moderate, compromise position located midway between the extremes represented by the other two positions.

Unfortunately for Berelson, the debate didn't end in 1961. As we shall see in Chapter 8, the Empiricus position did become the "dominant paradigm" among mass communication researchers for about two decades. But it was widely ignored outside of academia. Media industry proponents and opponents have continued their struggle with seemingly studied ignorance of what Empiricus had to say. They paid attention to the findings of media researchers only when they supported their views. Since these findings documented "limited effects," they were routinely condemned by Academicus for underestimating the impact of media. On the other hand, even modest effects on specific audience subgroups were considered unlikely by Practicus (except, of course, by advertising and marketing researchers, but more on that later).

Early Examples of Mass Society Theory

Now we'll summarize several of the first examples of mass society theory. This set of theories is by no means complete. Rather, these perspectives combine ideas that were developed by others and represent how people in a given culture at a particular point in time thought about their social world. The examples described and discussed were influential at the time they were written and provided important reference points for later theorists. It is important to remember, too, that even where not specifically mentioned, the emerging mass media were clearly implicated in each.

In subsequent chapters we will deal with development of later theories that grew out of mass society theory. These continued to gain popularity until late into the 1950s. By 1965 however, mass society theory, in its classic formulation, was collapsing—inherent flaws had become obvious even to adamant supporters. Fear of totalitarianism had ebbed—at least within academia. If mass culture was going to cause the end of civilization, it was already too late.

Although most assumptions of mass society theory have been challenged and discarded, the debate over mass culture endures. In the last three chapters of this book we will consider important new theories that articulate innovative ideas about mass culture. These inevitably draw upon older notions about mass society and mass culture but most reject the simplistic assumptions and criticisms of earlier eras. The newer theories no longer see elite high culture as the standard against which all others must be measured. Totalitarianism is no longer feared as inevitable. Instead, attention is focused on the inherent biases of media when it comes to developing new forms of culture. Media are no longer seen as corrupting and degrading high culture. Rather, they are viewed as limiting or disrupting cultural development. Media don't subvert culture but they do play a major and sometimes counterproductive role in cultural change.

Should current theories of mass culture be labeled as mass society theories? Or should we officially declare mass society theory dead? Although some contemporary theorists clearly continue to draw on mass society notions, most are aware of their limitations. Our preference here is to limit use of the term "mass society theory" to formulations that (a) were developed prior to 1970 and (b) fail to account for the findings of media effects research.

Gemeinschaft and Gesellschaft

Among the originators of mass society notions was a German sociologist, Ferdinand Tönnies. Tönnies sought to explain the critical difference between earlier forms of social organization and European society as it existed in the late Nineteenth Century. He proposed a simple dichotomy—*Gemeinschaft* or folk society and *Gesellschaft* or modern, industrial society. In folk society, people were bound together by strong ties of family, tradition, rigid social roles—basic social institutions were very powerful. "A collective has the character of a *Gemeinschaft* insofar as its members think of the group as a gift of nature created by a supernatural will" (Martindale, 1960, p. 83). Although folk society had important strengths as well as serious limitations, Tönnies emphasized the former. He argued that most people yearn for the order and meaning provided by folk society. They often find life in modern societies to be troublesome and unmeaningful.

In *Gesellschafts* people are bound together by relatively weak social institutions based upon rational choices rather than tradition. For example, when you take a job you sign a formal contract based on a personal decision on your part. You don't sign it because you are bound by family tradition to work for a certain employer. You make a more or less rational choice. You agree to perform a particular job in return for a salary. The contract lasts as long as you and your employer meet its conditions. If you fail to show up for work often enough, you'll be fired. If you employer goes broke and can't pay you, you'll stop working for him or her.

The marriage vow is another example of how important social institutions have been affected by the transition to modernity. In folk societies, these vows were defined as lifelong commitments that ended only with the death of spouses. Marriage partners were chosen by the heads of families using criteria determined by tradition and family needs. If you violated marriage vows you were likely to be ostracized by everyone in the community. In these social orders, families endured crises and people found ways of surviving within them. In modern societies, families are much more fragile. Marriage vows are often violated and though offenders may endure many negative consequences, they are not condemned by the society at large (a divorced man, Ronald Reagan, became President of the United States with almost no mention of that fact). A variety of factors has combined to make single parent families common rather than the exception in our contemporary social order.

Over the years, media have been continually accused of breaking down folk societies (Gemeinschaft) and encouraging the development of amoral, weak social institutions (Gesellschaft). Vice President Quayle reflected these views when he charged that a "cultural elite" was systematically subverting family values. Glamorizing a single-parent birth in prime time set a bad example that could undermine family values and weaken society. By doing this, he reasoned, the cultural elite (the media) was indirectly responsible for social disorder like the riots in South Central Los Angeles.

Mechanical and Organic Solidarity

The French sociologist, Émile Durkheim offered a theory with the same dichotomy as that of Tönnies but with a fundamentally different interpretation of modern social orders. He compared folk societies to machines in which people were little more than cogs. These machines were very ordered and durable but people were forced by a collective consensus to perform traditional social roles. People were bound by this consensus to one another like the parts of a great engine — *mechanical solidarity.*

Durkheim compared modern social orders to animals rather than machines. As they grow, animals undergo profound changes in their physical form. They begin life as babies and progress through several developmental stages on their way to adulthood and old age. The bodies of animals are made up of many different kinds of cells — skin, bone, blood — and these cells serve very different purposes. Similarly, modern social orders can undergo profound changes and therefore the people in them can grow and change along with the society at large. In Durkheim's theory, people are like the specialized cells of a body rather than the cogs of a machine. They perform specialized tasks and are dependent upon the overall health of the body for their personal survival. Unlike machines, animals are subject to diseases and physical threats. But they are capable of using mental processes to anticipate threats and cope with them. Durkheim used the term *organic solidarity* to refer the social ties that bind modern social orders together.

Social orders with organic solidarity are characterized by specialization, division of labor, and interdependence (Martindale, 1960, p. 87). Be warned, though, it is easy to confuse Durkheim's labeling of mechanical and organic solidarity since we naturally associate machines with modernity. Remember that he uses the metaphor of the machine to refer to folk society — not modern society.

Durkheim's praise for organic solidarity has been echoed in the many theories that have extolled the virtues of new media and new technology. Proponents of new media almost always argue that communications technology will permit important new social bonds to be formed. Another example from the 1992 Presidential campaign shows how much we continue to expect from new media. Ross Perot argued that we should create an "electronic democracy" in which the people can directly communicate with their leaders. He proposed establishing "electronic town halls" where the people would be able to decide what they want government to do for them. These arguments assume that these new mediated relationships would be an improvement over older forms of representative democracy.

book

It would be a mistake to view Durkheim as a naive optimist concerning the rise of modern society. His most enduring book was entitled *Suicide*. It documented rising suicide rates in those countries where traditional religious and social institutions had lost their preeminence. In these nations, Durkheim argued, people experienced high levels of anomie or normlessness. In his later work, Durkheim showed growing concern for the declining strength of common morality (Ritzer, 1983, p. 99). People are no longer bound by traditional values but are free to follow their personal passions and needs. For him, these problems were best viewed as social pathologies that could be diagnosed and cured by a social physician, in other words, a sociologist like himself (Ritzer, 1983, p. 110). Unlike conservatives who demanded a return to old social orders or radicals who called for revolution, Durkheim believed that scientifically chosen reforms would solve the problems inherent in modernity.

Mass Society Theory in Contemporary Times

Although mass society theory has very little support among contemporary mass communication researchers and theorists, its basic assumptions of a corrupting media and helpless audiences have never completely disappeared. Attacks on the pervasive, dysfunctional power of media (such as those offered by Vice President Quayle) have persisted and will persist as long as dominant elites find their power challenged by media.

In the same year as Quayle's attacks on the "Hollywood elite," for example, two books were published that echoed him. Moreover, not only did these works firmly rearticulate mass society notions, but they also amply demonstrated its many limitations (for example, distrust of "average people" and the presumption that the authors' values are the "right values"). Medved's (1992) *Hollywood vs. America: Popular Culture and the War on Traditional Values* argues precisely what its title would imply. The other, *Carnival Culture: The Trashing of Taste in America* (Twitchell, 1992), views modern mediated society this way:

~ get

> Here the barter is simpler: pay up and see what you want. Redemption can wait. If modern culture may be seen in terms of a competition for audience between high and low entertainment, between art and vulgarity, between the

Church and the Carnival, then the Carnival is having its day. Mardi Gras is less and less dependent on Lent. The paperback book, the Cineplex 16, the audiocassette, the videocassette, the compact disk, and the coaxial cable have allowed a huge audience to attend the ceremonies of entertainment, and a huge amount of money to be made by those who can gauge what the mass audience desires. In the twentieth century, especially since the 1960s, the gatekeeper/cleric has wandered away and the carnival barker/program-mer has taken his place. "Step right up, folks, right this way and see . . . " In the beginning was the Word, but in the end it will be the Image. (pp. 2–3)

Summary

Criticism of media and new media technology is not a new phenomenon. For more than a century now, new media industries have inspired harsh criticism from a variety of sources. There has been much to criticize. Mass entertainment content has pandered to the full range of popular tastes and passions. Early news media (and today's supermarket tabloids) attracted huge audiences by printing speculative, over-dramatized stories. The most important, continuing criticism of media took the form of mass society theory. Tönnies and Durkheim helped frame a debate over the fundamental nature of modernity that has not ended. For mass society theorists and media apologists, media were symbolic of modernity — representing either the worst or the best of modern life.

Early mass society theory argued that media are malignant forces that have the power to directly reach, transform, and corrupt the minds of individuals so that their lives are ruined and vast social problems are created. Through media influence, people are atomized, cut off from the civilizing influences of other peo-ple or high culture. Totalitarianism inevitably results as ruthless, power-hungry dictators seize control of media to promote their ideology.

Initially, mass society theory gained wide acceptance. But in time people questioned its unqualified assertions about the media's power to corrupt and debase individuals. Mass society notions enjoyed longer acceptance in Europe where commitments to traditional ways of life and high culture have been stron-ger and where distrust of average people and democracy runs deeper. For the past forty years, American media researchers have been skeptical of the absolute power of media. In subsequent chapters, we will show how their skepticism was grounded upon empirical observation. In study after study, researchers found it difficult to demonstrate that media could directly and routinely influence what people thought or did.

The debate over the role of media in modern life has not ended. Though many American scholars were satisfied with the answers supplied by empirical research, European theorists were not. Many old questions about the power of media have recently been revived. Cogent new theories argue that media do play an important role in the development and maintenance of culture. The revival of this debate has reinvigorated media theory and research.

Discussion Questions

1 Discuss the current competition within the media industries, for example, network television versus cable television and newspapers versus electronic news. How will the outcome of this competition affect your life or your career choice?

2 Do you expect that your life will be significantly better when new media technologies (that is, high definition television and multimedia) currently under development become widely available? Will you be willing to pay more for these media services? Will these services improve or degrade the quality of your life?

3 Why do you think the development of mass media aroused so much fear in the past? How justified were these fears? If you had lived in the 1930s, do you think you would have blamed media for causing the rise of Nazism or Communism? As you read through the various criticisms of media, do any strike you as still being valid? Are there any you find ridiculous?

4 Do you agree with former Vice President Quayle's view of the media or the view articulated in the Medved book or *Carnival Culture*? Why or why not?

Significant Names

Emile Durkheim

Ferdinand Tönnies

Herbert Marcuse

Significant Readings

Arato, Andrew and Eike Gebhardt, eds. (1978). *The Essential Frankfurt School Reader.* New York: Urizen Books.

Bauer, Raymond A. and Alice H. Bauer (1960). "America, Mass Society and Mass Media." *Journal of Social Issues,* 10: 3–66.

Kornhauser, William (1959). *The Politics of Mass Society.* New York: Free Press.

Important Terms

Robber Barons

Wire Services

Penny Press

Yellow Journalism

Functional Displacement

Mass Society Theory

Big Brother

Mass Culture

Gemeinschaft

Gesellschaft

Mechanical Solidarity

Organic Solidarity

Chapter 4

The Rise of Media Theory in the Age of Propaganda

Imagine that you have gone back in time to the beginning of this century. You live in a large, metropolitan area along the East Coast of the United States and you are a second or third generation American. You are a white, middle class, Anglo-Saxon Protestant. Your city is growing rapidly with new neighborhoods springing up daily to house waves of new immigrants from poorer nations in Eastern Europe and the Far East. These people speak strange languages and practice strange cultures. Many claim to be Christians but they don't behave like any Christians you've ever met. Most keep to themselves in ghetto neighborhoods in which there are many social problems.

Most disturbing of all, these people seem to have no sense of what it means to live in a free and democratic nation. They are governed by political bosses who turn them out to vote for what you perceive to be corrupt, party machine candidates. If you pay attention to gossip (or read the right books or magazines), you hear about groups like the Mafia or Cosa Nostra. You also hear (or read in your mass newspaper) that various extremist political groups are active in these ghettos, spreading all sorts of discontent among these ignorant, irresponsible aliens. Many of these nefarious groups are playing upon the newcomers' loyalties to foreign nations. What would you do about this situation?

Well, you might want to start an America for Americans movement to purge these foreigners from the sacred soil of your homeland. If you are of a more liberal bent, you might be reluctant to do away with these people (even though they do represent a threat to your way of life). As a Progressive person, you want to convert these people away from their obviously misguided beliefs. You want them to adopt better forms of government as practiced by responsible officials, people similar to you demographically and culturally. You are aware that greedy employers are exploiting these people with 16-hour work days and child labor, but you believe that's why they should join mainstream political parties and be responsible citizens. Perhaps, you figure, if they would only abstain from alcohol and adopt more rational forms of religion, that might help them see their problems more clearly.

Unfortunately, most of these recent arrivals don't seem to respond well to efforts designed to help them. Movements to eradicate them seem to make them only more determined to survive. Resistance grows ever more determined and is accompanied by violence on both sides. Now what do you do? You could become a Prohibitionist and successfully ban the sale of liquor. But this only creates a market for bootleggers. The power of organized crime is strengthened rather than reduced. Political party bosses flourish.

Or you could become a political Progressive and work to break up gigantic interstate monopolies at the same time that you attempt to ban subversive labor unions. You might advocate the use of violence to break illegal strikes. But breaking up monopolies does little to help the poor immigrants. Labor unions grow ever larger and more militant. How will these people ever become true Americans and be absorbed into the American melting pot?

Now imagine that you are one of those aliens. How do you cope with life in the world's greatest democracy—you turn to your family and the friends of your family. Your cousin is a member of the political machine. He promises a patronage job—if you vote for his boss. You fight exploitation by joining labor unions that promise to correct bad working conditions. But above all, you practice the culture you grew up with and you stay within the confines of the ghetto where this culture is practiced. You resent Prohibition and see nothing wrong with consuming alcohol occasionally. You listen to family members and local political bosses who can do things for you and can be trusted to keep their promises.

Throughout this century, the United States has been a nation of many cultures. At any given point in time, people in specific racial and ethnic groups have been exploited and feared. Some of these groups have escaped the ghettos and their children have been absorbed into the amorphous American middle class. Other groups have been less successful. Some members of dominant cultural groups have attempted to assist these subordinate groups but their efforts have been only partially successful. Too often, their work was actually quite self-serving—not selfless. They sought to protect their way of life from the threats posed by other cultures and life styles. This led them to adopt solutions that only made problems worse. Put yourself back there in time. Take which ever role you choose. How comfortable would you be? What would you do? How would you feel about the changes around you?

Overview

The situation just described was an ideal breeding ground for violent social conflict. This battle was waged in the streets and through the ever expanding mass media. A war of words was fought in the media by yellow journalists and muckrakers; battle lines were drawn between defenders of immigrant groups and representatives of existing elites. The war was not confined to polite newspaper editorials or human interest feature stories. It was a struggle for the heart and soul of the nation (Brownell, 1983; Altschull, 1990). Nor was the battle confined to America. In Europe, conflict across social class lines was even more intense and deadly.

In the United States, advocates on all sides were convinced of the Truth and Justice of their causes. Their way was the American way, the only Right way, the only True way. They were opposed by the forces of Evil and Chaos. Mass-mediated propaganda spread throughout America, across Europe, and around the world. Everywhere it has deeply affected politics and culture for most of the twentieth century.

In this chapter, we will discuss how political propaganda was used and then survey some of the theories that were developed to understand and control it. Along with the normative theories discussed in the next chapter, these were the first true media theories. Within mass society theory, media were seen as only one of many disruptive forces. But in propaganda theories, media became the focus of attention. These theories specifically analyzed media content and speculated about its influence. They sought to understand and explain the ability of messages to persuade and convert thousands or even millions of individuals to extreme viewpoints.

Propaganda commanded the attention of early media theorists because it threatened to undermine the very foundation of the American political system and of democratic governments everywhere. By the late 1930s, many if not most American leaders were convinced that democracy wouldn't survive if extremist propaganda was allowed to be freely distributed. But censorship of propaganda meant imposing significant limitations on that essential principle of Western democracy, communication freedom. This posed a terrible dilemma. If strict censorship were imposed, this might also undermine democracy. Propaganda theorists sought to address and resolve this dilemma.

At first, some experts were optimistic that the American public could be educated to resist propaganda. After all, propaganda violates the most basic rules of

fair, democratic political communication. It freely uses lies and deception to persuade. If people could be taught to critically evaluate propaganda messages, they
should learn how to reject propaganda messages as unfair and false. These
experts believed that public education could save democracy. But optimism about
the power of public education faded as both Nazism and Communism spread
from Europe to America during the 1930s. More and more Americans, especially
first generation immigrants from Europe, turned away from American-style
democracy and instead chose to listen to totalitarian leaders who promised social
justice and jobs. They joined social movements based on propaganda imported
more or less directly from Europe. In the United States, rallies were held to celebrate Hitler or Stalin and to denigrate inferior races and Wall Street Bosses.

Propaganda experts became convinced that even if public education was a
practical means of resisting propaganda, it would simply take too long. Time was
running out as the Depression deepened. It appeared likely that a Nazi or Communist leader would seize power before public education had a chance to
succeed. So propaganda theorists abandoned idealism in favor of ideas they
regarded as realistic and based on scientific fact. Propaganda must be resisted by
whatever means possible. Even though the threat of propaganda was great, there
might be a silver lining to this cloud. If we could find a way to harness the power
of propaganda to promote good and just ideals, then we would not only survive
its threat but have a tool that could help build a better social order. This was the
promise of what came to be called *White Propaganda*—a strategy that used
benign propaganda techniques to fight "bad" propaganda and promote objectives
that elites considered good. After World War II ended, these white propaganda
techniques provided a basis for the development of promotional communication
methods that are widely used today.

The Origin of Propaganda

Propaganda was not an American invention. The term was originated in the sixteenth century during the Counter-Reformation. It was first used by the Society
for the Propagation of the Faith—the Jesuits. The term propaganda has since
come to refer to the no-holds-barred use of communication to propagate specific
beliefs and expectations. The ultimate goal of propagandists is to change the way
people act. To do this though, they must first change the way people conceive of
themselves and their social world. A variety of communication techniques are
used to guide and transform popular beliefs. During the 1930s, the new media of
radio and movies provided propagandists with powerful new tools.

The propagandist believes that the end justifies the means. Therefore, it is
not only right but necessary that half-truths and outright lies be used to convince people to abandon ideas that are "wrong" and adopt those favored by the

propagandist. Propagandists also rely on what is referred to as *disinformation* to discredit their opposition. False information is spread about opposition groups and their objectives. Often the source of this false information is concealed so that it can't be traced to the propagandist.

As U.S. propaganda theorists studied it, they came to differentiate black, white, and gray propaganda. Black propaganda involved deliberate and strategic transmission of lies—its use was well illustrated by the Nazis. White propaganda involved intentional suppression of potentially harmful information and ideas, combined with deliberate promotion of positive information or ideas to distract attention from problematic events. Gray propaganda involved transmission of information or ideas that may or may not be false. The propagandist simply made no effort to determine their validity and actually avoided doing so—especially if dissemination of the content would serve his or her interest. Today we might find offensive the attribution of labels like "black" and "white" to the concepts of bad and good propaganda. But keep in mind one of this book's constant themes: these ideas are products of their times.

Propagandists then and now live in an either/or, good/evil world. Traditional elite propagandists at the turn of the century had two clear alternatives. On one side there was truth, justice, and freedom—in short, the American way—and on the other side there was falsehood, evil, and slavery—Totalitarianism. Of course, Communist and Nazis propagandists had their own versions of truth, justice, and freedom. For them the American vision of utopia was at best naive and at worst likely to lead to racial pollution and cultural degradation. The Nazis used propaganda to cultivate extreme fear and hatred of minority groups. In *Mein Kampf*, Hitler traced the problems of post World War I Germany to the Jewish people and other ethnic or racial minorities. Unlike the American elites, he saw no reason to bother converting these groups—they were Evil Incarnate and therefore should be exterminated. Nazi propaganda films used powerful negative imagery to equate Jews with rats and to associate mental illness with grotesque physical deformity while positive images were associated with blond, blue-eyed people. The threat to the Aryan or Master race was dramatized quite effectively. All opposition to these depictions was suppressed.

Thus, for the totalitarian propagandist, mass media were conceptualized as a very practical means of mass manipulation—an effective mechanism for controlling large populations so that the dominant majority came to have and act upon certain beliefs and attitudes. If people came to share the views of a propagandist, they were said to be converted—they abandoned old views and took on those promoted by propaganda.

Propagandists typically held elitist and paternalistic views about their audiences. They believed that people needed to be converted for their "own good" not just to serve the interest of the propagandist. Propagandists often blamed the

---

Box 4a A Few Words from a Master Propagandist

In his book, *The War That Hitler Won*, Robert Herzstein described a speech made in 1928 by the Nazis' master propagandist, Joseph Goebbels. Herzstein wrote, "Goebbels started out from the premise that the aim of propaganda was political success, not intellectual depth. The role of the propagandist was to express in words what his audience felt in their hearts. The propagan-

dist must feel the totality of the National Socialist idea in every aspect of his listeners . . . Goebbels believed that being in power gave a party or an idea the right to use that power . . . 'In politics power prevails, not moral claims of justice,' Goebbels stated. He thus saw propaganda as a pragmatic art, the means to an end, the seizure of total power" (1978, p. 69).

---

people for the necessity of engaging in lies and manipulation. They thought people to be so irrational or so illiterate or so inattentive that it was necessary to coerce, seduce, or trick them into learning bits of misinformation. The propagandists' argument was simple: If only people were more rational or intelligent, we could just sit down and explain things to them, person to person. But most aren't—especially the ones who need the most help. Most people are children when it comes to important affairs like politics. How can we expect them to listen to reason? It's just not possible.

The propagandist also uses similar reasoning for suppressing opposition messages: Average people are just too gullible. They will be taken in by the lies and tricks of others. If opponents are allowed to freely communicate their messages, a stand-off will result in which no one wins. Since propagandists are convinced of the validity of their cause, they must stop opponents from blocking their actions.

Propaganda Comes to America

From the viewpoint of the American old-line elites during the early years of this century, propaganda was a subversive form of communication invented by crazy Europeans who insisted on killing each other in endless, meaningless wars. There was widespread suspicion about propaganda. Americans were aware that modern propaganda techniques had been used with startling effectiveness to assemble massive armies during World War I. Never before had so many people been mobilized to fight a war. Never before had so many died so quickly under such harsh conditions.

After World War I, the propaganda battle not only continued, but it also spread beyond Europe. During the 1920s, radio and movies provided powerful new media for propaganda messages. Nations sought to spread their influence using propaganda. New political movements attracted members using propaganda. In the United States, the battlelines in the propaganda war were quickly drawn. On one side was the American Establishment, the traditional elite that dominated all the major social institutions and organizations, including the major political parties and established social groups. On the other side were a broad range of social movements and small, extremist political groups. Many of these were local variants of groups that were much larger and more significant in Europe. From the point of view of the old-line elite, these groups were suspect. Foreign subversion was a constant fear. The elite believed the influence of these movements and groups had to be curbed before they ruined the American way of life.

Extremist propagandists, whether foreign-based or domestically grown, found it increasingly easy to reach and persuade audiences during the 1930s. Only a part of this success, however, can be directly attributed to the rise of the powerful new media. In the United States, movies and radio were controlled by the existing elites. Extremists were often forced to rely on older media like pamphlets, handbills, and political rallies. But when the social conditions were right and people were receptive to propaganda messages, even older, smaller media could be quite effective.

American elites watched with increasing horror as extremist political groups consolidated their power in Europe and proceeded to establish totalitarian governments. Fear grew that these groups could and would come to power in the United States. In several American universities, researchers began to systematically study both foreign and domestic propaganda—searching for clues to what made it effective. Money for this research came from a variety of government agencies and private foundations, most notably military intelligence agencies and the Rockefeller Foundation.

We will review the propaganda theories of three of the most prolific, imaginative and complex thinkers of their time: Harold Lasswell, Walter Lippmann, and John Dewey. Given the number of books these men wrote, it is impossible to provide a complete presentation of their work. Instead, we will highlight some of their most influential and widely accepted ideas. In nearly every case, these men later refined or even rejected many of these ideas. Our objective in presenting their theories is to show how thinking about media evolved during a very critical period in world history—not to demean these individuals or to denigrate their work.

Most of the propaganda theories that developed during the 1930s were strongly influenced by three theories: behaviorism, Freudianism, and magic bullet theories. Some combined all three. Before presenting the ideas of the major propaganda theorists, we will first look at the three theories that influenced their development.

Behaviorism

Stimulus-response psychology was first popularized by John B. Watson, an animal experimentalist who argued that all human action is merely a conditioned response to external, environmental stimuli. Watson's theory became known as *behaviorism* in recognition of its narrow focus upon isolated human behaviors. Behaviorists rejected widely held views in psychology that assumed that higher mental processes (that is, conscious thought or reflection) ordinarily control human action. In contrast to such *mentalist* views, they argued that the only purpose served by consciousness was to rationalize behaviors *after* they are triggered by external stimuli. Behaviorists attempted to purge all mentalist terms from their theories and to deal strictly with observable variables—environmental stimuli on the one hand and behaviors on the other. By studying the associations that existed between specific stimuli and specific behaviors, they hoped to discover previously unknown causes for action.

Behavioristic notions were frequently used by early media theorists. They saw the media as providing external stimuli that triggered immediate responses. For example, these notions could be applied to the analysis of the Nazi propaganda films described earlier. The powerful ugly images presented of Jews or the mentally ill could be expected to trigger negative responses.

Freudianism

Freudian theory, on the other hand, was very different from behaviorism, though Sigmund Freud shared Watson's skepticism concerning people's ability to exercise effective conscious or rational control over their actions. Freud spent considerable time counseling middle class women who suffered from hysteria. During hysterical fits, seemingly ordinary individuals would suddenly "break down" and display uncontrolled and highly emotional behavior. It was not uncommon for quiet and passive women to scream and become violent. Often these outbursts occurred in public places at times when the likelihood of embarrassment and trouble for themselves and others was maximized.

To explain this apparently irrational behavior, Freud decided that the self that guides action must be fragmented into conflicting parts. Normally, one part, the rational mind or *Ego*, is in control but sometimes other parts become dominant. Freud speculated that human action often is the product of another, darker side of the self—the *Id*. This is the egocentric, pleasure seeking part of ourselves that we, the Ego, must struggle to keep under control. The Ego relies upon an internalized set of cultural rules (the *Superego*) for guidance. Caught between the primitive Id and the overly restrictive Superego, the Ego fights a losing battle. When the Ego loses control to the Id, hysteria or worse results. When the

Superego becomes dominant, people turn into unemotional, depressed social automatons who simply do what others demand.

Propaganda theorists used Freudian theory to develop very pessimistic interpretations of media influence. For example, propaganda would be most effective if it could appeal directly to the Id and stimulate it to overwhelm the Ego. Behaviorism and Freudianism were often combined to create theories that viewed the individual as incapable of rational self control. People were seen as highly vulnerable to media manipulation; media stimuli and the Id could trigger actions that the Ego and the Superego were powerless to stop. Afterwards, the Ego merely rationalizes actions that it couldn't control and experiences guilt about them. Accordingly, media could have societywide, instantaneous influence on even the most educated, thoughtful people. This view seemed to explain the situation in Nazi Germany. Prior to the rise of Hitler, Germany was considered to be among the most cultured and civilized nations. Somehow a cultured elite had been converted to Nazism. An entire nation had been turned into barbarians. Did Freudian theory explain this situation?

Magic Bullet Theories

By the 1920s, a variety of simplistic propaganda theories had been developed. In them, media stimuli were assumed to operate like magic bullets that penetrated people's minds and instantly created associations between strong emotions and specific concepts. By carefully controlling these magic bullets, propagandists felt that they could condition people to associate good emotions, such as loyalty and reverence, with their own country and associate bad emotions, such as fear and loathing, with their enemies. The propagandists saw average people as powerless to resist this influence.

Magic bullet theories assumed what behaviorism was never able to adequately demonstrate—that external stimuli, like those conveyed through mass media, can condition anyone to behave in whatever way a master propagandist wanted. People were viewed as powerless to consciously resist manipulation. No matter what their social status or how well educated people are, the magic bullets of propaganda penetrate their defenses and transform their thoughts and actions. In these theories, the rational mind was a mere façade, incapable of resisting powerful messages. People have no ability to screen out or criticize these messages. The messages penetrate to their subconscious mind and transform how they think and feel.

If magic bullet theories were valid, we would indeed live in a scary world. Imagine a nationwide audience of typical Americans listening to their favorite radio program. Suddenly a master propagandist breaks in with a message, "Everyone paint your faces purple!" The next day, riots break out as people demand that the government make available purple paint distribution centers. The price of a paint brush skyrockets to sixty dollars apiece. Havoc reigns! Sounds like an old science fiction movie, doesn't it? But from the turn of the century through the 1950s, similar tales of mass conversion were taken seriously. After all, it happened in Germany, Russia, Japan and Italy, didn't it?

good pt.

The advocates of the magic bullet theory cite numerous examples of the apparent power of media. Although many of these were from Europe, some were American. One of the most frequently cited examples occurred in October, 1938, when Orson Welles, the producer of a weekly CBS radio network program, played a not-so-funny Halloween joke on his listeners. The show was to be a dramatization of an H.G. Wells novel about an invasion from Mars. It began, however, with an elaborate ruse, simulating a live dance music show from a New York hotel. The show was repeatedly interrupted by phoney news bulletins: A spaceship had been observed. It had landed in New Jersey. Strange creatures were emerging from it. Then, the fictitious reports ceased and real life panic broke out in several cities; especially those were near the fake landing site. Critics of the power of radio interpreted this as proof of the validity of magic bullet notions. We will return to this example later and discuss why it may not provide conclusive proof about the power of media.

Lasswell's Propaganda Theory

Harold Lasswell's theory of propaganda combined behaviorism and Freudianism into a particularly pessimistic vision of media and their role. The power of propaganda was due not so much to the substance or appeal of specific messages but rather to the vulnerable state of mind of average persons. He argued that the economic depression and escalating political conflict had induced widespread psychosis and this made people susceptible to even crude forms of propaganda. According to Floyd Matson (1964, pp. 90–93), Lasswell concluded that even relatively benign forms of political conflict were inherently pathological (Lasswell, 1934). When conflict escalates to the level it did in Germany during the Depression, an entire nation could become psychologically unbalanced and vulnerable to manipulation. Lasswell argued that the solution was for social researchers to find ways to "obviate conflict." This necessitates controlling those forms of political communication that lead to conflict. Matson stated, "In short, according to the psychopathology of politics, the presumption in any individual case must be that political action is maladjustive, political participation is irrational, and political expression is irrelevant" (1964, p. 91).

Lasswell himself rejected simplistic magic bullet theory. He argued that propaganda was more than merely using media to lie to people to control them. People need to be slowly prepared to accept radically different ideas and actions.

Communicators need a well-developed, long-term campaign strategy in which new ideas and images are carefully introduced and then cultivated. Symbols must be created and people must be gradually taught to associate specific emotions with these symbols. If these cultivation strategies are successful, they create what Lasswell referred to as *collective* or *master symbols* (Lasswell, 1935). Master symbols are associated with strong emotions and possess the power to stimulate beneficial large-scale, mass action if they are used wisely. In contrast with magic bullet notions, Lasswell's theory envisioned a long and quite sophisticated conditioning process. Exposure to one or two extremist messages would not likely have significant effects.

Lasswell argued that successful social movements gain power by propagating master symbols over a period of months and years using a variety of media. For example, the emotions we experience when we see the American flag are not the result of a single, previous exposure to the flag. Rather, we have observed the flag in countless past situations in which a limited range of emotions were induced and experienced. The flag has acquired emotional meaning based on all of these previous experiences. When we see the flag on television with patriotic music in the background, some of these emotions may be aroused and reinforced.

Lasswell believed that past propagation of most master symbols had been more or less haphazard. For every successful propagandist, there were hundreds who failed. Although he respected the cunning way that the Nazis used propaganda, he was not convinced that they really understood what they were doing. He regarded Hitler as a mad genius who benefited from the psychoses induced in the German people by economic depression and political conflict. When it came to using media, Hitler was an evil artist but not a scientist. Lasswell proposed combatting Hitler with a new science of propaganda. Power to control delivery of propaganda through the mass media would be placed in the hands of a new elite, a scientific technocracy that would be pledged to using its knowledge for good rather than evil.

Matson (1966, p. 87), a severe critic of Lasswell's theory, has argued

> His contemplative analysis of "skill politics and skill revolution" has disclosed to Lasswell that in our own time the most potent of all skills is that of propaganda, of symbolic manipulation and myth-making—and hence that the dominant elite must be the one which possesses or can capture this skill.

Matson went on to quote from Lasswell (1966, p. 89):

> It is indisputable that the world could be unified if enough people were impressed by this (or by any other) elite. The hope of the professors of social science, if not of the world, lies in the competitive strength of an elite based on vocabulary, footnotes, questionnaires, and conditioned responses [sic], against an elite based on vocabulary, poison gas, property, and family prestige.

In a world where rational political debate is impossible because average people are prisoners of their own psychoses (remember behaviorism and Freudianism) and therefore subject to manipulation by propagandists, Lasswell argued, the only hope for us as a nation rested with social scientists who could harness the power of propaganda for Good rather than Evil. It is not surprising, then, that many of the early media researchers took their task very seriously. They believed that nothing less than the fate of the world lay in their hands.

Lippmann's Theory of Public Opinion Formation

Lasswell's vision of a benevolent technocracy was shared by many other members of the social elite, especially within major universities. Although Lasswell's work was never widely read, his views were shared by leading academics and opinion leaders, including one of the most powerful opinion makers of the time — Walter Lippmann, a nationally syndicated columnist for the New York *Times*.

Lippmann shared Lasswell's skepticism about the ability of average people to make sense of their social world and make rational decisions about their actions. In *Public Opinion* (Lippmann, 1922), he pointed out the discrepancies that necessarily exist between "the world outside and the pictures in our heads." Because these discrepancies were inevitable, Lippmann doubted that average people could govern themselves as classic democratic theory assumed they could. The world of the 1930s was an especially complex place and the political forces were very dangerous. People simply couldn't learn enough from media to help them understand it all. Even if journalists took their responsibility seriously, they couldn't overcome the psychological and social barriers that prevented average persons from developing useful "pictures in their heads."

Lippmann's ideas raised serious questions about the viability of democracy and the role of a free press in it. What do you do in a democracy if you can't trust the people to cast informed votes? What good is a free press if it is literally impossible to effectively transmit the most vital forms of information to the public? The fact that Lippmann made his living working as a newspaper columnist lent credibility to his pessimism. In advancing these arguments, he directly contradicted the libertarian assumptions (see Chapter 5) that were the intellectual foundation of the American media system.

Like Lasswell, Lippmann believed that propaganda posed such a severe challenge to American media that drastic changes in our political system were required. Since the public was vulnerable to propaganda, some mechanism or agency was needed to protect them from it. A benign but enormously potent form of media control was necessary. Self censorship by media probably wouldn't be sufficient. Lippmann shared Lasswell's conclusion that the best solution to these problems was to place control of information gathering and distribution in the hands of a benevolent technocracy—a scientific elite—that could be trusted to use scientific methods to sort fact from fiction and make good decisions about who should receive various messages. To accomplish this, he proposed the establishment of a quasi-governmental intelligence bureau that would carefully evaluate information and supply it to other elites for decision-making. This bureau could also determine which information should be transmitted through the mass media and which information people were better off not knowing.

Reaction Against Early Propaganda Theory

The propaganda theories of Lasswell and Lippmann prompted public debate. A prominent opponent of their ideas was a philosopher, John Dewey. In a series of lectures (Dewey, 1927), he outlined his objections to Lippmann's views. Throughout his long career, Dewey was a tireless and prolific defender of public education as the most effective means of defending democracy against totalitarianism. He refused to accept the need for a technocracy that would use scientific methods to protect people from themselves. Rather, he argued that people could learn to defend themselves if they were only taught the correct defenses. He rejected simplistic magic bullet notions and asserted that even rudimentary public education could enable people to resist propaganda methods.

Dewey's critics said he was an idealist who talked a lot about reforming education without actually doing much himself to implement concrete reforms (Altschull, 1990, p. 230). Dewey did no better when it came to reforming the media. He argued that newspapers needed to do more than simply serve as a bulletin board for information about current happenings. They should serve as vehicles for public education and debate. They should focus more on ideas and philosophy and less on descriptions of isolated actions. They should teach critical thinking skills and structure public discussion of important issues. His efforts to found such a paper never got very far, however.

James Carey (1989, pp. 83–84) contends that Dewey's ideas have continuing value. He argues that Dewey anticipated many of the concerns now being raised by cultural studies theories (see Chapter 12). In one very important respect, Dewey's ideas about the relationship between communities and media were quite innovative. Lasswell and Lippmann saw media as external agencies, as conveyor belts that deliver quantities of information to isolated audience members. In Chapter 11, we will discuss in detail Lasswell's classic linear model of mass communication: Who says what to whom through what medium with what effect. For Dewey such models were far too simplistic. They ignored the fact that effective media must be well integrated into the communities they serve; media are at the center of the complex network of relationships that define a community. Media should be understood not as external agents but as servants that facilitate public discussion and debate; as guardians and facilitators of the public forum in which democratic politics are conducted.

Dewey believed that communities, not isolated individuals, use communication (and the media of communication) to create and maintain the culture that bonds and sustains them. When media assume the role of external agents and work to manipulate the "pictures in people's heads," they lose the power to serve as credible facilitators and guardians of public debate; they become just another competitor for our attention. The potentially productive interdependence between the community and media is disrupted and the public forum itself is likely to be destroyed. This argument concerning the alienation of media from communities is now of considerable interest (see Chapters 12 and 13) and foreshadows contemporary debate over the proper role of media within communities.

Libertarianism Reborn

By the end of the 1930s, pessimism about the future of democracy was widespread. Most members of the old-line elites were convinced that totalitarianism couldn't be stopped. They pointed to theories like those of Lasswell and Lippmann as proof that average people could not be trusted. The only hope for the future lay with technocracy and science.

In the next chapter, we will trace the development of theories that arose in opposition to technocratic views. Advocates of these ideas didn't base their views of media upon social science, rather they sought to revive older notions of democracy and media. If modern democracy was being threatened, then maybe the threat was the result of having strayed too far from old values and ideals. Perhaps these could be restored and modern social institutions could somehow be purified and renewed. Theorists sought to make the libertarianism of the Founding Fathers relevant to democracy. In doing so, they created views of media that are still widely held.

Summary

The first half of the twentieth century was a highly traumatic period in which the basic principles of democracy were tested. The power of mass media was demonstrated by totalitarian propagandists who used media to convert millions to their ideas. Though Nazi and Communist propagandists wielded media with apparent effectiveness, the basis for their power over mass audiences was not well understood. Early theorists argued that propaganda messages were like magic bullets that could easily and instantly penetrate even the strongest defenses. No one was safe from their power to convert. Later theorists like Harold Lasswell held that propaganda typically influenced people in slow and subtle ways. It created new master symbols that could be used to induce new forms of thought and action. Both magic bullet and Lasswell's theories assumed that media could operate as external agents and be used as tools to manipulate essentially passive mass audiences. As we shall see in Chapter 7, this conception of media endured long after early propaganda theories were abandoned. Other, more optimistic, concepts of media's role also were developed.

Discussion Questions

1   Explain what you think is meant by propaganda. Give some examples from your own experience.

2   Is the use of propaganda ever justified? If so, should limitations be placed on it? Is deliberate lying or deception ever justified?

3   Discuss the dilemma that propaganda created during the 1930s. Which was worse — censorship by our own elites or the threat posed by subversive totalitarian propaganda? Is censorship of communication always a threat to democracy?

4   Discuss Harold Lasswell's view that people can be conditioned to associate strong emotions with master symbols. Think of a symbol that you find very powerful and consider the emotion that it arouses in you. How did this symbol come to have this meaning for you? Did media messages or interactions with other people influence you?

5   John Dewey argued that public education was the best means of resisting propaganda. Why did so many propaganda experts reject his views as idealistic and impractical? Do you think that average people can be educated to resist the influence of propaganda? Why or why not? How about yourself, are you able to resist propaganda?

Significant Names

John Dewey

Sigmund Freud

Walter Lippmann

Harold Lasswell

Significant Readings

Dewey, John (1927). *The Public and its Problems*. New York: Henry Holt,

Lasswell, Harold D. (1927). *Propaganda Technique in the World War*. New York: Knopf.

Lippmann, Walter (1922). *Public Opinion*. New York: Macmillan.

Important Terms

Propaganda

Disinformation

Behaviorism

Freudianism

Master Symbols ⸺   *p. 68*

Magic Bullet Theory

Chapter 5

Normative Theories of Mass Communication

Next time you visit the local supermarket, glance at the tabloids prominently displayed next to the cashier. The headlines are predictable: Somewhere aliens from outer space have invaded the earth; somewhere else ancient treasure, frozen mammoths, or the relics of a lost civilization have been uncovered. Often, animals are found that can read, do arithmetic, or talk. And of course, there are endless reports about the kinky and bizarre exploits, sexual and otherwise, of television and movie stars. Not even death could stop the stories about Elvis Presley.

Have you ever asked yourself how can someone print this stuff if it isn't true? Then again, if it *is* true, why doesn't the local newspaper or network television cover it? The world depicted by the *National Enquirer* is a very different place than the one viewed through the eye of CBS news.

There's no mystery why the supermarket tabloids print what they do. Sex, crime, death, celebrities, the occult, strange animals, and aliens all sell newspapers. But have *you* ever been tempted to buy one of these papers? What headlines might have caught your eye or excited your curiosity or titillated your imagination? It probably wasn't one for a story about the national debt or a congressional debate over health care reform.

If these seamy stories sell newspapers, why don't mainstream media operations cover them as well? This chapter addresses this question. We will show how these differences in news content arose as some media practitioners created new definitions for news and new ways of producing and distributing it. As we saw in

Chapter 3, during the yellow journalism era, most newspapers used news definitions and production and distribution strategies resembling those employed by the tabloids of today. But after the turn of the century, a crusade began among some news industry people and various social elites to clean up the media and make newspapers more respectable and credible. The watchword of this crusade was *professionalism* and its goal was elimination of shoddy and irresponsible news content. With rare exceptions, like supermarket tabloids and some "reality television" news shows, the values of today's news media and the media system as a whole were shaped by this crusade.

Some sort of theory is needed to guide the task of media reform. This theory should be able to answer questions such as these:

- Should media do something more than merely distribute whatever content will earn them the greatest profits in the shortest time?
- Are there some essential public services that media should provide even if no immediate profits can be earned?
- Should media become involved in identifying and solving social problems?
- Is it necessary or advisable for media to serve as watchdogs and protect consumers against business fraud and corrupt bureaucrats?
- What should we expect media to do for us in times of crisis?

These broad questions about the role of media are linked to issues concerning the day-to-day operation of media. How should media management and production jobs be structured? What moral and ethical standards should guide media workers? Are there any circumstances when it is appropriate or even necessary to invade people's privacy or risk ruining their reputations? If someone threatens to commit suicide in front of a television camera what should a reporter do — get it on tape or try to stop it? Should a newspaper print a story about unethical business practices even if the company involved is one of its biggest advertisers? Should television networks broadcast a highly rated program even if it routinely contains high levels of violence?

Answers to questions like these are found in *normative theory — a type of theory that describes an ideal way for a media system to be structured and operated.* Normative theories are different from most of the theories we will review in this book. They don't describe things as they are nor do they provide scientific explanations or predictions. Instead, they describe the way things should be if some ideal values or principles are to be realized. Normative theories come from many sources. Sometimes they are developed by media practitioners themselves. Sometimes they are developed by social critics or academics. Most normative theories develop over time and contain elements drawn from previous theories. This is especially true of the normative theory that currently guides American mass media, which is a synthesis of ideas developed over the past three centuries.

In the United States, a clear distinction is made between normative and social scientific theories. Normative theories describe ideal roles for media, recommend ideal practices, and envision ideal consequences. Scientific theories are based on empirical observation and provide useful descriptions and explanations of phenomena. As we will see in Chapter 13, critical theorists object to this differentiation. In their view, critical theories are needed that envision ideal roles for media *and* then use these ideals to critique existing roles or practices. Empirical observations can be made to assess whether ideal values are being served. The goal of this critical research is reform or transformation of practices to achieve ideal goals. Thus, if successful, critical theory and research could guide development of new roles for media and identify useful changes in bureaucratic structure and production practices. Critical theory may offer an important alternative to traditional normative theory. We will consider this possibility in Chapters 13 and 14, but for now, the point is a simple one: Normative theories are not grounded on empirical observation but rather on what *should be*.

It may be useful to take a few minutes now, before you read the remainder of this chapter, to think about your views concerning the role of media for yourself, your community, your state, your nation, and your world. What are the most important things that media should and shouldn't do? What standards of behavior should media practitioners follow as they perform these tasks? Is it permissible to do beneficial things but use questionable or unethical practices? For example, should reporters deliberately lie or engage in burglary to expose corrupt business practices? What about using a hidden camera to catch a corrupt politician taking a bribe? What about the high percentage of entertainment programming on television? Should there be less entertainment and more content that informs and educates?

Overview

This chapter will introduce you to a variety of normative theories of media including some that are questionable or even objectionable. We will proceed from earlier forms of normative theory to more recent examples. Our attention will focus on the normative theory that is predominantly used to guide and legitimize most large media in America — *social responsibility theory*. For some time now, the debate over normative theory has been muted in the United States. Social responsibility theory has seemingly provided such an ideal standard for media that further debate was considered unnecessary. The past 30 years have seen unprecedented growth and consolidation of control in the media industries and, as a result, gigantic conglomerates dominate the production and distribution of media content. Yet even these conglomerates have found that social responsibility theory provides practical guidelines for their operations and serves to legitimize what they do.

We will assess why social responsibility theory has enduring appeal for American media practitioners. We will contrast it with theories popular in other parts of the world. Then we will speculate about its future. As new industries based on new media technologies emerge, will social responsibility theory continue to guide them or will alternatives develop? Social responsibility theory is suited to a particular era of national development and to specific types of media. As the media industries change, it may have to be substantially revised or replaced. The chapter ends with consideration of some possible alternatives.

The Origin of Normative Theories of Media

Since the beginning of the twentieth century, the role of mass media in American society, as we've already seen, has been hotly debated. Sharply conflicting views have been expressed. At one extreme are people who argue for what we will term *radical libertarian* ideals. These people believe that there should be no laws governing media operations. They are *First Amendment Absolutists* who take the notion of "free press" quite literally to mean that all forms of media must be totally unregulated. They accept as gospel that the First Amendment dictate that "Congress shall make no law . . . abridging the freedom of speech or of the press" means exactly what is says. As Supreme Court Justice Hugo Black succinctly stated, "No law means no law."

At the other extreme are people who believe in direct regulation of media, most often by a government agency or commission. These include advocates of *technocratic control*, people like Harold Lasswell and Walter Lippmann. They argue that media practitioners can't be trusted to communicate responsibly or to use media to serve vital public needs. Some sort of oversight or control is necessary to assure that important needs are satisfied. Their views are taken most seriously during times of crisis when we need media to serve specific needs.

As we saw in Chapter 4, the advocates of control based their arguments on propaganda theories. According to them, the threat posed by propaganda was so great that information gathering and transmission had to be placed under the control of wise persons — technocrats who could be trusted to act in the public interest. These technocrats would be highly trained and have professional values and skills that guaranteed that media content would serve socially valuable purposes, for example, stopping the spread of totalitarianism or informing people about natural disasters or a disease like AIDS.

Other proponents of regulation based their views on mass society theory (see Chapter 3). They were troubled by the power of media content to undermine high culture with trivial forms of entertainment. Their complaints often centered around the way that sex and violence were presented by media. They also objected to the trivialization of what they consider to be important moral values.

Thus, both propaganda and mass society theories can be used to lobby for media regulation. In both perspectives, media are viewed as a powerful, subversive force that must be brought under the control of wise people, those who can be trusted to act in the public interest. But who should be trusted to censor media? Social scientists? Religious leaders? The military? The police? Congress? The Federal Communications Commission? Although many powerful people believed in the necessity of controlling media, they couldn't reach consensus on who should do it. Media practitioners were able to negotiate compromises by pointing out the dangers of regulation and by offering to engage in self-regulation — to become more socially responsible.

The advocates of regulation were opposed by people who favored various forms of libertarianism. Eventually, social responsibility theory emerged from this debate. It represents a compromise between views favoring government control of media and those favoring total press freedom. This didn't satisfy everyone, but it did have broad appeal, especially within the media industries. Even today, most media practitioners use some variant of social responsibility theory to justify their actions. To fully understand social responsibility theory we must review the ideas and events that led to its development. First, we will review libertarian theory, including its recent variants. Then we will trace the debate over regulation of radio in 1927 and the movement to professionalize media. We will consider how social responsibility theory finally emerged from the debate over the regulation of newspapers in the 1940s. Finally, we will evaluate social responsibility theory and contrast it with other theories.

The Origin of Libertarian Thought

Modern libertarian thought can be traced back to sixteenth century Europe — an era when feudal aristocracies exercised arbitrary power over the lives of most people. It was also an era rocked by major social changes. International trade and urbanization undermined the power of a rural aristocracy. A variety of social movements arose, including the Protestant Reformation, that demanded greater freedom for individuals over their own lives and thoughts (Altschull, 1990).

Libertarian theory arose in opposition to *authoritarian theory* — an idea that placed all forms of communication under the control of a governing elite or authorities (Siebert, Peterson, and Schramm, 1956). Authorities justified their control to protect and preserve a divinely ordained social order. In most countries, control rested in the hands of a king who, in turn, granted royal charters or licenses to media practitioners. Practitioners could be jailed for violating charters. Charters or licenses could be revoked. Censorship of all types was possible. Authoritarian control tended to be exercised in arbitrary, erratic ways. Sometimes, considerable freedom might exist to publicize minority viewpoints and culture as long as authorities didn't perceive a direct threat to their power. Unlike totalitarianism, authoritarian theory doesn't prioritize cultivation of a homogeneous, national culture. It only requires acquiescence to a governing elite.

In rebelling against authoritarian theory, early libertarians argued that if individuals could be freed from the arbitrary limits on communication imposed by Church and State, they would "naturally" follow the dictates of their conscience, seek truth, engage in public debate, and ultimately create a better life for themselves and others (McQuail, 1987; Siebert, Peterson, and Schramm, 1956). They blamed authorities for preserving unnatural, arbitrary social orders. They believed strongly in the power of unrestricted public debate and discussion to create more natural ways of structuring society.

In *Aeropagetica*, a powerful libertarian tract published in 1644, John Milton asserted that in a fair debate good and truthful arguments will always win out over lies and deceit. If this were true, it followed, then a new and better social order could be forged using public debate. This idea came to be referred to as Milton's *self-righting principle* and it continues to be widely cited by contemporary journalists as a rationale for preserving press freedom (Altschull, 1990). It is a fundamental principle within social responsibility theory.

Unfortunately, most early libertarians had a rather unrealistic view of how long it would take to find the "truth" and establish an ideal social order. This ideal order was not necessarily a democracy and it might not always permit communication freedom. Milton, for example, came to argue that the "truth" had been found by Oliver Cromwell and its validity had been demonstrated by his battlefield victories. Because he was convinced that Cromwell had created the ideal social order, Milton was willing to serve as the chief censor in Cromwell's regime. He expressed few regrets about limiting what Catholic leaders could communicate (Altschull, 1990).

When it became clear during the eighteenth century that definitive forms of "truth" couldn't be quickly or easily established, some libertarians became discouraged. Occasionally, they drifted back and forth between libertarian and authoritarian views. Even Thomas Jefferson, author of the Declaration of Independence, wavered in his commitment to press freedom and his faith in the self-righting principle. He voiced his deep frustration with scurrilous newspaper criticism during the second term of his presidency. Nevertheless, he reaffirmed Milton's self-righting principle in a letter written in retirement (Altschull, 1990, p. 117).

Libertarian ideals are at the heart of America's long-term experiment with democratic self government. The revolution of the American Colonies against Britain was legitimized by libertarian ideals — recall Patrick Henry's famous statement, "Give Me Liberty or Give Me Death." The newly formed United States was one of the first nations to explicitly adopt libertarian principles in the Declaration of Independence and the Bill of Rights. The latter asserts that all individuals have natural rights that no government, community, or group can unduly infringe upon or take away. Various forms of communication freedom — speech, press, and assembly — are listed as among the most important of these rights. The ability to express dissent, to band together with others to resist laws that people find to be wrong, to print or broadcast ideas, opinions, and beliefs — all of these rights are proclaimed as central to democratic self government.

But despite the priority given to communication freedom, it is important to recognize that many restrictions have been placed on communication. Libel laws protect against the publication of information that will damage reputations. Judges can issue gag orders to stop the publication of information that they think will interfere with a defendant's right to a fair trial. Other laws and regulations protect against false advertising, child pornography, and offensive language. The limits to communication freedom are being constantly renegotiated. In some eras, the balance shifts toward expanding freedom and at other times, freedom is curtailed. Whenever new media technologies are invented, it is necessary to decide how they should be regulated. The debate over communication freedom never ends.

Why is it necessary to place limits on communication freedom? The most common reason for limiting communication freedom is a conflict over basic rights. For example, where do the rights guaranteed to you by the Constitution end and those of another person begin? Do you have the right to shout "Fire" in a crowded movie theater if there is no fire? If you did, many other people would be hurt — don't they have a right to be protected against your irresponsible behavior? Similar questions arise when groups attempt to stir up hatred and resentment against racial or ethnic minorities. Does a Klansman have the right to tell lies about African Americans or gays? What about the false propaganda used by Hitler against the Jews? Shouldn't such irresponsible forms of communication be controlled? The larger issue, the one that goes beyond that of communication freedom, is the question of fundamental human rights and how best to maximize them at a given point in history. As we shall see in Chapter 14, these questions are at the heart of the current debate over what some term political correctness and others regard as minority empowerment and cultural sensitivity.

What about free press rights? Just how far should newspapers and broadcast stations be permitted to go in exercising their rights? Should they be allowed

Box 5a You Make the Call on Racist Television

Confronting the issue of "Hate TV," the newspaper *USA Today* ran the following editorial and the accompanying opposing view from economist and writer, Julianne Malveaux on January 6, 1989, p. 10A. With whom do you side? Why?

EDITORIAL

Don't Trample Rights to Get at 'Hate TV'

Like any TV talk show, the program begins with soft music. The host, in a three-piece suit, introduces the guests. But that's about as respectable as it gets. The host, former grand dragon of the Ku Klux Klan, heads the White American Political Association and White Aryan Resistance. It's a hate show. Not "shock TV" like that hosted by Phil, Oprah, Geraldo, Morton, and Sally Jesse. But hate. They're showing up on public-access cable TV in communities across the USA. Some fantasize about white supremacy. Some claim blacks and Jews spread the AIDS virus. That's so absurd no one with any sense would believe it. But some local government officials are overreacting to these warped people and to their warped views.

They want to censor them. They . . . want to keep them off TV channels that cable systems have to make available for public use. That's not the democratic way. As mean-spirited and despicable as the white supremacists and the garbage they peddle are, they have a right to broadcast if they aren't obscene and don't incite violence.

The mayors of Cincinnati and Pocatello, Idaho, tried to eliminate their public-use channels when the Klan showed up with a tape. Fear of racist shows almost caused Jackson, Miss., not to renew its public-access channel. Kansas City pulled the plug on its public-use channel and substituted another with more control of editorial content, rather than broadcast *Klansas Kable*. Next Wednesday, the city will be sued by the KKK, represented by the American Civil Liberties Union. Local officials and organizations in communities with public-access TV are watching the case closely.

If Kansas City can get by with eliminating its channel, others will try. That would be a big mistake. Then no one would have access to public TV. And that would give the Klan's kleagles, klaverns, cyclops, and wizards veto power over responsible, beneficial programs. Without the public-use channels, Vietnamese immigrants in Cupertino, Calif., couldn't see news from their homeland. Senior citizens and the deaf couldn't produce their own shows in Somerville, Mass. And special programs couldn't be produced by and for Chicago's handicapped. Without public-use TV, much of the ethnic, cultural and educational programming that commercial TV can't afford would never be produced. Important information would be denied the aged and the handicapped and the civic-minded.

In Austin, Texas, and Spokane, Wash., responsible organizations rallied when "hate TV" came to their communities. They countered with live talk shows and call-in programs and documentaries. They neutralized the haters. That's the right way. Free speech means free speech. For everybody. Public-access TV means public access. For everybody. Don't make martyrs out of haters by censoring them. Don't give them life-and-death control over public-use TV. Let them crawl out into the open. Let everybody see them. Let everybody hear their bizarre, sick messages. Let the sunlight shine on their hatred. It disinfects.

Copyright 1989, *USA Today*.
Reprinted with permission.

Box 5a continued

AN OPPOSING VIEW

Censoring "Hate TV" Protects Our Rights

Should the Ku Klux Klan and other white supremacists be allowed to use public-access cable TV or radio to spread their message of hate? Does broadcasting a message of racial intolerance serve any useful purpose? I think not! The race-hate message was one that Klan members once preached in the dark, shielding themselves with hoods, thus reaching only a lunatic fringe. But now, apparently with the sanction of the Federal Communications Commission, these racists have taken to the airwaves and cable wires.

Is it wrong to blame the FCC? NAACP Western Regional Director James Martin says deregulation is part of the problem and that '80s programmers respond to market concerns, not ethical ones. Ten years ago, you would not have heard the "n-word" over the air or on cable. Today, thanks to hate TV and radio, such utterances are regular.

Those who broadcast hate TV and radio attempt to present themselves in the shadow of the civil rights movement. Thus, the National Association for the Advancement of White People is formulated as a shadow of the National Association for the Advancement of Colored People. There are groups like the White American Political Action Committee to mimic the Black American Political Action Committee.

But the Niagara movement, which in 1909 formed the NAACP, promoted black rights because the law prevented black people from the full use of civil, political, and economic prerogatives. Grandfather clauses, segregated schools, restrictive covenants, and redlining made the organization of the NAACP necessary. These groups argued for full participation, not the race-hating exclusion that white supremacist groups advocate. As a card-carrying member of the American Civil Liberties Union, I am aware of colleagues who argue that the Klan has the same right to free speech as anyone else. But does someone have the right to cry "fire!" in an crowded theatre? To use the n-word and promote race hate when the gossamer thread of race relations is almost at breaking point after Forsyth County, Howard Beach, Eleanor Bumpers, and Tawana Brawley?

If lawmakers favor upholding the dignity and integrity of all people, if they are willing to enforce this principle where they can, they will say an empathic "no" to hate television and radio. Our Congress, our FCC, and local government bodies can put a stop to the pandering of hate. The viewers and listeners of our nation deserve much better.

Julianne Malveaux in *USA Today*,
January 6, 1989, p. 10A
Reprinted by permission of the author.

to invade your home, publish erroneous information about you, or deceive you with false advertising? Do publishers have the right to publish anything that will earn profits or should some limits be placed on them? If so, who should place and enforce those limits? If laws are written to protect individuals from irresponsible media, can such laws become a means of censoring the press?

The Marketplace of Ideas: A New Form of Radical Libertarianism

Though libertarian thought dates from the founding of the United States, it has undergone many transformations. An important variant emerged in the 1800s during the penny press and yellow journalism eras. Throughout this period, public confidence in both business and government was shaken by recurring depressions, widespread corruption, and injustice. Large companies, most notably in the oil, railroad, and steel industries, created nationwide monopolies to charge unfair prices and reap enormous profits. Workers were paid low salaries and forced to labor under difficult or hazardous conditions. Public respect for newspapers also ebbed as publishers pursued profits and created news to sell papers. Several social movements, especially the Progressive and Populist movements, sprang up to call for new laws and greater government regulation (Brownell, 1983; Altschull, 1990). Anti-trust legislation was enacted to break up the big monopolies. Libertarians feared that these laws and regulations would go too far. They sought to rekindle public support for libertarian ideals.

Some media practitioners developed a cogent response to Progressive and Populist criticisms. They argued that media should be regarded as a *self-regulating marketplace of ideas*. This idea is a variation of a fundamental principle of capitalism—the notion of a self-regulating market. In classical capitalist theory as formulated by Adam Smith, there is no need for the government to regulate markets. An open and competitive marketplace should regulate itself. If a product is in high demand, prices will "naturally" rise as consumers compete to buy it. This encourages other manufacturers to produce the product. Once demand is met by increased manufacturing, the price falls. If one manufacturer charges too much for a product, then competitors will cut their prices to attract buyers. No government interference is necessary to protect consumers or to force manufacturers to meet consumer needs. Another term used to refer to these ideas is the *laissez-faire doctrine*.

According to marketplace of ideas theory, the laissez-faire doctrine should be applied to mass media; that is, if ideas are "traded" freely among people, the correct or best ideas will prevail. The *ideas* compete and the best will be "bought." But there are some difficulties in applying this logic to our large, contemporary media. Media content is far less tangible than other consumer products. The meaning of individual messages can vary tremendously from one person to the next. Just what is being traded when news stories or television dramas are "bought" and "sold?" When we buy a newspaper, we don't buy individual stories, we buy packages of them bundled with features like comics and horoscopes. We can choose to ignore anything in the package that we find offensive. When we watch television, we don't pay a fee to the networks. Yet buying and selling are

Box 5b A Stirring Defense of Free Expression

Concurring with the majority in the 1927 Supreme Court decision in *Whitney v. California*, Justice Louis Brandeis penned this stunning defense for freedom of expression:

Those who won our independence believed that the final end of the State was to make men free to develop their faculties; and that in its government the deliberative forces should prevail over the arbitrary. They valued liberty both as an end and as a means. They believed liberty to be the secret of happiness and courage to be the secret of liberty. They believed that freedom to think as you will and speak as you think are means indispensable to the discovery and spread of political truth; that without free speech and assembly discussion would be futile; that with them, discussion affords ordinarily adequate protection against the dissemination of noxious doctrine; that the greatest menace to freedom is an inert people; that public discussion is a political duty;

and that this should be a fundamental principle of the American government. They recognized the risks to which all human institutions are subject. But they knew that order cannot be secured merely through fear of punishment for its infraction; that it is hazardous to discourage thought, hope, and imagination; that fear breeds repression; that repression breeds hate; that hate menaces stable government; that the path of safety lies in the opportunity to discuss freely supposed grievances and proposed remedies; and that the fitting remedy for evil counsels is good ones. Believing in the power of reason as applied through public discussion, they eschewed silence coerced by law—the argument of force in its worst form. Recognizing the occasional tyrannies of governing majorities, they amended the Constitution so that free speech and assembly should be guaranteed.

(Gillmor and Barron, 1974, pp. 21–22.)

clearly involved with network programs. Advertisers buy time on these shows and then use the programs as vehicles for their messages. When they buy time they buy access to the audience for the show; they do not necessarily buy the rightness or correctness of the program's ideas. Sponsors pay more to advertise on programs with large audiences. Clearly, the media marketplace is a bit more complicated than the marketplace for refrigerators or toothpaste.

In the American media system the marketplace of ideas was supposed to work like this. Someone comes up with a good idea and then transmits it through some form of mass communication. If other people like it, then they buy the message. When people buy the message, they pay for its production and distribution costs. Once these costs are covered, the message producer earns a profit. If people don't like the message, then they don't buy it and the producer goes broke trying to produce and distribute it. If people are wise message consumers, then the producers of the best and most useful messages will become rich and develop large media enterprises while the producers of bad messages will fail. Useless media

Box 5c Which Model of the Marketplace?

The Market Place of Ideas sees the operation of the mass media system as analogous to that of the self-regulating product market. Take this example and judge for yourself the goodness-of-fit.

Product Producer	Product	Consumer
Model 1		
A product producer	produces a product as efficiently and inexpensively as possible	for its consumers who wield the ultimate power, to buy or not to buy.
Model 2		
Hersheys	produces candy efficiently and inexpensively on a production line	for people like us. If we buy the candy, Hersheys continues to make similar candy in a similar way.
Model 3		
NBC	produces people using programs, their production line,	for advertisers. If they buy NBC's product, NBC continues to produce similar audiences in similar ways.

What do these models imply about the quality of candy in America? What do they say about the quality of television?

will go broke. If the purveyors of good ideas succeed, then these ideas should become more easily available at lower cost. Producers will compete to supply them. Similarly, the cost of bad ideas should rise and access to them should lessen. Eventually, truth should win out in the marketplace of ideas just as it should triumph in the public forum envisioned by the early libertarians. According to marketplace of ideas theory, the self-righting principle should apply to mass media as well as to public debate.

Since the marketplace of ideas is self-regulating, there is no need for a government agency to censor messages. Audiences won't buy bad messages and therefore irresponsible producers will go broke. But what if advertiser support permits bad messages to be distributed for free—maybe people will be less discriminating if they don't have to directly pay to receive such messages? What if the bad messages are distributed as part of a large bundle of messages (that is, a newspaper or television news program)? If you want the good messages, you also pay to subsidize the bad messages. What is bad for you may be good for someone else. You may not like horoscopes or soap operas but you have friends who do.

But just how useful is marketplace of ideas theory? After all, government regulation of the consumer marketplace is now generally accepted as necessary. Few people question the need for consumer protection laws or laws regulating unfair business practices. Since the consumer marketplace benefited from regulation, why not regulate the marketplace of ideas? From 1930 onward, this question has been asked more and more frequently by media critics. Even so, marketplace of ideas theory still enjoys some support within the media industries.

Government Regulation of Media — The Federal Radio Commission

During the 1920s and 1930s, a new normative theory of mass communication began to emerge that rejected both radical libertarian and technocratic control notions. One source of this theory was Congressional debates over government regulation of radio. In 1927, these debates led to the establishment of the Federal Radio Commission (FRC), which was the forerunner of the Federal Communication Commission (FCC). As the debates raged, some people—especially Progressive and Populist politicians—argued that the excesses of yellow journalism proved that self-regulation wasn't enough. Over-dramatized and fictitious news were so profitable that publishers couldn't resist producing it. Without some sort of regulation, radio was not likely to serve the public interest as well as it should. Even so, Progressives were cautious about turning control of radio over to government technocrats. A compromise solution was sought.

By the 1920s, government regulation of public utilities had become widely accepted as a means of ending wasteful competition while preserving private enterprise. Before government regulation of power companies or telephone companies, cities were blanketed with competing networks of wires. Anyone who wanted to telephone people on other networks had to buy phones from all the competing companies. The cost of building totally independent networks increased the cost of phone service and electricity. The solution to these problems was to allow one company to have a monopoly on supplying these needed services. In return for being granted a monopoly, the company submitted to government regulation of prices and services. In this way, public utilities were created with government commissions to oversee their operation. Could a government commission be used to regulate radio as a public utility?

Proponents of a radio commission pointed out the similarities between the early radio industry and the early telephone and power industries. Although broadcasters didn't need to cover a city with wires to send radio signals, they did need to be able to use a particular frequency for their transmission signal. If another broadcaster used this same frequency, she or he would cut into the original broadcast and disrupt it. Initially, radio manufacturers were the only companies who could afford to build large and powerful radio stations. Stations were built to stimulate public interest in the new medium and create a market for radio receivers. But the big stations soon faced growing competition from a variety of sources, including radio enthusiasts who set up stations in their living rooms and garages. Larger cities were blanketed with competing signals. Those who had invested money in the construction of large stations appealed to government to help protect their investment. They requested government regulation as a means of ending competition from stations they thought to be inferior. The public, too, was growing weary of the constant interference in and unpredictability of radio broadcasts. Secretary of Commerce Herbert Hoover himself was moved to remark, "This is one of the few instances where the country is unanimous in its desire for more regulation" (Barnouw, 1966).

In the debate over the establishment of the Federal Radio Commission, one especially important philosophy was championed by Secretary Hoover — the airwaves belong to the people. If airwaves are public property like other national resources (national forests, for example), then privately operated stations can never own them. Instead, they must be licensed from the people and used in the public interest. If a license holder violates the public trust, her or his license can be revoked. The FRC was created to act on behalf of the public. It was given a mandate to make certain that radio stations provided important services to the public in return for the privilege of using public airwaves. The broadcasters were required to serve the "public interest, convenience, or necessity. Unlike public utilities however, the FRC had no mandate to regulate industry profits. Stations were free to compete against each other and to earn the largest profits possible as long as they continued to provide certain basic public services such as news bulletins or community service programming. Moreover, the FRC had no ability to directly censor content but it could punish stations that broadcast prohibited content with fines or loss of their license.

The radio industry was the first media industry to ask for and submit to government regulation. The relative success of the FRC encouraged efforts to regulate other media industries. Government censorship of movies was widely advocated, especially by religious groups. Over the years, the movie industry has adopted various forms of self-censorship in an effort to avoid government regulation. As the threat of propaganda grew, even regulation of newspapers was seriously considered. In 1942, for example, the Hutchins Commission on Freedom of the Press was established to weigh the merits of newspaper regulation (we'll say more about this later).

Professionalization of Journalism

As pressure for government regulation of media mounted in this century, industry leaders responded with efforts to professionalize. As noted in Chapter 3, Pulitzer and Hearst established professional awards. The industry lobbied for and subsidized the establishment of professional schools to train media practitioners. Rather than cede control of media to a government agency, media managers went on record with pledges to serve public needs. In 1923, the American Society of Newspaper Editors adopted a set of professional standards entitled "The Canons of Journalism." Since then virtually every association of media practitioners has adopted similar standards. In doing so, they are emulating professionals in fields like law and medicine. These standards typically commit media practitioners to serving the public as effectively as possible.

Industry codes of ethics began to formalize another important notion about the role of media—that of a watchdog guarding the welfare of the public. This

---

Box 5d   The ASNE Canons of Journalism and Statement of Principles

Here are the American Society of Newspaper Editors' "Canons of Journalism" adopted in 1924. They are followed by the ASNE's *Statement of Principles* that were adopted in 1975 to replace the Canons. What changes in our society, in journalism, and in the media in general occurred between 1924 and 1975 that might have required the change? How well does your favorite newspaper conform to the Statement? How about your favorite television news show?

CANONS OF JOURNALISM

I. *Responsibility.* The right of a newspaper to attract and hold readers is restricted by nothing but considerations of public welfare. The use a newspaper makes of the share of public attention it gains serves to determine its sense of responsibility, which it shares with every member of its staff. A journalist who uses his power for any selfish or otherwise unworthy purpose is faithless to a high trust.

II. *Freedom of the Press.* Freedom of the press is to be guarded as a vital right of mankind. It is the unquestionable right to discuss what ever is not explicitly forbidden by law, including the wisdom of any restrictive statute.

III. *Independence.* Freedom from all obligations except that of fidelity to the public interest is vital.

1. Promotion of any private interest contrary to the general welfare, for whatever reason, is not compatible with honest journalism. So-called news communications from private sources should not be published without public notice of their source or else substantiation of their claims to value as news, both in form and substance.

2. Partisanship in editorial comment which knowingly departs from the truth does violence to the best spirit of American journalism; in the news columns it is subversive of a fundamental principle of the profession.

Box 5d continued

IV. *Sincerity, Truthfulness, Accuracy.* Good faith with the reader is the foundation of all journalism worthy of the name.

1. By every consideration of good faith a newspaper is constrained to be truthful. It is not to be excused for lack of thoroughness or accuracy within its control or failure to obtain command of these essential qualities.

2. Headlines should be fully warranted by the contents of the articles which they surmount.

V. *Impartiality.* Sound practice makes clear distinctions between news reports and expressions of opinion. News reports should be free from opinion or bias of any kind.

This rule does not apply to so-called special articles unmistakably devoted to advocacy or characterized by a signature authorizing the writer's own conclusions and interpretations.

VI. *Fair Play.* A newspaper should not publish unofficial charges affecting reputation or moral character without opportunity given to the accused to be heard; right practice demands the giving of such opportunity in all cases of serious accusation outside judicial proceedings.

1. A newspaper should not invade private rights or feelings without sure warrant of public right as distinguished from public curiosity.

2. It is the privilege, as it is the duty, of a newspaper to make prompt and complete correction of its own serious mistakes of fact or opinion, whatever their origin.

VI. *Decency.* A newspaper cannot escape conviction of insincerity if while professing high moral purpose it supplies incentives to base conduct, such as are to be found in details of crime and vice, publication of which is not demonstrably for the general good. Lacking authority to enforce its canons, the journalism here represented can but express the hope that deliberate pandering to vicious instincts will encounter effective public disapproval or yield to the influence of a preponderant professional condemnation.

STATEMENT OF PRINCIPLES

ARTICLE I: Responsibility

The primary purpose of gathering and distributing news and opinion is to serve the general welfare by informing the people and enabling them to make judgments on the issues of the time. Newspapermen and women who abuse the power of their professional role for selfish motives or unworthy purposes are faithless to that public trust.

The American press was made free not just to inform or just to serve as a forum for debate but also to bring an independent scrutiny to bear on the forces of power in the society, including the conduct of official power at all levels of government.

ARTICLE II: Freedom of the Press

Freedom of the press belongs to the people. It must be defended against encroachment or assault from any quarter, public or private.

Journalists must be constantly alert to see that the public's business is conducted in public. They must be vigilant against all who would exploit the press for selfish purposes.

ARTICLE III: Independence

Journalists must avoid impropriety and the appearance of impropriety as well as any conflict of interest or the appearance of conflict. They should neither accept anything nor pursue any activity that might compromise or seem to compromise their integrity.

Box 5d continued

ARTICLE IV: Truth and Accuracy

Good faith with the reader is the foundation of good journalism. Every effort must be made to assure that the news content is accurate, free from bias and in context, and that all sides are presented fairly. Editorials, analytical articles and commentary should be held to the same standards of accuracy with respect to facts as news reports.

Significant errors of fact, as well as errors of omission, should be corrected promptly and prominently.

ARTICLE V: Impartiality

To be impartial does not require the press to be unquestioning or to refrain from editorial expression. Sound practice, however, demands a clear distinction for the reader between news reports and opinion. Articles that contain opinion or personal interpretation should be clearly identified.

ARTICLE VI: Fair Play

Journalists should respect the rights of people involved in the news, observe the common standards of decency, and stand accountable to the public for the fairness and accuracy of their news reports.

Persons publicly accused should be given the earliest opportunity to respond. Pledges of confidentiality to news sources must be honored at all costs, and therefore should not be given lightly. Unless there is clear and pressing need to maintain confidences, sources of information should be identified.

These principles are intended to preserve, protect, and strengthen the bond of trust and respect between American journalists and the American people, a bond that is essential to sustain the grant of freedom entrusted to both by the nation's founders.

---

role was first articulated by muckraking journalists about the turn of the century. It assumes that media should continually scan the social world and alert the public to problems. Initially, this conception of media was viewed with skepticism by yellow journalists. However, muckraking investigations of corruption proved so popular that eventually the role became widely accepted. In some ambitious formulations of this role, the media are envisioned as an independent social institution—a Fourth Estate—charged with making certain that all other institutions—government, business, religion, family—serve the public. This perspective assumes that once people are informed about wrong-doing, incompetency, or inefficiency, they will take action against it. The masthead of the old Cleveland *Press* put it in these words, "Give light and the People will find their way."

In joining the trend toward professionalization, media practitioners, like doctors and lawyers before them, pledged to uphold standards of professional practice. They promised to weed out irresponsible people and give recognition to those who excel. Those who violate standards are to be censured. In extreme cases, they are barred from professional practice.

Limitations of Professionalization

As an alternative to direct government regulation, media professionalization worked rather well. Certain limitations, however, lead to recurring problems:

1   **Professionals in every field, including journalism, have been reluctant to identify and censure colleagues who violate professional standards.** To do so is often seen as admitting that embarrassing problems exist. Public trust in all professionals might be shaken if too many people are barred from practice. Professional societies tend to operate as closed groups in which members are protected against outside threats and criticism. Attacks from outsiders are routinely dismissed as unwarranted even when evidence against a practitioner mounts. Often, action is taken only in extreme cases when it cannot be avoided. Even then, news media either avoid covering the case or provide brief and superficial coverage.

2   **Professional standards can be overly abstract and ambiguous.** They may be difficult to implement and enforce. Mission statements and broad codes of ethics are notoriously vague. When should journalists engage in aggressive surveillance of government and when should they simply reprint press releases? In the Canons of Journalism adopted by the American Society of Newspaper Editors, editors vowed, "By every consideration of good faith a newspaper is constrained to be truthful. It is not to be excused for lack of thoroughness or accuracy within its control or failure to obtain command of these essential qualities." This standard rules out deliberate printing of lies, but just how much effort must a journalist make to confirm the truth of a story? How much thoroughness or accuracy is possible under deadline pressures? Should there be two confirming sources, or three, or four?

   During the Watergate scandal, the two Washington *Post* reporters who broke many important stories were required by their editor to have at least two and ideally three sources to confirm the truth of stories. When this proved difficult to do, they would call a potential source, read a story, and ask the source to simply hang up if they could confirm it. In this way, a failure to deny a story served to confirm it. Some press critics argue that this was at best a questionable practice.

   Thus, simply vowing to be truthful doesn't mandate that reporters must always engage in time-consuming, aggressive investigative journalism. Editors must make choices concerning allocation of resources. Increasingly, the news we read consists of edited corporate and government public relations press releases. How do editors decide when to stop rewriting press releases and start engaging in surveillance? There may be no reason to doubt the truth of press releases unless a reporter takes the time to conduct an independent investigation. But what if an investigation might lead a large advertiser to cancel its account with the paper? Why risk finding answers that would be embarrassing? In the news business, telling the truth can sometimes be difficult and expensive. Since professional standards are vague, there is nothing that forces journalists to endanger relationships with friendly sources or their profit margins in order to print truth.

A major limitation of the surveillance mission of the press is that it doesn't allow the press itself to be scrutinized by an independent agent. There is no formal press watchdog and journalists have strongly resisted establishing one. And although publications like the *Columbia Journalism Review* and the *Washington Journalism Review* provide regular critical examination of the profession, no one can demand that the press conduct an investigation or demand that one be stopped. Some newspapers have recognized this problem by hiring an ombudsman — a person who takes in complaints about news coverage and conducts internal investigations. Sometimes, the ombudsman writes columns reporting her or his findings, but these are rarely very hard hitting and tend to be buried deep in Sunday editions.

3   **In contrast with medicine and law, media professionalization doesn't include standards for professional training and licensing.** Other professions mandate that practitioners receive long and closely monitored professional training. For example, doctors and lawyers undergo from 4 to 10 years of specialized training in addition to completing 4 years of college. But media practitioners are unwilling to set standards for professional training and have strongly resisted efforts to license journalists. They argue that these requirements would inevitably be used by government to control the press. If the press is to remain free from control, then it must be free to hire anyone — no matter how untrained or unqualified. Anyone should be able to claim the title of journalist, start a newspaper, and exercise his or her free press rights. No government agency should be able to step in and shut down a paper just because some of its reporters or editors are unlicensed.

Arguments against specialized training and licensing of media practitioners fail to consider how these standards are enforced in other professions. Licensing has not brought doctors and lawyers directly under government control. Even when government agencies issue licenses, professional associations effectively control the standards used to determine who will get a license.

4   **In contrast with other professions, media practitioners tend to have less independent control over their work.** Media practitioners don't work as autonomous practitioners and therefore have difficulty assuming personal responsibility for their work. They tend to work within big, hierarchically structured bureaucracies. Individual reporters, editors, producers, or directors have only a limited ability to control what they do. Reporters are given assignments by editors, advertising designers work for account executives, and television anchors and camera operators follow the instructions of news directors. Editors, account managers, and directors are all responsible to higher management. In these large bureaucracies, it is difficult to assign responsibility. Those at lower levels can claim that they are only "following orders," while people at higher levels can simply disavow any knowledge of what was going on below them.

5   **In the media industries, violation of professional standards rarely has immediate, directly observable consequences.** Thus, it is hard for critics to cite violations or to identify the harm that has been done. Unethical conduct might even do some good. Two cases come to mind. In 1980, Janet Cooke, a reporter for the Washington *Post*, wrote a series of news stories about ghetto children that were nominated for a Pulitzer Prize (Altschull, 1990, pp. 361–364). Later these stories were found to be based on fabricated interviews. Cooke had taken personal details and comments from several people and then woven them together to create a fictitious interviewee. The resulting stories had great dramatic impact (argued her defenders) but violated professional standards of truth and accuracy. Cooke was fired and the Pulitzer Prize was returned. The *Post* expressed profound embarrassment.

In 1993, an NBC news program broadcast a story depicting an automobile crash test. The report showed a test in which a General Motors pickup truck was struck on its side by another vehicle. Soon after impact, the truck burst into flames supposedly because of a faulty design. What the report didn't say was that the test had been rigged to virtually guarantee an explosion. Though the design of the truck may well have increased the likelihood of such an explosion, NBC journalists would probably have had to stage a large number of crashes before they got one on tape. The news story may well have been successful in making its point with viewers but it definitely violated professional standards. Eventually, the NBC vice president for news resigned under pressure. Like the *Post*, NBC was embarrassed.

But what were the immediate consequences of these violations of professional standards? No one died. No one went to jail needlessly. The stories might actually have been effective in convincing the public that there were serious problems in the Washington D.C. ghettos and in their driveways — more effective than stories based on verbatim interviews or statistics on actual crashes.

Social Responsibility Theory of the Press: A Postwar Compromise

Despite moves toward professionalization and self-regulation, pressure for greater government regulation of media mounted throughout World War II and continued during the anti-Communist agitation that followed. In response,

Henry Luce, CEO of Time Inc., provided funding for an independent commission to make recommendations concerning the role of press. The Hutchins Commission on Freedom of the Press was established in 1942 and released a major report of its findings in 1947 (Davis, 1990; McIntyre, 1987). Its members consisted of leaders from many areas of society including academics, politicians, and heads of social groups.

Commission members were sharply divided between those who held strongly libertarian views and those who thought some form of press regulation was necessary. Those who favored regulation were fearful that the "marketplace of ideas" was much too vulnerable to subversion by antidemocratic forces. Several of these proponents of regulation were guided by notions about public communication developed by social researchers at the University of Chicago—the *Chicago School*.

The Chicago School envisioned modern cities as "Great Communities" made up of hundreds of small social groups—everything from neighborhood social organizations to citywide associations. For these Great Communities to develop, all of the constituent groups had to work together and contribute. These were referred to as *pluralistic groups* in recognition of their cultural and racial diversity (Davis, 1990).

The Chicago School opposed marketplace of ideas notions and argued that unregulated mass media inevitably served the interests and tastes of large or socially dominant groups. Small, weak, pluralistic groups would be either neglected or denigrated. The theory also maintained that ruthless elites could use media as a means of gaining personal political power. These demagogues could manipulate media to transmit propaganda to fuel hatred and fear among a majority and unite them against minorities. Hitler's use of media to arouse hatred of the Jews was seen as a prime example.

To prevent this tyranny by the majority and to mandate support for pluralistic groups, some Commission members favored creation of a public agency—a Press Council—that would be made up of people much like themselves and that would have the power to prevent publication of hate propaganda. It might have required that newspapers devote a certain portion of their coverage to minority groups. Or it might have required that these groups be given regular columns in which they could publish whatever they wanted. Does this sound like an unusual or absurd requirement? The FCC imposed similar requirements in 1972 when it mandated that cable operators in major urban areas provide public access channels.

Commission members recognized that such regulations might impose additional costs on newspapers. If this happened, then they favored government subsidies to cover these expenses. By serving pluralistic groups, media would strengthen them and enable them to make a contribution to the Great

Community. This fostering of pluralism and restraint on propaganda was seen as essential to preventing the spread of totalitarianism in the United States.

Although the majority of Hutchins Commission members had some sympathy for Chicago School ideas, they opposed any direct form of press regulation (McIntyre 1987; Davis 1990). The Commission members faced a serious dilemma. On the one hand, they recognized that the marketplace of ideas was not self-regulating and that newspapers were doing less than they could to provide services to minority groups. However, commission members feared that any form of press regulation would open the door to totalitarian control of media—the very thing they were trying to prevent.

The situation seemed quite dire at the time. Without some form of regulation, a ruthless and cunning demagogue might be able to use hate propaganda to gain power in the United States. But establishing a national press council might put too much control in the hands of existing elites and they might abuse it. Ultimately, the majority of Hutchins Commission members decided to place their faith in media practitioners and called on them to redouble their efforts to serve the public. They wrote a lengthy report to provide guidance to media practitioners.

The synthesis of ideas put forward in the Hutchins Commission report has become known as the *Social Responsibility Theory of the Press* (Siebert, Peterson, and Schramm, 1956). This theory restated old principles and repeated ideas expressed in various media codes of ethics. For example, it emphasized the need for an independent press that scrutinizes other social institutions and provides objective, accurate news reports. The most innovative feature of social responsibility theory was its call for media to be responsible for fostering productive and creative "Great Communities." It said that media should do this by prioritizing cultural pluralism—by becoming the voice of all of the people—not just elite groups or groups that had dominated national, regional, or local culture in the past.

In some respects, social responsibility theory is a radical statement. Instead of demanding that media be free to print or transmit whatever their owners want, social responsibility theory imposes a burden on them. Just as libertarianism arose as an alternative to authoritarian ideas, social responsibility theory is a response to totalitarian ideas. *Totalitarian media theories*, such as those developed by the Nazis or by Soviet Communists (Siebert, Peterson, and Schramm, 1956), called for suppression of pluralistic groups and exalted the necessity for propagating a strong centralized political culture—a thousand-year Reich or a Soviet Socialist People's Republic. Direct control of the media by the dominant political party was seen as essential to prevent deviant, disruptive views from being expressed by enemies of the people. The Party, whether it is National Socialist or Soviet Communist, must be trusted with total control over media so that it can educate the masses and lead them into a utopian future.

In contrast with totalitarian theories, social responsibility theory appealed to the idealism of individual media practitioners and tried to unite them in the service of cultural pluralism—even when this might reduce their profits or antagonize existing social elites. It challenged their ingenuity to come up with new ways of serving their communities. It encouraged them to see themselves as front-line participants in the battle to preserve democracy in a world drifting inexorably toward totalitarianism. By helping pluralistic groups, they were building a wall to protect democracy from external and internal foes. Denis McQuail (1987) summarized the basic principles of social responsibility theory as:

- Media should accept and fulfill certain obligations to society.
- These obligations are mainly to be met by setting high or professional standards of informativeness, truth, accuracy, objectivity, and balance.
- In accepting and applying these obligations, media should be self-regulating within the framework of law and established institutions.
- The media should avoid whatever might lead to crime, violence, or civil disorder or give offense to minority groups.
- The media as a whole should be pluralist and reflect the diversity of their society, giving access to various points of view and to rights of reply.
- Society and the public have a right to expect high standards of performance, and intervention can be justified to secure the, or a, public good.
- Journalists and media professionals should be accountable to society as well as to employers and the market.

The Cold War Tests Social Responsibility Theory

The first major test of social responsibility theory occurred during the 1950s with the rise of anti-Communist sentiments during the Cold War. Mainland China fell to the communists in 1949. At the same time, most of Eastern Europe was coming under communist control in a series of staged popular uprisings and coups. Soviet development of nuclear weapons was aided by spies who stole important secrets. World War II had stopped one form of totalitarianism but had unleashed another that appeared to be even stronger and more deadly. A generation of American politicians, including Richard Nixon and John F. Kennedy, gained national prominence by aggressively opposing the spread of Soviet communism.

The vanguard for opposition to communism was led by Joseph F. McCarthy, as discussed in Chapter 3. Though McCarthy presented himself as a crusader for democracy, he soon exhibited all the traits of the classic demagogue. He successfully used propaganda techniques to draw national attention to himself and stimulate widespread public hatred and suspicion of people or minorities whom he linked, most often inaccurately, to communism. McCarthy charged that many in both government and the media were communist agents or sympathizers and drew strong support from anti-Communist groups across the nation. Congressional investigations of media practitioners were launched by the House Un-American Activities Committee, or HUAC.

Media executives responded to pressure from anticommunist groups and from Congress by "blacklisting" many people who were accused, even in the absence of evidence, of communist leanings. Prominent practitioners were barred from working in the media. Ultimately, there was little evidence of any widespread conspiracy to subvert democracy in the United States. Though there were Soviet agents at work in the United States, their numbers and effectiveness were never as great as the anticommunist groups asserted.

This Red Scare episode illustrates how difficult it can be for journalists to adhere to social responsibility theory in crisis situations. Most journalists initially hailed McCarthy as someone taking an heroic stand against the Red Menace. His dramatic pronouncements provided ideal material for big headlines and popular front-page news stories. As long as McCarthy confined his witch hunt to Reds in federal bureaucracies, many reporters printed his charges without criticism. When he began to look for Pinkos and communist sympathizers in the media, more journalists began to have misgivings. But by then his popularity was so great that it was risky for them to oppose him, so most cowered. Months of Congressional hearings passed before significant media criticism of McCarthy appeared. Edward R. Murrow is credited by many with taking the initiative to produce a television news documentary that finally exposed McCarthy's propaganda tactics to public scrutiny.

How should media have reacted if they took social responsibility theory seriously? Should they have made a greater effort earlier to investigate the truth of McCarthy's frequent and dramatic allegations? They would have risked charges that they were pro-Communist or the unwitting dupes of the Communists. But by waiting they risked the possibility that McCarthy would seize political power and use it to suppress all forms of dissent including media criticism. Without a journalist of Edward R. Murrow's stature to confront McCarthy, the United States might have turned toward McCarthy's brand of fascism.

Using Social Responsibility Theory to Guide Professional Practice

Social responsibility theory has proved quite durable, even if its full implications are rarely understood by working journalists. Most journalists take seriously the central values of social responsibility theory such as pluralism and cultural diversity. There is little evidence, however, that they have developed an effective means of promoting these values through their work. For example, journalists continue to define the routine work of community and minority groups as unnewsworthy. All too often inflammatory remarks made by militant group leaders are widely publicized with no information about the social conditions that prompt the remarks.

If social responsibility theory is to remain a viable normative theory, greater effort may be needed to implement it. Compared to the vast amount of research done on media effects, relatively little research has examined whether existing news production practices actually serve the societal goals that they are intended to serve. For example, one of the primary goals is communicating accurate information about important events to average people. The findings of research on this goal are quite mixed. For example, evidence indicates that people don't learn much from news reports and what they do learn is quickly forgotten (Graber, 1987). People become easily confused by stories that are poorly structured or use dramatic but irrelevant pictures. Findings from this research have had little or no impact upon the practice of journalism. They have been largely ignored or misinterpreted by media practitioners (Davis and Robinson, 1989).

In the 1970s and 1980s, sociologists published a series of studies that raised important questions about the value of routine news production practices (Epstein, 1973; Tuchman, 1978; Gans, 1979; Fishman, 1980; Glasgow University Media Group, 1976, 1980; Bennett, 1988). Most of this research has been ignored or dismissed by journalists as biased, irrelevant, and misguided. It deserves a more careful reading. Gaye Tuchman, for example, presents a well-developed argument concerning the role played by media in the discovery and cultivation of social movements. She conceptualizes news production practices as "strategic rituals" and believes that these practices appear to satisfy the requirements imposed by social responsibility norms but fall far short of achieving their purpose. For example, journalists ritualistically construct "balanced" stories in which opposing views are contrasted. But these rites may actually undermine rather than advance pluralism. She maintains that "balanced stories" about minority groups frequently contain statements from social or political leaders that subtly or blatantly denigrate groups and their ideas. The emotionally charged opinions of little-known group leaders are contrasted with reasoned pronouncements from well-known, credible officials. Little effort is made to contextualize new groups in terms of their broader goals or their culture. Instead, news reports tend to focus on dramatic events staged by isolated group members.

Tuchman also cites early news coverage of the women's movement in the 1960s and early 1970s to illustrate her criticisms. The movement first achieved national prominence with a rally in which bras were purportedly burned (in supposed imitation of the burning of draft cards by antiwar protesters). She maintains that bras may have been brandished but were never burned. The news reports unfairly labeled the women's movement as an extremist group in the same category with the people burning draft cards. Instead of assisting the movement and enabling it to contribute to the larger society, these stories and those that followed hindered it. Pluralism was frustrated rather than advanced.

Is There Still a Role for Social Responsibility Theory?

Although U.S. media have developed many professional practices in an effort to implement social responsibility theory, the long-term objective — the creation of "Great Communities"— has never seemed more elusive. Our cities have undergone decades of urban renewal, yet slums remain and in some cities they continue to spread. There have been national "wars" to combat poverty, crime, pollution, disease (from polio to cancer to AIDS), and drugs. But the quality of life for many city dwellers has not improved. Ethnic and racial subcultures are still widely misunderstood. Minority group members continue to be discriminated against and harassed. There is evidence that hate groups are increasing in size and that their propaganda is effectively reaching larger audiences.

Does this mean that social responsibility theory is wrong? Has it been poorly implemented? What responsibility can or should media practitioners assume on behalf of the Great Communities that they serve? More important, how should this responsibility be exercised? With helicopters circling over riots scenes? With inflammatory coverage of hate groups? With boring coverage of the routine work of neighborhood associations? With endless listing of bad news about crime and disease? Was there merit in the Chicago School arguments concerning coverage of pluralistic groups? If so, what forms might that coverage take? Should group members be allowed some direct control over what is printed about them in newspapers or broadcast on television?

Our society's experience with local access channels on cable television suggests that it is not easy to use media to support pluralistic groups. In 1972, the Federal Communications Commission for the first time required local cable companies to provide local access channels in an effort to serve pluralistic groups, and although these *local origination* or *mandatory access* rules have been altered, suspended, and otherwise tinkered with over the last twenty years, they have generally failed to serve their intended purpose. Very few people watch the access channels and few groups use them. In Kansas City, the city council recently found itself embroiled in controversy over its proposal to shut down the local access channel to prevent it from being used by the Ku Klux Klan (KKK) to transmit hate propaganda (see Box 5a). The KKK is one of several hate groups whose strategy is to use local access channels across the country as a vehicle for their propaganda. How did an experiment intended to promote pluralism degenerate into one that threatens to do just the opposite?

Since the report of the Hutchins Commission on Press Freedom in 1947, there has been relatively little effort to develop a normative theory of media in the United States. Social responsibility theory emerged at a time of world crisis and when democracy itself was clearly threatened. Will the end of the Cold War and the establishment of a "New World Order" bring forth a new normative theory? Do our domestic crises provide sufficient motivation for rethinking social responsibility theory or developing a new normative theory? It is useful to examine some alternative normative theories that are being practiced in other parts of the world. In Chapters 13 and 14, we will discuss critical theory and consider its role in developing normative theory.

Other Normative Theories

McQuail (1987) cites a number of normative theories of media that have been developed in other parts of the world. These include development media theory and democratic-participant media theory. Each assigns a particular social role to media. *Development media theory* advocates media support for an existing political regime and its efforts to bring about national economic development. By supporting government development efforts, media aid society at large. This theory argues that until a nation is well-established and its economic development well underway, media must be supportive rather than critical of government. Journalists must not pick apart government efforts to promote development but rather assist government in implementing such policies. U.S. journalists have been critical of this view. They believe that it is an updated version of authoritarian theory and that media should never surrender the power to criticize government policies even if it risks causing the policies to fail.

Democratic-participant theory advocates media support for cultural pluralism at a grass-roots level. Media are to be used to stimulate and empower pluralistic groups. Unlike social responsibility theory, which assumes that mass media can perform this function, democratic-participant theory calls for development of innovative, "small" media that can be directly controlled by group members. If they cannot afford such media, then government subsidies should be provided to them. Existing small media should be identified and subsidized. Training programs should be established to teach group members how to operate small media.

Both of these alternative theories recognize the need for some form of government intervention into the operation of media. Development media theory envisions setting up government agencies that (a) monitor training and licensing of media practitioners; (b) control development of media institutions; (c) regularly censor media content prior to distribution; and (d) issue regular guidelines for day to day operation of media. Although varying degrees of self-regulation are encouraged, media practitioners are not trusted by government officials to carry out their responsibilities without guidance and constant monitoring.

Democratic-participant theory provides a very different role for government. This theory has been most fully developed in western Europe and is part of a grass-roots revival of historically significant cultural and ethnic groups. The rise of nation states in Europe over the past two centuries led to suppression of many local and regional cultures. Often, nation states were artificial creations that arbitrarily lumped together antagonistic groups. Cultural or ethnic minorities were routinely discriminated against, and their languages and their religions were banned. The scenes of bloody ethnic battles in Bosnia that filled the world's television screens in 1993 and 1994 strongly but sadly make this point. Centuries-old ethnic identities sparked this tragic confrontation.

Democratic-participant theory argues that surviving remnants of ethnic groups should be given access to media and allowed to revive or stabilize their culture. In Wales, for example, Welsh language programming has been successfully aired for several years. Proponents argue that it has restored local and regional pride.

Ironically, the unification of Europe into the European Union (E.U.) has encouraged such experiments with ethnic group media. A united Europe no longer needs strong nation states as protection against invasion or subversion. Minorities don't have to be suppressed for nation states to survive. The E.U. as a whole has tended to be respectful of minority cultures even when these cultures are not respected by member nations. The end of the Cold War reduced external threats even further and brought increased lobbying on behalf of minority cultures. The E.U. has taken important steps to guarantee equal rights to ethnic groups and even to encourage that they be given access to various forms of mass media. New technologies that lower the cost of media while increasing their effectiveness in serving small groups should encourage this trend. But where will it lead — to a Europe that is Balkanized into ethnic enclaves much like it was during the Middle Ages or to a united Europe energized by cultural pluralism?

If democratic-participant theory were to be adopted in the United States, it could inspire the creation of hundreds of small media outlets for specific ethnic groups. For example, at relatively low cost, a network of Native American media could be established that would span the continent. These media could help strengthen individual tribes while increasing their awareness of and respect for cultural diversity within their own "Great Community." Already many tribes have small media operations and there is interest in expanding and interconnecting these outlets. Some broadcast in Native American languages. There is growing cooperation among Native American media practitioners that is fostered by the Native American Journalists Association. Could a stronger Native American community have benefits for the larger society?

Summary

During the 1940s, social responsibility theory emerged as the predominant normative theory of media practice in the United States. It represents a compromise between radical libertarian views and technocratic control notions. Control over media content was placed in the hands of media practitioners who were expected to act in the public interest. No means existed to compel practitioners to serve the public, however. They were free to decide what services were needed and to monitor the effectiveness of those services.

Since its articulation by the Hutchins Commission, most media practitioners have made good faith efforts to understand and abide by the tenets of social responsibility theory. This theory is generally taught to all people who complete training in journalism programs. As such, when media practitioners are questioned about their work, most provide explanations that are based on social responsibility notions. In addition, many different news production practices have been developed in an effort to implement these ideas. As media expanded to serve mass audiences that included many different minorities, they found that social responsibility had practical as well as theoretical value. By tailoring news and entertainment to have broad appeal and minimize its offensiveness, vast audiences were created.

Recently, media critics such as Tuchman (1978) and W. Lance Bennett (1988) have charged that media services to minority groups and social movements have actually impeded or subverted group activities. They argue that ritualistic balancing of news combined with overdramatized coverage has popularized false impressions of groups or reinforced negative stereotypes. Groups get little real assistance from media. Most media services are aimed at demographic segments favored by advertisers—not at those groups in greatest need of help. Media have chronicled the decay of cities but have done less to create "Great Communities." Their target audiences are generally in the affluent suburbs, not the inner city ghettos. The harshest critics of social responsibility theory argue that it is an ideology that simply serves to legitimize and rationalize the status quo (Altschull, 1990). We will consider these criticisms in Chapter 13.

Defenders of media respond to these charges by arguing that it was never media's role to get directly involved with minority groups—services to the mass audience must take precedence over services to small, isolated groups. In any case, democracy has survived the threat of totalitarianism and media can claim some credit for that. Media also take credit for the very strong consumer marketplace that has dominated American society and culture for the past several decades. This marketplace serves the needs of all who can pay the cost of the goods and services it provides.

Recent changes in media technology and world politics make it reasonable to reassess the utility of social responsibility theory as currently applied. Small media can be provided to ethnic or racial groups at low cost. The rise of thousands of small groups need not be seen as a threat to national security if there is little to fear from external enemies. The rise of media networks to interconnect and serve Native Americans, African Americans, Hispanics, or Asian Americans might enhance rather than threaten our social order. To make these changes, however, we must reformulate the normative theory upon which our media system is grounded. This will require a critical reexamination of social responsibility theory and careful consideration of alternatives. Their risks as well as benefits should be weighed. We will return to this issue in later chapters.

Discussion Questions

1 Explain what is meant by a normative theory of media and give some examples.

2 What are the most important services that media provide for you? How would you react if one or more of these services were stopped? For example, it may soon be possible for media entrepreneurs to make more money selling National Football League games using a pay-per-view system than they already do using regular network and cable television. How would you react to that?

3 Should minority groups be protected from hate propaganda? What is your position on the situation in Kansas City regarding use of its access channel by the Klan? Rather than close its existing access operation, the city opened a second channel to allow for "more speech." What do you think of this solution?

4 How well do you think major media outlets serve minority groups? Do you agree or disagree with the media critics who charge that most news coverage harms rather than helps minority groups or social movements?

5 Develop a new normative theory of media. State at least three important services that media should offer even though little or no profit can be earned by providing them. The theory should justify providing these services. Do you think there should be government subsidies so that the media can afford to provide these services? How would you monitor and compel media outlets to provide mandated services?

Significant Names

John Milton

Joseph McCarthy

Hutchins Commission

Gaye Tuchman

Significant Readings

Altschull, J. Herbert (1990). *From Milton to McLuhan: The Ideas Behind American Journalism.* New York: Longman.

 Barnouw, Erik (1966). *A History of Broadcasting in the United States: A Tower of Babel, Vol. I.* New York: Oxford University Press.

Bennett, W. Lance (1988). *News: The Politics of Illusion,* 2d edition. New York: Longman.

Brownell, B.A. (1983). "Interpretations of Twentieth-Century Urban Progressive Reform." In D.R. Colburn and G.E. Pozzetta, eds., *Reform and Reformers in the Progressive Era.* Westport, CT: Greenwood Press.

McIntyre, Jeryln S. (1987). "Repositioning a Landmark: The Hutchins Commission and Freedom of the Press." *Critical Studies in Mass Communication,* 4: 95–135.

Tuchman, Gaye (1978). *Making News: A Study in the Construction of Reality.* New York: Free Press.

Important Terms

Normative Theory

Social Responsibility Theory

Libertarianism

Radical Libertarianism

Fourth Estate

Technocratic Control

Marketplace of Ideas

Self-Righting Principle

Chicago School

Mandatory Access Rule

Laissez-Faire

SECTION *Three*

Emergence of a Scientific Perspective on Mass Communication

1951   *Innis's* The Bias of Communication
Murrow's "See It Now" premieres

1953   *Hovland, Janis, and Kelley's* Communication and Persuasion

1954   *Murrow challenges McCarthy on television*

1957   *Mills's* Power Elite

1958   *TV quiz show scandal erupts*

1959   *Mills's* The Sociological Imagination

1960   *Kennedy and Nixon meet in Great Debates*
TV in 80% of all U.S. homes
Klapper's Effects of Mass Communication

1961   *Key's* Public Opinion and American Democracy
Kennedy makes nation's first live TV presidential press conference
Berelson's "Great Debate on Cultural Democracy"
Schramm team's Television in the Lives of Our Children *published*

1962   *Festinger's cognitive dissonance article appears*
Kraus's Great Debates

Chapter 6

Limited Effects Theory

On a peaceful evening in late October 1938, many Americans were listening to a ballroom dance music program on the CBS radio network when the show was interrupted by a series of news bulletins. Early announcements told of strange astronomical observations and sightings of lights in the sky. The reports grew steadily more ominous. An alien spaceship had landed and was attacking the military forces that surrounded it. Transmissions from the scene ended suddenly and were followed by an appeal from the Secretary of the Interior for calm in the face of the alien threat. In cities across the nation Americans reacted with alarm.

In that year, the medium of radio was still new, but it had become enormously popular. Networks had been established only a few years earlier. Listeners were starting to rely on the new medium for news. Radio news was free and easily accessible and provided compelling, on-the-spot reports of fast-breaking situations. In a very troubled era, with many unusual and threatening events, such as impending war in Europe, people listened to radio for the latest reports of bad news. Orson Welles, a young radio program producer, conceived a radio theater program in which simulated news bulletins would be used to play a Halloween joke on the entire nation. Borrowing freely from a novel by H.G. Wells entitled *War of the Worlds*, Welles and script writer Howard Koch created a radio drama in which listeners heard a series of compelling eyewitness reports of the alien invasion. Afraid that the program might be too dull, Koch embellished the script with allusions and authentic detail (Lowery and DeFleur, 1988).

As reports of panic came into his New York broadcast studio, Welles resisted efforts to interrupt the show, although during a scheduled program break, he did remind listeners that they were tuned in to a radio drama.

The last half of the program recounted the aftermath of the invasion. News bulletins gave way to a monologue from the sole human survivor. He told of the aliens' ultimate defeat by bacteria. Since this portion of the program was clearly fantasy, Welles saw no need to provide additional announcements. For many listeners, it was too late anyway. As soon as they heard the early bulletins they fled their homes and aroused their neighbors.

The invasion from Mars panic was seen by many elite observers as definitive proof of mass society theory. If a single radio program could induce such widespread panic, obviously concerted propaganda campaigns could do much worse. The American masses were clearly at the mercy of any demagogue who could gain control of the airwaves. Sooner or later, some bully would seize the opportunity and take power, as Hitler had done in Germany. Propaganda would be used to win a close election. Once sufficient control was gained, opposing political parties would be crushed.

At Princeton University, a group of social researchers set out to determine why the Welles broadcast had been so influential (Cantril, Gaudet, and Herzog, 1940). Their research found that many people acted too hastily after hearing only the first fragmentary reports of the invasion. The simulated news bulletins were trusted without question, especially the eyewitness reports and interviews with phony experts. The people who were most upset by the program didn't stay glued to their radios waiting for updates. In this era, before portable and car radios had become commonplace, these people lost touch with the program once they left their homes. Word of mouth spread news of the ersatz invasion through entire neighborhoods. Often, people who heard about the invasion from others didn't think to turn on their radios to check out the news for themselves. They trusted their neighbors and acted. But even though the researchers found considerable evidence of panic, they also found that most people were not taken in by Welles's practical joke. Most people possessed critical ability that led them to check the validity of the broadcast, so they had little trouble disconfirming news of the invasion. Only listeners who tuned in late and for just a few minutes were likely to be upset. The researchers concluded that these people had one or more psychological traits that made them especially susceptible to media influence: emotional insecurity, phobic personality, lack of self-confidence, and fatalism.

Here we can see the importance of understanding *levels of analysis* (Chapter 1). Because the *War of the Worlds* researchers were investigating media effects at the more micro, or individual level, they argued that their research showed *limited effects* because only a *limited* number of listeners were *directly* affected by the broadcast. Had they been more macro, or societally focused, they may well have taken that same evidence and argued that there were widespread social ramifications: many people were fooled (although only a small number behaved dysfunctionally, for example, hiding in the hills), people discussed the program for weeks, neighbors who had never met were now talking, the population in general became more aware and possibly more suspicious of radio's power, and so on. None of these is a limited effect on society.

The Princeton University researchers, led by Hadley Cantril, were part of a vanguard of social scientists who slowly transformed our view of how media influence society. Within twenty years of the *War of the Worlds* broadcast, the way social researchers looked at mass media was radically altered. Media were no longer feared as instruments of political oppression and manipulation, but instead viewed as a relatively benign force with much potential for social good. The power of media over the public was seen as limited—so limited, that no government regulations were deemed necessary to prevent manipulation. The public itself was viewed as very resistant to persuasion and extremist manipulation. The belief was that most people were influenced by others rather than by the media; opinion leaders in every community and at every level of society were responsible for guiding and stabilizing politics. It was argued that only a very small minority of people had psychological traits that made them vulnerable to direct manipulation by media. Media were conceptualized as relatively powerless in shaping public opinion in the face of more potent intervening variables like people's individual differences and group memberships. This new view of media arose and persisted even though television had transformed and dominated the media landscape.

So what lesson can be drawn from the *War of the Worlds* incident? If mass society theory is wrong and the limited effects perspective also missed the mark, how should we interpret it? This is not an easy question to answer. In later chapters, we will introduce some new perspectives on media that provide more useful insight. These remind us that though most people didn't panic, they could well have been influenced in subtle but important ways.

Overview

How and why did such a radical transformation in media theory take place in such a short period of time? In this and the two following chapters we will trace the rise of what became the dominant paradigm in American media research for several decades. In this chapter we will describe the work of researchers who were led by Paul Lazarsfeld, a colleague of Cantril at Princeton University. Lazarsfeld later moved to Columbia University and pioneered the use of sophisticated surveys to measure media influence on how people thought and acted. These surveys provided definitive evidence that media rarely had powerful, direct influence on individuals. The effects were quite limited in scope—affecting only a few people or influencing rather trivial thoughts or actions. These findings eventually led to a perspective on media that was referred to as *limited effects perspective*.

In Chapter 7, we will review experimental studies of the persuasive power of media, focusing on the work of Carl Hovland. Like Lazarsfeld, Hovland was a methodological innovator who introduced new standards for evaluating media influence. He too found that media lacked the power to instantly convert average people away from strongly held beliefs. Even in laboratory situations where the potential for media influence was exaggerated, only modest effects were discovered. Many factors were actually found to limit media influence.

Finally, in Chapter 8, we will consider how proponents of limited effects were able to establish this perspective as the dominant way of looking at media. Data from an impressive array of elaborate empirical studies were assembled into an important series of classic reports (for example, Klapper, 1960; Bauer and Bauer, 1960; Katz and Lazarsfeld, 1955; Campbell, et al, 1960; DeFleur and Larsen, 1958).

Paradigm Shifts

One way of interpreting what happened to media theory during the two decades from 1940 to 1960 is to view it as a *paradigm shift*. Thomas Kuhn (1962), a science historian, has argued that the way science progresses is through these radical breaks in theory. For a period of time, a single theoretical perspective or paradigm dominates most research. These paradigms can encompass many closely related theories. Each theory shares certain common assumptions (We listed the assumptions for mass society theory in Chapter 3. You will find a list of assumptions for the limited effects perspective in Chapter 8). A paradigm summarizes and is consistent with all known facts. It provides a useful guide for research as long as its basic assumptions are accepted. Most researchers find it easy to work within such a framework. Many are unaware of alternatives or find other ideas or contradictory findings easy to dismiss.

Though paradigms exercise great influence over the course of scientific research, shifts inevitably occur because no paradigm can provide an adequate explanation for all observations. Sometimes, small opposition research communities emerge to develop and investigate alternate theories. Their work is usually ignored or severely criticized, but sometimes they are able to conclusively demonstrate the validity of their perspective. Sometimes researchers committed to a dominant paradigm uncover important findings that are inconsistent with it. As they explore these findings, more and more contradictory data are obtained. Eventually, they make an effort to account for these inconsistencies and develop a new body of theory. Sometimes an important role is played by scientific iconoclasts—people who rebel against key assumptions in the dominant paradigm or who are convinced that new research methods should be used. Iconoclasts often work in isolation as they develop alternate perspectives; the value of their ideas and findings may not be recognized until decades after the original research was done.

Thus, the discovery of inconsistent facts, the appearance of iconoclasts, and the formation of competing research communities can precipitate paradigm shifts. But they do so only after long and sometimes bitter scientific controversies. Scientific communities frequently resist theoretical innovation. The work of iconoclasts or deviant research communities is likely to be dismissed as erroneous or simply ignored as unimportant. As new perspectives are pitted against dominant paradigms, dramatic confrontations can result.

The Paradigm Shift in Mass Communication Theory

The people who led the paradigm shift in mass communication theory during the 1940s and 1950s were primarily methodologists—not theorists. Lazarsfeld and Hovland were convinced that we could best assess the influence of media by employing objective, empirical methods to measure it. They argued that new research methods such as experiments and surveys made it possible to observe the effects of media. These observations would permit definitive conclusions to be reached and would guide the construction of more useful theory.

Both Lazarsfeld and Hovland were trained in the empirical research methods that had been developed in psychology. In addition, Lazarsfeld spent time as a social statistician in Austria. Working independently, they demonstrated how their research techniques could be adapted to the study of media effects. Both were successful in convincing others of the validity of their approach. Lazarsfeld secured funding that enabled him to conduct expensive, large-scale studies of media influence at Columbia University. After conducting propaganda experiments during World War II, Hovland established a large research center at Yale where hundreds of persuasion experiments were conducted. Both Columbia and Yale became very influential research centers that attracted some of the best social researchers of the time.

Neither Lazarsfeld nor Hovland set out to revolutionize mass media theory. Both had much broader objectives. During the war years, they were drawn into media studies as part of the larger effort to understand the power of propaganda and the threat it posed. Unlike many colleagues who were willing to assume that media were quite powerful, Lazarsfeld and Hovland were determined to conduct empirical research that could assess this influence. They hoped that if this power could be better understood it might be controlled and used for good purposes.

Both Lazarsfeld and Hovland argued that scientific methods provided the essential means to control media's power. They were impressed by the tremendous accomplishments being made in the physical sciences. In fields like physics and chemistry, the ability of science to understand and control the physical world was being vividly demonstrated. Some of the most striking examples could be found in new military technology—amazing aircraft, highly destructive bombs, and unstoppable tanks. These weapons could be used for either good or evil, to defend democracy or bolster totalitarianism. Along with Lasswell, Hovland, and Lazarsfeld believed that if democracy was to survive, it would have to produce the best scientists and these women and men would have to do a better job of harnessing technology to advance their political ideology.

Hovland and Lazarsfeld believed that a key goal of science is control. Physical science permits us to control the physical world and social science should therefore permit us to control the social world. Scientific theories should provide causal explanations of both physical *and* social events. Once a society understands why these events take place, it can find ways to control them. For example, Hovland studied persuasive communication to better understand how to use persuasive messages to change attitudes. He sought the "magic keys" to persuasion.

But as both men conducted their research, they found that media were not as powerful as mass society theory indicated. Often, media influence over public opinion or attitudes was hard to locate. Media influence was typically less important than that of factors such as social status or education. Those media effects that were found seemed to be isolated and were sometimes contradictory. Despite the weak findings, funding for additional research proved easy to secure. Study after study provided growing insight into the limited power of media.

During the 1950s, the new paradigm began to take shape. Across America, new research centers modeled after those at Yale and Columbia opened. By 1960, many of the "classic studies" were published. They became required reading for a generation of communication researchers. This new paradigm dominated during the 1960s and remained quite strong through the 1970s.

Much of the empirical research on mass communication that you will find in books or journals is based on this paradigm. As we discuss the early research, we will illustrate the factors that combined to make development of the paradigm possible. We list these factors here and we will refer to them in later sections.

1 **The refinement and broad acceptance of empirical social research methods was an essential factor in the emergence of the new paradigm.** Throughout this period, empirical research methods were effectively promoted as an ideal means of measuring social phenomena. They were declared to be the only "scientific" way of dealing with social phenomena. Other approaches were dismissed as overly speculative, unsystematic, or too subjective. Because so few people at the time understood the limitations of empirical research methods, findings

and the conclusions derived from empirical studies were often accepted uncritically. When these outcomes conflicted with past theories, the older theories were questioned.

2   **People who advocated mass society theories were successfully branded by empirical social researchers as "unscientific."** Mass society theory advocates were accused of being fuzzy-minded humanists, doomsayers, political ideologues, or biased against media. Mass society notions lost some of their broad appeal, however, as the threat of propaganda gradually faded in the late 1950s and 1960s.

3   **Social researchers exploited the commercial potential of the new research methods and gained the support of private industry.** One of the first articles written by Lazarsfeld after arriving in the United States was on the use of survey research methods as a tool for advertisers (Kornhauser and Lazarsfeld, 1935). Surveys and experiments were promoted as a means of probing media audiences and interpreting consumer attitudes and behaviors. Most of Hovland's persuasion studies had more or less direct application to advertising and marketing. Lazarsfeld coined the term "administrative research" to refer to these applications. He persuasively argued for the use of empirical research to guide administrative decision-making. As the new methods became more widely accepted in industry, jobs became available for those trained in social research methods. Academic programs expanded to provide this training and became centers for applied social research. The Bureau of Applied Social Research, founded by Lazarsfeld at Columbia University, became a model for other universities.

4   **The development of empirical social research was strongly backed by various private and government foundations, most notably the Rockefeller Foundation and the National Science Foundation.** This support was crucial, particularly in the early stages, because large-scale empirical social research required much more funding than previous forms of social research. Without support from the Rockefeller Foundation, Lazarsfeld might never have come to the United States or been able to develop and demonstrate the validity of his approach.

5   **After empirical research began to show that media were not as threatening and all-powerful as implied by mass society theory, media companies were encouraged to finance more empirical research.** In time, both CBS and NBC formed their own social research departments and employed many outside researchers as consultants. Two of the most influential early media researchers were Frank Stanton and Joseph Klapper—the former collaborated with Lazarsfeld on numerous research projects and the latter was Lazarsfeld's student. During their careers both men headed social research at CBS. Funding for academic research

continued even after mass society theory had lost influence and the pressure for media regulation had lessened. As media corporations grew larger and earned sizable profits, they could afford to fund empirical research—especially when that research helped to justify the status quo and block moves to regulate their operations. Media funding and support were vital to the development of commercial audience ratings services such as Nielsen and Arbitron. These companies pioneered the use of survey research methods to measure the size of audiences and guide administrative decision-making in areas such as advertising and marketing.

Media support was also crucial to the growth of various national polling services such as Gallup, Harris, and Roper. Media coverage of polls and ratings data helped establish their credibility in the face of widespread commonsense criticism. During the 1940s and 1950s, most people were skeptical about the usefulness of data gathered from small samples. They wondered, for example, how pollsters could survey just three hundred or twelve hundred people and draw conclusions about an entire city or nation. To answer these questions, media reported that opinion polls and ratings were valid because they were based on "scientific" samples. Often, there was little explanation of what the term "scientific" meant in this context.

6 **Empirical social researchers were successful in establishing their approach within the various social research disciplines—political science, history, social psychology, sociology, and economics.** These disciplines, in turn, shaped the development of communication research. As the various communication disciplines developed, empirical social researchers from the more established social sciences provided leadership. Social science theories and research methods assumed an important, often dominant place within university journalism, speech communication, and broadcasting departments. Empirical research became widely accepted as the most scientific way to study communication even though it proved difficult to find conclusive evidence of media influence. Grants were more readily available for empirical research than for other types of studies. Empirical research tended to attract the brightest, most ambitious, and most productive researchers.

The Two-Step Flow of Information and Influence

Paul Lazarsfeld was not a theorist, yet by promoting empirical research he did more than any of his peers to transform social theory. In his view, theory must be strongly grounded in empirical facts. He was concerned that macroscopic social theories, including the various mass society theories, were too speculative. He preferred a highly *inductive* approach to theory construction—that is, research should begin with empirical observation, not with armchair speculation. After the facts are gathered, they are sifted and the most important pieces of information are picked out. This information is used to construct empirical generalizations—assertions about the relationships between variables. Then, researchers can go back out and gather more data to see if these generalizations are valid.

This research approach is quite cautious and inherently conservative. It avoids sweeping generalizations that go beyond empirical observations and demands that theory construction be "disciplined" by data collection and analysis. Theory should never get too far removed from data. The research process proceeds slowly—building step by step on one data collection effort after another. Eventually a large number of empirical generalizations will be found and tested.

Theory is gradually created by combining generalizations to build what Lazarsfeld's colleague Robert Merton (1957) referred to as *middle range theory*. Unlike earlier forms of grand social theory—mass society theory, for example—middle range theory is made up of empirical generalizations that are solidly based on what Lazarsfeld referred to as empirical facts. In this era, most social researchers thought that this was how theories were developed in the physical sciences. They hoped that by emulating physical scientists, they would be just as successful in controlling phenomena. If so, the scientific methods that produced nuclear bombs might also eliminate poverty, war, and racism.

During the presidential election campaign of 1940, Lazarsfeld had his first major opportunity to test the validity of his approach. He designed and executed what was, at the time, the most elaborate field experiment ever conducted. Using funding he had obtained from the Rockefeller Foundation, *Life Magazine,* and Elmo Roper, Lazarsfeld assembled a large research team in May, 1940. He sent this group to Erie County, Ohio—a relatively remote region centered around the town of Sandusky along the shores of Lake Erie, west of Cleveland. The total population of the county was 43,000. By the time the research team left in November, more than 3,000 people had been personally interviewed in their homes. Six hundred were selected to be in a panel that was interviewed seven times—once every month from May until November. Assuming an average household size of five people, one out of every three households in the county was visited by an interviewer.

Erie County was chosen because it was considered to be an average American locality. Though Sandusky residents tended to vote Democrat, the surrounding rural area was strongly Republican. The 1940 election was notable in two ways—it was the first time that a President had sought election to more than two terms and it took place as the Nazis were invading and occupying most of Western Europe. Franklin Roosevelt ran on a peace platform promising to keep the nation out of war. His opponent was Wendell Willkie—a self-made business success who promised more efficient government. Roosevelt was elected by a large majority in both Erie County and the nation.

Lazarsfeld's methodological conservatism is obvious from his research design. He considered it necessary to interview four control groups of 600 people in addition to his panel of 600. He was concerned that the people in his original panel might answer his questions differently because they were being reinterviewed so often. Therefore, every time he interviewed his panel members, he also interviewed another 600 people chosen at random in the area. The answers from the panel were compared to those provided by the control groups, so he determined that the responses given by panel members were not affected by the frequent interviews. His final report concentrated on the original 600 panel members.

In his data analysis, Lazarsfeld focused attention on changes in voting decisions. As people were interviewed each month, their choice of candidates was compared to the previous month. Over the course of six months, several types of changes were possible. Lazarsfeld created labels for each: *Early Deciders* chose a candidate in May and never changed during the entire campaign. *Waverers* chose one candidate, then were undecided or switched to another candidate, but in the end they voted for their first choice. *Converts* chose one candidate but then voted for his opponent. *Crystallizers* had not chosen a candidate in May but made a choice by November.

Lazarsfeld used a very long and detailed questionnaire that dealt extensively with exposure to specific mass media content such as candidate speeches. This focus was not surprising given Lazarsfeld's considerable background and interest in radio research. If propaganda was as powerful as mass society theory predicted, these questions should have allowed him to pinpoint media influence. If mass society theory was valid, he should have found that most voters were either Converts or Waverers. He should have observed people switching back and forth between candidates. Those who showed the most change should have been the heaviest users of media.

But Lazarsfeld's results directly contradicted mass society theory. Fifty-three percent of the voters were early deciders. They chose one candidate in May and never changed. Twenty-eight percent were crystallizers—they eventually made a very predictable choice and stayed with it. Fifteen percent were waverers, and only eight percent were converts. He could find little evidence that media played an important role in influencing the crystallizers, the waverers, or the converts. Media use by those in the latter two categories was lower than average and very few of them reported being specifically influenced by media messages. Instead, these voters were much more likely to say that they had been influenced by other people. Many were politically apathetic. They failed to make clear-cut voting decisions because they had such low interest. Often, they decided to vote as the people closest to them voted—not as radio speeches or newspaper editorials told them to vote.

Lazarsfeld argued that the most important influence of mass media was to reinforce a vote choice that had already been made. Media simply gave people more reasons for choosing a candidate that they already favored. For some voters, the crystallizers for example, media helped activate existing party loyalties. Republicans who had never heard of Willkie were able to at least learn his name. But Lazarsfeld found very little evidence that media converted people. Instead, the converts were often people with divided loyalties—in Lazarsfeld's terminology they were "cross-pressured." They had group ties that pulled them in opposing directions. Willkie was Catholic so religion pulled some people toward him and pushed others away. Most Republican voters were rural Protestants—to vote for Willkie they had to ignore his religion. The same was true of urban Catholic Democrats—they had to ignore religion to vote for Roosevelt.

But if media weren't directly influencing voting decisions, what was their role? As Lazarsfeld worked with his data he began to formulate an empirical generalization that ultimately had enormous importance. He noticed that some of the hard-core early deciders were also the heaviest users of media. They even made a point of seeking out and listening to opposition speeches. On the other hand, the people who made the least use of media were most likely to report that they relied on others for help in making a vote decision. Lazarsfeld reasoned that the heavy user/early deciders might be the same people whose advice was being sought by other, more apathetic voters. The heavy user/early deciders might be sophisticated media users who held well-developed political views and used media wisely and critically. They might be capable of listening to and evaluating opposition speeches. Rather than be converted themselves, they might actually gain information that would help them advise others so that they would be more resistant to conversion. Thus, these people might act as *gate-keepers*—screening information and only passing on items that would help others share their views. Lazarsfeld chose the term *opinion leader* to refer to these individuals. He labeled those who turned to opinion leaders for advice as *opinion followers*.

Lazarsfeld designed his next two major studies to directly investigate the empirical generalizations that emerged from the 1940 research. He didn't want to speculate about the attributes of opinion leaders or their role—he wanted empirical facts. But to conduct his research, he needed money. He demonstrated his grantsmanship skills by obtaining funding from an unlikely source—McFadden Publications—a publisher of magazines primarily targeted at middle and lower class women. McFadden was having problems selling advertising for these magazines. Most manufacturers of consumer products and clothing at that time were skeptical about marketing directly to lower class women. One widely believed notion was that the purchasing decisions of lower-class people were strongly influenced by higher-status persons. The lower-class Smiths tried to keep up with the Jones — their middle-class neighbors. If this were true, it would be useless to advertise directly to the Smiths. Instead, advertising should be targeted at the Jones. If the Jones were influenced, the Smiths would follow. But was this conventional wisdom correct? Did lower-class people look to their middle-class neighbors in making consumer decisions? Lazarsfeld convinced McFadden that his research could answer this question. If he found that there were opinion leaders at all levels of social class, this data could be used by McFadden to sell advertising.

Lazarsfeld came up with an innovative, yet methodologically sound research design. In 1943, he sent a research team headed by one of his graduate students, C. Wright Mills (more about him in Chapter 8), to Decatur, Illinois, to interview more than 700 housewives. Decatur, a city in the heartland of America, was widely viewed as representative of most small to medium-sized cities. A "snowball" sampling technique was used. An initial sample of women was contacted. During their interview, they were asked the names of people who influenced their thinking on marketing, movies, fashions, and politics. Subsequently, these influential people were interviewed. In this way, Lazarsfeld hoped to identify and study those who had been named by others as opinion leaders. Their nomination by others was taken as factual evidence of their opinion leader status.

More than ten years passed before the Decatur research was published. With the assistance of a coauthor, Elihu Katz, *Personal Influence* was finally published in 1954. This book was quite influential in conceptualizing how people use media and formally advanced the *two-step flow hypothesis*, integrating it with ideas developed in social psychology, especially small group theory. Katz and Lazarsfeld reported that opinion leaders existed at all levels of society and that the flow of their influence tended to be horizontal rather than vertical. Opinion leaders influenced people like themselves rather than those above or below them in the social order. Opinion leaders differed from followers in many of their personal attributes — they were more gregarious, used media more, were more socially active — but they often shared the same social status.

A critical examination of *Personal Influence* must consider the limitations imposed by McFadden sponsorship. Had Lazarsfeld been free to focus on political communication and to include both men and women, this study might have been more useful. The choice of marketing, fashion, and movies as foci was questionable from the point of view of theory construction because these might have been special cases. For example, was the flow of influence different for politics than it was for these areas? Political opinion leaders tended to be older and of higher social status than followers. Thus, in the case of politics, the two-step flow may have actually been more vertical than horizontal.

Box 6a Election Campaign Studies

The Lazarsfeld approach to political campaign research has been replicated periodically since 1948. Though Lazarsfeld himself was involved with only one replication, in 1948, (Berelson, Lazarsfeld, and McPhee, 1954), the Center for Political Studies (CPS) at the University of Michigan has conducted biannual studies of national election campaigns (Campbell, et. al., 1954; Campbell, et. al., 1960). The CPS studies are widely respected because they employ sophisticated survey research methodology. Each is based on a national sample of more than one thousand people. Long and detailed interviews are conducted in respondents' homes. Powerful statistical techniques are used to analyze the data. Until recently, the Michigan research largely confirmed Lazarsfeld's original assessments about the role of mass media. Social and demographic variables like political party affiliation, social status, age, sex, race, and group membership were found to be more important in predicting how people will vote than was their use of mass media. Recently, however, these variables have become less powerful predictors. Party affiliation, once the strongest predictor, has become rather weak partly due to sharp declines in party affiliation. In fact, current thinking sees voting as very volatile—different factors are more or less important depending on the specific election.

Limitations in the Lazarsfeld Model

The Lazarsfeld research approach has several important deficiencies that its defenders have been slow to recognize. Although these deficiencies don't invalidate specific findings, they do force us to be very careful in their interpretation. We must recognize what is and is not being measured by such survey research:

1 **Surveys can't measure how people actually use media on a day-to-day basis.** Surveys can only record how people *report* their use of media. As our experience with surveys has grown we have identified some common biases in reports of media use. For example, more educated people tend to underestimate media influence on their decisions while less educated people may overestimate it. Estimates of influence tend to be strongly linked to people's perceptions of various media. For example, since television is widely viewed by educated people as a less socially acceptable medium (that is, the boob tube), they are less willing to admit being influenced by it.

2 **Surveys are a very expensive and cumbersome way to study people's use of specific media content such as their reading of certain news stories or their viewing of specific television programs.** Since Lazarsfeld's early work, most

research has dealt with overall patterns of media use rather than use of specific content. Critics have charged that this means that media content is being ignored. The impact of powerful individual messages isn't routinely assessed; only the amount of use being routinely made of a given medium. We can learn a great deal from studying patterns of media use. There are important research questions, however, that can only be addressed if use of specific content is studied.

3 **The research design and data analysis procedures developed by Lazarsfeld are inherently conservative in assessing the power of media.** Media influence is gauged by the amount of change media cause in an effect variable (that is, voting decision) after statistically controlling a set of social and demographic variables. Under these conditions, media are rarely found to be strong predictors of effects. Overall patterns of media use tend to be strongly associated with social and demographic variables like age, sex, social status, education, and so forth. When these variables are statistically controlled, there is little impact (variance) left for media-use patterns to explain. Does this mean that media use really isn't very powerful? Or is such a conclusion a methodological artifact?

4 **Subsequent research on the two-step flow has produced highly contradictory findings.** Most theorists who still find this conceptualization useful talk about multistep flows. These flows have been found to differ greatly according to the type of information being transmitted and the social conditions that exist at a particular point in time (Rogers, 1983). Although information flow from media to audiences has general patterns, these patterns are subject to constant change. Powerful messages could radically alter patterns of flow.

5 **Although surveys can be useful for studying changes over time, they are a relatively crude technique.** In 1940, Lazarsfeld interviewed people once a month. Considerable change could occur during a 30-day period that isn't measured. Listening or reading that took place days earlier could well be misreported. People tend to selectively remember and report what they think they should be doing rather than what they actually do. If surveys are done more often and at closer intervals, they can become intrusive. But the primary reason these surveys aren't conducted is that they are too expensive.

6 **Surveys omit many potentially important variables by focusing only on what can be easily or reliably measured using existing techniques.** Too often these variables are dismissed as unimportant or unduly speculative. Because they are hard or impossible to measure, their very existence may be questioned. This greatly limits theory construction because entire categories of variables are necessarily eliminated.

Limited Effects Theory

Two popular labels for the perspective on media that developed out of Lazarsfeld's work are *indirect effects theory* and *limited effects theory*. These labels call attention to key generalizations about the role of media in society. Here we offer some of the most important generalizations that have emerged from the survey research work conducted between 1945 and 1960. In the next chapter we will provide a discussion of the findings that resulted from persuasion research. Then, in Chapter 8 we will show how these were combined to create a paradigm.

1 **Media rarely have any direct influence upon individuals.** Most people are sheltered from direct manipulation by propaganda by their family, friends, coworkers, and social groups. People don't believe everything they hear or see in the media. They turn to others for advice and critical interpretation. This assumption contradicts mass society notions that viewed people as isolated and highly vulnerable to direct manipulation.

2 **There is a two-step flow of media influence.** Media will only be influential if the opinion leaders who guide others are influenced first. Since these opinion leaders are sophisticated, critical media users, they are not easily manipulated by media content. They act as an effective barrier to media influence.

3 **By the time most people become adults they have developed strongly held group commitments such as political party and religious affiliations that individual media messages are powerless to overcome.** These commitments cause people to reject messages even if other group members are not present to assist them. Media use tends to be consistent with these commitments. For example, voters with Republican affiliations subscribe to Republican magazines and listen mostly to Republican politicians on radio.

4 **When media effects do occur, they will be modest and isolated.** Huge numbers of people across the land will not be converted. Rather, small pockets of individuals may be influenced—usually those who are somehow cut off from the influence of other people or whose long-term group commitments are undermined by social crises.

Summary

The research approach pioneered by Lazarsfeld has had a lasting influence upon media theory and research. It is cautious and based on the use of empirical research methods. Theory is constructed inductively using findings from many different research projects. Every effort is made to avoid overgeneralization and undue speculation. Care is taken to make certain that the correct sources of various effects are identified. The possible influence of media is weighed against the possible influence of other factors. When this approach is used, the typical finding is that media have limited or indirect effects. Other factors are more powerful and the specific effects linked to media tend to be trivial.

The limited effects perspective may have gained popularity partly because it provided a comforting answer to the question that troubled social elites throughout the 1930s. When propaganda threatened to subvert democracy, limited effects theory argued that most people could not be directly reached and influenced by typical propaganda messages. This reassuring argument was based on empirical facts, not on speculative notions about the subversive power of propaganda or how media might corrupt culture.

Limited effects theory actually placed little faith in the rationality of individuals or in their ability to critically evaluate propaganda. This theory is quite pessimistic about the intellect and the motivation of average people. During the 1950s and 1960s, study after study found most people to be politically ignorant and apathetic. Average people saw little relevance between politicians and their daily lives. When people did pay attention to politics it was for the wrong reasons. They were drawn to it as a dramatic contest, passively observing politics as though it were a football game or the March Madness of the NCAA basketball playoffs. Only a small proportion of the population was found to have regular, active involvement in politics. The collective wisdom and political knowledge of the electorate was concentrated in these people—the opinion leaders.

According to limited effects notions, the opinion leaders are the mainstay of the American political system. Typical people have little ability to screen out and resist propaganda. Instead, opinion leaders must intervene and assist others so that they reject it based upon their group loyalties.

This vision is both reassuring and troubling. It implies that bad propaganda will be screened out but it also suggests that potentially positive influences of media will also be rejected. People will reject fascist or communist propaganda but they will also ignore messages designed to reduce racism or increase understanding of other cultures. Instead, they can be expected to cling to the beliefs and values of the groups they grow up in no matter how personally limiting or demeaning these may be. For example, women reared in a strongly patriarchal culture will join groups that support this culture even though it severely limits their options in life and places them in subordinate roles. Most people are viewed as having little capacity to weigh and evaluate the information provided by media. They have to rely upon the guidance of others—the opinion leaders.

Opinion leaders are central to the limited effects perspective, but just who are these individuals and how much can we trust them? The future of the nation is in the hands of leaders who are spread out across the land and throughout the social hierarchy. Can they be trusted to always reject bad propaganda—or do they have weaknesses that master propagandists might be able to exploit? Just who are they? Are they better educated, more socially concerned, and more politically wise or are they people who mindlessly resist all innovative ideas—both good and bad—in favor of traditional culture? This debate over the attributes and role of opinion leaders will be traced in Chapter 8.

Discussion Questions

1   What are the key similarities and differences in how mass society theory and the limited effects perspective view people.

2   Describe some of the major assertions of the limited effects perspective in your own words. Do you agree with them?

3   To what extent do you personally depend upon opinion leaders to help you sort out your thoughts on topics such as politics, movies, fashion, or consumer products. For example, how did you make your last decision to attend a movie?

4   How have you come to envision your own future, the career you will pursue, the lifestyle you will live, the relationships you will develop with other people? Are your ideas consistent with the social groups you grew up in or are they different? To what extent has media content influenced your thinking?

5   Is there anything wrong with a democratic political system in which most people depend upon others to tell them how to vote? Can democracy work only if most people are well informed about politics and politically active? Why or why not?

Significant Names

Orson Welles

Hadley Cantril

Thomas Kuhn

Robert Merton

Significant Readings

Campbell, Angus, G. Gurin, and Warren E. Miller (1954). *The Voter Decides.* Evanston, IL: Row, Peterson.

Cantril, Hadley, Helen Gaudet, and Herta Herzog (1940). *Invasion from Mars.* Princeton: Princeton University Press.

Katz, Elihu, and Paul F. Lazarsfeld (1955). *Personal Influence: The Part Played by People in the Flow of Communications.* New York: Free Press.

Klapper, Joseph (1960). *The Effects of Mass Communication.* New York: Free Press.

Kuhn, Thomas (1970). *The Structure of Scientific Revolutions,* second edition. Chicago: University of Chicago Press.

Lazarsfeld, Paul F., Bernard Berelson, and Helen Gaudet (1944). *The People's Choice: How the Voter Makes Up His in a Presidential Campaign.* New York: Duell, Sloan & Pearce.

Important Terms

Paradigm Shift

Inductive

Middle Range Theory

Opinion Leaders

Gate-Keepers

Two-Step Flow

Chapter 7

Attitude Change Theories

Remember back to the 1991 war in the Persian Gulf. Before the shooting began, the American public was evenly divided on whether our country should actually engage Saddam Hussein's military forces. That quickly changed. Polls taken in the days immediately after the start of hostilities showed that Americans now favored war, 80 percent to 20 percent. How could the public's attitude on something as serious as war change so rapidly? Was it the desire to rally behind the men and women who were risking their lives in an alien land? To what extent was this rally fueled and sustained by overwhelmingly positive media reports?

Media coverage of the Gulf War was one-sidedly positive partly because journalists were subjected to tight control. The military had learned lessons in Vietnam and had developed very effective strategies for restricting the press and making certain that events were covered as the military wanted. Most journalists spent the war confined to areas assigned to them. Those who violated restrictions were arrested. Journalists were so anxious for stories that the military was able to plant false information in news reports to mislead Hussein about invasion plans (Ottosen, 1992). Media critics and some journalists have expressed concern about this coverage and what it portends for coverage of future conflicts (Dennis, 1991). Did the press cooperate too much with government? Should major news media have worked together to effectively challenge censorship at the very start of the war? Should there have been more coverage of anti-war viewpoints and more pictures of the bloody consequences of fighting? Devotees of CNN will remember the frequent military briefings with their lovely, exciting pictures of very smart bombs neatly taking out their steel and concrete targets with great precision and apparently little damage to human beings. But was Saddam Hussein really another Adolf Hitler as George Bush claimed and as many Americans came to believe?

After August 1990, Americans changed their minds about some very important matters relatively quickly and these changes persisted throughout the war. Except for those very few people who were actually in Saudia Arabia and Kuwait or the even fewer people who knew Hussein personally, people changed their minds because of information and pictures provided by the mass media. How should we assess the role of media in this situation and gauge its impact on public opinion? Can we assume that media always have limited effects and that it doesn't really matter how the war was covered? If so, why should we worry about military censorship and control over coverage? Why waste money even sending journalists to the front? The military proved that it is quite capable of furnishing dramatic videos of war highlights. All journalists need to do is sit in New York and edit these into attractive packages.

In this chapter we will continue to trace the emergence of the limited effects perspective. This perspective predicts that media coverage of the war shouldn't have had much direct impact on opinions. Media might communicate information and reinforce some existing opinions or crystallize the views of a few people who hadn't quite made up their minds and were pulled in different directions. Most people, however, should have been resistant to significant changes in their outlook. But were they? The poll results raise questions that quantitative media research and the limited effects perspective can't adequately answer.

Overview

People have been interested in attitude change as long as people have held attitudes. Aristotle's *Rhetoric*, written three hundred years before the birth of Christ, was devoted to the development of skills that we now call persuasion and attitude change. When he wrote, "We believe good men more fully and more readily than others," he was discussing what we now refer to as source credibility. When Abraham Lincoln said "You can fool some of the people all of the time and all of the people some of the time; but you can't fool all of the people all of the time," he was discussing what contemporary communication theorists label resistance to persuasion.

Although persuasion and attitude change have been speculated about almost since the beginning of recorded history, systematic study of these phenomena began only in this century. As noted in Chapter 4, propaganda threatened to subvert democracy, but many social researchers like Harold Lasswell believed that if it could be brought under control it might be used to produce beneficial social changes. Some social researchers believed themselves to be in a race against time—much like the developers of the atom bomb. If the "magic keys to persuasion" couldn't be quickly found, totalitarianism would overrun the world. If they could be detected, then a new world of peace, justice, and equality might be created. In 1953, Carl Hovland and his colleagues wrote:

> During recent years the study of the effectiveness of communication has become a subject of major interest in human relations research. In part this may be ascribed to the important role of mass communications in the economic, political and social organizations of modern society . . . Executives in many organizations feel the need to improve their communications systems in order to achieve widespread acceptance of the standards and values necessary to the success of their enterprises. In the sphere of international relations, numerous practical communications problems are posed by the "cold war," particularly for government policy makers who wish to increase our "influence" on the people in foreign countries and to counteract potentially disruptive foreign propaganda. Also, a major concern of agencies such as UNESCO is in developing mass educational programs that will be effective in breaking down psychological barriers which prevent mutual understanding between nations. A similar need has long been apparent to leaders within our own country who have worked to counteract racial, ethnic, and religious prejudices interfering with the consistent operation of democratic values (Hovland, Janis, and Kelley, 1953, p. 1).

In this chapter we will examine a body of thought that matured with that of the Lazarsfeld survey-fueled public opinion research. While the direct effects model of media influence was being challenged by Lazarsfeld and his colleagues, psychologists interested in how individuals develop, maintain, and change attitudes were attacking it from a different front. We'll see that this perspective developed partly as a result of World War II and the challenge to the Libertarian ideal of good and rational people posed by Nazi propaganda successes. We'll also investigate how the psychologists' methodology (experiments) led to the conclusion of limited media effects. We'll look at the assumptions of these attitude change researchers and detail their conceptualization of selective processes as "shields" against media influence. Finally, as we did in the previous chapter, we'll offer some evidence of the limitations of this limited effects view.

Behaviorism and the Magic Bullet Theory

Rather ironically, the initial breakthrough in the study of attitudes was achieved by behaviorists — psychological researchers who rejected all "mentalist concepts" such as attitude. Behaviorists demonstrated that animals, and to some extent people, could be conditioned to react in specific ways to environmental stimuli. As we explained in Chapter 4, their work encouraged the development of *magic bullet theory* — a perspective that argued that media had the power to condition people's emotional reactions and shape their behavior. Eventually, more sophisticated theories evolved like those of Harold Lasswell and Walter Lippmann. All shared important assumptions with mass society theory. They assumed that average people were vulnerable to media manipulation. Various forms of censorship and technocratic control were thought necessary to protect people from their own weaknesses and to preserve democracy.

World War II and the Study of Attitudes

World War II provided the "laboratory" for the development of a cohesive body of thought on attitude change and, by obvious extension, media and attitude change. The United States entered this war convinced that it was as much a psychological battle as it was a shooting war. The Nazis had demonstrated the power of the Big Lie. We needed to be able to mount an effective counter-offensive. But before we could confront the Japanese and the Germans, we had to turn our attention to the home front. During the 1930s there were powerful isolationist and pacifist sentiments in the United States. These movements were so strong that in the election of 1940 Roosevelt promised to keep the United States out of the war, even though the Nazis were conquering much of Western Europe. Aid to Britain was handled secretly. Until the bombing of Pearl Harbor, peace negotiations were conducted with the Japanese.

Thus, the war provided three important motivations for people interested in attitude research. For one thing, the success of the Nazi propaganda efforts in Europe challenged the democratic and very American notion of the people's wisdom. It seemed that powerful bad ideas might overwhelm inadequately defended good ideas. Strategies were needed to counter Nazi propaganda and defend American values. Early in the war, for example, Carl J. Friedrich (1943), a consultant to the Office of War Information, outlined the military's ongoing research strategy: detect psychological barriers to persuasion *and* assess how effectively a given set of messages could overcome those barriers.

A second war-provided research motivation was actually more imperative. Large numbers of men and women from all parts of the country and from all sorts of backgrounds had been rapidly recruited, trained, and tossed together in the armed forces. Remembering that this was before television, universalized higher education, and the country's urbanization, it is easy to see that the military needed to determine what these soldiers were thinking and to find a way to intellectually and emotionally bind them — Yankee and Southerner, Easterner and Westerner, city boy and country girl — to the cause.

The third motivation was simple convenience: where the military saw soldiers in training, psychologists saw subjects, well-tracked subjects. As Major General Frederick Osborn, Director of the Army's Information and Education Division, wrote in his foreword to Volume I of the series of monographs produced from this research, "The citizen army of the United States offered an exceptional opportunity for the effective use of the new scientific methods devised and taught in the years immediately preceding the war. Not only did the Army contain all the diverse elements of young American men, in numbers adequate for valid statistical results, but each of these men was indexed for various items of personal background of a kind important in drawing samples" (Stouffer, et al., 1949, p. vii).

The availability of a large number of people about whom already existed large amounts of background information proved significant because it helped define the research direction of what we now call attitude change theory. Major General Osborn may have been correct when he enthused, "Never before had modern methods of social science been employed on so large a scale, by such competent technicians. Its value to the social scientist may be as great as its value to the military for whom the original research was done" (Stouffer, et al., 1949, p. vii). But equally important to those social scientists was that this groundbreaking research set the tenor for their work for the next two decades.

Carl Hovland and the Experimental Section

The Army's Information and Education Division had a Research Branch. Inside the Research Branch was the Experimental Section, headed by psychologist Carl Hovland. Its primary mission "was to make experimental evaluations of the effectiveness of various programs of the Information and Education Division" (Hovland, Lumsdaine, and Sheffield, 1949, p. v). At first, the Experimental Section focused on documentary films and the War Department's orientation movie series, *Why We Fight*. But because of the military's increasing use of media, it also studied "other media . . . quite diverse in character" (p. vi). As the researchers themselves wrote (p. vii), "The diversity of topics covered by the research of the Experimental Section made it unfeasible to publish a single cohesive account of all the studies. However, it did appear possible to integrate the group of studies on the effects of motion pictures, film strips, and radio programs into a systematic treatment concerning the effectiveness of mass communication media." They called their account *Experiments on Mass Communication* and it clearly bore the mark of group leader Hovland.

With his background in behaviorism and learning theory, Hovland's strength was in identifying the essential elements of attitude change and devising straightforward experiments employing *controlled variation*. He took some piece of stimulus material (a film, for example), and systematically isolated and varied its potentially important elements independently and in combination to assess their effects.

To meet the military's immediate needs, the Experimental Section began with evaluation research, that is, testing whether or not the *Why We Fight* film series met its indoctrinational goals. Prevailing notions about the power of propaganda implied that the researchers would find dramatic shifts in attitude as a result of viewing the films. According to some versions of mass society theory, every soldier, no matter what his or her background or personality, should have been easily manipulated by the messages in the films. Military training should have induced an ideal form of mass society experience. Individual soldiers were torn from their families, jobs, and social groups. They were isolated individuals, supposedly highly vulnerable to propaganda.

But Hovland's group found that the military's propaganda wasn't as powerful as had been assumed. They discovered that although the movies were successful in increasing knowledge, they were not as effective in influencing attitudes and motivations (their primary function). Even the most effective films served primarily to strengthen existing attitudes. Conversions were rare. Typically, only the attitudes specifically targeted by films showed changes. More global attitudes such as optimism or pessimism about the war were resistant to change. Of some scientific importance, however, was the Experimental Section's analysis of the films in terms of viewer demographics (for example, intellectual ability and educational attainment; remember, this was a very well documented group of subjects).

The fact that the films produced little attitude change and that what change there was was influenced by people's individual differences directly contradicted mass society theory and its assumption that propaganda could radically change even strongly held beliefs and attitudes. If isolated soldiers being hurriedly prepared for battle were resistant to the most sophisticated propaganda available, were average people likely to be more susceptible? As with Lazarsfeld's research, these empirical facts contradicted the prevailing theoretical paradigm and implied that it would be necessary to develop new conceptualizations.

A second outcome of the initial evaluation work was important in determining the direction of future attitude change theory. In examining one of the three films in the series, the 50-minute *The Battle of Britain*, Hovland and his colleagues found that, although initially more effective in imparting factual information than in changing attitudes about the British, as time passed, factual knowledge decreased but attitudes toward the British actually became more positive. Time, the researchers discovered, was a key variable in attitude change. Possibly propaganda effects were not as instantaneous as mass society theory or behavioristic notions suggested. Hovland's group formulated various explanations for these slow shifts in attitude. Perhaps when soldiers were less focused on the film itself (attitudes were measured that second time after nine weeks had passed), they may have responded more generally to questions about their British allies. Or maybe after seeing the film they may have become more attuned to other pro-British information that came their way during the next nine weeks. Maybe the information they learned about the British brought about a slow change in attitude.

With no precise way to scientifically answer the question of why the passage of time produced increased attitude change in the direction of the original media stimulus, Hovland and his research team developed a new type of research design—controlled variation experiments—"to obtain findings having a greater degree of generalizability. The method used is that of systematically varying certain specified factors while other factors are controlled. This makes it possible to determine the effectiveness of the particular factors varied" (Hovland, Lumsdaine, and Sheffield, 1949, p. 179).

One of the most important variables the researchers examined was the presentation of one or both sides of a persuasive argument. Using two versions of a radio program, they presented a one-sided argument (that the war would be a long one) and a two-sided argument (the war would be long, but the alternative view was addressed). Of course, those who heard either version showed more attitude change than those who had heard no broadcast, but there was no difference between the groups who had listened to the two versions. Hovland had anticipated this. Accordingly, he had assessed the men's initial points of view. What his work demonstrated was that one-sided messages were more effective with people already in favor of the message; two-sided presentations were more effective with those holding divergent perspectives. In addition, Hovland looked at educational level and discovered that the two-sided presentation was more effective with those people who had more schooling.

These results were both a source of pessimism and optimism to would-be propagandists. They demonstrated that propaganda messages designed for and distributed to everyone had only limited power. They also indicated that it might be possible to increase the effectiveness of propaganda by tailoring messages for specific groups and targeting them as specific audiences. For example, send one-sided messages to audiences that already hold a particular attitude but direct two-sided messages to audiences who disagree with this attitude. Target two-sided messages toward better educated people and develop one-sided messages for the less educated. The basis for current-day promotional communication strategies was laid.

Thus, this group of psychologists determined that attitude change was a very complex beast and that aspects of the messages themselves can and often did interact with aspects of the people receiving them. An enormous number of significant research questions suddenly could be posed. What happens, for example, when two-sided presentations are directed toward people who are initially predisposed against a position but have low levels of education? Such questions fueled several decades of persuasion research and challenged two generations of researchers.

Further evidence of the complexity of the interrelationship between media, messages, and audiences was provided by some of the last research conducted by the Hovland group before the end of the war. One-sided and two-sided films were produced that explained the necessity for invading Japan. These were shown to soldiers with both low and high education levels. As with the radio experiments, the two-sided film was more effective with educated soldiers. When they were asked which film they perceived as more like propaganda, however, they chose the two-sided film. The educated soldiers said the two-sided film was more deceptive because it put forward weak, straw-man positions against the invasion and then quickly dismissed these in favor of stronger arguments favoring invasion. There was another unanticipated side effect: For some uneducated soldiers, the two-sided film had a boomerang effect—it converted them so that they rejected the necessity for invasion. When these men were questioned, the researchers found that they had never before heard any reasons against invasion and found them persuasive, even though these arguments were deliberately designed by the message producers to be weak. Persuasion researchers were clearly facing a difficult challenge in trying to probe such a contradictory process. The simple assumptions of direct effects of media messages had been conclusively rejected.

The Communication Research Program

The concept of attitude change was so complex that Hovland proposed and conducted a systematic program of research that occupied him and his colleagues in the post-war years. Funded by the Rockefeller Foundation, Hovland established the Communication Research Program at Yale University. Its work centered on the four groups or categories of variables that Hovland considered central to attitude change: the Communicator, the Content of the Communication, Audience Predispositions, and Audience Responses. Hovland expressed this grouping a bit more succinctly when he borrowed Harold Lasswell's "well-known formula of *who says what to whom with what effect*" (Hovland, Janis, and Kelley, 1953, p. 12) to explain the bases of the Yale group's investigations.

These researchers produced scores of scientific articles and a number of significant books on attitude and attitude change, but the most important was the 1953 *Communication and Persuasion*. Organized around the study of the four crucial variables in Lasswell's formula, the psychologists examined a number of issues. Although a close reading of their original work is the best way to grasp the full extent of their findings, here is a general statement of that seminal research.

1 The Communicator (Who): Arguing that "the nature of the source may affect the way in which the audience responds," Hovland and his group studied the power of source credibility, which they divided into _trustworthiness_ and _expertness_. As you might expect, they found that high-credibility communicators produced increased amounts of attitude change; low-credibility communicators produced less attitude change. But what happens in this situation: a very trustworthy communicator, for example your favorite uncle, offers very inexpert arguments, perhaps a faulty argument for why the Yankees are a better baseball team than the Red Sox? Hovland's group found that you will tend to _dissociate_ the source and the content. As they described it, dissociation "reduces or eliminates the direct influence of the source on acceptance of the content. To the extent that the recipient is able to dissociate source and message, the acceptance of the message will be independent of the source" (Hovland, Janis, and Kelley, 1953, p. 41–42). In other words, you will ignore the fact that your uncle is the source of this argument and consider it on its own merits. In which case, you will, of course, reject it. Unless you are a Yankees fan. Then, you will most likely fail to detect the faulty logic in the argument and simply go on believing what you want to believe.

2 Content of the Communication (Says What): Hovland and his colleagues examined two general aspects of content, the nature of the appeal itself and the organization of that appeal.

Focusing specifically on fear-arousing appeals, the Yale group again showed just how complex the process of attitude change could be. The logical assumption is that stronger fear arousing presentations will lead to greater attitude change. This is referred to as a positive, linear relationship. As one variable increases, the other will also increase. This relationship was found to be true to some extent, but . . . well, actually there are a number of "buts." The message's effectiveness is related to how "vividly" the communicator describes the threat and its outcome—but only if audience members are not already in a heightened state of alarm. Effectiveness can also be related to the vagueness or lack of specificity in the appeal—but that depends on the receiver's evaluation of the communicator, not only the evaluation already held, but also that made during the presentation of the fear appeal itself. We also have to take into account what the receiver already knows about the subject at hand. If he or she already has some information about the issue, that information may serve to _inoculate_ him or her against the effects of the threat. If the threat is difficult to comprehend, then prior information may increase attitude change. For the Yale group, it was like peeling the layers of an onion. Every new finding led them to yet another set of variables that had to be considered alongside other variables. Although all of this was heuristic—it produced more and better research questions—it was also frustrating. The magic keys of persuasion kept slipping away.

Their look at the organization of the arguments was a bit more straightforward. Should a communicator explicitly state an argument's conclusions or leave them implicit? In general, the explicit statement of the argument's conclusion is more effective, but not invariably. Less trustworthy communicators, it might be assumed, are less effective when drawing conclusions for their listeners. Higher-intelligence audiences may be more responsive when allowed to make their own conclusions. Of course, personality factors might intervene; for example, highly suggestible folks are more influenced by explicit presentations. But we can't forget the nature of the issue at hand. If the issue is one of greater importance to the audience (highly ego involving), it is better to let members of the audience make up their own minds. Hovland and his colleagues produced a relatively straightforward hypothesis on the question of implicit or explicit conclusions: "In persuasive communications that present a complicated series of arguments on impersonal topics, it is generally more effective to state the conclusion explicitly than to allow the audience to draw its own conclusions" (Hovland, Janis, and Kelley, 1953, p. 105).

The Yale Group also revisited the one side versus both sides question. They came to a similar conclusion. Over time, a two-sided presentation is more effective in producing attitude change when the audience is initially opposed to the communicator's point of view and when, regardless of initial orientation, the audience is later confronted by discrepant information. One-sided arguments are more effective when the audience initially agrees with the communicator or is less well educated.

Could there be other content questions? Certainly. In 1925 psychologist Frederick Hansen Lund offered his Law of Primacy in Persuasion. Simply stated, when an audience is presented with two or more differing arguments on an issue, the first will be the most effective. Hovland and his followers questioned this belief. They formulated a series of experiments to examine the issue of _primacy versus recency_. Hovland's group saw this as actually two different questions. The first was whether, when only one side of the issue is to be presented, it is better to use the strongest arguments at the outset (anticlimax order) or at the end (climax order)? Their findings suggested that if the audience is initially disinterested in the issue, it is more effective to present the strongest points early. If the audience is familiar with the issue and has deep concern about it, the climax order works best.

The second version of the primacy versus recency debate has to do with the issue Lund thought he had decided in 1925: when both sides of an issue are to be offered, which is more effective, that which is offered first (primacy) or that offered last (recency)? After varying such factors as the audience's motivation to learn, the degree of acceptance of each proposition by the audience, attitudes

Box 7a Factors in Attitude Change

This model from Irving Janis (1959) and his Yale University colleagues summarizes the Yale Group's inventory of factors that enter the persuasion process. As you can see, persuasion and attitude change is no simple matter!

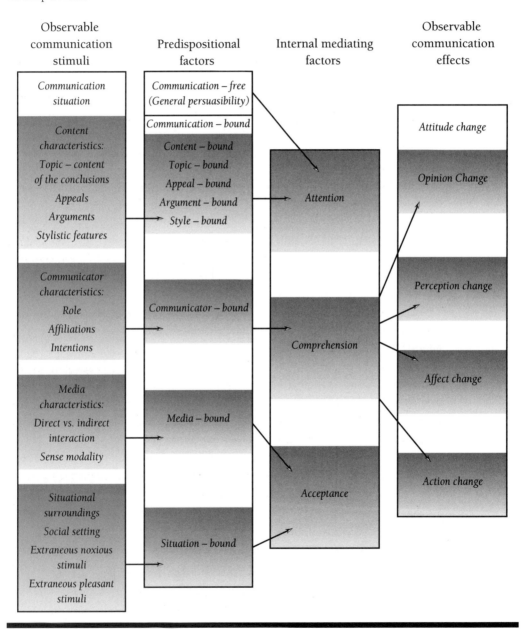

toward the communicator, the audience members' initial predispositions, and any public pronouncements on the issue they might have made, Hovland, Janis, and Kelley (1953, p. 129) concluded, "it is doubtful it will ever be meaningful to postulate a Law of Primacy . . . which states that the material presented first will be more effective than that presented second. It may turn out empirically that 'primacy' is obtained more frequently than 'recency,' but if so it is due to special combinations of events which can produce either primacy or recency, or equal effectiveness of both." This is another indecisive conclusion — like having more layers of an onion to be peeled.

3   Audience Predispositions (To Whom): Of course, regardless of how well a persuasive message is crafted, not all people are influenced by it to the same degree. The Yale group examined this phenomenon in terms of the personal importance of the audience's group memberships and individual personality differences among people that might influence their susceptibility to persuasion.

Testing the power of what they called "counternorm communications," Hovland and his cohorts demonstrated that the more highly people value their membership in a group, the more closely their attitudes will conform to those of the group and, therefore, the more resistant they will be to change. If you attend a Big Ten university and closely follow your school's sports teams, it isn't very likely that anyone will be able to persuade you that the Atlantic Coast Conference fields superior athletes. If you attend that same Big Ten college but care little about its sports programs, you might be a more likely target for opinion change, particularly if your team loses to an ACC team in dramatic fashion.

The question of individual differences in susceptibility to persuasion is not about a person's willingness to be persuaded on a given issue, rather it is about those personality factors that render someone *generally* susceptible to influence. Intelligence is a good example. It is easy to assume that more intelligent people would be less susceptible to persuasive arguments, but this isn't the case. More intelligent people are *more* likely to be persuaded if the message they receive is based on solid, logical arguments. Self esteem, aggressiveness, and social withdrawal were several of the other individual characteristics the Yale Group tested. But as with intelligence, each failed to produce the straightforward, unambiguous relationship that might have seemed warranted. Why? None of a person's personality characteristics operates apart from his or her evaluation of the communicator, his or her judgments of the message, or his or her understanding of the social reward or punishment that might accompany acceptance or rejection of a given attitude. As we'll see, this colored our understanding of media effects for decades.

4   Responses (With What Effect): What the persuasion researchers wanted to know was how opinion change is assisted or impeded by overt expression and what factors extend or diminish the staying power of that change. With their usual list of mediating influences and other provisos, they concluded that "under certain conditions active participation induced by role playing (or by other devices) tends to augment the effectiveness of persuasive communications" (Hovland, Janis, and Kelley, 1953, p. 228).

The factors that mitigate the persistence of attitude change also proved to be inextricably related to the other aspects of the communication situation. These factors were things like the nature of the communicator, the nature of the material, the degree of initial learning or acceptance, the type of retention required, the predispositions of the audience, and, of course, experiences subsequent to the initial communication.

Emergence of the Media Effects Focus

From the 1950s to the 1990s, persuasion research influenced the study of media. Following the models provided by the early persuasion studies as well as those of Lazarsfeld's group, empirical media research focused heavily on the study of media *effects*. This focus was very practical and pragmatic. Sponsors could be found to pay for a variety of different types of effects studies, ranging from the influence of advertising (paid for by advertisers) to the effects of television violence (paid for by the Surgeon General). This sponsorship was critical and permitted the development of a large number of communication research centers dedicated primarily to media effects research. Compared to other forms of media study, effects research was accorded higher scientific status and its practitioners were viewed as constituting an elite subgroup—especially by those who were unaware of the limitations of this research. Melvin DeFleur wrote (1970, p. 118), "The all-consuming question that has dominated research and the development of contemporary theory in the study of the mass media can be summed up in simple terms—namely, 'what has been their effect?' That is, how have the media influenced us as individuals in terms of persuading us."

Although the individual findings of effects research were enormously varied and even contradictory, two interrelated empirical generalizations emerged. These generalizations are completely consistent with the limited effects perspective outlined at the end of Chapter 6 and thus served to buttress it. They assert that the influence of mass media is rarely direct because it is almost always mediated by: (a) *individual differences* and (b) *group membership or relationships*. These two factors normally serve as effective barriers to media influence. Study after study confirmed their existence and expanded our understanding of how they operate. DeFleur (1970) summarized this body of research when he offered "specific formulations that summarize contemporary thinking about the effects of mass communication."

Two of these formulations clearly owe their existence to persuasion and attitude change theory:

1 **Individual differences theory** argued that, because people vary greatly in their psychological make-up and because they have different perceptions of things, media influence differs from person to person. More specifically, "media messages contain particular stimulus attributes that have differential interaction with personality characteristics of members of the audience" (DeFleur, 1970, p. 122).

2 **Social categories theory** "assumes that there are broad collectivities, aggregates, or social categories in urban-industrial societies whose behavior in the face of a given set of stimuli is more or less uniform" (DeFleur, 1970, p. 122–123). In addition, people with similar backgrounds (for example, age, gender, income level, religious affiliation) will have similar patterns of media exposure and similar reactions to that exposure. This set of generalizations derives partly from Lazarsfeld's work, but its validity has been demonstrated by both surveys and the attitude change researchers' experiments.

In the next chapter we will see how these theories combined to form a paradigm. This paradigm provided a broad perspective on media and society that we will discuss in detail. It is important to note that this early research tended to underestimate the power of media due in part to methodological limitations. In Chapter 6, we summarized the limitations of survey research. We will do the same at the close of this chapter for communication experiments.

The Selective Processes

One of the central tenets of attitude change theory that was adopted (in one way or another or under one name or another) by influential mass communication theorists from Lazarsfeld to Joseph Klapper to DeFleur, is the idea of *cognitive consistency*. We noted in Chapter 6 that Lazarsfeld found that people seemed to seek out media messages consistent with the values and beliefs of those around them. This finding implied that people tried to preserve their existing views by avoiding messages that challenged them. As persuasion research proceeded, more direct evidence of this was sought. Cognitive consistency was defined as "a tendency (on the part of individuals) to maintain, or to return to, a state of cognitive balance, and . . . this tendency toward equilibrium determines . . . the kind of persuasive communication to which the individual may be receptive" (Rosnow and Robinson, 1967, p. 299). These same authors wrote, "Although the consistency hypothesis is fundamental in numerous theoretical formulations . . . of all the consistency-type formulations it is Leon Festinger's *theory of cognitive dissonance* which has been the object of greatest interest and controversy" (1967, p. 299–300).

Festinger explained that the bedrock premise of dissonance theory is that information that is not consistent with a person's already-held values and beliefs will create a psychological discomfort (dissonance) that must be relieved; people generally work to keep their knowledge of themselves and their knowledge of the world somewhat consistent. More specifically he said, "If a person knows various things that are not psychologically consistent with one another, he will, in a variety of ways, try to make them more consistent" (Festinger, 1962, p. 93). Collectively, these "ways" have become known as the *selective processes*. Some psychologists consider these to be defense mechanisms that we routinely use to protect ourselves (and our egos) from information that would threaten us. Others argue that they are merely routinized procedures for coping with the enormous quantity of sensory information constantly bombarding us. Either way, the selective processes function as complex and highly sophisticated filtering mechanisms that screen out useless sensory data while quickly identifying and highlighting the most useful patterns in this data.

In arguing that "the (mass) communication itself appears to be no sufficient cause of the effect," Klapper (1960, pp. 18–19) offered his conclusion that "reinforcement is or may be abetted by predispositions *and the related processes of selective exposure, selective perception and selective retention.*" His explanation of how these selective processes protect media content consumers from media's impact neatly echoes Festinger's own presentation. Wrote Klapper (1960, p. 19), "By and large, people tend to expose themselves to those mass communications that are in accord with their existing attitudes and interests. Consciously or unconsciously, they avoid communications of opposite hue. In the event of their being nevertheless exposed to unsympathetic material, they often seem not to perceive it, or to recast and interpret it to fit their existing views, or to forget it more readily than they forget sympathetic material."

Here are the three forms of selectivity that were studied by attitude change researchers. Keep in mind that these notions have since been widely criticized and should be interpreted very carefully. We will point out some of the major limitations as we discuss each.

Selective exposure is people's tendency to expose themselves to or attend to media messages that they feel are in accord with their already-held attitudes and interests and the parallel tendency to avoid that which might be dissonance-creating. Democrats will watch their party's national convention on television, but go bowling when the GOP gala is aired. Lazarsfeld, Berelson, and Gaudet (1944, p. 89), in their Erie County voter study, discovered that "about two-thirds of the constant partisans (Republicans and Democrats) managed to see and hear more of their own side's propaganda than the opposition's . . .

But—and this is important—the more strongly partisan the person, the more likely he is to insulate himself from contrary points of view."

This finding illustrates the danger of inferring the existence of an underlying psychological process based upon survey data. In retrospect, we now realize that during the 1940s it was quite common for people to have media use patterns that were strongly linked to their social status and group affiliation. Newspapers still had strong party connections. Most were Republican. Thus, Republicans read newspapers with a strongly Republican bias and Democrats either read Democrat newspapers or learned how to systematically screen out pro-Republican content. Radio stations tried to avoid most forms of political content but occasionally carried major political speeches. These weren't hard to avoid if you knew you didn't like the politics of the speaker. As media have changed during the intervening four decades, newspapers have become much less partisan and the demographics of their audiences have changed. Today, mainstream broadcast and print media create political news stories that avoid or carefully balance presentation of politically biased content. It has become harder and harder for people to screen out partisan ideas. Candidates increasingly target their campaigns at independent voters by playing down their partisan ties and emphasizing their ability to rise above partisan politics and serve everyone. Not surprisingly, research has documented a steady decline in selective exposure to political information. The obvious content cues that once enabled consumers to avoid or screen out messages are gone.

Selective retention is the process by which people tend to remember best and longest information that is consistent with their preexisting attitudes and interests. Name all the classes in which you've earned the grade of "A." Name all the classes in which you've earned a "C." The A's have it, no doubt. But often you remember disturbing or threatening information. Name the last class you almost failed. Have you managed to forget it and the instructor or are they etched among the things you wish you could forget? If selective retention always operated to protect us from what we don't want to remember, we would never have any difficulty forgetting our problems. Although some people seem able to do this with ease, others tend to dwell on disturbing information. Should we assume that their ability to engage in selective retention has somehow broken down? As we will see in Chapter 11, information processing theory provides a broader perspective that explains these inconsistencies.

Keeping in mind that these processes are not discrete (you cannot retain that to which you have not been exposed), *selective perception* is the mental or psychological recasting of a message so that its meaning is in line with a person's beliefs and attitudes. Klapper offers the famous Allport and Postman (1945) study of rumors as one example of how selective perception works. These two psychologists showed a picture of a fight aboard a train to some people. The combatants

Box 7b Allport and Postman Selective Perception Experiment

The Gordon Allport and Leo Postman experiment on selective perception that we discuss in these pages has become legend in mass communication theory circles. Here is the drawing that their subjects saw in 1945. (Reprinted by permission of the New York Academy of Sciences.)

were a Caucasian male grasping a razor and an unarmed African American male. Those who saw the scene were then asked to describe it to another person who, in turn, passed it on. In 1945 America, the knife inevitably passed into the hands of the Black man. Allport and Postman (1945, p. 81) concluded, "What was outer becomes inner; what was objective becomes subjective."

As with the other notions of selectivity, selective exposure proved to be a useful way of initially conceptualizing experimental findings. The attitude researchers who documented its operation were good scientists. But as with the other forms of selectivity, their findings were based on people's use of a very different set of media and very different forms of media content than we know today. In the 1940s and 1950s, movies were primarily an entertainment medium; radio disseminated significant amounts of news, but typically as brief, highly descriptive reports that expressed no partisan opinion; newspapers were the dominant news medium; and television did not exist. Television moved all the media away from dissemination of information toward the presentation of images and symbols. Most contemporary movies sacrifice storyline and character development for exciting and interesting visuals; your favorite radio station (plus your second and third choices) probably present minimal news, if any; newspaper stories are getting shorter and shorter, the graphics more colorful and interesting, and more than a few papers across the country regularly present pictures snapped from a television screen in their pages. It's not surprising that we process information very differently today than our grandparents did in the 1940s.

Let's transport the valuable Allport and Postman experiment to our times to explain why the selective processes, categorized by the attitude theorists and quickly appropriated by mass communication theorists, might be less useful now in understanding media influence than they were in Allport and Postman's time.

If a speaker were to appear on television and present the argument, complete with charts and "facts," that a particular ethnic group or race of people was inherently dangerous, prone to violent crime, and otherwise inferior to most other folks, the selective processes should theoretically kick in. Sure, some racists would tune in and love the show. But the vast majority of Americans would not watch. Those who might happen to catch it would no doubt selectively perceive the speaker as stupid, sick, beneath contempt. Three weeks later, this individual would be a vague, if not nonexistent memory.

But what if television news—because it is easier to cover violent crime rather than white-collar crime and because violent crime, especially that committed downtown near the studio, provides better pictures than a scandal in the Savings and Loan industry—were to present inner-city violence to the exclusion of most other crime? What if entertainment programmers, because of time, format, and other pressures (Gerbner, 1990), continually portrayed their villains as, say, dark, mysterious, different? Do the selective processes still kick in? When the ubiquitous mass media that we routinely rely upon repeatedly provide homogeneous and biased messages, where will we get the dissonant information that activates our psychological life preservers? *good questions*

Today, fifty years after the Allport and Postman study, would the knife still find its way from the white man's hand into the black man's? Why was our country (police and government officials, the media, we) so willing to accept Charles Stuart's account in 1990 of how a black man had shot his pregnant wife as the expectant parents left their birthing lesson in Boston (See Box 7c)? Later chapters *yes* that deal with theories that view mass communication as more symbolically, rather than informationally, powerful will address these questions.

Box 7c Charles Stuart: Allport and Postman Revisited

On the night of October 23, 1990, expectant father Charles Stuart phoned Boston's 911 emergency service from his car. "My wife's been shot. I've been shot," he gasped, "It hurts. And my wife has stopped gurgling. She's stopped breathing." The tape of his frantic, desperate call was played on local and national radio and television. A news crew, who happened to be traveling with the emergency team that responded to the plea, caught the gruesome scene in pictures: the 30-year-old pregnant woman, dead, her head smashed by the assailant's bullet, blood flooding the young couple's automobile.

But fortunately Stuart was able to describe the beast who had committed this atrocity. He was a raspy-voiced black man, dressed in a jogging suit, brandishing a snubbed-nose .38. The shootings occurred in a dark street in Boston's racially-mixed Mission Hill District. The city's mayor, Raymond Flynn, ordered all available detectives onto the case. Police and prominent government officials attended Carol Stuart's funeral and visited severely wounded Charles in the hospital. Flynn called him a hero.

Soon, police were randomly stopping 200 men a day for questioning and frisking. What made them suspicious? They were young and black.

Boston NAACP president, Louis Elisa, likened the atmosphere in the city to that of a "lynch-mob." Prominent African American community leader, Reverend Charles Smith, accused the media of "overkill" in their reports showing "the worst of what black people are supposed to be." Still, police arrested William Bennett, an unemployed black man with a long criminal record. Justice was done.

Not quite. Three months later, about to be exposed by the police, Charles Stuart committed suicide by plunging into the frozen Mystic River and drowning. He had killed his wife and shot himself to collect insurance money and set up a new life with his mistress.

How did this happen? Even though federal crime statistics show that one-third of all the women murdered in America are killed by their husbands, how was this diabolical man able to fool the police, the media, and the public so dramatically and for so long? How was one man able to move police to terrorize innocent people? Allport and Postman had the answer in 1945. *Time Magazine* (January 22, p. 10) had it in 1990: By identifying the killer as a black man, Stuart "raised the curtain on a drama in which the press and police, prosecutors, politicians and the public played out their parts as though they were following the script for the television movie that CBS will make about the case. Instead of suspicion, Stuart was showered with sympathy. The media apotheosized the couple as starry-eyed lovers out of Camelot cut down by an urban savage."

The Hovland-Lazarsfeld Legacy

The wealth of empirically based knowledge generated by persuasion research and, more important, the often conflicting, inconclusive, and situationally-specific research questions it inspired, have occupied many if not most communication researchers until the present. Together with the survey research findings produced by Lazarsfeld, these data challenged and ultimately undermined mass society notions. In the next chapter we will discuss how a new and quite powerful paradigm emerged that claimed to be based on all of this data. Miller and Burgoon (1978, p. 29) acknowledged the powerful initial influence of the new paradigm when they commented with regard to the Hovland work, "The classic volumes of the 'Yale Group' . . . were accorded a seminal status comparable to that conferred on the Book of Genesis by devoted followers of the Judeo-Christian religious faith."

This body of work deserves recognition but not reverence. It was thorough, sophisticated, and groundbreaking—but it was not Truth. Along with the research of Lazarsfeld, it spawned literally thousands of research efforts on and dozens of intellectual refinements of the process of communication. But now, several decades later, we have only begun to put this work into perspective and understand its limitations as well as its considerable merits. Though the new paradigm shed important light upon the process of communication it failed to illuminate all aspects of the process. The beam it cast was narrow, obscuring some of important features of the process while highlighting some trivial properties. Thus, its contribution to our overall understanding of the role of mass media in the society at large was at best misleading, and at worst erroneous.

Limitations of the Experimental Persuasion Research

Like the research approach developed by Lazarsfeld, the Yale approach also had important limitations. Here they are listed and compared to those described for the Lazarsfeld research.

1. Experiments were conducted in laboratories or other artificial settings to control extraneous variables and manipulate independent variables. But it was often difficult to generalize these results to real life situations. Many serious errors were made in trying to generalize from laboratory results. Also, most experiments take place over relatively short time periods. Effects that don't take place immediately were not found. Hovland found long-term effects only because the military trainees he was studying were readily accessible over a longer time period. Most researchers don't have this luxury. Some are forced to study "captive" but atypical populations like students or prisoners.

2. Experiments have the opposite problems from surveys when studying the immediate effects of specific media messages. As noted in Chapter 6, it is cumbersome if not impossible to study effects of specific messages using surveys. By contrast, experiments are ideally suited to studying the immediate effects of specific media

content on small or homogeneous groups of people. They aren't, however, suited to studying the cumulative influence of patterns of overall media use within large, heterogeneous populations. For example, we have begun to find that members of ethnic groups who use different combinations of media show markedly different long-term effects. This type of influence cannot be studied using simple, short-term experiments. Instead, very complex and expensive research is required. Such research typically won't be conducted unless it is likely to have an immediate payoff for the sponsor, that is, to determine how to more effectively market products to a specific ethnic group.

This limitation of experimental research has produced serious biases in the findings that have accumulated. Since the study and comparison of the influence of individual media was difficult, research often failed to distinguish results based on messages delivered through a mass medium (like film) from those generated in research dependent on messages presented by speakers (for example, an adult speaking about the value of woodcrafts to a group of Boy Scouts) or by printed expressions of opinion. As a result, the persuasion research directed attention away from the power of the media themselves and focused attention on message content. As late as 1972, for example, Alan Elms wrote "The medium itself may indeed be the principal message in certain artistic productions or entertainments; it is seldom so in communication designed (with any sort of competence) to be persuasive" (p. 184). But if serious lectures extolling young American soldiers to trust the Brits could have done the job, why did the Army commission the movie *Battle of Britain*? If a classmate told you that he'd heard that the Berlin Wall had fallen would you be really convinced or would you want to see it for yourself on CNN or the network news? Clearly, the medium can largely be the message when we are considering persuasion. But it wasn't until much later that this proposition was seriously considered.

3   Like the Lazarsfeld approach, the Hovland work is also inherently cautious in assessing media influence, but for very different reasons. Lazarsfeld insisted on comparing the power of media to the influence of other social and demographic variables. These other variables were usually stronger. In an experiment, other variables aren't statistically controlled as is done in analyzing survey data; control is exercised by excluding variables from the laboratory and by random assignment of research subjects to treatment and control groups. But in controlling for extraneous variables, the researchers often eliminated factors that we now know to be crucial in reinforcing or magnifying media influence. For example, we now know that conversations with other people during or immediately after viewing television programs are likely to strengthen a broad range of media effects. If a researcher eliminates conversation from the laboratory, she or he will systematically underestimate the power of media in situations where personal conversations are otherwise likely.

4 Throughout this chapter we have described many instances where persuasion research produced apparently contradictory findings. Often these apparent conflicts were resolved by later work in which research questions were redefined to include additional variables. Sometimes it was necessary to rethink key variables like source credibility. L. Erwin Atwood (1984), for example, was interested in source credibility in news. But what he discovered is that every agent in the news-making process possessed its own specific degree of credibility. He wrote, "The definition of a source depends upon the system level under consideration . . . the provider of the original details, the bylined writer, the news service and the newspaper, magazine, and television or radio station" (p. 4). A CBS network news story about a movie star's temper tantrums should convince a lot more people than a similar story in the *Midnight Enquiring Star*. Individuals may differ greatly in how they assess credibility of media content. Some of us pay attention to newspaper bylines or come to trust the television network star reporters. Others simply trust or distrust specific media — or the media in general. The early persuasion experiments weren't designed to differentiate source credibility in this way.

5 Like surveys, experiments are a very crude technique for examining the influence of media over time. Conceivably, a researcher could set up an experimental group and bring it back to a laboratory after weeks or months. But this ongoing experimentation could easily affect or bias the results. Imagine yourself as the subject, required to come into a laboratory every few days over a period of several months so that you can watch films in which women are violently attacked, raped, or murdered. What do you suppose your long-term reaction to these movies would be? Would it be the same as if you were a fan of such movies and regularly sought them out? Research like this has found that male subjects become desensitized to violence against women. They show a greater likelihood to blame rape victims rather than the rapists for causing this crime. What does this research prove? That a persistent researcher can turn an average male into an insensitive animal if he or she can just get him to sit through enough scenes of torture and mayhem? Or does it demonstrate that college students attending biweekly violence film-fests will eventually get bored and stop being aroused by every violent episode? Would you as a male subject be more likely to blame real life rape victims or are you simply more likely to blame the victims that you see on videotapes in the laboratory? Long-term effects of generic forms of media content have been quite hard to establish and have fueled legitimate debates among some of the most skilled researchers.

6 As with surveys, there are many variables that experiments cannot explore. For example, some real-life conditions are far too complex to be simulated in laboratories. In other cases, it would be unethical or even illegal to manipulate certain independent variables. One of the most infamous experiments in persuasion research involved a study of how far people would go in obeying authority. Stanley Milgram (1963) demonstrated that in a laboratory setting people could be induced to administer electrical shocks that they thought were likely to kill or maim another person. The techniques he used have since become extremely controversial among social science researchers because of the potential psychological harm to subjects (see Box 7d).

What about brainwashing? Should we experiment with that? We did during the 1950s. Today, you could easily land in jail if you attempted the manipulations that were done then by our government intelligence agencies using drugs, sleep deprivation, and physical isolation to manipulate experimental subjects and make them highly vulnerable to manipulation. We justified this research because the North Koreans were brain washing captured soldiers and we wanted to know if there were ways of making our personnel resistant to their techniques. Did the end justify the means? Can such forms of persuasion be studied in the laboratory?

Contemporary Attitude and Persuasion Research

Although the work of the war and post-war years had the greatest impact on shaping mass communication theory, much attitude change research continues today. Two of the most interesting and valuable manifestations are actually re-articulations of existing knowledge on attitudes recast in provocative ways. The first is Martin Fishbein's (1967) *expectancy-value theory*. Stephen Littlejohn (1989, p. 84) explained it succinctly,

> (T)here are two kinds of belief, both of which are probability statements. The first is what (Fishbein) terms *belief* in a thing. When one believes *in* something, he or she predicts a high probability of existence. The second kind of belief, *belief about* is the predicted probability that a particular relationship exists between the belief object and some other quality or thing. Again, this is a probability situation, and one's belief is the predicted probability of the existence of a particular relationship . . . Attitudes differ from beliefs in that they are *evaluative*. Attitudes are correlated with beliefs and predispose a person to behave in a certain way toward the attitude object. Attitudes are learned as part of one's concept formation. They may change as new learnings occur throughout life . . . Fishbein sees attitudes as hierarchically organized. In other words, general attitudes are predicted from specific ones in a *summative* fashion. An attitude toward an object is the sum of the specific factors, including beliefs and evaluations, in the family hierarchy.

A second influential attitude change theory is John Cacioppo and Richard Petty's (1985) *elaboration likelihood model*. This approach sees attitude formation as a function of the directness of information processing. Information that is dealt

Box 7d Milgram's Electrical Shock Experiments

Stanley Milgram was a psychology professor and researcher at Yale University in New Haven, Connecticut. In the early 1960s he conducted a series of experiments on obedience in which subjects recruited through a newspaper were told to administer electrical shocks to another person. Milgram wanted to see how far individuals would go in hurting other people if they were told that they were free of responsibility. He was testing the I'm-only-following-orders hypothesis, testing to what lengths people would go if they could claim that they were doing someone else's bidding. Most of the subjects in his studies continued giving shocks well after the man receiving them asked, even begged them to stop. Some went as far as to kill the man because Milgram's associate, an "authority figure," ordered them to keep giving shocks. No one ever really died, of course. The man never received the shocks, he was acting. He simply watched an indicator that told him how much electricity he was supposed to be getting. He would yell at the appropriate time, beg that the experiment be stopped, and then feign death when the shocks reached a specified level of intensity.

The experiments were ingeniously designed. The unwitting subject would be introduced to Milgram's accomplice, the actor. The two people would sit together waiting their turn to work at what they were told was a memory task. The actor would let on that he had a heart condition and that maybe he should withdraw; but no, he'd decide to participate after all. It was only an exercise in memorizing lists of words, he'd say. Milgram even went as far as to give the subject a small jolt of electricity so the unsuspecting volunteer would know what his partner, the actor, would feel each time he erred when asked to repeat the memorized words. When the experiment ended, either with the supposed death of the accomplice or the subject's unwillingness to go on delivering shocks, there was a debriefing. The subject was allowed to meet the much alive accomplice to see that he was, indeed, unhurt and the experiment's purpose was then explained.

We'll let Milgram's student-at-the-time, psychologist Alan Elms, explain what happened then. "Milgram, in exploring the external conditions that produce such destructive obedience, the psychological processes that lead to such attempted abdication of responsibility, and the means by which defiance of illegitimate authority can be promoted, seems to me to have done some of the most morally significant research in modern psychology. A number of ministers who have based sermons on this research, and the Germans and Israelis who were the first to publish translations of Milgram's papers, apparently agree," he wrote (Elms, 1972, p. 146–147). "But by an odd twist of moral sensibilities, the Milgram studies have themselves been more extensively attacked on ethical grounds than any other recent psychological research. Part of the criticism has come simply from coffee-break moralizers, who feel their own vague personal codes of ethics to have been somehow bruised. But the studies have also been used as stepping-off points for serious discussions of the psychologist's ethical responsibilities, both to his research participants and to society at large."

with directly, or through the *central route*, is highly elaborated; that is, the subsequent attitude change is the product of extensive, careful examination and scrutiny. The resulting attitude will be more permanent and change-resistant. Information that is processed through a more *peripheral route* undergoes more casual evaluation or, in other words, less elaboration. As might be obvious, these ideas are of particular interest to advertising and marketing professionals who are as concerned with depth of attitude as they are in changing it.

Summary

Although people have long been interested in attitudes, the development of the mass media and, especially, World War II galvanized serious systematic evaluation of what we now call attitude change theory. The war provided the need for the research as well as an available pool of subjects.

Carl Hovland and the Experimental Section of the Army's Information and Education Division were the leaders in, at first, evaluation research of existing media fare and later, studies of persuasion using controlled variation. When the war ended, Hovland established the Communication Research Program at Yale University. The Yale Group focused attitude research on the four variables it considered most central to attitude change: the Communicator, the Content, Audience Predispositions, and Audience Responses. In doing so, they investigated issues such as source credibility, fear appeals, inoculation, the organization of arguments, one- and two-sided appeals, primacy versus recency, value of group membership, individual personality factors, and duration of opinion change.

This important communication research, however, may have diverted attention away from a fuller understanding of *mass* communication. For one thing, the research ignored the power of the media themselves, or at least it did not pay significant attention to differences between individual media and their presentations. More important, this research helped cement the prevailing notion that media had limited effects (if any at all) because people's individual differences and group affiliations protected them from media influence. This position was popularized contemporarily by Lazarsfeld in the Voter Studies, and as we shall see, by Klapper and his reinforcement theory. This position also formed the basis for the writing of later theorists like DeFleur, who synopsized several theories of mass communication including individual differences, social control, and cultural norms. The first two of these theories suggest minimal or limited media effects and the last, a more powerful mass media. These theories are excellent examples of where our knowledge of mass communication stood in those 10 or 15 years after the Yale Group was formed. More important, though, they should be seen as the logical product of their time because attitude change theory was developed and legitimized during the same period as the Lazarsfeld group's view of mass communication that also positioned media as relatively powerless to produce significant individual or societal effects.

Cultural norms theory, however, demonstrates the direction that thinking about mass communication eventually took — and anticipated the challenge that the limited effects paradigm would face. DeFleur initially offered cultural norms theory as "more controversial" and as having "received little in the way of explicit formulation." His low regard for this newfangled notion was evident in his admonition that "it appears to be the basis for much criticism of the media for their purported 'harmful' effects" and in the definition he offered. Cultural norms theory, he wrote,

> postulates that the mass media, through selective presentations and the emphasis of certain themes, create impressions among their audiences that common cultural norms concerning the emphasized topics are structured or defined in some specific way. Since individual behavior is usually guided by cultural norms . . . with respect to a given topic or situation, the media would then serve *indirectly* to influence conduct (1970, p. 129).

One product of attitude change research that played a major role in people's thinking about media was the idea of cognitive consistency and its related notions of cognitive dissonance and the selective processes. Klapper, for one, depended heavily on the concepts of selective exposure, selective retention, and selective perception to explain why media served as agents of reinforcement rather than as agents of change.

The foundation for the new paradigm had been laid but the seeds of its destruction were also present.

Discussion Questions

1 Did you personally experience a change in opinion on the 1991 Gulf War once the shooting began? Why or why not? Do you think the media influenced your attitudes at all in that event?

2 Do you remember the Charles Stuart event? Would you have been taken in if you were a Boston law officer or reporter? Why or why not?

3 Do you consider yourself a persuasive person? If you do, what skills make you persuasive?

4 Do you consider yourself immune to persuasion? If you do, what makes you that way?

5 Can you offer any recent examples of your own selective exposure? Selective retention? Selective perception?

Significant Names

Carl Hovland

Leon Festinger

Bernard Berelson

Gordon Allport

Melvin DeFleur

Irving Janis

Joseph Klapper

Martin Fishbein

Hazel Gaudet

Significant Readings

Allport, Gordon W. (1967). "Attitudes." In M. Fishbein, ed., *Readings in Attitude Theory and Measurement*. New York: John Wiley and Sons.

DeFleur, Melvin L. (1970). *Theories of Mass Communication*. New York: David McKay Company.

Hovland, Carl I., Irving L. Janis, and Harold H. Kelley (1953). *Communication and Persuasion*. New Haven: Yale University Press.

Hovland, Carl I., Arthur A. Lumsdaine, and Fred D. Sheffield (1949). *Experiments on Mass Communication*. Princeton: Princeton University Press.

Lazarsfeld, Paul F., Bernard Berelson, and Hazel Gaudet (1948). *The People's Choice: How the Voter Makes Up His Mind in a Presidential Campaign*. New York: Duell, Sloan & Pearce.

Important Terms

Experiment

Controlled Variation

Source Credibility

Primacy

Recency

Individual Differences

Social Categories

Cognitive Dissonance

Selective Processes

Cultural Norms

Selective Exposure, Retention, and Perception

Elaboration Likelihood Model

Expectancy-Value Theory

SECTION *Four*

The Limited Effects Paradigm Emerges

1961   *Key's* Public Opinion and American Democracy
Kennedy makes nation's first live TV presidential press conference
Berelson's "Great Debate on Cultural Democracy"
Schramm team's Television in the Lives of Our Children *published*

1962   *Festinger's cognitive dissonance article appears*
Kraus's Great Debates

1963   *JFK assassinated*
Bandura's aggressive modeling experiments first appear
Networks begin one half hour newscasts

1964   *McLuhan's* Understanding Media

1965   *Color comes to all three commercial TV networks*
Comsat satellite launched

1966   *Mendelsohn's* Mass Entertainment
Berger and Luckmann's Social Construction of Reality

1967   *Merton's* On Theoretical Sociology
Stephenson's Play Theory

1969   *Blumer coins "symbolic interaction"*

1971   *Bandura's* Psychological Modeling

1972   *Surgeon General's Report on Television and Social Behavior released*
McCombs and Shaw introduce "agenda-setting"
Gerbner's Violence Profile initiated
FCC requires cable companies to provide "local access"

1973   *Watergate Hearings broadcast live*

1974   *Blumler and Katz's* Uses of Mass Communication
Noelle-Neumann introduces "spiral of silence"
Goffman pioneers frame analysis
Home use of VCR introduced

Chapter 8

The Limited Effects Paradigm Emerges

No informed person can say simply that television is bad or good for children.

For some *children, under* some *conditions,* some *television is harmful. For* other *children under the same conditions, or for the same children under* other *conditions, it will be beneficial. For* most *children under* most *conditions,* most *television is probably neither particularly harmful nor particularly beneficial* (Schramm, Lyle, and Parker, 1961, p. 1)

[handwritten margin note: important quote (often cited)]

In the United States, the Golden Age of television began in the 1950s and continued throughout the 1960s. New television stations went on the air daily. Sales of television sets soared and rooftop antennas became a status symbol. The highly successful introduction of color television during the 1960s confirmed the popularity of the new medium. People were willing to pay high prices and cope with sets that delivered unstable, inferior pictures.

In the space of two decades, the everyday life of the nation was radically altered. Visits with friends and extended family members declined sharply as more and more Americans, especially children, stayed at home to watch television. During popular programs, neighborhood streets and playgrounds were deserted.

[handwritten margin note: paraphrase (condense)]

But how was the new medium affecting the nation? Were there negative effects, slowly undermining our mental ability or moral fiber? Among some social elites, mass society arguments resurfaced in new forms. Book after book catalogued speculation about the insidious influences of the mass culture being disseminated by television. Some warned that television was distracting attention from important things in life and turning us into passive couch potatoes. The civilizing influence of high culture was being undermined by the mindless entertainment on television. How could we be good citizens if we relied on television for information? Some experts argued that within a few years, people's ability to read and write might disappear entirely—television would make literacy obsolete. But would a nation of illiterates be capable of self-government? How could such a country continue to produce scientists, doctors, or teachers?

Special attention was directed at television's influence on children. Would television so radically alter their experience that enormous social problems might be created in the space of one generation? According to Lawrence Freedman, "Psychiatrists have raised grave questions concerning the pathological implications of prolonged watching of television with its associated surrender of personal, physical, and intellectual ability. They see passivity merging into autism, and predisposing to dependent, schizoid, and withdrawn personalities" (1961, p. 190). Others worried that television violence would lead to widespread juvenile delinquency.

Not surprisingly, these fears spawned numerous research projects. One of the most ambitious was directed by Wilbur Schramm, Jack Lyle, and Edwin Parker (1961). In the late 1950s, Schramm was a rising star among empirical media researchers (see Chapter 14 for a description of Schramm's career). He had founded one of the first research centers for the scientific study of communication at the University of Illinois and had been hired to establish a similar center at Stanford University. With a large grant from the National Educational Television and Radio Center, he and his Stanford colleagues set out to demonstrate that social science research techniques could provide needed insight into the role of television in the lives of American children.

From 1958 to 1960, the Stanford team conducted 11 studies in 10 different cities. Interviews were conducted with 6,000 children and 2,000 parents. Schramm and his team published their findings in 1961 in a format designed to be read by parents as well as other researchers (all research design and data analyses were placed in methodological appendices). Their book provides a classic example of both the strengths and the limitations of the limited effects paradigm, which had been under development for almost two decades by the time Schramm and his colleagues undertook their work. They used newly refined empirical research methods, primarily survey interviews, to address a full range of questions about the influence of television on children. Computerized data analysis permitted the researchers to examine literally thousands of relationships between variables to isolate those that were statistically significant.

The Stanford team conducted its research without using a single, well-articulated theoretical framework. Instead, in keeping with the limited effects paradigm, it relied upon a welter of empirical generalizations that had emerged from earlier studies, including notions about selectivity and individual differences.

These were combined with others from diverse sources including Freudian psychology and behaviorism. Although Schramm and his team were guided by these ideas, like most limited effects researchers they preferred not to be "biased" by any well-developed theoretical framework. Rather, their ultimate goal was to construct a theory based upon systematic empirical observation. To this end they worked inductively, identifying consistencies in their data and then summarizing and interpreting them. The essence of their conclusions was stated in the first two paragraphs of their book. We repeated these conclusions on the first page of this chapter. Television adversely affects some children, under some conditions but not most children under most conditions.

The team recognized that some readers wouldn't consider this a satisfactory answer to their concerns. Parents didn't want to know what television did to most children—they wanted to know what it might do to their child. The Stanford approach couldn't explain media's influence on individual children, but it did seek to rule out simplistic, mass society conceptions of media subversion. According to the researchers, the effect of television could most usefully be viewed as "an interaction between characteristics of television and characteristics of viewers."

Unfortunately, in 1960 we knew very little about the nature of this interaction. Therefore, the obvious solution was to do more research that investigated interrelationships between these variables. The researchers were optimistic about the potential of their work. They hoped that modern data analysis techniques would permit causal connections to be efficiently explored so that definitive conclusions about television uses and effects could be reached. Researchers believed that a useful theory of television effects based on hard, empirical facts could be constructed. In the meantime, we could reassure ourselves that whatever television was doing to us, it wasn't doing too much to most of us under most conditions.

In their analysis of the Schramm, Lyle, and Parker study, Lowery and DeFleur (1988) pointed out that throughout their book, Schramm and his team offered an implicit theory that allayed the fears of troubled parents and included comforting, traditional child-rearing truisms. In case after case, specific empirical findings were interpreted as proving the wisdom of these homilies. All was quite simple: "good" parents had only to do what their family and friends told them to be the right thing and they would have nothing to fear from the new medium. In this view, childhood was seen as an unstable period when children were plagued by wild emotions and drawn toward strange fantasies, so it was not surprising that they were attracted by television that played upon these emotions and fantasies. Children hadn't yet learned self-discipline and conformity; they didn't know what was good for them. Parents must provide the discipline and guidance necessary to get children through these crises so that they can mature into rational, responsible adults. Thus, Schramm and his colleagues asserted that the arrival of television hadn't radically altered child-rearing. It had merely eliminated some old problems (reading comic books) and substituted new ones. They advised that although television may aggravate some child-rearing problems, these could be handled if parents provided a little extra care and understanding. In the words of Lowery and DeFleur:

> In short, some children could be "damned" by exposure to television. Those who could be "saved" were those who enjoyed the WASP world of love, security, and middle class values. These were the simple solutions to the potential problems of television (1988, pp. 269–270).

These solutions were offered despite the fact that the data collected and analyzed by the researchers provided only indirect and superficial evidence in support of them. As Lowery and DeFleur (1988) noted, all of the studies were cross-sectional (conducted at one particular point in time), but the Schramm team tried to draw firm conclusions about developmental changes in children that take place overtime. To do so, they were forced to compare children at different ages and in different cities who had grown up while the medium of television itself was undergoing many changes. On the basis of this circumstantial evidence, the researchers evaluated middle-class child-rearing practices and concluded that they would effectively counteract any potential threat posed by television—a comforting message for troubled parents, but hardly good social science. The television industry and the U.S. government also found this message both plausible and self-serving, because it absolved both from taking actions that would have threatened profits or proved politically controversial.

An interesting note of historic irony is that the most persuasive (and potentially damning) early research on children's ability to learn aggression from the media was being conducted at this same time on Schramm's very same Stanford University campus by psychologist Albert Bandura (for example, Bandura, Ross, and Ross, 1963). This should offer some hint as to the power of the dominant limited effects paradigm to structure mass communication scientists' interpretation of results.

Overview

During the 1960s and into the 1970s, the limited effects paradigm dominated American mass communication research. The increasing hegemony of a new theoretical paradigm normally goes unheralded, even by its major adherents. Unlike political ideologies, social theories normally aren't debated in public forums. Unlike new cars or brands of toothpaste, they aren't unveiled in front of television cameras before nationwide audiences. As the preceding chapters illustrated, new paradigms are created by loosely knit research communities with inspiration from key individuals like Lazarsfeld and Hovland. Communities form at a handful of universities and their influence gradually spreads outwards. Their members share a common perspective that is acquired through collaboration on research and through graduate education. Fledgling researchers are trained to use specific theories and research methods.

As research communities evolve, the paradigm on which they are based gradually matures. At a certain point, if a particular community grows in size and produces widely accepted research, it publishes landmark studies—like the work of Schramm's team. These studies solidify the paradigm's dominance over rival perspectives.

In this chapter, we will discuss several of the "classic" studies that heralded the growing importance and utility of the limited effects perspective. Like the research by Schramm's Stanford group, these studies demonstrated the power of the paradigm and its ability to produce findings that had immediate, practical value. These findings addressed important, troubling questions concerning the role of media. But all too often, researchers overgeneralized and made sweeping assertions and recommendations based on very marginal and tangential evidence. The view that media had limited effects was one that foundation, corporate, and government sponsors also found comforting. The most successful researchers were good entrepreneurs who sold their approaches and their findings to these sponsors. We will place these studies into historical perspective and gauge their continuing impact upon communication research.

Building a Paradigm

In discussing the development of scientific paradigms, Thomas Kuhn (1962) argued that although great individuals inspire paradigm shifts, the grunt work necessary to solidify an innovative perspective is done by technicians—people who competently execute individual research projects. Each project forms yet another building block for the paradigm. Master researchers such as Lazarsfeld and Hovland are like architects who draw plans for a skyscraper: Without the work of thousands of individual researchers, their blueprints would be useless.

Like buildings, once paradigms are constructed they take on a life of their own—they reify the dreams of their builders. Unfortunately, reality rarely conforms to the dreamers' fondest hopes. By 1960, the limited effects paradigm was like a half-constructed skyscraper. Thousands of surveys and experiments had been conducted in accordance with the plans devised by the master architects. A structure, much like a framework of steel girders for a skyscraper, had been built but many details remained to be filled in. The research we've been discussing outlines this structure: media influence *some* people, under *some* conditions, but not most people under most conditions. But which media influence which people under which conditions? To answer this question, the paradigm needed to be elaborated and that required lots of research.

Unlike a physical building, you can't see a paradigm. To be serviceable, the limited effects paradigm had to be *envisioned*—an effort had to be made to look at all the pieces of research and locate consistencies in them. Then, new theories had to be created that accounted for these consistencies. In this respect, our discussion of research in the two preceding chapters might have been a bit misleading. With the benefit of hindsight, we identified key findings and discussed the most important ideas. We ignored, however, countless studies that proved useless at best and obfuscating at worst. Until the late 1950s, social researchers were plagued by a myriad of competing conceptualizations and findings. Once the limited effects paradigm solidly emerged, it quickly gained popularity among empirical researchers because it summarized the bulk of existing findings. Those that didn't fit were relegated to obscurity.

The paradigm, before dominating, passed through a crucial period of development. A new generation of researchers, led by people like Wilbur Schramm, reinterpreted the work of their predecessors and built upon it. New research was conducted and new theories were developed that were consistent with the paradigm. Most researchers in this second generation had either been trained by pioneer empirical researchers or were strongly influenced by their writing. (See Chapter 14 for a discussion of those who influenced Wilbur Schramm.)

The effort to find meaning in the welter of individual empirical studies could have failed. Even with superior resources, researchers might have lost confidence, misinterpreted findings, or based their theories on misleading findings. Given the cost of conducting empirical research, corporate, foundation, and government sponsorship was especially essential during this stage. In addition to paying for this research, sponsorship by elite funding agencies such as the Rockefeller Foundation, the Columbia Broadcasting System, or the National Science Foundation legitimized the paradigm.

In the late 1950s, the utility of the limited effects paradigm was not obvious to all or even most social researchers. Many were troubled by its dependence upon induction and its rejection of speculative theory. There were strong reactions against its proponents. Often, these judgments were ill-conceived—based upon misinterpretations of the new paradigm and prejudices against quantitative research. But occasionally the criticisms were made by people who were knowledgeable about both the paradigm's strengths and limitations. Perhaps the most intelligent and devastating criticism was offered by C. Wright Mills, a Harvard sociologist. Mills had been personally tutored by Lazarsfeld and served as field director for the survey of housewives in Decatur in 1943. In the early 1950s, he abandoned empirical social research and eventually labeled it "abstracted

162

empiricism." He argued that it stifled the "sociological imagination" (Mills, 1959) and produced highly misleading insights into the social order. He was especially concerned that the new paradigm tended to produce findings that justified the status quo. Since Mills believed that radical changes were needed in the American social order, he viewed the paradigm as overly conservative and inhibiting. The basis for his criticisms and the consequences of his challenge will be discussed later in this chapter.

Robert Merton: Master Paradigm Maker

Most of the disciples of the paradigm's architects followed their mentors but did little to advance development of the paradigm. They were content to simply conduct empirical research and address the many research questions that kept springing up. They felt little need to step back and get perspective on what they were doing. But a few more ambitious or thoughtful disciples tried to take stock of what had been done. They saw a need to formulate long-term objectives for empirical social research. They wanted to know how all of the individual research findings might be added up or collated. To do this, new theories were needed. As these theories were created, the outlines of the paradigm became clearer.

Fortunately for these would-be theorists, a master theorist guided and inspired their work. Robert Merton could truly claim to bridge the world of grand sociological theory in the tradition of Émile Durkheim, Karl Marx, and Max Weber and the world of microscopic sociological observation as practiced by Lazarsfeld, Hovland, and Schramm. Merton was educated at Harvard by a grand social theorist, Talcott Parsons, himself a student of Weber. Merton was convinced that empirical research would only succeed if it eventually led to the construction of a body of abstract theory. In the late 1940s, when most empirical researchers were content to write grants, conduct field studies, run experiments, and report data, Merton began writing about the necessity of constructing a paradigm to support the empirical approach to research (Merton, 1949).

A colleague of Lazarsfeld at Columbia University, Merton consulted on Lazarsfeld's empirical projects, including those involving mass media. Merton himself led a research project that investigated the effectiveness of an 18-hour marathon radio broadcast (featuring singer Kate Smith) in stimulating listeners to call in and buy millions of dollars worth of government war bonds (Merton, et. al., 1946). From the beginning of their association, Merton labored to place empirical findings into a broader theoretical perspective. Lazarsfeld and Merton formed a team in which the latter devoted his attention to theory construction and the former focused on developing new techniques for data collection and analysis.

add to my list

The book that made Merton's reputation as a sociologist was *Social Theory and Social Structure* (1949). His work on the art of paradigm construction continued through the 1950s and 1960s and culminated with the publication of *On Theoretical Sociology* (1967). Over more than two decades, Merton tutored a host of thoughtful and reflective empirical researchers. He gave them a perspective from which to interpret their work and he taught them the necessity of combining induction with deduction. More than any other individual, Merton provided a conceptual foundation for the new paradigm.

Merton was a strong advocate for what he called "theories of the middle range." Unlike grand social theories (that is, mass society theory) that attempted to explain all forms of social action, *middle-range theories* were designed to explain only limited domains or ranges of action that had been or could be explored using empirical research. According to Merton:

> Some sociologists still write as though they expect, here and now, formulation of *the* general sociological theory broad enough to encompass the vast ranges of precisely observed details of social behavior, organization, and change and fruitful enough to direct the attention of research workers to a flow of problems for empirical research. This I take to be a premature and apocalyptic belief. We are not ready. Not enough preparatory work has been done (1967, p. 45).

Merton found his model for social science in physics. He argued as follows:

i (ask Hugh to comment on)

> What characterizes physics is an array of special theories of greater or lesser scope, coupled with the historically-grounded hope that these will continue to be brought together into families of theory . . . If the science of physics, with its centuries of enlarged theoretical generalizations, has not managed to develop an all-encompassing theoretical system, then *a fortiori* the science of sociology, which has only begun to accumulate empirically grounded theoretical generalizations of modest scope, would seem well advised to moderate its aspirations for such a system (1967, pp. 47–48).

Merton described middle-range theory as follows:

1. Middle-range theories consist of limited sets of assumptions from which specific hypotheses are logically derived and confirmed by empirical investigation.

2. These theories do not remain separate but are consolidated into wider networks of theory, as illustrated by theories of level of aspiration, reference-group, and opportunity-structure.

3. These theories are sufficiently abstract to deal with differing spheres of social behavior and social structure, so that they transcend sheer description or empirical generalization . . .

4. This type of theory cuts across the distinction between micro-sociological problems . . .

5. The middle-range orientation involves the specification of ignorance. Rather than pretend to knowledge where it is in fact absent, it expressly recognizes what must still be learned in order to lay the foundation for still more knowledge (1967, p. 68).

Middle-range theory provided a useful rationale for what most empirical researchers, including media scientists, were already doing (Merton, 1967, p. 56). Many were determined to ignore what they considered unnecessary theoretical baggage and to focus on developing and applying empirical research methods. They believed that the future of social science lay in producing and collating empirical generalizations. Following the examples set by Lazarsfeld and Hovland, researchers conducted endless surveys and experiments, gathering data to support or reject individual generalizations and constantly discovering new research questions requiring yet more empirical research. Merton argued that all this research work would eventually be brought together to first create an array of middle-range theories and then to construct a comprehensive theory that would have the power and scope of theories in the physical sciences. Moreover, when it was finally constructed, this theory would be far superior to earlier forms of social theory that were not empirically grounded.

Thus, middle-range theory provided an ideal rationale for limited effects research. It implied that eventually all of the individual effects studies would add up and a broad perspective on the role of media could be constructed. Yet middle-range theory had important shortcomings that were not immediately apparent. Countless empirical generalizations were studied, but the effort to combine them into broader theories proved more problematic than had been expected. Numerous interesting and useful middle-range theories were created. But broader theories based on middle-range notions had crucial limitations. We will point these out as we present each theory and then discuss them in detail at the end of the chapter. We will show how each of these theories is consistent with the underlying limited effects paradigm. We will conclude with a discussion of the problems of middle-range theory and the limited effects paradigm.

The Functional Analysis Approach

In *Social Theory and Social Structure*, Merton proposed what he called a "paradigm for functional analysis." The paradigm outlined how an inductive strategy centered around the study of social artifacts (such as the use of mass media) could eventually lead to the construction of theories that explained the "functions" of these items. Merton derived his perspective on functional analysis from careful examination of research in anthropology and sociology. Functional analysis assumes that a society can be usefully viewed as a "system in balance." That is, the society consists of complex sets of interrelated activities, each of which supports the others. Every form of social activity is assumed to play some part in maintaining the system as a whole.

One feature of functional analysis that appealed to Merton and his followers was its apparent *value neutrality*. Older forms of social theory had characterized various parts of society as either "good" or "evil" in some ultimate sense. For example, mass society theory saw media as disruptive and subversive, a negative force that somehow had to be brought under control. Functionalists rejected such thinking and instead argued that empirical research should investigate both the functions and dysfunctions of media. Then a systematic appraisal could be made of the overall impact of media. They believed that social science had no basis and no need for making value judgments about media. Rather, empirical investigation was necessary to determine whether specific media perform certain functions for the society.

This notion can be further illustrated by a functionalist analysis of primitive tribal society. According to functionalists, all the activities and practices of the tribe can be assumed to be interrelated in such a way that the tribe is able to survive in and adapt to a specific physical environment. All practices that contribute to maintaining the tribe can be said to be *functional* rather than good. Any practices that are disruptive or harmful are by definition *dysfunctional* rather than evil. Some individual practices will be found to be functional in certain respects but dysfunctional in others. Some tribal members will be helped or harmed under some conditions. As long as functional practices dominate and dysfunctional practices are kept to some minimum, the tribe will flourish—it can be said to be "in balance" because the functional practices balance out the dysfunctional ones. Merton also distinguished *manifest* functions—those consequences that are intended and readily observed—and *latent* functions—those that are unintended and less easily observed.

This functional analysis was widely adopted as a rationale for many mass communication studies during the 1950s and 1960s. Researchers tried to determine whether specific media or forms of media content were functional or dysfunctional. Manifest and latent functions of media were investigated. In 1959, Charles Wright published the first mass communication theory textbook that popularized the functional analysis framework for media research. He retained this focus on functional analysis through the third edition of this work (1986, pp. 12–27). The list of functions grew with every edition.

In the various editions of his textbook, Wright provided an overview of research using the functional analysis paradigm. He referred to Harold Lasswell (1948) and argued that Lasswell's famous list of the most important media activities could be studied using functional analysis: "(1) surveillance of the environ-

Box 8a Wright's Functional Analysis of Media Effects

In the third edition of his *Mass Communication: A Sociological Perspective*, Charles Wright offered this scheme for identifying latent and manifest functions and dysfunctions. He called it the Partial Inventory for Hypothetical Effects of Mass Communications, by System (Manifest and Latent Functions and Dysfunctions).   (© 1986 McGraw-Hill, Inc. Reprinted by permission of the publisher.)

Mass-Communicated Activity: Surveillance (News)

	Society	Individual	Specific Subgroups	Culture
Functions	Warning: Natural dangers; attack; war Egalitarian feelings Instrumental: News essential to the economy and other institutions Ethicizing Status conferral on social issues Agenda-setting	Warning Instrumental Adds to prestige: Opinion leadership Status conferral Agenda-setting	Instrumental: Information useful to power, agenda-building Detects: Knowledge of subversive and deviant behavior Manages public opinion: monitors: controls Legitimizes power; status conferral	Aids cultural contact Aids cultural growth
Dysfunctions	Threatens domestic stability: News of "better" societies Risks panic Widens knowledge gap between social strata	Anxiety: privatization; apathy; narcotization	Threatens power: News of reality; "enemy" propaganda; exposés	Permits cultural invasion

Mass-Communicated Activity: Correlation (Editorial Selection, Interpretation, and Prescription)

	Society	Individual	Specific Subgroups	Culture
Functions	Aids mobilization Impedes threats to social stability Helps prevent possible panic Agenda-setting	Provides efficiency: Assimilating news Impedes: Over-stimulation: anxiety; apathy; privatization Agenda-setting	Helps preserve power	Impedes cultural invasion Maintains cultural consensus
Dysfunctions	Increases social conformism: Impedes social change if social criticism is avoided; fosters spiral of silence	Weakens critical faculties Increases passivity	Increases responsibility	Impedes cultural growth

Box 8a continued

Mass-Communicated Activity: Socialization

	Society	Individual	Specific Subgroups	Culture
Functions	Increases social cohesion: Widens base of common norms, experiences, and so on	Aids integration: Exposure to common norms	Extends power: Another agency for socialization	Standardizes Maintains cultural consensus
	Reduces anomie	Reduces idiosyncrasy		
	Continues socialization: Reaches adults even after they have left such institutions as school	Reduces anomie		
Dysfunctions	Augments "mass" society	Depersonalizes acts of socialization		Reduces variety of subcultures

Mass-Communicated Activity: Entertainment

	Society	Individual	Specific Subgroups	Culture
Functions	Respite for masses	Respite	Extends power: Control over another area of life	
Dysfunctions	Diverts public: Avoids social action	Increases passivity		Weaken esthetics: "Popular culture"
	Cultivates mass conformity	Lowers "tastes"		
		Permits escapism		Cultural "pollution"

ment; (2) correlation of the parts of society in responding to the environment and (3) transmission of the social heritage from one generation to the next (Wright, 1986, pp. 4–5)." We'll discuss this further in Chapter 10.

Functional analysis can be quite complicated. Various forms of media content can be functional or dysfunctional for society as a whole, for specific individuals, for various subgroups in the society, or for the culture. Thus, news that alerts society to a corrupt politician is functional for the society but dysfunctional for the politician. If the politician is a member of an ethnic group—say Irish or Italian—public hostility might be aroused against the group and the news would be dysfunctional for the group. Thus, the functions for society may be offset by the dysfunctions for individuals or for particular minority groups. Individuals may have to endure things that are dysfunctional for them personally as long as these are functional for the society as a whole.

This example illustrates one of the key problems with functional analysis. It rarely permits any definitive conclusions to be drawn about the overall functions or dysfunctions of media. In general, functional analysis produces conclusions that largely legitimize or rationalize the status quo. Researchers can easily avoid drawing controversial conclusions by simply noting that dysfunctions may be balanced by functions. For example, existing forms of media content and the industries that produce them can be assumed to be functional. After all, if society isn't literally falling apart, then it must be in balance. If it is in balance, then we can deduce that the overall influence of factors such as media must either be positive or only slightly negative. Effects that are obviously negative can be found to be offset by positive effects. If we eliminate the negative effects, then we might also eliminate the positive effects that balance them. Are we willing to pay that price? Researchers were usually content to point to the existence of such balanced effects and then conclude that there was little that could or should be done about them.

As we noted in the two preceding chapters, the early effects research found media influence to be quite modest and therefore implied that media couldn't be too dysfunctional. For example, Schramm's Stanford researchers found that although viewing of certain forms of violent television content encouraged some children to be aggressive, this was offset by most children showing little or no influence. Some might even learn how to anticipate and cope with aggressive peers. Thus, as far as the social system as whole is concerned, it is possible to conclude that violent television content doesn't make much difference despite being dysfunctional for a few children (those "damned" by their "bad" parents to be manipulated by television violence).

This reasoning might not sound very scientific. This is because functional analysis sometimes provides a means of dressing up an informed guess about media's role in pseudoscientific language, complete with summaries of data and citations to literature. If the data show media doing something that is apparently harmful, a researcher can point out that they also do or may be doing good things that offset the harm. Whatever harm television violence does to some children is compensated for by the positive or "prosocial" influence of programs like "Sesame Street." Many adults turn to violent programming for entertainment; should they be deprived of this content and the pleasure it affords just because a few children are adversely affected?

Thus, research based on the functional analysis paradigm tends to offer "balanced" conclusions. It contrasts and weighs various functions and dysfunctions and typically concludes that in the final analysis, media are doing as well as might be expected—given the circumstances under which they operate.

Information Flow Research

During the 1950s, many surveys and field experiments were conducted to assess the flow of information from media to mass audiences. Two major types of research were done. Scholars in journalism schools studied how quickly people found out about individual news stories (Funkhouser and McCombs, 1971). Other researchers with federal government grants studied how quickly and effectively various forms of civil defense information could be disseminated (DeFleur and Larsen, 1958). The overall objective of both bodies of work was to assess the effectiveness of media in transmitting information to mass audiences. The research was patterned after persuasion research, but investigated whether information was learned instead of measuring shifts in attitudes. Cognitive rather than affective effects were studied. Survey research rather than controlled experiments were used to gather data.

As we've seen, persuasion research had identified numerous barriers to persuasion. News flow research focused on determining whether similar barriers impeded the flow of information from media to typical audience members. Some barriers investigated included level of education, amount of media use for news, interest in news, and talking about news with others. The researchers differentiated between "hard" and "soft" news. Hard news typically included news about politics, science, world events, and community organizations. Soft news included sports coverage, gossip about popular entertainers, and human interest stories about average people.

The news flow research found that most Americans learned very little about hard news from news media because they were poorly educated, made little use of media for hard news, had low interest in hard news, and didn't talk to other people about hard news (Davis, 1990). Except for major news events such as President Eisenhower's heart attack or the assassination of President John F. Kennedy, most people didn't know or care much about national news events. Soft news generally was more likely to be learned than hard news, but even the flow of soft news was not what might have been hoped. The most important factor that accelerated or reinforced the flow of news was the degree to which people talked about individual news items with others. News of the Kennedy assassination reached most people very rapidly because people interrupted their daily routine to tell others about it (Greenberg and Parker, 1965). Learning about most hard news events rarely reached more than 10 to 20 percent of the population and was forgotten by those people within a few days or weeks.

Studies of the flow of civil defense information identified similar barriers (DeFleur and Larsen, 1958). In most cases, the public was even less interested in mundane civil defense information than they were in politics. In a series of field experiments, hundreds of thousands of leaflets were dropped on small, isolated towns in the state of Washington. The researchers wanted to determine how effective they would be in warning people about incoming Soviet bombers. For example, one set of leaflets announced that a civil defense test was being conducted. Every person who found a leaflet was instructed to tell someone else about it and then drop the leaflet in a mailbox.

The researchers were disappointed that relatively few folks read or returned the leaflets. Children were the most likely to take the leaflets seriously. To get the most useful effect, eight leaflets had to be dropped for every resident of a town. In one city, the researchers were pleasantly surprised by good results only to learn that a local civil defense volunteer group had organized an effort to distribute and return the leaflets. Even the 1950s Cold War threat of Soviet bombers was not enough to mobilize people to talk to their neighbors.

Speculating that people were ignoring the leaflets because they only warned of a hypothetical attack, the researchers designed another field experiment in which people were supposed to tell their neighbors about a slogan for a new brand of coffee. Survey teams visited homes in a small town and told people that they could earn a free pound of coffee by teaching their neighbors the coffee slogan. The survey team promised to return the following week and if they found that neighbors knew the slogan, then both families would receive free coffee. The experiment produced mixed results. On the one hand, almost every neighboring family had heard about the coffee slogan and tried to reproduce it. Unfortunately, many gave the wrong slogan. The researchers reported interesting distortions of the original slogan; many people had shortened it, confused it with similar slogans, or recited garbled phrases containing a few key words. The research confirmed the importance of motivating people to pass on information, but suggested that even a free gift was insufficient to guarantee the accurate flow of information. If word of mouth was crucial to the flow of information, the possibility of distortion and misunderstanding was high. Even if media deliver accurate information, the news that reaches most people may be wrong.

Limitations of Information Flow Theory

The most important limitation of information flow theory is that it is a simplistic, linear, source-dominated theory. Information originates with authoritative or elite sources and then flows outward to "ignorant" individuals. Barriers to the information flow are to be identified and overcome and little effort is typically made to consider whether the information has any value or utility for average audience members. Audience reactions to messages are ignored unless they form a barrier to information flow. Then, they must be studied only so that they can be overcome. Like most limited effects theories, information-flow theory assumes that the status quo is acceptable. Elites and authorities are justified in trying to disseminate certain forms of information and average people will be better off if they receive and learn it. Barriers are assumed to be bad and where possible must be eliminated.

Diffusion Theory

In 1962, Everett Rogers combined the information-flow research findings with studies on the flow of information and personal influence in several fields including anthropology, sociology, and rural agricultural extension work. He developed what he called *diffusion theory*, which can be seen as an important extension of Lazarsfeld's original idea of the two-step flow. Rogers assembled data from numerous empirical studies to show that when new technological innovations are introduced, they will pass through a series of stages before being widely adopted. First, most people will become *aware* of them, often through information from mass media. Second, the innovations will be adopted by a very small group of innovators or *early adopters*. Third, opinion leaders learn from the early adopters and try the innovation themselves. Fourth, if opinion leaders find the innovation useful, they encourage their friends—the opinion followers. Finally, after most people have adopted the innovation, a group of laggards or late adopters make the change. This process was found to apply to most American agricultural innovations.

Diffusion theory is an excellent example of the power and the limitations of a middle-range theory. Diffusion theory successfully integrates a vast amount of empirical research. Rogers reviewed thousands of studies. Diffusion theory guided this research and facilitated interpretation of it, but also had many implicit assumptions limiting its utility. Like information flow theory, diffusion theory is a *source-dominated* theory that sees the communication process from the point of view of an elite that has decided to diffuse an innovation. This theory "improves" upon information flow theory by providing more and better strategies for overcoming barriers to innovations.

Diffusion theory assigns a very limited role to mass media: Media mainly creates awareness of new innovations. Only the early adopters are directly influenced by media content. Others adopt innovations only after being influenced by other people. Rogers recommended that diffusion efforts be led by *change agents*, people who could go out into rural communities and directly influence early adopters and opinion leaders. Media were used to draw attention to innovations and as a basis for group discussions led by change agents. This strategy was patterned after the success of agricultural extension agents in the American Midwest. Thus, diffusion theory was consistent with other versions of limited effects thinking.

Roger's theory was enormously successful. The United States Agency for International Development (USAID) used the strategy to spread agricultural innovations in the Third World. During the Cold War of the 1950s and 1960s, the United States competed against the U.S.S.R. for influence in the developing nations (recall the quote from Hovland, Janis, and Kelley in Chapter 7). The hope was that by leading a Green Revolution and helping them better feed themselves, America would gain their favor. But to help them do this, the United States needed to convince peasants and rural villagers to adopt a large number of new agricultural innovations as quickly as possible. Roger's diffusion theory became a training manual for that effort. Change agents from around the world were brought to Michigan State University to learn the theory from Rogers himself. Many of these people became academics in their home countries, and unlike many U.S. theories, diffusion theory spread through the universities of the developing nations while agricultural innovations were spreading in their fields. In many parts of the world, Roger's theory became synonymous with communication theory.

Diffusion theory represented an important advance over earlier limited effects theories. Like the other classic work of the early 1960s, this theory drew from existing empirical generalizations and synthesized them into a coherent, insightful perspective. Diffusion theory was consistent with most findings from effects surveys and persuasion experiments, and above all, it was very practical. In addition to guiding Third World development, diffusion theory laid the foundation for various promotional communication and marketing theories (see Chapter 11).

But diffusion theory's limitations were also serious. (Most of these are summarized in more detail at the end of this chapter in our discussion of the limitations of the limited effects paradigm.) Diffusion theory had some unique drawbacks stemming from its application. For example, it facilitated the adoption of innovations that were sometimes not well understood or even desired by adopters. For example, a campaign to get Georgia farm wives to can vegetables was initially judged to be a great success until it was found that very few women were using the vegetables. They mounted the glass jars on the walls of their living rooms as status symbols. Most didn't know any recipes for cooking canned vegetables—and those who tried using canned vegetables found that family members didn't like the taste. This experience was duplicated around the world; corn was grown in Mexico and rice was grown in Southeast Asia that no one wanted to eat; farmers in India destroyed their crops by using too much fertilizer; farmers adopted complex new machinery only to have it break down and stand idle after change agents left. Mere diffusion of innovations didn't guarantee long-term success.

Klapper's Phenomenistic Theory

In 1960, Joseph Klapper finally published a manuscript originally developed in 1949 as he completed requirements for a Ph.D. at Columbia University and worked as a researcher for CBS. *The Effects of Mass Communication* was a compilation and integration of all significant media effects findings produced through the mid-1950s and was intended for both scholars and informed members of the public. Klapper was concerned that average people exaggerated the power of media. Though informed academics (that is, empirical researchers) had rejected mass society theory, too many people still believed that media had tremendous power. He wanted to calm their fears by showing how limited media actually were in their ability to influence people.

Klapper introduced what he called *phenomenistic theory*. It argued that media rarely have any direct effects and are relatively powerless when compared to other social and psychological factors such as social status, group membership, strongly held attitudes, education, and so forth. According to Klapper:

1. Mass communication *ordinarily* does not serve as a necessary and sufficient cause of audience effects, but rather functions among and through a nexus of mediating factors and influences.

2. These mediating factors are such that they typically render mass communication as a contributory agent, but not the sole cause, in the process of reinforcing existing conditions (1960, p. 8).

These arguments were not very original, but Klapper expressed them forcefully and cited hundreds of findings to support them. His book came to be viewed as a definitive statement on media effects — especially by those outside the media research community.

Klapper's theory is often referred to now as *reinforcement theory* because a key assertion is that the primary influence of media is to reinforce (not change) existing attitudes and behaviors. Instead of disrupting society and creating unexpected social change, media generally serve as agents of the status quo, giving people more reasons to go on believing and acting as they already do. Klapper argued that there simply are too many barriers to media influence for drastic changes to occur except under very unusual circumstances (see Chapter 9).

An Apology for Mass Entertainment

Another major compilation of media research findings was published by Harold Mendelsohn in 1966. As a young researcher, Mendelsohn was tutored by Lazarsfeld and served as the field director for the 1940 Erie County study. *Mass Entertainment* was intended as a scholarly examination of the role of television entertainment in American society. Like Klapper, Mendelsohn was concerned

---

Box 8b   Joseph Klapper's Phenomenistic Theory

Joseph Klapper's own summary of his reinforcement or phenomenistic theory makes it clear that his ideas are very much at home in the limited effects paradigm. The following is drawn directly from his landmark work, *The Effects of Mass Communication*, published in 1960 (p. 8).

Theoretical Statements

1   Mass communication *ordinarily* does not serve as a necessary and sufficient cause of audience effects, but rather functions among and through a nexus of mediating factors and influences.

2   These mediating factors are such that they typically render mass communication a contributing agent, but not the sole cause, in a process of reinforcing the existing conditions.

3   On such occasions as mass communication does function in the service of change, one of two conditions is likely to exist. Either:

a. The mediating factors will be found to be inoperative and the effect of the media will be found to be direct; or

b. The mediating factors, that normally favor reinforcement, will be found to be themselves impelling toward change.

4   There are certain residual situations in which mass communication seems to produce direct effects, or directly and of itself to serve certain psycho-physical functions.

5   The efficacy of mass communication, either as a contributory agent or as an agent of direct effect, is affected by various aspects of the media and communications themselves or of the communication situation.

Your Turn

Can you find hints in Klapper's overview of his theory's links to the dominant paradigm of its time?

---

that the influence of media was widely misunderstood. He blamed elite critics of media (mostly mass society theorists) for continuing to foster misconceptions about mass entertainment. He charged that these critics were protecting their own self-interests and were ignoring empirical research findings. His book reviewed various mass society criticisms of mass entertainment and rejected them all. He dismissed most criticisms as prejudiced speculation that was inconsistent with empirical data. According to Mendelsohn, mass society critics were too paternalistic and elitist. They were upset because television entertainment attracted people away from the boring forms of education, politics or religion that they, themselves, wanted to promote. Mendelsohn argued that average people needed the relaxation and harmless escapism that television entertainment offered. If television entertainment weren't available, people would find other releases from the tensions of daily life. Television simply served these needs more easily, powerfully, and efficiently than other alternatives.

Instead of condemning television, Mendelsohn argued that the critics should acknowledge that it performs its function very well and at extremely low cost. He was concerned that critics had greatly exaggerated the importance and long-term consequences of television entertainment and asserted that it had a very limited and ultimately quite minor social role. Television entertainment did not disrupt or debase high culture, it merely gave average people a more attractive alternative to operas or symphony concerts. It did not distract people from important activities like religion, politics or family life, rather it helped them relax so that they could later engage in these activities with renewed interest and energy.

Mendelsohn cited numerous psychological studies to support his conclusions. He admitted that a small number of people might suffer because they became addicted to television entertainment. These same people, however, would most likely have become addicted to something else if television weren't available. Chronic couch potatoes might otherwise become lounge lizards or romance novel fans. Compared to these alternatives, he viewed addiction to television as rather benign: It didn't hurt other people and might even be slightly educational.

Mendelsohn's book provides an excellent example of how limited effects research and its findings can legitimize the status quo. Harmful effects are balanced by an overwhelming number of positive effects. Who can judge whether the harm being done is great enough to warrant making changes? Congress? The Courts? The Public? When the evidence is mixed, the best course of action would appear to be inaction.

Elite Pluralism

All of the preceding efforts at paradigm construction were limited in scope compared to the development of *Elite Pluralism*. This idea was spawned in part as an effort to make sense of the voter research initiated by Lazarsfeld. In their report on the 1948 election campaign (Berelson, Lazarsfeld, and McPhee, 1954), Lazarsfeld and his colleagues noted important inconsistencies between their empirical observation of typical voters and the assumptions that classical democratic theory made about those same people. If the Lazarsfeld data were right, then classical democratic theory must be wrong. If the Lazarsfeld data were wrong, then what did this mean for the long-term survival of our social and political order? Was our political system a facade for a benign ruling class? Could a democratic political system continue to flourish if most citizens were politically apathetic and ignorant?

In characteristic fashion, the Lazarsfeld group offered a guardedly optimistic assessment. They asserted that classical democratic theory should be replaced with an up-to-date perspective based on empirical findings. Classical democratic theory assumed that everyone must be well informed and politically active. The new perspective was based on empirical data that showed that average people didn't know or care very much about politics. Voting decisions were more likely to be based on personal influence than on reasoned consideration of the various candidates. People voted as their friends, family, and coworkers told them to vote, not as a political theorist would have liked them to vote.

The Lazarsfeld group argued that voter apathy and ignorance weren't necessarily a problem *for the political system as a whole*. In their view, a political system in which most people voted based on long-standing political commitments or alliances would be a stable system even if these commitments were based on prejudice and were held in place by emotional bonds to family and friends. In their view, the important factor was not the quality of voting decisions but rather their stability. We are better off if our political system changes very slowly over time as a result of gradual conversions, they argued. We don't want sudden changes that could occur if everyone made a rational, informed decisions using information from media. For example, there would be tragic consequences if many people based their vote decisions on bad or biased information from media. Nor could our political system handle the high levels of political activism that would occur if everyone took a strong interest in politics.

These arguments imply rejection of libertarian theory. If voters don't need to be informed or if informing them might actually lead to political disorder, then there is no need for communication media to deliver information. Research findings demonstrated that uncensored and independent media typically failed to diffuse political information to most people. If so, then what political role should media be expected to play? To reinforce the status quo except in times of crisis? Was there really a need for media to serve as a public forum as libertarian theory had assumed? If so, how should this forum operate and what resources would be necessary to make it work effectively? Limited effects research findings implied that such a public forum would serve little purpose except for the handful of people who were already well informed about politics and already engaged in political activity. These conclusions directed researchers away from the study of mass media and the formation of media policy and toward political parties, political socialization, and the institutions of government such as legislatures, political executives such as the President, and the legal system. These topics soon dominated the research agenda in political science.

The political perspective implicit in these arguments became known as *Elite Pluralism*. During the 1960s, elite pluralism was widely debated in political science and strongly challenged traditional forms of democratic theory. Elite pluralism claimed to be scientific because, in contrast with classical democratic theory, it was based on empirical data. One of its best formulations was provided by V.O. Key in *Public Opinion and American Democracy* (1961). Like Lazarsfeld, Key was optimistic in the face of apparently discouraging voter data. His book emphasized the strength and enduring value of the American political system, even if it fell short of being a classical democracy.

In some respects, elite pluralism is as contradictory as the two terms that make up its label. "Elite" implies a political system in which power is ultimately in the hands of a small group of influential persons, a political elite. "Pluralism" refers to cultural, social, and political diversity. It implies a political system in which many diverse groups are given equal status and representation. Can there be a political system that is based on both of these principles — a system in which power is centralized in the hands of the few but in which the rights and status of all minority groups are recognized and advanced? V.O. Key not only argued that it is possible to combine these two principles, but he also cited study after study that he interpreted as demonstrating that our political system already accomplished this.

Like the other examples of limited effects theory, elite pluralism assumes that media have little ability to directly influence people. Thus, media alone can't fundamentally alter politics. Elite pluralism rejects libertarian notions and argues that media, in the name of stability, should reinforce political party loyalties and assist the parties to develop and maintain large voter coalitions. Media shouldn't be expected to lead public opinion but rather reinforce it. If change is to occur, it must come from the pluralistic groups and be negotiated and enacted by the leaders of these groups.

It is important to recognize that in constructing his perspective on American society, Key, like most limited effects researchers, went far beyond the small insight provided by his data. Although the ideas he advanced were consistent with the data available to him, other conclusions were equally reasonable. But when Key wrote his book, this was not well understood. His ideas gained widespread acceptance as a definitive interpretation of the data and his talents as a writer also lent force to his theory.

C. Wright Mills and The Power Elite

Opposition to elite pluralism came from both the political left and the right. Most classical democratic theorists were offended by and disdainful of elite pluralism. They argued that even if the present political system was not a "true" democracy, efforts should be made to move the system in that direction. Either we should recapture the essence of democracy as envisioned by the Founding Fathers or we should take steps to break the power of existing elites. To opponents, elite pluralism was a rationalization of the status quo that provided no direction for future development. But in an era when respect for normative and grand social theories was declining, it was hard for classical democratic theorists to defend their views against a "scientific" theory like elite pluralism.

Strong opposition to elite pluralism came from the political left and was spearheaded by C. Wright Mills, whom we introduced earlier as a Harvard sociologist and rebel Lazarsfeld protégé. Mills rejected the argument that elite pluralism was more scientific than other forms of political theory. Based on his knowledge of survey research, he was deeply skeptical of the data marshaled in its support. He argued that in American society, political power was not decentralized across a broad range of pluralistic groups. Instead, he believed that power was centralized in a small group of military-industrial-complex leaders whom he called *The Power Elite* (1957). This elite was not representative of pluralistic groups. Rather it was isolated from them and typically acted against their interests.

For almost a decade, the followers of Mills and those of Key were arrayed against each other. In this conflict, Key and his allies had many crucial advantages. Their research had larger and more secure funding from government agencies and private foundations. As such, elite pluralists successfully defended their claim of being more scientific in their research. Ultimately, Mills brought his own perspective into question by backing Fidel Castro's revolution in Cuba. Then, in 1962, he was killed in a tragic motorcycle accident. Criticism of elite pluralism was muted for more than a decade.

In *The Power Elite* and other books Mills raised many disturbing questions about American politics. If elite pluralism was operating so effectively, why were so many minority groups receiving so little help? Why did average people feel so powerless and apathetic? Why did people choose to remain ignorant about politics? Why did the same people serve over and over again as leaders of supposedly independent social institutions? Why were the interests of the few so often pursued at the expense of average people? Why did political parties and other social institutions make no determined efforts to educate people about their interests or to mobilize them to take actions that might serve those interests? Why did mass media tend to merely reinforce the status quo rather than inspire people to take action against race- and social class-based discrimination? Mills proved prophetic because these same issues surfaced a decade later as part of a broad-based challenge to American social science and the American political system. Those same questions are again resurfacing in the wake of the "Reagan Revolution," the South Central Los Angeles riots, and the rise of populist political candidates like H. Ross Perot in 1992.

Assumptions and Drawbacks of the Limited Effects Paradigm

The several views of media's impact detailed in this chapter are all part of the limited effects paradigm. This perspective on the media's power and influence is based on a number of assumptions and it has numerous limitations that we have already discussed. The assumptions are as follows:

1 **Empirical social research methods can be used to generate theory through an inductive research process.** Exploratory, descriptive research is expected to produce empirical generalizations that can later be combined to form middle-range theories. Eventually, middle-range notions can be combined to create broad, powerful social theories that are firmly grounded in empirical facts.

2 **The role of mass media in society is quite limited; media primarily reinforce existing social trends and only rarely initiate social change.** The media will cause change only if the many barriers to their influence are broken down by highly unusual circumstances. The empirical mass communication research discussed in this and the preceding two chapters supports this assumption. In study after study, little evidence of strong media influence was found. Even evidence of reinforcement was often lacking.

3 **When media are responsible for social change, these changes are often dysfunctional; they disrupt a stable and benign social order.** Such social changes occur only when unusual social circumstances prevail and media tend to exacerbate these abnormal conditions. For example, widespread unemployment could cut large numbers of workers off from the influence of their coworkers and drastically alter their relationships with family and friends. These people might become vulnerable to extremist propaganda. Similarly, in the hours immediately after the South Central Los Angeles riots began in 1992, people were highly dependent upon media for news reports. Media critics have argued that these reports may well have exacerbated the problem by exciting people and drawing them to the scene.

   Given the potentially disruptive influence of media, it is important to conduct research to detect and guard against such harmful episodes. This type of research has produced little evidence that media can produce large-scale, continuing disruption. Rather, evidence indicates that there are certain types of individuals who can be adversely affected by media under certain unusual or rare conditions. These people are unlikely to do much harm to anyone but themselves, however.

4 **Mass media's role in the lives of individuals is limited, but it can be very dysfunctional for some types of people.** Media provide a convenient and inexpensive source of entertainment and information. But neither use has much long-term or important impact on the daily life of most people. Almost all information is either ignored or quickly forgotten. Entertainment mainly provides a temporary distraction from work, allowing people to relax and enjoy themselves so that they can go back to work refreshed. People who are adversely affected by media

tend to have severe personality or social adjustment problems; they would be deeply troubled even if media weren't available.

5 **The U.S. political and social system is both stable and equitable.** Although not democratic in the classical sense, the U.S. System is nevertheless a viable and humane system that respects and nurtures cultural pluralism while preserving social order. There is no need for radical reform. Media play a limited but nonetheless useful role within the larger society. Potentially harmful effects can be detected and prevented should any appear.

Summary

We've seen many of the limitations of the limited effects perspective in Chapters 6 and 7, but here they are briefly listed, accompanied by some new concerns.

1 **Both survey research and experiments have serious methodological limitations that were not adequately recognized or acknowledged.** Empirical researchers were anxious to popularize their approach and sometimes made exaggerated claims for it. Naive people outside the empirical research community made false assumptions about the power and utility of this type of research. When empirical researchers were directly challenged in the late 1960s, they were slow to acknowledge limitations of their work and reacted defensively. Criticism was met with counter-criticism, which provoked a hostile confrontation that still impedes objective assessment of the merits of the claims made on both sides.

2 **The methodological limitations of early empirical social research led to findings that systematically underestimated the influence of mass media for society and for individuals.** Researchers like Lazarsfeld and Hovland were inherently cautious. They didn't want to infer the existence of effects that might not be there — *spurious effects*. The methods they developed were designed to guard against this, but they took the risk of overlooking or dismissing evidence that could have been interpreted as an argument for significant media effects. In their conclusions, they often failed to emphasize that there were many types of media effects that they might be overlooking because they had no way of measuring them.

3 **Early empirical social research centered around whether media had immediate, powerful, direct effects; other types of influence were ignored.** This focus was justified for two reasons. First, the mass-society paradigm, which had been dominant, asserted that such effects existed and should be easy to observe. This paradigm needed to be evaluated and the early research did so. Second, the early research methods were best suited to studying immediate, direct effects. Only later were techniques developed that permitted other types of influence to be empirically assessed.

4   As the limited effects paradigm gained strength, social theories were developed that ignored or assigned a very limited role to media. Most social scientists became less interested in studying the mass media, and the focus of media research was narrowed to those domains where media were more confidently thought to have some possibility for influence. Research focused on groups thought to be especially vulnerable to influence—children, old people, social isolates, and the psychologically disturbed. Average people were assumed to be well insulated against significant influence. Only recently has an effort been made to construct theories that assign more important roles to media.

Although the limited effects paradigm had many failings, it is worth noting its contributions.

1   The limited effects paradigm effectively supplanted mass society theory as the dominant perspective on media. Thus, it lessened unjustified fears about massive, uncontrollable media effects. This had beneficial results for media practitioners. Most important, it helped ease pressures for direct government censorship of media and permitted useful forms of self-censorship to be implemented by media practitioners.

2   The paradigm prioritized empirical observation and downgraded highly speculative forms of theory construction. It demonstrated the practicality and utility of empirical research and inspired development of a broad range of innovative methods for data collection as well as new techniques for data analysis. These empirical techniques have proved to be powerful and useful for specific purposes. If the paradigm had not become dominant, we might not have devoted the time and resources necessary to develop these techniques.

3   Although the limited effects paradigm ultimately turned many established social scientists away from media study, it provided a useful framework for research done in university and college journalism schools and speech departments during the 1950s and 1960s. In hindsight we can see that the paradigm was, to some extent at least, a self-fulfilling prophecy. It asserted that media had no socially important effects. This belief was based on research findings provided by crude data collection and analysis methods. These methods can now be interpreted as having grossly underestimated the influence of media. Unfortunately, by the time more sophisticated research techniques were developed, most social researchers in the established disciplines of sociology, psychology and political science had stopped looking for important media effects. During the 1960s and 1970s, the work of mass communication researchers was viewed with considerable skepticism. What was there that we didn't already know about the role of media? Quite a lot, as we shall see.

Discussion Questions:

1 If Klapper had examined media influence at the macro, or societal level, would he have been as likely to classify "reinforcement" as a limited or minimal effect? Why or why not?

2 Consider the role of media in your own life. Would you say that media generally have a very limited influence upon your thoughts and actions? What about other people? Would media be more likely to influence them? Why or why not?

3 List some factors that have been identified as barriers to media influence. Do any of these protect you from being influenced by media?

4 Do you agree with critics who charge that there is an inherent conservative or status quo bias in the limited effects paradigm? Why or why not?

5 We criticized several of the studies in this chapter because researchers overgeneralized their conclusions based on very limited research findings. Explain what is meant by overgeneralization and give an example.

Significant Names

C. Wright Mills

Everett Rogers

V.O. Key

Joseph Klapper

Harold Mendelsohn

Charles Wright

Significant Readings

DeFleur, Melvin L. and Otto N. Larsen (1958). *The Flow of Information.* New York: Harper & Brothers.

Key, V.O. (1961). *Public Opinion and American Democracy.* New York: Alfred A. Knopf.

Klapper, Joseph (1960). *The Effects of Mass Communication.* New York: Free Press.

Kuhn, Thomas (1970). *The Structure of Scientific Revolutions,* second edition. Chicago: University of Chicago Press.

Mendelsohn, Harold (1966). *Mass Entertainment*. New Haven: College and University Press.

Merton, Robert K. (1949). *Social Theory and Social Structure*. Glencoe, IL: Free Press.

Merton, Robert K. (1967). *On Theoretical Sociology*. New York: Free Press.

Mills, C. Wright (1957). *The Power Elite*. New York: Oxford University Press.

Mills, C. Wright (1959). *The Sociological Imagination*. New York: Oxford University Press.

Rogers, Everett M. (1983). *Diffusion of Innovations*. New York: Free Press.

Schramm, Wilbur, Jack Lyle, and Edwin Parker (1961). *Television in the Lives of Our Children*. Stanford, CA: Stanford University Press.

Wright, C.R. (1986). *Mass Communication: a Sociological Perspective*, third edition. New York: Random House (updated version of his 1949 book).

Important Terms

Paradigm

Middle Range Theory

Diffusion

Manifest and Latent Functions

Functional Analysis

Information Flow Theory

Source-Dominated Theory

Change Agent

Phenomenistic Theory

Reinforcement Theory

Elite Pluralism

Power Elite

Chapter 9

Social Learning and the Violence Theories

Summer of 1991 saw, as most summers do, the release of a dozen new hit movies. At the Entertainment Cinemas in Quincy, Massachusetts, three of the more notable of that season's offerings were playing: *Return to the Blue Lagoon*, a movie about two teenagers discovering their sexuality; *Bill and Ted's Bogus Journey*, featuring two semi-literate adolescents' battle against Death and world domination; and *Body Parts*, a film true to its name.

A fourth picture, one of the year's top-grossing movies, was absent. *Boyz N the Hood*, a film about African-American families fighting to raise their children amidst the blight of urban drugs and crime, was not being shown. Why not? Quincy public officials had asked the theater owners not to play the movie because it might "attract the wrong element." In other words, they were concerned about violence. The themes of the movie—strength lives in friends and family; drugs, gangs, and violence are wrong—didn't matter to Quincy's town leaders. "Historically the movie has been nothing but trouble," argued Police Captain Frederick Laracy in the Quincy *Patriot Ledger*. "Under a controlled environment, the movie is probably an educational movie," added City Councilperson Michael Cheney, "Unfortunately we don't have that kind of control."

So, imagine yourself a parent having to make a choice. *Blue Lagoon*? Do you want to explain the boy/girl thing to your seven-year-old? *Bogus Journey*? But Mom and Dad, why do I have to study? Bill and Ted didn't and now they're rich and famous! *Body Parts*? You deal with your youngster's nightmares. Maybe *Boyz* offered the right message for your child—drugs and violence are bad. But maybe it does it in a way that depicts these bad things in a dramatic fashion. What do you do?

Overview

By the mid 1960s the recurring debate over media effects was raging again. As in previous eras, media practitioners, particularly the television industry, were pitted against various elites and interest and advocacy groups, including viewers (in this case, many parents). The dominant concern was the effect of violent content on children. The issues in the debate were predictable: Was direct FCC regulation of television content needed to curb violence on television? Should the industry impose some form of self-censorship on the presentation of violence? Just how harmful was the viewing of violent content by average children? Could viewing violence trigger aggressive acts or lead to delinquency and crime? It was hoped that media research could address answer these questions. From the late 1960s through the 1970s, television violence research flourished and attracted some top social science researchers.

The rise of television violence research took place at the same time that the limited effects paradigm became dominant. Many theories and research findings discussed in this chapter fit rather nicely within the limited effects paradigm. But these conceptualizations and findings were greeted with considerable skepticism outside the social research community. How could a pervasive medium like television that was viewed by most children for more than four hours a day have such limited influence? Media researchers were continually forced to defend and explain their findings.

This chapter will focus on the development of the most important television violence theories. We will consider the broader social and intellectual context in which they appeared, examine how research using them was conducted, and summarize key findings. Theories that explain the influence of televised violence also tend to explain how other forms of content might influence children. While doing research on the effects of violence, researchers gained insight into how other types of effects might occur. We will point out the broader implications of the violence research and also give some consideration to the politics underlying this research (Melody, 1973). The television networks watched this research closely and sponsored key studies. Violent content was very popular throughout this period and the networks might have lost millions in advertising revenue had they been forced to curtail the amount they aired. The limited effects paradigm served their interests well and frustrated their critics.

We'll begin with a brief synopsis of research prior to 1965. Early research into the effect of media on children was dominated by the mass society paradigm and its findings contrast sharply with later work. The changes illustrate the consequences of the paradigm shift from mass society theories to the limited effects paradigm. Researchers in the 1930s found movie violence to have many troublesome effects on average children. But by the 1970s, effects researchers had become much more optimistic about influence of media on children. For example, the worst effects of television violence were likely to be confined to a small fraction of the adolescent boys from bad homes who were predisposed to be aggressive. Ironically, these reassuring findings were offered at a time when the social world was becoming increasingly unstable, when urban violence was escalating, and when violence by and against social movements was growing. Critics continued to question whether televised violence might be linked in some way to this instability.

Media Violence in the Mass Society Era

In 1933, when the mass society paradigm was dominant, traditional elites were confronted by increased violence among young people; decreased church attendance; the apparent growth of disrespect for parents, teachers, and other authority figures; and, at the same time, the introduction of Hollywood "talkies" and their immediate acceptance by the public, especially by those youngsters from urban, illiterate (or newly literate) immigrant families. Blame for the former ills was laid on the latter technology. The most notable investigation of the link between the new gangster movies and juvenile delinquency and other antisocial behavior was underwritten by the Payne Fund (Blumer and Hauser, 1933). In a series of reports, the researchers "proved" many disturbing associations between media use and delinquency.

The Payne Fund studies represent an important stage in the development of media research. In 1928, a group of prominent social researchers was invited by William H. Short, Executive Director of the Motion Picture Research Council, to study the influence of television on children (Lowery and DeFleur, 1988, p. 33). In all, thirteen separate studies were conducted using virtually every social research method available at the time. They ranged from surveys and experiments to content analyses and autobiographies. Despite the differing methodologies, the conclusions of the various studies were strikingly similar. Virtually every one found movies to have important and predominantly negative influences on children. For example, movies were found to disrupt sleep patterns, challenge and erode moral values, overstimulate emotions, change attitudes for both good and ill, and provide compelling but troublesome models for personal action. According to Shearon Lowery and Melvin DeFleur (1988), the Payne Fund studies helped intensify the public pressure on the movie industry for some form of regulation or censorship. Ultimately, the industry strengthened its Production Code and rigorously enforced it with strong self-censorship by the powerful Hays Commission. The most widely criticized representations of sex, crime, and violence content were curbed and direct government intervention was avoided.

After the limited effects paradigm became dominant in empirical social research in the 1960s, the Payne Fund studies were something of an embarrassment. They clearly didn't fit the paradigm. Yet the research had been conducted by respected scientists, including pioneers of empirical research like L.L. Thurstone, who developed one of the first scales for measuring attitudes. One interpretation offered by Lowery and DeFleur (1988) was that movies may actually have been very powerful when they were first introduced—after all, no previous medium had the ability to physically dominate sight and hearing simultaneously. Effects on children should have been more likely than effects on adults. So maybe the Payne Fund researchers were right. But times have changed and now we live in a world where audiovisual presentations are ubiquitous. They may well have lost much of their power to routinely compel our attention, arouse our emotion, and guide our action.

There is another possibility. The Payne Fund researchers expected to find strong media influence and they may have knowingly or unknowingly structured their research in ways that increased the likelihood that they would find what they expected. Standards for empirical research that guard against subtle biases were just being developed. Researchers had little understanding of how these biases could be introduced into the design and administration of both experiments and surveys. For example, survey question ordering and wording can cue respondents to provide answers that fit researcher expectations. Interpretation of survey responses made by children and adolescents is especially difficult since most young people are anxious to cooperate but have trouble making sense of abstract questions, difficulty recalling previous actions, and difficulty making predictions about future actions.

Some of the most conclusive early findings were seemingly provided by attitude change experiments. For example, Ruth Peterson and L.L. Thurstone (1933) reported statistically significant shifts in important attitudes after children viewed various movies. The 11 experiments they conducted showed similar results. They concluded that movies could indeed affect how children perceived African Americans, war, criminals, or the Chinese. Even more disturbing was evidence that adverse effects on attitudes endured for months after the experiments were conducted.

Does this research contradict the limited effects paradigm? Let's reinterpret it as a limited effects advocate might. Many aspects of this research can be questioned. First, the experiments were conducted in a way now considered inappropriate. Large groups of children watched movies and then were asked to fill out questionnaires. We now know that experimental groups should be kept small to minimize the influence individuals have on one another. Children under the age of 10 should be questioned by an interviewer who can help them make sense of difficult items. Second, though the attitude change results were statistically significant, their practical importance can be questioned. In most cases, the researchers measured an average shift of about 1 point on a 10-point measurement scale. With groups of 100 to 600 subjects, these shifts were statistically significant. But a shift of one point hardly represents a conversion from one viewpoint to another. Finally, there is a strong possibility that the initial attitudes of the children were poorly formed, weakly held, and not based on personal experience. The children used in the experiments had little or no personal experience with African Americans, Chinese, criminals, or war. They lived in homogeneous, relatively isolated, midwestern communities. The pretest showed that many children initially had strong positive attitudes toward African Americans. After seeing *The Birth of a Nation* with its negative depiction of African Americans, their views spread across the full range of the scale and became more bipolar. We now know that such results are common when initial attitudes are poorly formed, not strongly held, and not based on personal experience. Thus, there may not have been any important effects but if there were, they were *limited*—they influenced only certain individuals who had certain types of preexisting attitudes.

So what overall interpretation should we place on the Payne Fund studies? Should we dismiss them as a misguided and biased effort to support mass society notions? Should we see them as a pioneering effort to address an important social problem and develop new research techniques to answer important questions? Do they provide unintended confirmation of limited effects notions or are they proof that movies were once a very powerful medium? Any or all of these interpretations may be appropriate. What we can definitely conclude is that the studies didn't provide definitive answers to the questions they set out to study. Though quite influential at the time they were published, their usefulness has faded (Wartella and Reeves, 1985).

A 1941 study by Mary Preston provides another example of early research on media and children. It reflected the influence of the Payne Fund research and mass society thinking in its focus on and interpretation of "children's reactions to movie horrors and radio crime." Preston detected "maladjustments" in a number of aspects of children's lives. Kids who were "addicted" to such media fare exhibited, among other maladies, callousness, nervousness, a morbid interest in gore, and even "daydreaming." She predicted, however, that these negative effects could be minimized by good health, a secure home life, satisfying peer relationships, and school success. Others at the time shared this belief—that movies, radio, and comic books were corrupting the nation's young people and only returning to traditional values could protect them (Davis, 1976).

Media Violence in the Limited Effects Era

By the 1950s media research on children had begun to clearly reflect the limited effects paradigm. Media portrayals of crime and other antisocial behavior became a focus of concern. Alberta Siegel (1956), for example, conducted an experiment designed to demonstrate that viewing film aggression could reduce levels of aggressive behavior in children—only to discover just the opposite. This led her to reject the "catharsis hypothesis" of media effects that was enjoying some popularity at the time. Her view, however, was a minority opinion among social researchers.

Robert Zajonc (1954) is more indicative of the times (and the limited effects paradigm). He studied 10- to 14-year-olds' identification with the heroes of serial radio space dramas. He learned that children overwhelmingly preferred to be like the successful radio characters, regardless of whether those heroes were "power oriented" or "friendship seeking." Zajonc wrote, however, that he doubted that a child would select a successful criminal as a model; a child would choose instead to identify with characters only as long as those characters' values were not too deviant from his or her already-held values. Of course, poorly socialized children or those who lacked appropriate adult role models might fail to develop consistent values and thus be vulnerable to media portrayals. Fortunately, relatively few such children were found in the early 1950s. This "yes . . . but" view of the effects of mediated violence is typical of the limited effects perspective that came to dominate the scientific literature.

Five years later, for example, Lotte Bailyn (1959) scrutinized the effects of reading comic books and discovered that heavy consumers of comics were also heavy consumers of movies and television. She concluded that people with certain preexisting problems and behavioral difficulties could suffer harmful effects, but that only a very small percentage of young people actually fit that description.

Most observers believed that the media did have some impact. But by the 1950s this influence was conceptualized as essentially benign or else offset by more dominant factors in children's lives such as their relationships with family members or peer groups. Often—as we saw in Chapter 8 in our consideration of the research conducted by Wilbur Schramm, Jack Lyle, and Edwin Parker (1961)—somewhat naive functionalist arguments were developed to provide a "balanced" interpretation of such effects. Good and bad functions of media offset each other just as other factors in children's lives offset the influence of media.

Many other researchers voiced cautiously optimistic views. Eleanor Maccoby (1954, p. 239), for example, wrote that the media "provide a child with experience which is free from real-life controls so that, in attempting to find solutions to a problem, he can try out various modes of action without risking the injury or punishment which might ensue if he experimented overtly." This benevolent view of media effects anticipated the more definitive interpretations offered in 1961 by Schramm, Lyle, and Parker, who labeled television at most a "contributing factor" and not a basic cause of youthful aggression and antisocial behavior. Most "normal" children, they argued, those with solid interpersonal relationships and a secure home, would be relatively free from television's more harmful effects. In "good" homes television could be used by wise parents to reinforce positive effects such as reading library books.

Clearly, these were simpler times; the 1960s changed not only that, but also how many social scientists came to view media's effects on children's aggressive and antisocial behavior.

The Sixties

In 1960, Joseph Klapper's *The Effects of Mass Communication* was published and became arguably the single most influential commentary on media's impact on individuals and society. Its primary thesis—that "mass communication ordinarily does not serve as a necessary and sufficient cause of audience effects, but rather functions among and through a nexus of mediating factors and influences" (1960, p. 8)—expressed the essence of the limited effects paradigm. This belief, that media at most could be agents of reinforcement, dominated media research in general and research on media and children in particular. That Dr. Klapper spent most of his professional life as Director of Social Research for the CBS television network and that the network provided grants for his research do not diminish its reliability. But they do suggest an orientation to or a view of the mass media that would have made a different interpretation quite difficult.

But Klapper's ideas, arguably credible for their time, deserve rethinking especially about research on media and children. Klapper based his conclusions on research done prior to the postwar restructuring of American society and prior to the "television generation." From 1960 to today, the factors that Klapper identified as posing important barriers to media influence (family, school, and church) have become less dominant in children's lives. As single-parent families and latchkey children became more common, the ability of parents to monitor and moderate media effects declined. At the same time, media have become more powerful and more specifically attuned to individual tastes and interests. Tiny black and white TV sets connected to one or two networks have given way to big-screen video units linked to tens or even hundreds of program channels.

The Sixties really began on August 6, 1945 when the United States dropped the atom bomb on Hiroshima, effectively ending World War II. That four-year global conflict forced cataclysmic changes in America's economic, industrial, demographic, familial, and technological character. Trends were unleashed that would be felt most powerfully in the 1960s.

The mass medium that transformed the 1960s had an inauspicious introduction as a novelty at the 1939 World's Fair in New York. Its tiny picture, poor sound quality, and high cost led some to doubt its future as a popular medium. During the next three years a small number of experimental television stations began broadcasting a very limited number and variety of programs to a minuscule audience. When the United States entered the war, television's already limited diffusion to the public halted, as the technologies and materials needed to improve and produce the medium went to the war effort. Technological research, however, did not stop. Therefore, when the war ended and materials were once again available for the manufacture of consumer goods, a technologically mature medium was immediately available. Anticipating not only this, but also dramatic changes in American society that would benefit the new medium, the four commercial radio networks—ABC, NBC, Mutual and CBS—were instantly prepared to move their hit shows and big stars to television. Television became a *mass* medium in 1960, reaching into 80% of all American homes.

This technological advance occurred simultaneously with profound alterations in American society. The war changed America from a primarily rural society that boasted an agriculturally based economy into a highly urban nation dependent on an industrially based economy. After the war more people worked regularly scheduled jobs (as opposed to the sunrise-to-sunset workday of farmers), and they had more leisure. More people had regular incomes (as opposed to the seasonal, put-the-money-back-into-the-land financial farmer existence), and they had more money to spend on that leisure. Because the manufacturing capabilities developed for the war were still in existence, the economy had the ability to mass produce items on which that money could be spent. Because there were more consumer goods competing in the marketplace, there was a greater need to advertise, which provided the economic base for the new television medium. Because non-Caucasian Americans had been enlisted to fight the war and to work in the country's factories, they began to demand their rightful share of the American dream. Because women entered the work force while the men were off to battle, it was more common and acceptable to have both parents working out of the home. Because people had moved away from their small towns and family roots, the traditional community anchors—church and school—began to lose their dominance in the social development of children who were present in the 1960s—in their teenage years—in inordinately large numbers due to the Baby Boom that occurred soon after the war ended.

A new social landscape took shape at precisely the same time that the new mass medium arrived. As in all periods of change, there were serious social problems. The rapid expansion in the number of teenagers brought sharp increases in delinquency and crime. The schools were blamed for not doing their job of educating children to be responsible citizens. Crime waves swept one city after another. Successive social movements captured the attention of the nation, especially the Civil Rights and the Anti-Vietnam War Movements. Political instability reached new heights with the assassinations of President John F. Kennedy, Dr. Martin Luther King, and Robert Kennedy. Young people were behaving strangely. Many were listening more to new, unfamiliar music and less to their increasingly "old fashioned, irrelevant" parents. Sociologists discovered the existence of a "generation gap" between conservative, middle-class parents and their increasingly liberal, even radical children.

Media's role in all of these changes was hotly debated. Although social researchers and media practitioners typically argued from the limited effects perspective, a new generation of media critics charged that media were corrupting children and disrupting their lives. Evidence mounted that families, schools, and churches had become less important to children. As Urie Bronfenbrenner (1970) said, the back yards were growing smaller and the school yards growing bigger. In other words, young people were being socialized more and more away from the home and outside the classroom. His own research demonstrated that, whereas parents and church had been the primary socializing agents for pre-war American adolescents, by the mid 1960s, media and peers shared top billing in the performance of that crucial function.

It is no surprise, then, that the media, particularly television, became the target of increasing criticism and the object of increasing scientific inquiry, especially where harmful effects were presumed. But these renewed efforts to probe the negative influence of mass media occurred when the limited effects paradigm was becoming dominant. An intense and continuing debate erupted between those social researchers who had confidence in that perspective and those who were skeptical of its conclusions despite the consistency of its empirical findings. Strong advocates of limited effects notions were accused of being paid lackeys of the media industries while overzealous critics of television were said to oversimplify complex problems and to ignore alternative causes.

The argument over the role of media in fomenting social instability and instigating violence reached a peak in the late 1960s. After disruptive riots in the Los Angeles suburb of Watts and in the cities of Cleveland, Newark, and Detroit, President Lyndon Johnson established a National Commission on the Causes and Prevention of Violence in 1968. The Commission offered some serious criticisms of media and recommended a variety of changes in both news reporting and entertainment content. Writing in the preface to the Commission's Staff Report, *Violence and the Media*, editor Paul Briand asked, "If, as the media claim, no objective correlation exists between media portrayals of violence and violent behavior — if, in other words, the one has no impact upon the other — then how can the media claim an impact in product selection and consumption, as they obviously affect the viewers' commercial attitudes and behavior? Can they do one and not the other?" (Baker and Ball, 1969, preface). This question reflected growing public and elite skepticism concerning limited effects assertions.

The federal government itself tried to locate new answers to this query by establishing the Surgeon General's Scientific Advisory Committee on Television and Social Behavior in 1969. Its purpose was to commission a broad range of

Box 9a U.S. Senate Hearings on the Surgeon General's Report on Television and Social Behavior

So much controversy was generated by the release and media interpretation of the Surgeon General's Report in 1972 (for example, the New York *Times* report on January 11 that was headlined "TV Violence Held Unharmful to Youth," Gould, 1972) that John O. Pastore of Rhode Island convened the U.S. Senate's Communications Subcommittee. He intended to clear the air about the true findings of Dr. Steinfield's Scientific Advisory Committee. The Surgeon General was certain in his understanding of the results, as we see on pages 193 and 194. But Pastore wanted a more definitive statement before the public. This exchange between the Senator and CBS's Joseph Klapper occurred on March 21, 1972, in Washington, DC.

Dr. Klapper: I have in mind programs which promote admiration for skills and abilities that do not involve the display of anti-social aggression, or of violence, including among such skills and abilities, the solution of interpersonal problems without resort to violence. This would all be undertaken in my hope, in an intensified effort, as I said, to maximize the pro-social potential of television.

Senator Pastore: May I interrupt you, Doctor? You talk about the responsibility of the parents, and I agree with you. You talk about the maxi-

mization of pro-social programs, I agree with you. But, why don't we talk about the minimizing of excessive violence? Why isn't that a part of the question? I mean, that is the thing that we are investigating here. I realize that there is a lot of good we can do through television, and television should do it, and that is their responsibility . . . But what we are bothered with here is excessive violence. Now, I realize that a family can do a great deal with a child and should do a great deal with a child, but we have to accept life the way it is. You are a scientist with the broadcasting industry, CBS . . . Don't you think there has been much violence on television that is unnecessary.

Dr. Klapper: Yes.

Senator Pastore: Now, why don't we cut that out? That is what I am talking about. That is what we should do, where we should start. And then all of the other studies you mention, of course, we ought to do them . . . But the question at hand is, does televised violence have to do with the aggressiveness of a child, in spite of everything else? And the question here is, is it something that can be helped, and that is a question we have to decide. If it can be helped, I say for goodness gracious, let's do it.

research on television effects that might determine whether television could be an important influence on children's behavior.

What did this collection of scientists conclude after two years and a million dollars of study? The Surgeon General, Jesse L. Steinfield, reported to a U.S. Senate subcommittee, "While the . . . report is carefully phrased and qualified in language acceptable to social scientists, it is clear to me that the causal relationship between televised violence and antisocial behavior is sufficient to warrant appropriate and immediate remedial action. The data on social phenomena such as television and violence and/or aggressive behavior will never be clear enough for all social scientists to agree on the formulation of a succinct statement of causality. But there comes a time when the data are sufficient to justify action. That time has come" (Ninety-Second Congress, 1972, p. 26).

But this report did little to end the controversy over television's effects. Industry officials and lobbyists worked hard to block development and implementation of new Federal Communications Commission regulations for children's programming. They cited inconclusive research and restated limited effects arguments. The dominant opposition to the industry was Action for Children's Television (ACT)—a Boston-based group that grew rapidly during the 1970s in response to growing public fears about television effects. Eventually the industry agreed to a self-imposed family viewing hour in which violent content was ostensibly minimized and, at the time, all three networks tightened their programming standards and worked closely with program producers to limit gratuitous violence.

Television Violence Theories

The most important outcome of the violence research was the gradual development of a set of middle-range theories. These summarized findings and offered increasingly useful insight into the media's role in the lives of children. Although these theories and the research they guided failed to conclusively demonstrate that viewing of violence has adverse, long-term effects on most children, they did indicate that some children could be harmed. In what we can now see as a good example of the conflict between micro- and macro-level media researchers, the effects debate centered around the total number of children harmed and whether this number was sufficiently threatening to the society to warrant censoring violence. Network research showed strong audience preferences for violence, and many popular action adventure dramas featured high levels of it. Network officials argued that the majority of Americans should have the right to watch what they liked even if it might be harmful to a few adolescent boys in bad families who were predisposed to being aggressive anyway (Melody, 1973).

Catharsis

The findings from the Surgeon General's Report on one aspect of the television violence debate, catharsis, were quite clear and generated significant agreement. Testified CBS's Joseph Klapper (Ninety-Second Congress, 1972, p. 60), "I myself am unaware of any, shall we say, hard evidence that seeing violence on television or any other medium acts in a cathartic or sublimated manner. There have been some studies to that effect; they are grossly, greatly outweighed by studies as to the opposite effect."

Yet *catharsis* (sometimes called *sublimation*) — the idea that viewing violence is sufficient to purge or at least satisfy a person's aggressive drive and, therefore, reduce the likelihood of aggressive behavior — has lived a long, if not thoroughly respectable life in mass communication theory.

Common sense and your own media consumption as well offer some evidence of the weakness of the catharsis hypothesis. When you watch couples engaged in physical affection on the screen, does it reduce your sexual drive? Do media presentations of families devouring devilish chocolate cakes purge you of your hunger drive? If viewing mediated sexual behavior does not reduce the sex drive and viewing media presentations of people dining does not reduce our hunger, why should we assume that seeing mediated violence can satisfy an aggressive drive? Moreover, think back to when you attend movies like *Alien*, *Dirty Harry*, *RoboCop*, any of the numerous "Rocky" films, or even *Boyz N the Hood*. Do you walk out of the theater a tranquil, placid person? Probably not.

Yet, it isn't difficult to see why the proposition seemed so attractive. For one thing, catharsis was originally articulated by the philosopher, Aristotle, to explain audience reaction to Greek tragedy. So it has developed a sort of intellectual validity based on tradition rather than observation. For another, catharsis suggested that television violence had social utility, providing young people with a harmless outlet for their pent-up aggression and hostility. Remember, in television's early days, many people were anxious to rationalize their use of this attractive, new medium.

There was even early scientific evidence suggesting that catharsis was, indeed, at work. Seymour Feshbach (1961) demonstrated what he said was catharsis by insulting college-aged men with "a number of unwarranted and extremely critical remarks" in an experimental setting and then having them watch either filmed aggression (a brutal prize fight) or a neutral film (on the spread of rumors). The men were then asked to evaluate the experiment and the insulting experimenter. The insultees who had seen the prize fight were less aggressive in their attitudes than those who had seen the other film.

But, as F. Scott Andison wrote in 1977 after reviewing twenty years' worth of scientific evidence, "We can conclude on the basis of the present data cumulation that television, as it is shown today, probably does stimulate a higher amount of aggression in individuals within society. Therefore, it seems reasonable to tentatively accept the 'TV violence as a stimulant to aggression' theory and to reject the . . .'cathartic' theories" (Andison, 1977 p. 323). Or, as James D. Halloran (1964–65), then-director of Britain's Center for Mass Communication Research at the University of Leicester, more directly put it, catharsis is a "phony argument."

But Feshbach apparently *did* demonstrate a reduction in aggression after the viewing in 1961 and he obtained similar results in a 1971 study (Feshbach and Singer) conducted with research funding from NBC. The research was conducted in a group home for preadolescent boys. For six weeks, half of the boys were restricted to watching television programs with little or no violence while the other half were allowed to watch violent content. A variety of behavioral measures indicated that the boys viewing the violent programs were less aggressive. These findings may not have been due to catharsis, however. The boys who were placed in the nonviolent programming group may have been frustrated because they were not allowed to watch some of their favorite shows. Heightened frustration might account for their increased aggressiveness.

Certain presentations of mediated violence and aggression can reduce the likelihood of subsequent viewer aggression. But catharsis is not necessarily in operation. Rather, viewers *learn* that violence may not be appropriate in a given situation. Think about the first Feshbach study we mentioned. Maybe those who had seen the brutal boxing match, who had seen unnecessary pain inflicted on another human, simply said to themselves, "Aggression is not a good thing." Their aggressive drive may not have been purged; but they may have simply learned that such treatment of another human is inappropriate. In other words, their inclination toward aggression (remember, they had been insulted) was inhibited by the information in the media presentation. This leads us to the theory that is generally accepted as most useful in understanding the influence of media violence — *social learning theory.*

Social Learning

There is no doubt that humans learn from observation. There has been some question, however, about how much and what kinds of behaviors people learn from the media. This debate has been fueled, in part, by a definitional problem. No one questions whether or not people can imitate what they see in the media. *Imitation* is the direct, mechanical reproduction of behavior. A television viewer sees a movie called *Fuzz* in which a gang of teenagers beats and sets afire a hobo. The next day, he beats a homeless man sleeping on a beach and sets him on fire. Or four teenagers rape two little girls four days after seeing a similar scene in the televised movie, "Born Innocent." Both true stories. Both imitation. The problem for mass communication theorists, however, is that these obvious examples of media influence, as dramatic as they may be, are relatively rare. Moreover, such gross examples of media influence lend substance to the argument that negative effects occur only in those "predisposed" to aggression, in other words, those crazy to begin with.

Identification, on the other hand, is "a particular form of imitation in which copying a model, generalized beyond specific acts, springs from wanting to be and trying to be like the model with respect to some broader quality" (White, 1972, p. 252). Although only one or a very few people may have imitated the killings seen in the televised programming mentioned above, how many others identified with the murderer? How many others might choose a different form of violence against someone they might encounter? How many others identified with the killers' mode of problem solving, although they might never express it exactly as did our video killers? Imitation from media is clearly more dramatic and observable than identification. But identification with media models may be the more lasting and significant of the media's effects (for a detailed discussion of this distinction and its importance to media theory, see Baran and Meyer, 1974).

The first serious look at learning through observation was offered by psychologists Neal Miller and John Dollard (1941). They argued that imitative learning occurred when observers were motivated to learn, when the cues or elements of the behaviors to be learned were present, when observers performed the given behaviors, and when observers were positively reinforced for imitating those behaviors. In other words, people could imitate behaviors that they saw; those behaviors would be reinforced and therefore learned.

Instead of presenting a means of understanding how people learn from models (including media models), however, Miller and Dollard were simply describing an efficient form of traditional stimulus-response learning. They assumed that individuals behaved in certain ways and then shaped their behavior according to the reinforcement they actually received. They saw imitation as replacing random trial-and-error behaviors. Imitation simply made it easier for an individual to choose a behavior to be reinforced for making it. The actual reinforcement, they argued, ensured learning. But this insistence on the operation of reinforcement limited their theory's application for understanding how people learn from the mass media. The theory's inability to account for people's apparent skill at learning new responses through observation rather than actually receiving reinforcement limited its applicability to media impact.

Two decades later, Miller and Dollard's ideas on social learning and imitation were sufficiently developed, however, to become valuable tools in understanding media effects. Where Miller and Dollard saw social learning as an efficient form of stimulus-response learning (the model provided information that helped the observer make the correct response to be reinforced), contemporary social learning theory argues that observers can acquire symbolic representations of the behavior, and these "pictures" provide them with information on which to base their own subsequent behavior (Bandura, 1971). Media characters (models) can influence behavior simply by being depicted on the screen. The audience member need not be reinforced or rewarded for exhibiting the modeled behavior.

Social Learning from Mass Media

Traditional or operant learning theory as developed by the early behaviorists (see Chapter 4) asserts that people learn new behaviors when they are presented with stimuli (something in their environment), make a response to those stimuli, and have those responses reinforced either positively (rewarded) or negatively (punished). In this way, new behaviors are learned, or added to people's *behavioral repertoire*— the individual's available behaviors in a given circumstance.

Two things are clear, however. First, this is an inefficient form of learning. All of us know, for example, how to deal with fire. If each of us had to learn our fire-related behavior individually, we would have overcrowded hospitals. According to operant learning theory, each of us, when presented with that stimulus (fire), would render a chance response (put our hand in it) and be negatively reinforced (burned). We would then add avoidance of fire to our behavioral repertoire. This is very inefficient. Instead we observe, in a variety of settings (mass mediated and otherwise), the operation of that stimulus, response, and reinforcement chain; and we, in turn, add avoidance to the store of behaviors that we can use when confronted in everyday life by the stimulus. In essence, then, we have substituted a representation of an experience for an actual (and, in this case, painful) experience.

A second obvious point is that we do not learn in only this manner. We have all experienced learning through observation even when we have not seen the stimulus/response/reinforcement chain; that is, when there has been no reinforcement, either to us or to the person in the representation. Observation of a behavior is sufficient for people to learn that behavior.

Modeling from the mass media, then, is an efficient way to learn a wide range of behaviors and solutions to problems that we would otherwise learn slowly or not at all, or pay too high a price to learn in the actual environment.

This social learning through the use of media representations operates in one or all of three ways (see Bandura, 1971, for an excellent extended discussion):

1 **Observational Learning**: Consumers of representations can acquire new patterns of behavior by simply watching these representations. All of us know how to shoot a gun, although many of us have never actually performed or been reinforced for that act. Many of us probably even think that we can hijack a plane. We have seen it done.

2 **Inhibitory Effects**: Seeing a model in a representation punished for exhibiting a certain behavior decreases the likelihood that the observers will make that response. It is as if the viewers themselves are actually negatively reinforced. We see the villain punished for evil deeds; we see J.R. Ewing hated by the people of

"Dallas" because of his meanness and greed. Our likelihood of responding to various real-world stimuli in similar ways is reduced. Experimental studies using film and video of people being punished for various behaviors have shown that these representations can inhibit in observers such things as aggression, exploratory behavior, and antisocial interaction with peers.

3 **Disinhibitory Effects:** A media representation that depicts reward for a threatening or prohibited behavior is often sufficient to increase likelihood that the consumer of the representation will make that response. A young man sees Sam on "Cheers" win a woman's attention with one of his usual displays of macho crudeness; he sees Fonzie on "Happy Days" surrounded by beautiful girls because of his adroit use of antisocial or eccentric behavior. Experimental studies using film and television representations of various threatening and prohibited encounters have successfully reduced fear of dentists, dogs, and snakes and increased aggression by reducing viewers' inhibitions toward such action.

Vicarious reinforcement is central to this notion of social learning through the mass media. Although observational learning can occur in the absence of any reinforcement, vicarious or real, whether observers actually make that learned behavior is a function of the *reinforcement contingencies* (positive or negative) they associate with it.

In one laboratory experiment, children were shown a film of a young boy pummeling large plastic punching doll (a BOBO doll) in various unique and novel ways while shouting "lickitstickit" and "wetosmacko," all in the absence of any reinforcement, either in the film or real life (Bandura, Ross, and Ross 1963). Observational learning seemed to occur. When put in a playroom, many of the children performed those same pummeling behaviors and shouted those same strange words.

Some, however, did not. All of the children probably learned this way of interpreting action, the behaviors, and words; but only some chose to act out or exhibit those behaviors. This is where the concept of vicarious reinforcement becomes important to our understanding of how learning from media representations affects our behavior. Vicarious reinforcement is the operation of reinforcement, although the observer is not actually reinforced. Observation of a model's or character's behavior-reinforcement combination often serves as an actual reinforcement for the observing individual. Observation may be sufficient for learning from the media, but the reinforcement contingencies we see associated with the represented behaviors may dictate whether we actually *use* these behaviors in our everyday life.

For, example, when we see a television character rewarded or punished for some action, it is as if we ourselves have been actually reinforced, either positively or negatively. This vicarious reinforcement tells us where to place the observationally learned behavior in our behavioral hierarchy—the likelihood that we will choose a given behavior. When presented with certain stimuli in our environment, we will be likely to choose a highly placed behavior for demonstration. One that promises punishment will be given a lower place in that hierarchy. We do not actually have to experience those rewards and sanctions; we have done it vicariously through the use of media representations.

Clearly there may be times when we ignore the negative vicarious reinforcement and perform a behavior that we have seen represented as associated with punishment, such as running into a burning house. In these cases, sufficient incentive is present in the actual environment (saving a child from the flames, for example) to move that behavior up the hierarchy to a point where we can choose it from among a number of alternatives.

Albert Bandura (1965) conducted what is now considered a classic experiment in modeling aggressive behavior from television, one that has direct bearing on several aspects of the media effects debate. He showed nursery school children a television program in which a character, Rocky, was either rewarded for aggression (given candy and a soft drink and called a "strong champion") or punished for those same behaviors (reprimanded, called a "bully," and spanked with a rolled-up magazine). Those who saw aggression rewarded showed more aggressive activity in a "free play" period (disinhibition) and those who saw it punished displayed less (inhibition). You can almost hear those people who believe that media have no effects on viewer aggression crowing, "See, the bad guy is punished, so media portrayals of violence actually reduce subsequent aggression." But Bandura went one step further. He then offered those in the inhibited group "sticker-pictures" for each of Rocky's aggressive acts they could demonstrate. Boys and girls alike could produce the "forbidden" behaviors. The environment offered them sufficient reward to demonstrate those observationally learned, but previously inhibited behaviors. The response to the "TV violence apologists," then, is simple: The bad guy is usually "out-aggressed" by the good guy who is rewarded for his or her more proficient display of aggression; and besides, that may not matter because the behaviors are observationally learned and can appear later when the conditions in the viewer's world call them (or similar ones) forward.

Social Learning as Middle-Range Theory

Social learning theory, explaining observers' identification with media models as well as the more visible direct imitation of them, came to dominate the thinking of media impact on individual behavior. This theory explained how people could learn from the media in the absence of actual or vicarious reinforcement and it explained how that vicarious reinforcement could increase (disinhibit) or decrease (inhibit) the likelihood that a behavior seen in the media would be made.

Social learning theory is an example of a useful, middle-range media effects theory that has helped us predict and interpret a wide variety of media influences. But in many ways, it succeeds by ignoring the larger social context in which learning occurs. Social learning theory conceptualizes a learning process in which a variety of external, societal factors are held constant. It has difficulty explaining why some media models are very potent while others are ignored. It recognizes but finds it difficult to conceptualize and study the manner in which children's understanding and use of media content interact with other aspects of their daily lives. How does learning from media models become a part of every-day experience and action? What are the long-term societal consequences of such learning? For example, we know that "Sesame Street" is successful in teaching children through the use of media models. The show's content is designed using social learning theory principles and its effectiveness has been closely studied using empirical research methods. But social learning theory can't explain or predict the long-term, societal consequences of "Sesame Street." The theory can't tell us whether the program actually helps ghetto kids adjust to middle-class schools (this was its original intent). "Sesame Street" critics argue that the program actually is of greater help to middle-class children and only *increases* the gap between them and ghetto children. Middle-class mothers value "Sesame Street" more and they work to reinforce the behaviors that their children learn from it. In ghetto families, these behaviors are more likely to be ignored or misunderstood. Thus, although social learning theory is widely accepted and useful, it remains middle-range and cannot address such macroscopic issues. On the other hand, as a good middle-range theory, it does suggest additional avenues of inquiry. Four of the most fruitful—aggressive cues, the effects of violent pornography, a developmental perspective of television viewing, and an active theory of television viewing—are discussed below.

Aggressive Cues

One direct outgrowth of social learning theory focuses on the *aggressive cues* inherent in media portrayals of violence. People who see mediated violence are believed to show higher levels of subsequent aggression. The question is when and against whom do they aggress? The answer is that media portrayals of violence are almost always in some dramatic context and that context provides information, or *cues*, that tell viewers when and against whom violence is acceptable.

Leonard Berkowitz (1965) produced an indicative piece of research, in which male college students were shown a film of a brutal boxing scene (the closing sequence of the movie, *The Champion*). To some it was presented in the context of a story that said the loser deserved his beating, that is, the violence against him was justified. In a second version of the tale, the defeated boxer was victimized, that is, the violence against him was unjustified.

The students were then given an opportunity to "grade" another student's design of "an original and imaginative floor plan for a house." Unbeknownst to them, all the subjects were given the same floor plan from that other student (who was actually Berkowitz's accomplice). In half the cases, that accomplice introduced himself as a "college boxer" and in the other as a "speech major." A "new form of grading" was to be used, grading by electrical shock: one shock was very good, ten was very bad. Of course, the accomplice did not actually get zapped; the shocks administered by the subjects were read by a metering device and the accomplice feigned a response. Any differences in shocking the other student would be the result of differences in what they had seen on the screen. To confuse matters even more, half the subjects were insulted (angered) by the experimenter before they began. What happened? The "college boxer" was shocked more than the speech major; the angered subjects gave more shocks regardless of whom they were shocking; and those who had seen the justified version of the film also gave more shocks. Berkowitz's conclusions? First, viewers' *psychological state* can lead them to respond to cues in programs that meet the needs of that state. Second, viewers who see justified violence not only learn the behavior, but also learn that it can be a good or useful problem solving device (disinhibition). Third, cues associated with a victim, in this case a boxer, can disinhibit viewers toward aggression against similar people in the real world. Berkowitz said, "The findings show that the film context can affect the observer's inhibitions against aggression and that the people encountered soon afterwards vary in the extent to which they can evoke aggressive responses from the observer" (Berkowitz, 1965, p. 368). In a later study (Berkowitz and Geen, 1966), Berkowitz produced similar results simply by having the real-world target of the viewers' aggression share the same first name (Kirk) as the victim in the film.

This idea of aggressive cues forms the core of some of the most interesting and controversial media violence research now being conducted. With the media violence-viewer aggression link generally accepted, contemporary attention has been turned to the issue of violence against a specific target—women.

Richard Frost and John Stauffer (1987, p. 29) wrote, "But even though members of an audience for a violent film or television program may not be moved to actual behavioral imitation, do they not experience different levels of emotional arousal? . . . Could arousal also be influenced by the type of violence being portrayed, such as violence against women as opposed to men . . . ?" Edward Donnerstein has been most visible in the investigation of this question. In a series of

Copy pg for 313 re: proof

Box 9b Dr. Leonard Berkowitz on the Value of Laboratory Experiments

When the National Commission on the Causes and Prevention of Violence held five days of "Mass Media Hearings" in 1968, much discussion centered on what was actually known about the television-violence link. Industry representatives argued that the research was too artificial to be useful and that no connection had been proved. Dr. Leonard Berkowitz, Professor of Psychology at the University of Wisconsin, addressed these issues in his statement on October 16 (Baker and Ball, 1969, p. 36–37).

"One very important point . . . has to do with whether anything is really ever proven. I would like strongly to support the contention that very few if any scientific statements are ever proven. All we can do really is to offer educated guesses and probability statements. I think on the basis of available research we cannot say that anything is proven, but we can say that we have a pretty good guess to make, and we can offer a probability statement that has some likelihood of holding up on subsequent testing . . .

One of the more important objections (to the findings) is that the laboratory research does not really involve aggression. Giving electrical shocks or beating up a BOBO doll is said not to be aggressive in nature. I think there are a variety of observations which can pretty well demolish that kind of objection. First of all, we have independent evidence that youngsters who are most aggressive in real life are the ones who display

this kind of laboratory behavior more characteristically. Second of all, there is evidence that training youngsters in the laboratory, for example even to beat up a BOBO doll, subsequently enhances their likelihood of going out into the playground and beating up their playmates. The laboratory behavior does carry over. And further, there is no doubt in my mind that our subjects regard the behavior, particularly the giving of electrical shocks, as aggressive. Dr. Klapper points out quite correctly that the laboratory situation attempts to lower restraints against aggression. We actually, for theoretical reasons, do want our subjects to be uninhibited. But, nevertheless, our subjects know darn well that they are shocking someone. And further, generally they are rather reluctant to attack someone. Among the indications of this . . . is that at the very end of the experiment, when we tell them they really didn't shock anyone, very often there is a burst of relieved laughter. They are happy to hear that they hadn't attacked anyone . . .

Now again the question might come up, can I prove this? I cannot. But . . . with fairly great consistency across many different studies, carried out in many different laboratories, they all seemed to add up to a probability statement that while not perfect, it is certainly not zero either . . . These results are based on both young children and college students as well, which to me adds to the significance of the findings.

experiments (Donnerstein and Berkowitz, 1981, for example), he demonstrated that a

> multiplicity of processes . . . can determine an audience's reactions to events in the mass media. Arousal level, lowered inhibitions, viewer's

interpretations and understandings, and stimulus-response associations all play some part . . . (T)he addition of aggression to the sex in pornographic materials is probably more dangerous (in terms of possible aggressive consequences) than the display of pure erotica . . . (T)his combination is appearing with increasing frequency (p. 722).

Donnerstein's comments make a crucial point that will lead us into the next chapter. He and coauthor Berkowitz wrote that one process that can influence the effects of the media's message is "viewer's interpretations and understandings." They are acknowledging that the audience, we as individuals, obviously has some say how any given medium or message influences us. Good mass communication theory, as we'll see, does not ignore the power of the people.

Donnerstein is at the center of a related but more controversial aspect of the issue of mediated violence against women, the effects of "aggressive-pornographic mass media stimuli." In a review of the available science on the question (Malamuth and Donnerstein, 1982), he and his coauthor wrote

Summary of findings to date

i

The data across the laboratory and field experiments discussed in this article support the proposition that exposure to mass media stimuli that have violent and sexual content increases the audience's aggressive- sexual fantasies, acceptance of aggression, beliefs in rape myths, and aggressive behavior. These findings were obtained both with unedited, commercially available stimuli (e.g., feature-length films) and with (specifically) edited stimuli . . . Effects were found directly following exposure as well as several days later. (p. 129–130).

In an article published that same year, Dolf Zillmann and Jennings Bryant (1982) examined the relationship between pornography and what they called "sexual callousness and the trivialization of rape." They demonstrated that "massive exposure to standard pornographic materials devoid of coercion and aggression seemed to promote such callousness" (p. 19). As their stimuli these researchers used 6 eight-minute porno films depicting heterosexual erotica. They measured callousness toward women through a post-exposure questionnaire to groups of college students who had seen various amounts of that stimuli. According to the researchers, the basic premise of this inquiry is that pornography demeans women and therefore leads to their devaluation by men who consume this "unrealistic" content. They wrote,

Indeed, pornography appears to thrive on featuring social encounters in which women are eager to accommodate any and every imaginable sexual urge of any man in the vicinity. These socially non-discriminating females are typically shown . . . to encourage and actively solicit the sexual behaviors that are dear to men but not necessarily to women (1982, p. 12).

But not everyone agrees with the logic or the values in the Zillmann and Bryant research. Ferrel Christensen (1986, p. 181), for example, wrote,

So perhaps it is not pornography but this society that "misrepresents reality" vis-á-vis female sexuality. Is the sexual conflict between men and women, with which we are all painfully familiar, more the product of false expectations (as Zillmann and Bryant claim) or of sexual repression? . . . The message of pornography need not be taken as 'women are like this' but rather as "it's all right for women to be sexually uninhibited."

Although this debate continues, Daniel Linz and Edward Donnerstein (1988) expanded the research question to include not only X-rated porn, both violent and nonviolent, but also R-rated horror or slasher movies like those featuring Jason and Freddy Kreuger, to produce a synopsis of contemporary knowledge on the issue. They concluded, "Subject empathy and sympathy (toward women) were affected by exposure to 'slasher' films that combine sex and violence but not by prolonged exposure to pornographic films . . . Subjects exposed to 'slasher' films showed significant declines in anxiety and depression (our primary indices of desensitization) with continued viewing" (pp. 180–181). They also editorialized on the value of this research (in doing so, they hint at the cultural and critical cultural theories that are the core of Chapters 12 and 13). Linz and Donnerstein wrote

It is misguided to single out pornography because of its negative message about women. This leaves the impression that if only we could eliminate pornography we would eliminate that material that most harms women in our society. Why limit ourselves to objecting to the demeaning depictions of women that appear only in a sexually explicit context? Our research suggests that you need not look any further than the family's own television set to find demeaning depictions of women available to far more viewers than pornographic material. (1988, p. 184).

The Developmental Perspective

One aspect of people's power to deal with television is their ability to comprehend it at different stages in their intellectual development. Logically, older children will "read" television differently than will younger children. As Ellen Wartella wrote, this *developmental perspective* "seeks to describe and explain the nature of the communicative differences between four year olds, six year olds, 10 year olds, etc., and adults" (1979, p. 7). This notion of developmental stages in children's communicative abilities was drawn from developmental psychology, especially the work of Jean Piaget, who argued that children, as they move from infancy through adolescence, undergo qualitative changes in the level of cognitive and intellectual abilities available to them. Although it might be easy to assume that older children's processing of television's messages is more developed and, therefore, somehow better at insulating them from television effects, this was neither the conclusion of developmental research, nor was it its goal.

Wartella said, "While questions of children's modeling of televised behavior has been the major focus of experimental and survey research" the developmental perspective asks "new questions and (deals with) different sorts of communication issues regarding children's learning from television and use of television" (1979, p. 8–9). Much of this research actually focused on differences in attention and comprehension at different stages of development to better tailor educational programming to specific groups of children.

Active Theory of Television Viewing

Presenting "a theory of visual attention to television which has as its central premise the cognitively active nature of television viewing," Daniel Anderson and Elizabeth Lorch (1983, pp. 27–28), as well as several others (for example, Bryant and Anderson, 1983, and Singer and Singer, 1983) challenged social learning theory's implication that "television viewing is fundamentally reactive and passive." This active theory of television viewing sees viewers in general—and in the violence debate, particularly children—as actively and consciously working to understand television content. They argue that by the age of two and half, children have sufficiently developed *viewing schema* that allow them to comprehend specific television content conventions. "Beyond two and a half years," they wrote, "visual attention to television increases throughout the preschool years . . . and may level off during the school-age years . . . We suggest this increase reflects cognitive development, increased world knowledge, and an understanding of the cinematic codes and format structures of television" (Anderson and Lorch, 1983, p. 13).

Those who argued for this active theory of viewing claimed that social learning theorists generally subscribe "to the proposition that the child is an active, cognitive, and social being (but) television is seen as providing such an exceptionally powerful influence that the child becomes reactive in its presence" (Anderson and Lorch, 1983, p. 5). This pessimistic view of children's viewing and cognitive abilities, they claimed, inevitably led social learning theorists to overestimate the power of the medium and underestimate the influence that individual viewers had in determining effects. Put another way, "reactive theory" assumed that attention caused comprehension and therefore, effects. Active theory assumes that comprehension causes attention and, therefore, effects (or no effects).

Summary

New media are always blamed for societal troubles that happen to occur at the time of their introduction. Yet most 1960s research that examined media effects on young people's aggression and antisocial behavior concluded that media influence was, if not inconsequential, at least tempered by traditional forces like church, family, and school. The 1960s, however, with the mass diffusion of a new, powerful medium—television—the clear presence of significant social upheaval, and a weakening of those traditional forces' influence over young people, gave rise to several penetrating looks at media and viewer aggression.

Catharsis, the idea that viewing violence substitutes for the actual demonstration of aggression by the viewer, was ultimately discredited.

Social learning theory proved to be a useful way of understanding how people learn behaviors from television, but it left many questions unanswered, especially as its insights were extrapolated from micro-level analyses (where they were initially formulated) to more macro-level explanations of effects.

Aggressive cues research attempted to add some specificity to social learning theory, as did the developmental perspective. Another conception of the young audience, active theory of television viewing, although not dismissing media effects, did suggest that viewers have more influence over their interaction with media than social learning theory seemed to imply.

Discussion Questions

1   What was your family's attitude toward television when you were growing up? Were there viewing rules for the children in your home?

2   Think back to when you were in your pre and early teen years. Which lessons from those days are still with you? Those from school, church, and family or those from media and friends? What are they?

3   What is your opinion on catharsis? Do you agree with the authors' example of your own movie attendance?

4   Can you think of an example of social learning from the media in your own life? Examples of imitation? Of identification?

5   Do you think that laboratory experiments demonstrating the link between televised violence and viewer aggression *really* tell us about what happens in the real world?

Significant Names

Albert Bandura

Elizabeth Lorch

Dorothy Singer

Jerome Singer

Leonard Berkowitz

Ellen Wartella

Daniel Anderson

Dolf Zillmann

Jennings Bryant

Edward Donnerstein

Significant Readings

Bandura, Albert (1971). *Psychological Modeling: Conflicting Theories*. Chicago: Aldine Atherton.

Bryant, Jennings and Daniel R. Anderson (1983). *Children's Understanding of Television: Research on Attention and Comprehension*. New York: Academic Press.

Liebert, Robert M., Joyce N. Sprafkin, and Emily Davidson (1982). *The Early Window: Effects of Television on Children and Youth*. New York: Pergamon.

Melody, William (1973). *Children's TV: The Economics of Exploitation*. New Haven, CT: Yale University Press.

Schramm, Wilbur, Jack Lyle, and Edwin Parker (1961). *Television in the Lives of Our Children*. Stanford, CA: Stanford University Press.

Important Terms

Catharsis

Social Learning Theory

Imitation

Identification

Behavioral Repertoire

Observational Learning

Inhibitory Effects

Disinhibitory Effects

Aggressive Cues

Vicarious Reinforcement

Developmental Perspective

Viewing Schema

Stimulus-Response Learning

Chapter 10

Using Media: Theories of the Active Audience

Why do you go to the movies? To pass time? To be entertained? To stay "up" on what's happening? To be able to talk about something other than exams when hanging around the student union? To get some ideas about how to act on a first date? To study the latest fashions? You can no doubt offer many more yourself, because each of us has many of his or her own reasons, not only for going to the movies, but also for watching television news, reading the sports page, playing rock n' roll tapes in the car but classical CDs at home — in short, for whatever media consumption activities in which we choose to engage.

This simple idea — that people put specific media and specific media content to specific use in the hopes of having some specific need or set of needs gratified — forms the basis of the theories we will review in this chapter. Unlike many of the perspectives we've examined already, those that we called active-audience theories do not attempt to understand what the *media do to people* but rather focus on assessing what *people do with media*. For this reason they are referred to as *audience-centered* rather than *source-dominated* theories.

Much of the empirical research that we reviewed in preceding chapters was "effects research" which assumed that media do things to people, often without their consent or desire. This research typically focused on negative effects — the bad things that happen to people because they use media. Effects were caused by a variety of content, from political propaganda to dramatized presentations of sex and violence. As effects research became more sophisticated, it demonstrated that most direct effects are limited.

In this chapter, we will consider a very different type of media effect—those we consciously or routinely seek every time we turn to media for some particular purpose. Study of these effects was slow to develop. Mass society theory and the response to it focused researchers' attention on the unintended, negative consequences of media. Audience members were seen as passively responding to whatever content media made available to them. There were some early critics of this viewpoint. For example, John Dewey (1927) argued that educated people could make good use of media. He saw the problem of propaganda as one that should be solved through public education rather than censorship: If people could be taught to make better use of media content, they wouldn't need to be sheltered from it. Despite such arguments, empirical research remained focused on locating evidence of how average people could be manipulated by media. Eventually, effects research found that people weren't as vulnerable to propaganda as had been predicted by mass society theory. They were protected from manipulation by opinion leaders and well-formed, intensely held attitudes. But even this seemingly optimistic conclusion was associated with a pessimistic view of the average person. If the barriers protecting them were broken down, individuals could be easily manipulated. Researchers were slow to develop the perspective that average people can be responsible media consumers who use media for their own worthwhile purposes—an active audience.

Overview

In this chapter we will examine how active-audience conceptualizations gained popularity among empirical researchers during the 1970s. Of course, the possibility of responsible audience activity was never totally ignored in early media research, but much of it gave audiences insufficient credit for selection, interpretation, and use of media content. We will see that the early development of the audience-centered theories was hampered by confusion of the ideas of "functions" and "functionalism" and by methodological and theoretical disputes. We will discuss what it means to be an active audience member and examine in detail several audience-centered approaches: uses and gratifications, play theory, agenda-setting, and the spiral of silence.

Many of the theories introduced in later chapters are also audience-centered theories. For example, in Chapter 12 you will find that audience-centered views of media have become popular among critical theorists who presume much more than limited effects. The theories introduced in this chapter are important because they were among the first to make a priority of the study of audience activity and to view that activity in a positive way. As we shall see, this doesn't mean that they ignored the possibility of long-term negative consequences. Active audiences can still be misled by poorly constructed or inaccurate media presentations. We will explain why the development of audience-centered theories challenged the limited effects paradigm.

The Active Audience

As early as the 1940s, the work of people like Herta Herzog, Paul Lazarsfeld, and Frank Stanton reflected at least the implicit concern for studying an active, gratifications-seeking audience.

Lazarsfeld and Stanton (1942) produced a series of books and studies throughout the 1940s that paid significant attention to how audiences used media to organize their lives and experiences. For example, they studied the value of early morning radio reports to farmers. As part of the Lazarsfeld and Stanton series, Bernard Berelson (1949) published a classic media use study of the disruption experienced by newspaper readers during a strike. He reported convincing evidence that newspapers formed an important part of many people's daily routine.

Herta Herzog, a colleague of Lazarsfeld, is often credited as the originator of the uses and gratifications theory, although she most likely did not give it its label. Her 1944 article entitled, "Motivations and Gratifications of Daily Serial Listeners," was the first published research to provide an in-depth examination of media gratifications. She interviewed 100 radio soap-opera fans and identified "three major types of gratification." They were (including her editorial comments) first, "merely a means of emotional release," "a second and commonly recognized form of enjoyment concerns the opportunities for wishful thinking," and the "third and commonly unsuspected form of gratification concerns the advice obtained from listening to daytime serials." Herzog wanted to understand why so many housewives were attracted to radio soap operas. In contrast with the typical effects research being done in Lazarsfeld's shop, Herzog didn't try to measure the influence that soap opera listening had on women. She was satisfied with assessing their reasons and experiences—their uses and gratifications.

One of the first college mass communication text books, *The Process and Effects of Mass Communication*, offered an early active-audience conceptualization. Author Wilbur Schramm (1954, p. 19) asked the question, "What determines which offerings of mass communication will be selected by a given individual?" The answer he offered is called the "fraction of selection," and it looks like this:

$$\frac{\text{Expectation of reward}}{\text{Effort required}}$$

His point was that people weigh the level of reward (gratification) they expect from a given medium or message against how much effort they must make to secure that reward. Review your own movie viewing, for example. Of course it's easier to watch a film at home on a rented video than it is to get in your car, drive to the theater, find a parking place, stand in line, pay a week's salary for two tickets, and spend another half-week's salary for some popcorn and a soda. Home videos are cheaper and more convenient: you can start and stop them when you want, you can look and dress how you want when you watch, and you always have the best seat in the house. All of this concerns only the denominator, effort required. We still go to the movies, though, because the reward we expect from our visit to the theater (the big screen, the better sound, the fun of an evening out, the social contact, the status of being among the first on our block to see the latest hit) makes the effort worthwhile. You can develop your own fractions for your own media use of all kinds, but the essence of Schramm's argument remains — we all make decisions about which content we choose based on our expectations of having some need met, even if that decision is to not make a choice — say between two early evening situation comedies, for example, because it's too much trouble to get up and change the channel — because all we really want is some background noise while we sit and daydream.

Limitations of Early Audience-Centered Research

If this is all so seemingly logical and straight forward, why didn't the early theories that saw audiences as active and important in the mass communication process quickly emerge as strong alternatives to limited effects theories? There are many possible answers to this question. We have seen how mass society theory exaggerated the influence of media and centered widespread public concern on negative media effects. Since the 1930s, government agencies, private foundations, and the media industry all have been willing to provide funding to study negative effects, but little money was available for the study of active audiences. Also, researchers thought that it was possible to study effects more objectively than media uses. For example, negative effects might be observed in a laboratory following exposure to media content. On the other hand, studying uses meant asking people to report on their subjective experience of content. During the 1940s and 1950s, social science researchers were determined to avoid approaches that didn't meet what they regarded as scientific standards. They chose to focus their efforts on developing what they thought would be definitive, powerful *explanations for the consequences* of media use. They didn't see much purpose or value in *describing and cataloguing people's subjective reasons* for using media.

For example, in the area of media and attitude change, early researchers hoped to find the magic keys to persuasion (see Chapter 7). The discovery of these keys would enable media to be used by benevolent communicators to eliminate all sorts of bad attitudes (that is, racism, fascism) and replace them with good attitudes (that is, middle-class values). This would provide many benefits to society—and to the researchers. The Cold War could be ended. Ethnic conflict could be avoided. A new era of peace could be initiated. Of course, there would be problems if these keys fell into the wrong hands (such as, Adolf Hitler or Joseph McCarthy), but that was another matter.

Thus, for these researchers, the study of people's reasons for using media was hard to do using available scientific methods, hard to fund, and unlikely to be productive. Most attitude researchers had strong behaviorist biases that led them to be suspicious of taking people's thoughts and experiences at face value. They regarded people's reasons for doing things as rationalizations for actions. The real reasons people acted as they did could only be determined by studying the stimuli they were exposed to and the responses that they learned for them.

Early active-audience research was widely criticized by social scientists as being too descriptive—it did little more than group people's reasons for using media into sets of arbitrarily chosen categories. Why one set of categories rather than another? Moreover, the categorization process itself was dismissed as too arbitrary and subjective. For example, Herzog placed her listeners' reasons into three categories—why not five? Where did her categories come from and how could we be certain she wasn't arbitrarily putting reasons into these categories? In contrast, experimental attitude change research used what most researchers regarded as a scientifically sound set of procedures. It produced causal explanations rather than simple descriptions of subjective perceptions. As long as this effects research (even that based on the limited effects model) offered the hope of producing significant new insight into the causal power of media, there was little motivation to test alternate approaches.

Confusion of Media Functions and Media Uses

In Chapter 8, we described functional analysis and its use by early media researchers. By the 1960s, notions of an active and gratification-seeking audience had been absorbed by and confused with functional analysis. Failure to adequately differentiate media uses from media functions impeded the design and interpretation of audience-centered research. Charles Wright explicitly linked the active audience to functionalism in 1959 textbook. Explained Wright (1959, p. 16), "Harold Lasswell, a political scientist who has done pioneering research in mass communications, once noted three activities of communication specialists: (1) surveillance of the environment, (2) correlation of the parts of society in responding to the environment, and (3) transmission of the social heritage from one generation to the next." To these, Wright added a fourth, entertainment.

These have become known as the Classic Four Functions of the Media, and we'll discuss them later, but what's more important immediately is how this linkage to functions influenced the development of active-audience theories.

Although Wright cautioned his readers to distinguish "between the consequences (functions) of a social activity and the aims or purposes behind the activity (p. 16)," *functions* were assumed by most communication theorists to be equivalent to (synonymous with) the aims or goals of the media industries themselves. As explained in Chapter 8, functionalism became equated with legitimation of the status quo. To the extent that active-audience notions were linked to functionalism, they were seen by critics as merely another way to rationalize the way things are.

Let's use the Classic Four Functions as an example. *Surveillance of the environment* refers to the media's collection and distribution of information. We know who was elected governor of Illinois because it was in the newspaper and we know whether or not to wear a sweater to school because the radio weatherperson said that it would be chilly today. *Correlation of parts of society* refers to the media's interpretive or analytical activities. We know that the failure of the Highway Bond Proposition means that gasoline taxes will rise to cover necessary road repair because of the editorial in the Sunday paper. *Transmission of the social heritage* relates to the media's ability to communicate values, norms, and styles across time and between groups. What were typical attitudes toward women in the 1930s? What did a normal American home look like in the 1950s? Any of two hundred old movies can answer the former question and "Leave It To Beaver" and "Father Knows Best" answer the latter. What's happening in French fashion today? Pick up a recent copy of *Paris Match*. Finally, *entertainment* means media's ability to entertain or amuse.

These seem like perfectly reasonable aims of the media; but there is a problem. These may be *aims* of given media organizations, but may not necessarily be the functions they serve for the people who consume those media, and these functions may be different from the intended uses of audience members. For example, you may intentionally watch an old black and white gangster movie to be entertained and you might even learn (unintentionally) a bit about how people at the time viewed lawlessness. But you might also, in the course of watching, inadvertently learn how to use a pistol. The filmmaker's aim was to entertain, but the use (the purpose) to which you ultimately put the content was much different. Transmission of the cultural heritage occurred (although that was not the filmmaker's aim), as did some learning of potentially dangerous behavior (although that, too, was no one's aim). In other words, the aim is not always the ultimate function. If we confine our research to an investigation of functions intended by media practitioners (their aims), we are likely to ignore many negative effects. Since much early functional analysis was restricted to *intended* functions (again, aims), critics have charged that it is too apologetic to the media industries.

Wright, realizing how his functions were misinterpreted, later wrote (1974, p. 205),

> Our working quartet of communications—surveillance, correlation, cultural transmission, and entertainment—was intended to refer to common kinds of activities that might or might not be carried out as mass communications or as private, personal communications. These activities were not synonymous for functions, which . . . refer to the consequences of routinely carrying out such communication activities through the institutionalized processes of mass communications.

To clarify even further, he added that in understanding how functionalism relates to mass communication, it is necessary to draw a distinction between functions (the consequences of routinely carrying out communication activities) and the effects of those activities.

The surveillance activity, its functions in our society, and the effects of those functions offer a good example of how functionalism was intended to be applied to media studies (and uses and gratifications). Newspapers and television news devote great amounts of energy and effort to covering political campaigns and delivering the product of that effort to their audiences. If readers and viewers ignore (that is, fail to use) the reports, no communication happens and the intended functions fail to occur. But if readers and viewers do consume the reports, then the intended function we've been calling surveillance of the environment should take place. Thus, media cannot serve their intended function unless people make certain uses of their content. For surveillance to occur, routine transmission of news information about key events must be accompanied by active audience use that results in widespread learning about those events. Thus, news media can achieve this societal level function only if enough audience members are willing and able to make certain uses of content.

As was implied in our earlier discussion of libertarianism (Chapter 5), one historically important and widely intended function of public communication is the creation and maintenance of an enlightened and knowledgeable electorate, one capable of governing itself. But many of us might argue that most current day news media transmit "infotainment" that actually serves a negative function (a dysfunction) in that it produces ill-educated citizens or citizens who actually become *less* involved in the political process because they substitute pseudo-involvement in overdramatized media depictions of campaign spectacles for actual involvement in real campaign activities (Edelman, 1988).

What we've done here, though, is confused intended functions with unintended effects, just as Wright warned us against. The intended function of the reporting of those events and our intended use of the reports may be consistent with a normative theory (libertarianism) that underlies our political and media system. The effects of that activity, however, may well be something completely different. As campaigns cater more and more to the time, economic, and aesthetic demands of the broadcast media (less complexity, more staging of campaign spectacles, less talk about complex and controversial issues, more reliance on negative ads, and so on), voters may become repelled by politics, which may create disrespect for government and increase the influence of well-organized special interest groups. Voters use of media can gradually change so that instead of seeking information that isn't there, they turn to media for the mesmerizing spectacles that are available. In this example, the intended function of media hasn't changed but its practical consequences have. Such gaps between intended functions and observed effects have impressed media critics and led them to be suspicious both of functional analysis and of theories that presume an active audience, those that can be categorized under what is now called the *uses and gratification approach.*

We will return to functional analysis in the next chapter and provide the latest formulation of it. Most researchers who use this approach today have adopted a systems-theory perspective, which allows a much clearer differentiation of various levels of analysis that were often confused in early functionalist theories.

Revival of the Uses and Gratifications Approach

Interest in the study of the audience's uses of the media and the gratifications it receives from them was rekindled during the 1970s as a response to the inconsequential and overqualified findings of run-of-the-mill effects research. As we have discussed earlier, by 1970 most of the important tenets of the limited effects paradigm had been worked out and demonstrated in study after study. In all of this research, media's role was found to be marginal in comparison with other social factors. But how could this be true when media audiences were so vast and so many people spent so much time consuming media? In particular, why were network television audiences continuing to grow? Didn't any of this media use have important consequences for the people who were engaging in it? If so, why didn't effects research document this influence? Was it overlooking something—and if so, what?

The limited effects paradigm had become so dominant that it was hard to ask questions about media that weren't stated in terms of measurable effects. There just didn't seem to be anything else worth studying. But if researchers restricted their research to the study of effects, all they could obtain would be predictable, modest, highly qualified results. Though they were frustrated by this situation, few could see any practical alternative.

The revival of interest in the uses and gratifications approach can be traced to three developments — one methodological and two theoretical:

1 **New survey research methods and data analysis techniques allowed important new strategies for conducting studies of and interpreting audience uses and gratifications to be developed.** Innovative questionnaires were developed that allowed people's reasons for using media to be measured more systematically and objectively. At the same time, new data analysis techniques provided more objective procedures for developing categories and for assigning reasons to them. These developments overcame some of the most serious methodological criticisms of earlier research.

2 **During the 1970s there was increasing awareness among some media researchers that people's active use of media might be an important mediating factor that made effects more or less likely.** These researchers argued that a member of an active audience can decide whether certain media effects are desirable and set out to achieve those effects. For example, you may have decided to read this book to learn about media theories. You intend the book to have this effect upon you and you work to induce the effect. If you lack this intent, use of the book is less likely to result in learning. Does the book cause you to learn? Or do you make it serve this purpose for you? If you hold the latter view, then you share the perspective of uses and gratifications theorists.

3 **Some researchers began expressing growing concern that effects research was focusing too much on unintended, negative effects of media while intended, positive uses of media were being ignored.** By 1975, we knew a lot about the influence of television violence on small segments of the audience but much less about the ways in which people were able to make media do things for them that they wanted.

Measuring Uses and Gratifications

How, then, does one measure the audience's media use and the gratifications it garners from that activity in a scientifically acceptable manner? Moreover, how does one do these things while avoiding the "sins" of the effects researchers (things like artificial laboratory settings and small samples of readers, listeners or viewers)? Surveys. That is, query large numbers of people about their media usage in more naturalistic settings (for example, their homes).

The product of this inquiry was, as might be expected, a number of lists of uses people make of the media and lists of the gratifications they seek from that use. As a counter to the source-dominated perspective, this work served a valuable purpose: it turned attention to audience members and gave them a voice in mass communication theory. Moreover, as Denis McQuail (1987, p. 73) claimed, this "growing inventory of gratifications, satisfactions and uses . . . shows a convincing degree of patterned regularity and predictability." In other words, the various surveys of various samples at various times showed enough consistency that researchers could be confident that their findings had some validity. But many critics of uses and gratifications see this as a shortcoming, and their criticism has several dimensions.

First, what do these lists tell us, for example, about the effects of using the media for "finding a basis for conversation and social interaction" (from McQuail's 1972 inventory). One response is that uses and gratifications is not particularly interested in effects, but offers a useful alternative to effects studies. Uses and gratifications research is concerned with what people want from and choose to do with media and media content. As Jack McLeod and Lee Becker (1981, p. 68) argued, "In limited effects models, although an individual was more autonomous as cast by the earlier powerful-media 'hypodermic' effects models, the person was active only in the sense of seeking consonant and avoiding discrepant information. The uses and gratifications research presents a much more positive image. The person follows his/her interests, choosing media content according to needs and synthesizes that content to satisfy those needs." Rather than being passively manipulated by media, individuals use media to induce effects that they desire.

A second criticism has to do with how uses and gratifications research is conducted. For one thing, it is difficult and expensive to demonstrate causality with surveys. Costly field experiments or long-term panel studies are needed. Since most uses and gratifications research is done on low budgets using surveys done at one point in time, no conclusive evidence can be found for causal relationships. Researchers are instead satisfied to find empirical associations that are interesting or fit their theoretical expectations. Although this research is considered inadequate or too elementary by some standards for social research, it has provided useful insight into media use.

Surveys of people's media uses and habits can happen in two general ways, each troubling to critics of uses and gratifications thinking. People are sometimes given lists of media uses and gratifications (even those drawn "from the literature . . . supplemented by additional items, based on our own insights into the specific functions of the media," as Elihu Katz, Michael Gurevitch, and Hadassah Haas, 1973, wrote) and asked to evaluate how important each item is to them or how central each is to their personal media use. But aren't folks completing these surveys responding to the researchers' cues? How many would say on their own, "Oh, yeah, I use television to learn about things I haven't done before?"

The second way these surveys are conducted is to simply ask people open-ended questions about media use and let them construct their own replies. The problems with this procedure are both practical and theoretical. From the practical viewpoint, researchers must still categorize based, obviously, on their own notions and values. The 1972 McQuail inventory already mentioned is an example. Among his "uses of the media" were the categories Sexual Arousal, Emotional Release, Filling Time, Getting Intrinsic Cultural or Aesthetic Enjoyment, Relaxing, Escaping From Problems, and Having a Substitute for Real-Life Companionship. All fairly common uses of the media. But where would you, if you were the researcher, put a young woman's freely offered response of "I watch 'Baywatch' to check out the good-looking guys?"

The theoretical problem in conducting these "open-ended" uses and gratifications surveys is a bit more difficult. The critics' point is a simple one: they refuse to believe that media audiences are very active or reflective. If you confront people with questions about media use, they will work hard to provide answers. If you give them lists of uses, they will choose some. But these answers and choices may well be meaningless; nothing more than post hoc rationalizations. They don't conclusively demonstrate that people actually think about their use of media and they can't establish that people's choices are based upon some personally important need or gratification. Thus, for those theorists who are skeptical about audience activity, this research proves little. They continue to reject the basic assumptions of uses and gratifications theory and regard its research findings as mere artifacts of the methods used to produce them.

The Active Audience Revisited

Are media audiences active? Mark Levy and Sven Windahl attempted to put the issue in perspective by writing:

> As commonly understood by gratifications researchers, the term "audience activity" postulates a voluntaristic and selective orientation by audiences toward the communication process. In brief, it suggests that media use is motivated by needs and goals that are defined by audience members themselves, and that active participation in the communication process may facilitate, limit, or otherwise influence the gratifications and effects associated with exposure. Current thinking also suggests that audience activity is best conceptualized as a variable construct, with audiences exhibiting varying kinds and degrees of activity (1985, p. 110).

Jay G. Blumler (1979) claimed that one problem in the development of a strong uses and gratifications tradition is the "extraordinary range of meanings" given to the concept of "activity." He identified several meanings for the term, including

- **Utility**: Media have uses for people and people can put media to those uses.
- **Intentionality**: Consumption of media content can be directed by people's prior motivations.
- **Selectivity**: People's use of media may reflect their existing interests and preferences.
- **Imperviousness to influence**: Audience members are obstinate; they may not want to be controlled by anyone or anything, even mass media. They actively avoid certain types of media influence.

Blumler's list summarized the forms of audience activity that the early uses and gratifications researchers studied. They related to overall choices of content and media use patterns. They did not, however, consider what people actually did with media content once they had chosen it. Recent research has begun to focus on this type of audience activity—the manner in which people *actively impose meaning* on content and *construct new meaning* that serves their purposes better than any meaning that might have been intended by the message producer or distributor. The television program "All In The Family" is a good example. Creator Norman Lear and his writers may have intended their show to be satire, poking fun at narrow-mindedness and bigotry, but a substantial portion of the audience chose not to look at it that way—the meaning that many people made from Archie Bunker's battles with his politically and socially liberal son-in-law was something completely different. They "read" Archie as correct and Mike as a dumb bleeding heart.

Two ways to clarify the issue are to distinguish between "activity" and "activeness" and to see the "active audience" as a relative concept. "Activity" and "activeness" are related, but the former refers more to what the audience does (for example, chooses to read the newspaper rather than watch television news), and the latter is more what the uses and gratifications people had in mind—that is, the audience's freedom and autonomy in the mass communication situation. This activeness, no doubt, is relative. Some audience members are more active, some are more passive. This is obvious; we all know too many couch potatoes, people who live their lives through the movies, or people who bend to every fad and fashion presented in the mass media. But we also know many people who fit none of these descriptions. An inactive user can become active. Our level of activity may vary by time of day and by type of content. We may be active users of books by day and passive consumers of late night movies.

What the uses and gratifications approach really does, then, is provide a framework for understanding when and how different media consumers become more or less active and what the consequences of that increased or decreased involvement may be.

The classic articulation of this framework remains that offered by Katz, Blumler, and Gurevitch (1974). These theorists detailed five elements, or basic assumptions, of the uses and gratifications model:

1 **The audience is active and its media use is goal oriented.** We've seen some confusion about exactly what is meant by "active," but clearly various audience members bring various levels of activity to their consumption (if nothing else, at least in choice of preferred medium in given situations or preferred content within a given medium).

2 **The initiative in linking his or her need gratification to a specific media choice rests with the audience member.** Francis Ford Coppola, or even Marlon Brando can't force you to see *Godfather III.* Dan Rather and Tom Brokaw cannot compel you to be a news junkie.

3 **The media compete with other sources for need satisfaction.** This is what Klapper meant when he said that media function "through a nexus of mediating factors and influences." Simply put, the media and their audiences do not exist in a vacuum. They are part of the larger society and obviously the relationship between media and audiences is influenced by events in that environment. If all of your needs for information and entertainment are being satisfied by conversations with your friends, then you are much less likely to turn on a television set or pick up a newspaper. When students enter college, their media use tends to sharply decline. In this new environment, media don't compete as well.

4 **People are self-aware enough of their own media use, interests, and motives to be able to provide researchers with an accurate picture of that use.** This, as we've seen earlier, is a methodological issue that is debated. As research methods are refined, however, researchers should be able to offer better evidence of people's awareness of media use. Evidence suggests that as media choices grow with the continued diffusion of technologies like VCRs and cable, people are being forced to become more conscious of their media use. You can blunder into watching television shows by flipping on a channel and leaving the set tuned to one station all night. But if you pay money to rent a video, you are more likely to make an active choice. You don't pick the first tape on the shelf. You scan over rows of tapes, weigh the merits of one versus another, read the backs of video boxes, and then settle on a tape. Your choice is much more likely to reflect your interests than when you "zone out" viewing one channel.

5 **Value judgments of the audience's linking its needs to specific media or content should be suspended.** For example, the "harmful effects" of consumer product advertising on our culture's values may only be harmful in the researcher's eyes. If audience members want those ads to help them decide what's "cool," that's their decision. This is perhaps the most problematic of Katz and his associates' assertions. Their point is that people can use the same content in very different ways and therefore the same content could have very different consequences. Viewing movies that show violent treatment of minorities could reinforce some people's negative attitudes and lead others to be more supportive of minority rights—remember our earlier example of the uses made of Archie Bunker. Although news reports of Rodney King being beaten by Los Angeles police will lead some to say that he got what he deserved, others worry that an erosion of his rights could eventually threaten their own. Each of us constructs our own meaning of such reports and that meaning ultimately influences what we think and do.

This synopsis of the perspective's basic assumptions raises several questions. What factors affect an audience member's level of activeness or her or his awareness of media use? What are the other things in the environment that influence the creation or maintenance of the audience's needs and their judgments of which media use will best meet those needs? Katz, Blumler, and Gurevitch (1974, p. 27) argued that the "social situations" that people find themselves in can be "involved in the generation of media-related needs" in any of the following ways:

1 **Social situations can produce tensions and conflicts, leading to pressure for their easement through the consumption of media.** You're going dancing with a group of friends next weekend, so you plan a steady diet of MTV so you can pick up on the latest steps, or you rent a video of *Dirty Dancing*, or you borrow a friend's magazine with an article on dance fads.

2 **Social situations can create an awareness of problems that demand attention, information about which may be sought in the media.** In our dance example, you notice that the most popular people in your circle of friends are those who are the most socially outgoing; you also see that they get invited to do things that you do not. You increase your consumption of style and fashion magazines to better understand the social scene.

3 **Social situations can impoverish real-life opportunities to satisfy certain needs, and the media can serve as substitutes or supplements.** Your student budget does not allow you to buy the "in" clothes or to pay the cover charge at the dance club, so MTV's "Dance Party" keeps you company on Saturday night. When you move to a new city, you may use media as a substitute until you make new friends.

4 **Social situations often elicit specific values, and their affirmation and reinforcement can be facilitated by the consumption of related media materials.** The fact that you are a single, young adult in college often means that you are part of a group that values dancing. And if you want to be reassured that is true, just check out VH1, MTV, "Soul Train," and most made-for-TV movies. These programs also promote dancing and will reinforce your attitude toward dancing.

5 Social situations can provide realms of expectations of familiarity with media, which must be met to sustain membership in specific social groups. What? You don't watch MTV? You don't know the name of Paul McCartney's backup band before he formed Wings? You haven't seen the latest dating flick?

Of course, if you see media as important sources of effects, you might ask if the mass media themselves might not have been instrumental in creating certain social situations (such as the one in our example) *and* for making the satisfaction of those situation's attendant needs so crucial *and* for making themselves, the media, the most convenient and effective means of gratifying those needs. But that is not of concern in uses and gratifications thinking, since the members of the audience personally and actively determine what gratifications of what needs will and will not occur from their own exposure to media messages. Cultural and critical cultural theorists disagree with this position, as we'll see in Chapters 12 and 13.

Play Theory

An excellent example of one approach to media that is compatible with the uses and gratifications approach is William Stephenson's *Play Theory of Mass Communication*. Stephenson (1967) proceeded from two basic assumptions. The first assumption is that the mass media and people interact in two ways. One is *social control*, which is manifested in our "inner beliefs and values." He identified these beliefs and values to be religion, customs, and political orientations. In addition, he argued that if media had any impact on these personally important values, it was in the realm of public opinion and, more important, that effect was limited: "From its beginnings, in 1924 or so, mass communication theory has concerned itself primarily with how the mass media influence the attitudes, beliefs, and actions of people. There was little evidence . . . however, that the mass media had any significant effects on the deeper or more important beliefs of people" (1967, p. 1). According to Stephenson, the second way that people and media interact is *convergent selectivity*, "new or non-customary modes of behavior, our fads and fancies, that allow us opportunities to exist for ourselves, to please ourselves, free to a degree from social control" (1967, p. 2).

His second important assumption was that people seek *communication pleasure*, "which holds that play has little gain for the player except self-enhancement." Audiences engage in what he called *subjective play*, for example media consumption, which produces personal (or subjective) self-satisfaction. He argued, therefore, that the "daily mix" of media content is repetitious, like a child's game, played over and over with variations on a number of recognizable themes. This means no work ("communication unpleasure") for the audience. But he saw this not as a flight from reality or as escapism. Rather, he viewed media as serving as a buffer against pressures of the real world that otherwise cause people anxiety. In this sense, he echoed Mendelsohn's mass entertainment ideas.

Stephenson offered advertising as the model for the media's convergent selectivity function of meeting audience "wants." His position was that commercial messages gratified people's desires by providing a range of choices from which they could select those things that brought them personal satisfaction: "When one buys this or that toothpaste, car, or cookie, one has a certain freedom to decide for himself, under conditions not available to him before" (1967, p. 2). Remember that Stephenson developed these ideas during the 1950s and 1960s when he worked as a consultant to advertising agencies. His theory provides a powerful rationalization for advertising. By playing up various options for product purchases, advertising makes those purchases more meaningful to us. It can bring meaning to an otherwise routine task. Imagine what it would be like to go into a supermarket stocked exclusively with generic products packaged in white boxes. There would only be one type of toothpaste and one type of soap. How much satisfaction would you get from picking up various generic items?

From a uses and gratifications point of view, it is quite logical for people to enjoy learning about consumption choices and then experience pleasure as they make these choices. Many people feel they need to know about fashions and they enjoy using media to keep up on them. Similarly, people enjoy using media to follow trends in other products from toothpaste to computers and cars. Play theory does not address questions like *why* people think they need to follow these trends or how self-satisfaction can reside in the choice of one cookie rather than another, or how advertising (and the media that carry it) have helped create a situation where such things matter at all (would you serve generic beer and potato chips at a party and if you did, would you hide the cans and bags?). Nor is Stephenson's assertion that play is "largely unproductive" without serious challenge, but these are issues for other parts of this book (see Chapter 12 for a critical theory perspective) and for you to evaluate yourself. What is important here is that play theory fits neatly into what is generally considered to be the uses and gratifications tradition: people use media to have personally important needs gratified and thus to some extent control any effects that may occur.

Uses and Gratifications and Effects

Some contemporary proponents of uses and gratifications argue that one enduring challenge for their school of thought is to make a link from gratifications to effects. Sven Windahl (1981) argued that a merger of uses and gratifications and the effects traditions was overdue and proposed what he called a "uses and effects" model that viewed the product of the use of media content as

Names

"conseffects." In a similar vein, Phillip Palmgreen, Lawrence Wenner, and Karl Rosengren (1985, p. 31) wrote, "studies have shown that a variety of audience gratifications (again, both sought and obtained) are related to a wide spectrum of media effects, including knowledge, dependency, attitudes, perceptions of social reality, agenda-setting, discussion, and various political effects variables."

and Blumler (1979) also presented his ideas on how the uses and gratifications and effects approaches could be harmonized. You'll notice that his perspective still centers responsibility for the control of effects with the consumer as opposed to the media. He wrote:

> How might propositions about media effects be generated from . . . gratifications? First, we may postulate that cognitive motivation will facilitate information gain . . . Second, media consumption for purposes of diversion and escape will favour audience acceptance of perceptions of social situations in line with portrayals frequently found in entertainment materials . . . Third, involvement in media materials for personal identity reasons is likely to promote reinforcement effects (pp. 18–19).

Three other recent theories that can be linked to active audience thinking — media system dependency theory, agenda-setting and the spiral of silence — provide useful examples of how the uses and gratifications approach can be related to questions of effects.

Media System Dependency Theory

In its simplest terms, media system dependency theory assumes that the more dependent a person is on having his or her needs gratified by media use, the more important will be the role media play in the person's life and, therefore, the more influence those media will have on that person. From a macroscopic, societal perspective, if more and more people become dependent upon media, then the overall influence of media will rise and media's role in society will become more central. Thus, there should be a direct relationship between the amount of overall dependency and the degree of media influence or centrality at any given point in time. Melvin DeFleur and Sandra Ball-Rokeach have provided a fuller explanation.

DeFleur and Ball-Rokeach presented a number of assertions (1975, pp. 261–263). First, the *"basis of media influence lies in the relationship between the larger social system, the media's role in that system, and audience relationships to the media."* Effects occur, not because all-powerful media or omnipotent sources will that occurrence, but because the media operate in a given way in a given social system to meet given audience wants and needs.

Second, *"the degree of audience dependence on media information is the key variable in understanding when and why media messages alter audience beliefs, feelings, or behavior."* The ultimate occurrence and shape of media effects rests with the audience members and is related to how necessary a given medium or media message is to them. The uses people make of media determine their influence.

Third, *in our industrial society, we are becoming increasingly dependent on the media (a) to understand the social world, (b) to act meaningfully and effectively in society, and (c) for fantasy and escape.* As our world becomes more complex, we not only need the media to a greater degree to help us make sense, to help us understand what our best responses may be, and to help us relax and cope, but also we ultimately come to know that world largely *through* those media. Note the emphasis on meaning making in this assertion. As we use media to make sense of the social world, we permit media to shape our expectations.

Finally, fourth, *"the greater the need and consequently the stronger the dependency . . . the greater the likelihood"* that the media and their messages will have an *effect.* Not everyone will be equally influenced by media. Those who have greater needs and thus greater dependency on media will be most influenced.

If we remember our discussion of what constitutes an active audience, we know that the best way to think of activity is to think of it as existing on a continuum, from totally inactive media consumers to totally active ones. DeFleur and Ball-Rokeach, because they tied audience activity to audience dependence, described media dependency in just that way. Moreover, they explained that an individual's (or society's) level of dependency is a function of (a) *"the number and centrality (importance) of the specific information-delivery functions served by a medium"* and (b) the degree of change and conflict present in society.

These assertions can be illustrated by an example involving media use during a crisis situation. Think of your own media use the last time you found yourself in a natural crisis, in other words, in a time of change or conflict (earthquake, tornado, hurricane, or serious rain or snow storm). Or what about your media use during a social crisis such as the Gulf War or the South-Central Los Angeles riots? You probably spent more time watching the television news and weather reports than you did watching comedy shows. But consider what would have happened if the electricity had failed during such a crisis. Then, the "number and centrality of television's information delivery functions" instantly would be reduced to a level below that of your transistor radio. So radio and radio news might become your medium and content of choice, respectively. And no doubt, if the crises deepened, your dependence would increase. So also might your attentiveness and willingness to respond as "directed" by that medium and its messages. For example, one aspect of the South-Central Los Angeles riots that we

Box 10a Fitting Theory to Reality: The Active Audience in Times of Crisis

by Kimberly B. Massey, Ph.D., Assistant Professor of Radio-TV-Film at San Jose State University in San Jose, California.

As you've been proceeding through this book of theories you might have stopped at some point and asked, "But which is the *correct* one? Are older theories (like rock bands) better just because they've withstood the test of time? Or are newer theories more complete because they take into account changes that have occurred in society and technology?" What should you believe? Which theory is right? And why do you have to know about so many anyway?

The answer to these questions may not make you feel any better: **It depends**.

When the 1989 Loma Prieta Earthquake hit the San Francisco Bay Area on October 17th, I was teaching at San Jose State University. It was fascinating to actually be a participant in a major news story while it was being covered by the mass media. By coincidence, I had given my class an assignment the week before in which I asked them to keep a media consumption diary. When we returned to campus ten days after the quake, most of my students had completed the task despite the fact that they, too, had been victims of the quake. I had stumbled into a media research project. I found myself with important data and I had to make a decision about what to do with it.

This is where theory comes into the picture. Obviously, looking at media coverage during crisis or disaster is not a new idea. In fact, there are numerous ways to approach such studies. Because of my data set (the media diaries), however, I was most interested in how audiences interacted with the media, so audience-oriented theory became my focus.

Media system dependency theorists, in particular, actually use disasters as an example of a high degree of structural instability that they claim increases the potential for mass media messages to achieve effects. But I was not interested in dependency's concentration on the interrelationships between audiences, media and society; I wanted a more micro-level understanding of the audience's media use. So I chose uses and gratifications with its focus on audience activity and use of media which is what my data represented: the quantity and quality of media consumption before, during, and after the quake.

So you see, it really does depend. It depends on where you are. It depends on what you know. It depends on the questions you ask. And the more options you have, especially when it comes to theory, the more clearly and confidently you can proceed. Good luck, future media scholars!

don't understand very well is the way different people used news broadcasts to guide their actions. Limited effects theory tells us that the coverage most likely didn't stimulate vast numbers of people to riot. But it is likely that many people turned to media, interpreted what they were told, and then acted. Some rushed to the scene while others left town. Most sat in front of their television sets. If coverage had been structured differently, could these actions have been changed?

Could potential rioters have been encouraged to be more responsible? Could others have been encouraged to take actions that would have stabilized the situation without endangering their lives?

Now consider your life as you moved into your teen years. Talk about change and conflict! The media were important in helping you determine any one of a thousand aspects of how to act meaningfully, to know what was happening, and for simple relief or escape.

DeFleur and Ball-Rokeach (1989, for example) refined and expanded their media system dependency theory a number of times to account for such "system change," but their thesis never varied much beyond their initial assertion that media can and do have powerful effects, even as explained in their theory, a uses and gratifications-oriented point of view. Dependency theory has more advantages and limitations than other uses and gratifications theories. Media dependency has been measured in a variety of ways and each has its drawbacks. It has not yet been conclusively demonstrated that the experience of media dependency by average people is strongly related to a broad range of effects. Can we be dependent upon media without experiencing dependency? Can we experience dependency when we are actually quite independent? Is this theory better at explaining the consequences of short-term, situationally induced dependency (that is, reaction to a crisis) rather than long-term, chronic dependency? Finally, the theory doesn't directly address the question of whether there is some ideal level of media dependency. Are Americans currently too dependent on media or too independent? Is the trend toward increased or decreased dependency? Will new media increase our dependency or make us more independent?

Accommodating the Limited Effects View

The same social, cultural, and political upheaval that moved the social learning theorists to expand their investigations of television's impact on individual social behavior (Chapter 9) also reinvigorated political communication and public opinion theorists' interest in media effects, especially those of news. With 30 or so years of hindsight we now can reasonably wonder why that interest ever waned. But we must remember that the limited effects perspective dominated thinking about media impact in this area as well. Lazarsfeld's voter studies and Hovland's propaganda and attitude research were influential throughout the 1960s and into the 1970s. Media were seen, at most, as *reinforcers* of attitude and opinion and rarely, if ever, as agents of change.

Throughout the relatively placid 1950s, a decade of unusual political stability, economic expansion, social calm, and uniform national pride, most social researchers could sustain their view of media as a secondary, largely benevolent force. The Red Scare raised questions about media's role but ultimately media, through the actions of Edward R. Murrow, met the challenge and halted McCarthy's threat. Media demonstrated social responsibility by participating in efforts to establish a national civil defense network. In most cities, competing, politically partisan newspapers disappeared, to be replaced by more responsible, though homogenized, monopoly newspapers. Television was in its infancy and not yet a source of major concern. After all, the wealthy people who could afford to buy television sets could be trusted to use it wisely. Most threats to social stability were external rather than internal.

The 1960s, though, forced a reconsideration of our beliefs about ourselves as a people, our media, and our political system. The media, especially with the rapid diffusion of television, were increasingly suspected of undermining social stability. Civil rights protests and ugly racist reactions filled the country's television screens. Rising crime statistics screamed from the front pages of newspapers. News magazines presented analyses of a seemingly interminable jungle war in Vietnam. Music changed. Drugs became a national concern. Young people appeared to be beyond control. The cities were set afire by unruly mobs. Police beat young people in front of television cameras at the Democratic National Party Convention in Chicago, and National Guardsmen killed college students at Kent State and Jackson State. Photos of the carnage were the front covers of *Time* and *Newsweek* and film was broadcast at 6 and 11.

All this put many mass communication theorists in a difficult position. James Lemert (1981, p. 6) wrote succinctly that social scientists were "beginning to reflect dissatisfaction with the ability of the traditional media effects approach to account for the social impact of mass media." In other words, even those steeped in the traditional scientific methods and committed to the traditional findings of the masters (Lazarsfeld, Hovland, Merton, Klapper) needed to explain the profound changes in the body politic that were becoming increasingly impossible to ignore. The groundbreaking work of those who had come before, however, could not be completely discarded. Science, especially social science, does not operate that way. Therefore, the political communication and public opinion theorists started investigating whether there could be important media effects while supporting the limited effects theories. They did this in two ways. First, some investigators shifted their attention from affective (attitude) and behavioral effects toward cognitive (knowledge) effects (Becker, et. al., 1975). Second, others began to change their research focus from the micro, personal effects level to the macro, societal effects level. The research reviewed later in this chapter and in Chapter 11 illustrates both of these trends.

Accommodating the dominant paradigm was indeed a formidable task for several reasons. To admit powerful media was to challenge not only years of scientific evidence to the contrary, but also to raise again the mass society threats that had been dismissed as irresponsible speculation. Still, this, in and of itself, was not the problem. If science could show otherwise, then so be it. The real obstacle was what Lemert called "the accumulated mental habits of decades of social research." We can see the bases of these mental habits in the well-known works of the researchers we called "the masters" earlier.

The measure of media effects for Lazarsfeld in the Voter Studies was *voting*, a behavior. Therefore, the inability to demonstrate a link between specific media messages and that specific behavior was tantamount to demonstrating the absence of media influence. The measure of effects for the attitude change research of Hovland's Yale Group was just that, attitude change. Therefore, the inability to demonstrate a consistent, enduring link between specific media messages, specific attitudes, and subsequent actions was tantamount to demonstrating the absence of media influence. Klapper, reviewing decades of scientific literature dominated by these social science mental habits (and conducted before the true advent of television), concluded that media are not normally sufficient cause of effects and that, if media had any effects at all, they were more than likely in the direction of reinforcement rather than change. But what else could he have concluded if accepting the presence of effects was dependent upon demonstrating conclusively that there were strong causal links between use of media, specific attitudes, and specific actions? Moreover, why was reinforcement not considered an effect, and a powerful one at that? And what if attitudinal or behavioral changes were shown? Klapper (1960, p. 8) wrote, "There are certain residual situations in which mass communication seems to produce direct effects, or directly and of itself, to serve certain psycho-physical functions." In other words, when effects did occur they were an anomaly, a departure.

What had occurred during the time that the limited effects paradigm dominated was that those working under its umbrella set a standard for themselves that they had to meet to accept the presence of media effects. But they left unanswered two important questions:

- Was observable behavioral or attitudinal change the only or best valid measure of media influence?

- Was the failure to demonstrate causal links between media use and various actions evidence of the absence of effects or rather was it evidence of researchers' inability to measure effects that did exist?

Two theories, agenda-setting and the spiral of silence, attempted to accommodate the philosophy of the limited effects perspective while addressing these questions. We'll deal with agenda-setting first, because as Stephen Littlejohn (1989, p. 272) argued, "It returns a degree of power to the media after an era in which media effects were thought to be minimal (and) second, its focus on cognitive effects rather than attitude and opinion change adds a badly needed dimension to effects research." As we review both theories, we will describe the many criticisms made of them. The amount of criticism they inspired is an indicator of how much they challenged the dominant paradigm. Read the criticisms carefully and form your own views of the relative usefulness of each. Both are still widely used and deserve attention. In Chapter 14, we will consider how a new paradigm could emerge from an integration of these and the theories presented in the next chapter.

Agenda-Setting

What were the crucial issues in the 1992 Presidential campaign? The United States was faced with a budget deficit that exceeded all the previous deficits combined. The recession refused to end. Dictators like Khadafy in Libya and Saddam Hussein in Iraq continued to consolidate their power and destabilize the Middle East. Proponents of a woman's right to reproductive choice clashed angrily and frequently with those who saw abortion as murder. The inner cities were in decay. American educational standards were diminishing. Billions were being spent on weapons systems despite the end of the Cold War. What do you remember from the mass media as the important issues and images of that campaign? What do you remember as the most important issues? The debate over Murphy Brown's single-motherhood? Candidate Bush visiting a supermarket? Candidate Clinton's marital and draft board difficulties? H. Ross Perot's efforts to escape the Navy because the sailors around him cursed? Of all the issues that should or could have been aired and examined, only a few became dominate. This is agenda-setting.

With or without the label, the idea of agenda-setting has been with us since the days of the penny press. Walter Lippmann, in *Public Opinion*, argued that the people do not deal directly with their environments as much as they respond to "pictures" in their heads. He wrote (1922, p. 16), "For the real environment is altogether too big, too complex, and too fleeting for direct acquaintance. We are not equipped to deal with so much subtlety, so much variety, so many permutations and combinations. And although we have to act in that environment, we have to reconstruct it on a simpler model before we can manage with it." If you remember our discussion of Lippmann in Chapters 4 and 5, then you know that he concluded that average people just can't be trusted to make important political decisions based on these simplified pictures. They have to be protected and the important decisions have to be made by technocrats who use better models to guide their actions. Thus, modern agenda-setting notions derive more or less directly from a mass society perspective. Critics have noted this connection.

Although he did not specifically use the term itself, Bernard Cohen is generally credited with refining Lippmann's ideas into the theory of agenda-setting. He wrote (1963, p. 13), "The press is significantly more than a purveyor of information and opinion. It may not be successful much of the time in telling people what to think, but it is stunningly successful in telling its readers what to think *about.* And it follows from this that the world looks different to different people, depending not only on their personal interests, but also on the map that is drawn for them by the writers, editors, and publishers of the papers they read." Parenthetically, it's hard to ignore the limited effects bias in Cohen's thinking. He first argued that the press is rarely successful in telling people what to think, but then said that the world looks different to different people depending on what the press offers them. Another way of interpreting this is that Cohen took a mass society perspective and revised it to make it compatible with the limited effects paradigm.

Cohen's writing became the basis for what we now call the agenda-setting function of the mass media. This perspective might have lingered in obscurity had it not been empirically confirmed by research conducted by Maxwell E. McCombs and Donald Shaw. They articulated their interpretation of agenda-setting (1972, p. 176): "In choosing and displaying news, editors, newsroom staff, and broadcasters play an important part in shaping political reality. Readers learn not only about a given issue, but how much importance to attach to that issue from the amount of information in a news story and its position . . . The mass media may well determine the important issues — that is, the media may set the 'agenda' of the campaign."

During September and October of the presidential election of 1968, these researchers interviewed one hundred registered voters who had not yet committed to either candidate (presumably these people would be more open to media messages). By asking each respondent "to outline the key issues as he saw them, regardless of what the candidates might be saying at the moment," they were able to identify and rank by importance just what these people thought were the crucial issues facing them. Then, these results were compared to a ranking of the time and space accorded to various issues produced by a content analysis of the television news, newspapers, newsmagazines, and editorial pages available to voters in the area where the study was conducted. The results? "The media appear to have exerted a considerable impact on voters' judgments of what they considered the major issues of the campaign . . . The correlation between the major item emphasis on the main campaign issues carried by the media and voters' independent judgments of what were the important issues was +.967," they wrote, continuing, "In short, the data suggest a very strong relationship between the emphasis placed on different campaign issues by the media . . . and the judgments of voters as to the salience and importance of various campaign topics" (McCombs and Shaw, 1972, p. 180–181).

This important and straight forward study highlights both the strengths and weaknesses of agenda-setting as a theory of media effects. It clearly establishes that there is an important relationship between media reports and the people's ranking of public issues. On the negative side, we can see that the logic of agenda-setting seems well suited for the question of news and campaigns, but what of other kinds of content and other kinds of effects? More important, though, is the question of the actual nature of the relationship between news and its audience. Maybe the public sets the media's agenda and then the media reinforce it. The McCombs and Shaw analysis, like most early agenda-setting research, implies a direction of influence from media to audience—that is, it implies causality. But the argument that the media are simply responding to their audiences can be easily made. Few newspeople have not uttered at least once in their careers, "We only give the people what they want." McCombs (1981) himself acknowledged these limitations.

It is important not to judge the utility of the agenda-setting approach based upon the earliest studies. Although these had many limitations, they have inspired other research that is providing intriguing if still controversial results. For example, Shanto Iyengar and Donald Kinder attempted to overcome some of the problems of earlier work in a series of experiments published in 1987. Because of the unanswered questions about causality, they lamented, "Agenda-setting may be an apt metaphor, but it is no theory. The lack of a theory of media effects has significantly impeded our understanding of how democracy works" (1987, p. 3). To develop such a theory they offered a *testable* "agenda-setting hypothesis: those problems that receive prominent attention on the national news become the problems the viewing public regards as the nation's most important" (1987, p. 16). Their series of experiments examined agenda-setting, the vividness of news reports, the positioning of stories, and what they called "priming."

- **Agenda-setting**: Iyengar and Kinder demonstrated causality. They wrote, "Americans' view of their society and nation are powerfully shaped by the stories that appear on the evening news. We found that people who were shown network broadcasts edited to draw attention to a particular problem assigned greater importance to that problem—greater importance than they themselves did before the experiment began, and greater importance than did people assigned to control conditions that emphasized different problems. Our subjects regarded the target problem as more important for the country, cared more about it, believed that government should do more about it, reported stronger feelings about it, and were much more likely to identify it as one of the country's most important problems" (Iyengar and Kinder, 1987, p. 112).

- **Vividness of presentation**: Iyengar and Kinder found that dramatic news accounts undermined rather than increased television's agenda-setting power. Powerfully presented, personal accounts (a staple of contemporary television news) may focus too much attention on the specific situation or individual rather than on the issue at hand.

- **Position of a story**: Lead stories had a greater agenda-setting effect. Two possible reasons were offered. First, people paid more attention to the stories at the beginning of the news and these were less likely to fall victim to the inevitable interruptions viewers experience when viewing at home. Second, people accepted the news program's implicit designation of a lead story as most newsworthy.

- **Priming**: This is the idea that even the most motivated citizens cannot take into account all that they know when evaluating complex political issues. Instead, people consider the things that come easily to mind, or as the researchers said, "those bits and pieces of political memory that are accessible." Their research strongly demonstrated that "through priming (drawing attention to some aspects of political life at the expense of others) television news (helps) to set the terms by which political judgments are reached and political choices made" (Iyengar and Kinder, 1987, p. 114). Writing in a later study, Iyengar (1991, p. 133) offered this distinction, "While agenda-setting reflects the impact of news coverage on the perceived importance of national issues, priming refers to the impact of news coverage on the weight assigned to specific issues in making political judgments."

Agenda-setting theory has emerged as a potentially heuristic but controversial perspective. Where Werner Severin and James Tankard (1982, p. 255) wrote, "At this point, the research on agenda-setting must be labeled inconclusive," Iyengar and Kinder (1987, p. 117) countered, "The power of television news—and mass communication in general—appears not to rest on persuasion but on commanding the public's attention (agenda-setting) and defining criteria underlying the public's judgments (priming)."

Agenda-setting, primarily an individual level effects perspective, has another interesting contemporary articulation as a more macro level theory—*agenda-building*, "the often complicated process by which some issues become important in policy making arenas" (Protess et. al., 1991, p. 6). Kurt Lang and Gladys Lang defined "agenda-building—a more apt term than agenda-setting—(as) a collective process in which media, government, and the citizenry reciprocally influence one another" (1983, p. 58–59). The Langs provided a useful case study of agenda-building during the Watergate crisis.

Agenda-building presumes cognitive effects (increases in knowledge), an active audience (as seen in the Lang and Lang definition), and societal level effects (as seen in both of the above definitions). Its basic premise—that media can have profound impact on how a society (or nation or culture) determines what are its important concerns and therefore can mobilize its various institutions toward meeting them — has allowed this line of inquiry, in the words of David Protess and his colleagues (1991), to "flourish."

> These studies have employed different methodologies to try to identify actors who might influence agenda-building processes, including political leaders, bureaucrats, interest groups, citizens, and the media. Some studies have focuses on agenda-building influences in specific social problem areas, such as child abuse and criminal victimization of the elderly. Others have examined institutional agenda-building. (p. 241)

The Spiral of Silence

A somewhat more controversial theory of media and public opinion is the concept of the *spiral of silence*. This can be regarded as another type of agenda-setting theory but one that is focused on macro-level rather than micro-level consequences. In the words of its originator, Elisabeth Noelle-Neumann (1984, p. 5), "Observations made in one context (the mass media) spread to another and encouraged people either to proclaim their views or to swallow them and keep quiet until, in a spiraling process, the one view dominated the public scene and the other disappeared from public awareness as its adherents became mute. This is the process that can be called a 'spiral of silence.'" In other words, because of people's fear of isolation or separation from those around them, they tend to keep their attitudes to themselves when they think they are in the minority. The media, because of a variety of factors, tend to present one (or at most two) sides of an issue to the exclusion of others, which further encourages those people to keep quiet and makes it even tougher for the media to uncover and register that opposing viewpoint.

Noelle-Neumann's focus is not with micro-level conceptualizations of the way that average people come to perceive the public agenda; rather she is concerned with the macro-level, long-term consequences of such perceptions. If various viewpoints about agenda items are ignored, marginalized, or trivialized by media reports then people will be reluctant to talk about them. As time passes, those viewpoints will cease to be heard in public and therefore cannot have impact upon political decision-making. Her arguments are especially noteworthy because she has a reputation of being one of the foremost public-opinion pollsters in Germany. In a series of empirical studies she has demonstrated links between media reports of viewpoints on issues and trends in what people are willing to say about those issues.

Think back to the 1991 conflict in the Persian Gulf. Before the United States began bombing the Iraqis, public opinion was evenly split as to whether war was the best solution for removing Saddam Hussein from Kuwait. Once hostilities began, however, opposition to the war disappeared from television screens and front pages. So, too, did many people's willingness to articulate their misgivings. How much opposition to the fighting did you hear from those around you in those few weeks of battle? Did it not exist or were people afraid of appearing "unpatriotic" or of "not supporting the troops?"

Noelle-Neumann (1973) argued that her perspective involves a "return to the concept of powerful mass media." She believes that the limited effects perspective was in error in its assertion that selective perception limits media to reinforcement effects—that people interpret media messages based on preexisting attitudes and beliefs and, therefore, reinforcement of those attitudes and beliefs is the result. Incorrect, she wrote, because "as regards the connection between selective perception and the effect of the mass media, one can put forward the hypothesis that the more restricted the selection the less the reinforcement principle applies, in other words the greater the possibility of mass media changing attitudes" (1973, p. 78).

The way news is collected and disseminated, she continued, effectively restricts the breath and depth of selection available to citizens. She identified three characteristics of the news media that produce this scarcity of perspective:

- **Ubiquity**: The media are virtually everywhere as sources of information.
- **Cumulation**: The various news media tend to repeat stories and perspectives across their different individual programs or editions, across the different media themselves, and across time.
- **Consonance**: The congruence or similarities of values held by newspeople influences the content they produce.

She identified six parts of working journalists' everyday lives as factors that produce this consonance:

1 The concurring assumptions and experiences held by all journalists at all levels and in all fields about the public's criteria for acceptance of their work in terms of both style and content.

2 Their common tendency to confirm their own opinions, to demonstrate that theirs is the proper interpretation, and to confirm that their predictions have indeed been correct.

3 Their dependence on common sources, such as the relatively few wire and news video services.

4 Their "reciprocal influence in building up frames of reference;" newspaper people watch what's on the television news, television news programs monitor one another, and broadcast newspeople scour the newspapers for consensus and information.

5 Their striving for acceptance from colleagues and superiors.

6 Their relative uniformity of views as a result of demographic and attitudinal attributes shared by the news profession's practitioners.

This view of media effects suggests that two different social processes, one macro level and one micro level, are operating simultaneously to produce effects. Audience members, because of their desire to be accepted, choose to remain silent when confronted with what they perceive to be prevailing counter opinion (this may not be audience activity as traditionally understood by uses and gratifications, but it is most certainly a very specific use made by audience members actively in search of a very specific gratification). Newspeople, because of the dynamics of their news-gathering function and their need to be accepted, present a restricted selection of news, further forcing into silence those in the audience who wish to avoid isolation. This led Klaus Merten (1985) to at first praise spiral of silence as composed of features that are "significant for any advanced social theory . . . The theory is a *dynamic* theory; that is, it possesses features of a process theory . . . (and) the theory relies heavily on an important structural feature of communication processes, *reflexivity in the social dimension*" (p. 33), but later to call it "a highly pretentious theory" (p. 42).

Katz (1983), in an essay critical of spiral of silence, summarized Noelle-Neumann's thinking this way:

> (1) Individuals have opinions; (2) Fearing isolation, individuals will not express their opinions if they perceive themselves unsupported by others; (3) A "quasi-statistical sense" is employed by individuals to scan the environment for signs of support; (4) Mass media constitute the major source of reference for information about the distribution of opinion and thus the climate of support/nonsupport; (5) So do other reference groups . . . (6) The media tend to speak in one voice, almost monopolistically; (7) The media tend to distort the distribution of opinion in society, biased as they are by the (leftist) views of journalists; (8) Perceiving themselves unsupported, groups of individuals—who may, at times, even constitute a majority—will lose confidence and withdraw from public debate, thus speeding the demise of their position through the self-fulfilling spiral of silence. They may not change their own minds, but they stop recruitment of others and abandon the fight; (9) Society is manipulated and impoverished thereby . . . (p. 89)

This understanding led Katz to conclude that these "more subtle, more sociological (macro level) definitions of effect" (p. 96) would have us "consider the dark side of mass communication. Even in the democracies, media—like interpersonal communication—can impose acquiescence and silence in defiance of the free flow of information" (Katz, 1983, p. 91). This commentary is especially noteworthy because it is offered by someone who helped pioneer uses and gratifications research and who coauthored a classic limited effects study based upon the data collected in Decatur (1955). Katz clearly was reluctant to accept Noelle-Neumann's assertions and discredited them by arguing that they are an updated version of mass society theory.

Spiral of silence has encountered other criticisms as well. Charles Salmon and F. Gerald Kline (1985) wrote that the effects explained by spiral of silence could just as easily be understood as the product of the bandwagon effect (everybody wants to join a winner) or of projection (people's natural tendency to use their own opinions to form perceptions of the general climate of opinion around them). In addition, these critics argued that individual factors, such as a person's degree of ego-involvement in an issue, should be considered (regardless of the climate of opinion surrounding you, if you feel very strongly about the issue, you may not want to remain silent, even if isolation is a threat). They call, too, for further examination of individual demographic differences that Noelle-Neumann suggested would combine to produce people who are more likely to speak out — males, younger people, and members of the middle and upper classes, for example.

Drawing on the notion that pluralistic groups can mediate media effects, Carroll Glynn and Jack McLeod (1985) faulted the spiral of silence for underestimating the power of people's communities, organizations, and reference groups in mitigating media influence on the larger society. Regardless of the consonant view of racial equality presented in the news, they might say, a Ku Klux Klan member would probably feel no great threat of alienation for expressing his views to his team mates between innings of a Klan softball game. Glynn and McLeod also questioned the generalizability of Noelle-Neumann's research (conducted almost exclusively in what was then West Germany) to the American situation and they raised the possibility of situations in which media can actually move people to speak up rather than remain silent.

Noelle-Neumann (1985) responded simply that the media, especially television, adopt a prevailing attitude in any controversy as a matter of course, and as a result, they present a "dominant tendency." Holders of the minority viewpoint are willing to speak out if they feel that they are supported by the media dominant tendency (as during the Civil Rights movement). Moreover, she offered an alternative perspective on the media's ability to increase speaking out in the face of rejection when she wrote, "It appears that the intensive articulation of a certain viewpoint in the media gives the followers of this viewpoint the advantage of being better equipped to express their point of view . . . The resulting willingness to talk has nothing to do with fear of isolation, it only makes talking easier. By using words and arguments taken from the media to discuss a topic, people cause the point of view to be heard in public and give it visibility, thus creating a situation in which the danger of isolation is reduced" (Noelle-Neumann, 1985, p. 80).

As with any theoretical proposition that challenges the prevailing view, spiral of silence and agenda-setting both suffered intense criticism and their adherents had to overcome a fear of isolation and rejection from others in the discipline, just as Noelle-Neumann might have predicted. Nonetheless, these articulations of a more powerful mass media helped move mass communication theory toward its more contemporary stance.

Some Final Words to Clear the Mist

Of all the chapters you have or will read in this book, this one no doubt will leave you the most unsatisfied. Social learning theory was easy: people learn from the mass media through a process called modeling; attitude change theory is simple, cognitive dissonance helps people protect themselves from persuasive messages. But uses and gratifications offered no such clear-cut explanatory mantras. Purists in that camp might even recoil at our discussion of media system dependency theory, agenda-setting, and spiral of silence in the same chapter. For example, Elihu Katz, one developer of uses and gratifications thinking, saw few links between his ideas and those of Noelle-Neumann. He found her work to be a throwback to mass society thinking, although she may well find his work to remain too strongly linked to limited effects notions. We included them with the audience-centered theories because each presumes some more or less active use of media content by audience members. Each of these theories developed at about the same time during the 1970s. Each was a response to limitations of the limited effects perspective. But there are many differences between these theories. These differences must be kept in mind as you weigh their value.

Part of the difficulty stems from how uses and gratifications theory came about. For one thing, the developers of uses and gratifications were interested in how people used media in situations like political or informational campaigns. Given that such people as Elihu Katz and Jay Blumler were of a political science and sociological bent, this was only natural. They were researching and writing when media were still viewed predominantly as *informational* rather than *symbolic* entities, so it was almost predestined that they would see a discriminating, reflective audience that selected the information that it wanted and needed. Think of it this way: uses and gratifications is easy to understand when we are talking about how people use the newspaper (discrete sections, each geared for a specific type of reader) or magazines (quite specific, demographically-targeted publications designed for very specific use by very specific groups of consumers). It becomes a bit harder to justify when we consider the more complex, symbolic media like movies and television in which the same ambiguous content may be interpreted in many different ways and thus serve fundamentally different purposes. Why do people watch cartoons on television, for example? What gratifications are realized from that consumption? You can think of a thousand reasons, no doubt, but did you distinguish between adults and children? And that's only one permutation. What about a program like "Twin Peaks" that can be interpreted as a mystery, a satire, a black comedy, a deconstruction of a soap opera, and on and on.

A second reason that uses and gratifications defies easy categorization is the difficulty it has in explaining media effects. Several authors we've cited told us that uses and gratifications developed as a "counter" to the effects research that was dominant at the time. Blumler (1979, p. 10) for example, wrote that it developed "at a time of widespread disappointment with the fruits of attempts to measure the short-term (media) effects on people." Palmgreen, Wenner, and Rosengren (1985, p. 12) wrote, "The dominance of the 'effects' focus in pre- and post- World War II communication research tended to overshadow . . . concern with individual differences." In a sense, uses and gratifications thinkers could not allow themselves the luxury of demonstrating or even postulating media-initiated effects because that would have been heresy to the then dominant paradigm.

Finally, and maybe as a result of the two issues just mentioned, uses and gratifications is best regarded not as a highly coherent, systematic conceptual framework but rather as a loosely structured perspective through which a number of ideas and theories about media choice, consumption, and even impact can be viewed. As Blumler himself said,

> There is no such thing as *a* or *the* uses and gratification theory, although there are plenty of theories about uses and gratification phenomena, which may well differ with each other over many issues. Together, they will share a common field of concern, an elementary set of concepts indispensable for intelligibly carving up that terrain, and an identification of certain wider features of the mass communication process with which such core phenomena are presumed to be connected (Blumer, 1979, p. 11–12).

So where do we go from here? How does someone who believes in the concept of an active audience but who is also working to understand mass communication do so but remain in the uses and gratifications fold? Four hints have been offered by Elihu Katz and Jay Blumler, two of the creators of the original 1974 volume that established the school, *The Uses of Mass Communication.* When asked to write the concluding comments for a book to celebrate the tenth anniversary of that work, they, along with the colleague who wrote the original volume's introductory chapter, had this advice:

> Philosophically, lingering traces of "vulgar gratificationism" should be purged from our outlook. This implies the following: (1) *Rejection of audience imperialism.* Our stress on audience activity should not be equated with a serene faith in the full or easy realization of audience autonomy . . . (2) *Social roles constrain audience needs, opportunities, and choices . . .* The individual is part of a social structure, and his or her choices are less free and

Box 10b Uses and Dependency Model

Alan Rubin and Sven Windahl created this "Uses and Dependency Model" to help us visualize how societal, medium, and audience factors interact to influence people's use of media and the consequences of that use. (Reprinted by permission of the Speech Communication Association.)

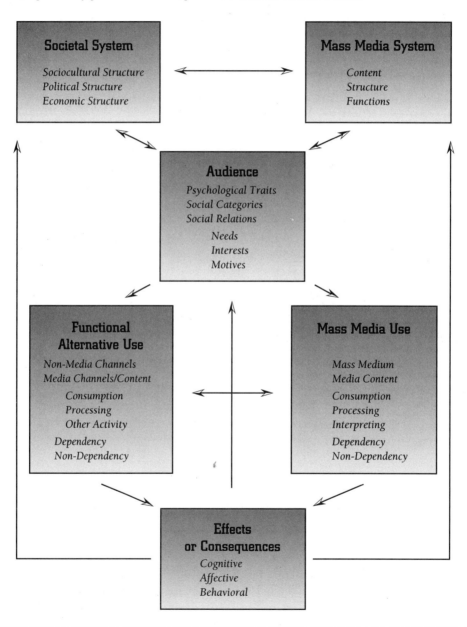

less random than a vulgar gratificationism would presume. (3) *Texts are also to some extent constraining.* In our zeal to deny a one-to-one relationship between media content and audience motivation, we have sometimes appeared to slip into the less warranted claim that almost any type of content may serve any type of function (Blumler, Gurevitch, and Katz, 1985, p. 259–260).

Their fourth assertion was that these three "propositions inject into the uses and gratifications paradigm an essential (but sometimes neglected) element of *realism*—without reducing . . . our normative commitment to the would-be active audience member and to the provision of media materials designed to enable him or her to realize his or her purposes."

Summary

The active audience perspective was developed as a counter to both mass society notions and the dominant limited effects paradigm. It argued that the media do not do things to people; rather, people do things with media. Its basic tenet is that audiences are active and make their own effects for themselves.

This uses and gratifications approach, however, has met resistance from some theorists because of questions about the definition of an active audience, the methods of conducting research within its framework, and because of its seeming basis in functional theory.

Uses and gratifications research is largely based on the survey method. If the theory's basic assumption is that people decide which media and which content best meet their needs, what better way to examine mass communication than by asking those who make those decisions? But this assumes that audience members are active participants in the process and can adequately articulate the reasons and outcomes of that activity.

Audience activity can be defined in a number of ways—utility, intentionality, selectivity, imperviousness to influence, and meaning construction for example—but activity should be seen as a relative concept, that is, some people are more active consumers than others.

Three other arguably audience-based theories show how the school of thought can explain or predict effects. Media system dependency theory is the idea that the basis of media influence rests in the relationship between the social system, the media's role in that system, and the relationship of the audience to those media and their content. The degree of dependence regulates the level of effects.

Agenda-setting and the spiral of silence are two theories that argued for powerful media effects when the limited effects perspective was dominant by asserting use, or at least discretion, on the part of audience members.

In attempting to move away from the demonstration of specific behaviors and attitude change as the only acceptable measures of media effects, agenda-setting postulated that the media do, indeed, influence public opinion by placing issues on individuals' mental or attentional agendas through their coverage of those issues (and noncoverage of others).

Although much survey research showed considerable relationships between the positioning, amount of time, and amount of attention different issues received in the media and people's judgments of the important issues of the day, some question remains as to the direction of that effect. Do media set people's agendas or do people set the media's agenda? Experimental investigations tend to support the notion that media are the agenda-setters.

Spiral of silence remains a bit more problematic. This is the idea that people who feel that they hold a minority position on an issue (largely because the media present the other view as dominant) will remain silent about that position for fear of being rejected by or isolated from those around them. This, in turn, makes it more difficult for the media to present their perspective—and the spiral continues.

Discussion Questions

1 How active a media consumer are you? Are you always thoughtful in your choice of individual television programs, for example?

2 How has your willingness and ability to be intentional in your media choices changed as you've grown older? Do you find yourself being more thoughtful in your choices at different times? When? With different media?

3 Are you more or less of an active participant in the mass communication process than others? Why do you think that?

4 If you accept play theory's idea that media only affect the unimportant aspects of your life (styles, fads, fancies), how do things like clothes, athletic shoes, cars, beers, and other products come to have so much value in our culture?

5 Where do you see audience activity in agenda-setting and spiral of silence? Do you agree or disagree with our placement of these perspectives in a chapter on audience-centered theory? Why?

6 When you enter the room where your television sits, do you turn it on and then flip around the channels, searching for something to watch or do you first examine some sort of listing to determine what you will watch and then turn the set to that choice? What does this say about uses and gratifications theory? What does this say about you as a media consumer?

Significant Names

Frank Stanton

Bernard Berelson

Jay G. Blumler

William Stephenson

Elihu Katz

Michael Gurevitch

Maxwell E. McCombs

Elisabeth Noelle-Neumann

Alan Rubin

Sandra Ball-Rokeach

Mark Levy

Sven Windahl

Shanto Iyengar

Donald Kinder

Kurt Lang

Gladys Lang

Elizabeth Perse

Lawrence Wenner

Philip Palmgreen

Significant Readings

Blumler, Jay G. and Elihu Katz, eds., (1974). *The Uses of Mass Communication: Current Perspectives on Gratifications Research*. Beverly Hills, CA: Sage.

DeFleur, Melvin L. and Sandra Ball-Rokeach (1975). *Theories of Mass Communication*, third edition. New York: David McKay.

Lippmann, Walter (1922). *Public Opinion*. New York: Macmillan.

Noelle-Neumann, Elisabeth (1984). *The Spiral of Silence*. Chicago: University of Chicago Press.

Stephenson, William (1967). *Play Theory of Mass Communication*. Chicago: University of Chicago Press.

Symposium: Agenda-Setting Revisited (1993). *Journal of Communication*, 43: 58–127.

Important Terms

Fraction of Selection

Classic Four Functions

Play Theory

Active Audience

Social Control

Uses and Gratification Approach

Convergent Selectivity

Dependency Theory

Agenda-Setting

Spiral of Silence

Agenda-Building

Chapter 11

Systems Theories of
Communication Processes

Early in World War II, a man who became a well-known behavioral psychologist, B.F. Skinner, was given an unusual task. The U.S. military wanted his assistance in developing a top secret weapon—a more accurate guided missile. Skinner knew nothing about missiles or about electronics. He was an expert in using behavioral conditioning techniques (see Chapter 7) to train animals to respond to specific stimuli. The problem that Skinner helped solve involved communication.

Early missiles were crude and inaccurate weapons. When fired at distant targets, they inevitably were thrown off-course by unanticipated winds or storms. The communication technology was at such an early stage of development that it was difficult to monitor weapons' trajectories and make in-flight corrections. More important, enemy forces could interfere with this communication and divert the missiles from their target. Skinner's job was to train pigeons so that they could guide missiles. The system that he helped design used colored lights to signal the birds when the missile went off-course. The pigeons were conditioned to peck at these lights until a change in colors indicated that the missile was back on-course.

This crude system for guiding missiles was an experiment that ultimately had little practical value. Before it could be implemented, it was replaced by superior systems based on electronic guidance mechanisms and sophisticated, ground-based communications technology. This illustrates the essential elements of a simple *system*, however. These systems *consist of a set of parts that are interlinked so that changes in one part induce changes in other parts*. System parts may be directly linked through mechanical connections or they may be indirectly linked by communication technology. Because all parts are linked, the entire system can change as a result of changes in only one element. Systems can be *goal directed* if there is a long-term objective that they are designed to accomplish. In this example, the missile is designed to reach a target. Some systems are capable of *monitoring the environment and altering their operations in response to environmental changes*.

Overview

This chapter will discuss how the notion of communication systems was developed and used by mass communication theorists. One important conception of communication systems originated with electronics engineers who developed systems that could be programmed to pursue goals, monitor the environment, and adjust actions so that the goals were achieved. These engineers were concerned with designing systems in which communication links functioned efficiently and transmitted information accurately. Communication was a means to an end. If a communication link didn't work properly, then the solution was obvious: Communications technology had to be improved so that desired levels of effectiveness and accuracy were achieved. Thus, in designing and engineering systems of this type, communication problems were solved by technological change. During the 1950s and 1960s there was optimism that important, societal-level communication problems might also be solved by improving the accuracy of message transmissions.

Systems models have important strengths but equally important limitations. In this chapter we will explain how various systems models developed and we will identify some of their applications. This is followed by a discussion of limitations. Our objective is not to deny the usefulness of systems models but to note the reasons why some social researchers and humanists reject them. You will have to weigh the merits of these criticisms. In the last half of this chapter, we will describe some current mass communication theories that were derived from and are to some extent based on systems notions. These theories address limitations of earlier models and are proving to be quite useful.

The Rise of Systems Theories

After World War II, social theorists became intrigued by systems notions as a way of conceptualizing both macroscopic and microscopic phenomena. Some decided that the idea of systems offered a heuristic means of constructing useful models of various social processes, including communication. Rather than merely adding more variables, these models fundamentally altered how relationships between variables were understood. In developing these models, theorists drew on a variety of sources. Walter Buckley (1967) traced systems notions to seventeenth century mechanical models, nineteenth century organic models, and early twentieth century process models. But most 1960s social systems theorists acknowledged that the greatest and most recent impetus toward the development of systems theories came from an engineering subfield known as *cybernetics*, the study of regulation and control in complex machines. Cybernetics investigated how communication links between the various parts of a machine can enable it to perform very complex tasks and adjust to changes taking place in its external environment.

Cybernetics emerged as an important new field during World War II, partly because of its utility for designing sophisticated weapons (Wiener, 1954, 1961). It proved especially useful for communications engineering—the design of powerful new communication systems for military applications, such as radar. Communications engineers had abandoned simple, linear models of the communication process by the 1940s. A circular but evolving communication process was conceptualized in which messages come back from receivers to influence sources that in turn alter their messages. These circular processes were referred to as *feedback loops*. In these systems, ongoing mutual adjustment is possible that ultimately leads to achieving a long-term objective or function.

Complex machines rely on feedback loops as a means of making ongoing adjustments to changes caused by the environment. Feedback loops enable sources to monitor the influence of their messages on receivers. But just as important, receivers can in turn influence sources. If the effects are not what is expected or desired, a source can keep altering a message until the desired feedback is obtained. As World War II progressed, machines were built that used ever more powerful forms of communication technology, such as radar and television cameras, to monitor the environment. These provided sophisticated means of detecting subtle changes so that a weapons system could achieve its objective. We will refer to these as *communication systems* if their function is primarily to facilitate communication. By this definition, the guided missile is not a communication system. It is a weapons system that contains a communication subsystem.

Mathematical Theory of Communication

Communications engineers also made another important breakthrough that is central to the current revolution in communications technology (Shannon and Weaver, 1949). Accuracy in message transmission is essential if systems are to operate effectively and achieve long-term goals. Even minor errors could compound over time and lead to serious problems. To address this situation, communications engineers developed a very sophisticated way of conceptualizing the flow of communication from one part to another within a system. The flow was referred to as a *signal* and each element in it was labeled an *information bit*. The ultimate information bit is a digital bit—one that is either present or absent. Methods of monitoring the accuracy of transmissions of bits were developed. The signal transmitted by one part was compared to the signal received by another. Any differences between the signal sent and the signal received were viewed as errors or *noise*. Because a signal can be composed of thousands or even millions of bits, some level of noise can usually be tolerated before it creates a problem. High levels of noise can be tolerated if a message is *redundant*, that is, if it contains many bits that carry the same information. All redundant bits must be lost or distorted before noise becomes a problem. Every communication link can be seen as a *channel* and every channel can be seen as having a certain capacity to transmit an accurate signal. This *channel capacity* may be quite high, permitting a very complex signal to be carried with few errors or it may be low, permitting only a very simple signal to be accurately transmitted. Obviously, it is better to have channels that can accurately transmit complex signals. When accuracy is a problem, redundancy can be increased, but this reduces efficiency because the same information is being sent more than once.

For example, when you listen to an AM radio, you hear static. The static is actually thousands of erroneous bits of information that have somehow entered the signal as it moves from the radio transmitter to your receiver. The importance of minimizing these errors in signal transmission depends on the purpose or function of the communication link. Your grandparents were much more tolerant of AM static than you are. If the static gets too bad you will decide that the channel isn't serving the purpose you intend and you may switch to an FM radio station. FM signals aren't as subject to the introduction of errors as the signal moves from transmitter to receiver, so you receive a more accurate transmission of the original signal.

This example illustrates a common trend in communication engineering. As technology develops, ways are found to reduce or even eliminate noise, improve efficiency, and increase channel capacity. The dominant strategy for doing this currently involves digital technology. A signal is first broken into or encoded into digital bits, the digitalized signal is transmitted and received, and then the original signal is reconstructed or decoded from the digital information. The channel capacity of existing communication links can be increased tremendously using digital technology. There is less need for transmission of redundant information so the links are more efficient.

Notions about signals, noise, bits, efficiency, redundancy and channel capacity have found their way into mass communication theory through a variety of sources. One of the first and most important books was the *Mathematical Theory of Communication* written by Claude Shannon and Warren Weaver in 1949.

Shannon was a research mathematician at Bell Telephone Laboratories and Weaver was a consultant on scientific projects at the Sloan Foundation. They believed that these new concepts would transform how all forms of communication were understood. They were optimistic that it might even be possible to remedy macroscopic, societal-level communication problems using these very microscopic notions. Their ideas came to be referred to as *information theory*.

The highest ambitions for Shannon and Weaver's information theory have yet to be realized. In communications technology and the design of communications systems, the theory has been enormously successful. Technology based on this theory is providing the building blocks for constructing an "information superhighway." Designers of this super communications system promise it will provide us with vast quantities of information at low cost in convenient, user-friendly formats.

But efficient, accurate transmission of information isn't enough. Entry into the information age has been accompanied by a troubling escalation in social problems. Ideally, systems notions could also provide a powerful way of conceptualizing complex, social systems and analyzing the role played by communication in them. Important social problems might be solved. Next, we'll consider two new forms of systems theory, *simulation models and second-order cybernetic theory*. These theories address the larger goals envisioned by Shannon and Weaver.

Modeling Systems

The term system is used in communication engineering and cybernetics to refer to any set of interrelated parts that can influence and control one another through communication and feedback loops. Any representation of a system, whether in words or diagrams, is a *model*. In systems, a change in one part affects all of the others because all are interconnected via channels. *Interdependence* and *self-regulation* are key attributes of systems. Each part may have a specialized role or function but all must interrelate in an organized manner for the overall system to operate properly and regulate itself so that goals are achieved. Systems can be relatively simple or quite complex. They may display a high or low level of internal organization. They can operate in a static fashion, or they can evolve and undergo profound change over time. They may operate in isolation or be interconnected with a series of other machines to form an even larger system.

Another key attribute of systems is that they are *goal-oriented*. That is, they constantly seek to serve a certain overall or long-term purpose. The pigeon-guided missile was designed to reach a target. We usually associate goals with thinking and planning. But, of course, machines can't think. Their goal orientation is built-in, hardwired, or otherwise programmed. Once a machine is started, it will seek its goal even if the goal is mistaken or can't be achieved. Like the robots in a bad science fiction movie, machines carry out their mission even if it makes no sense.

A Simple Systems Model

Although complex systems can be hard to describe and understand, the basic principles of a self-regulating system can be illustrated by looking at the way the furnace or air conditioner in your home operates. Both of these are parts of a self-regulating system that uses a simple feedback loop to adjust to the external environment. Both the furnace and the air conditioner communicate with a thermostat that monitors the environment and signals them when they need to turn on or off. As long as the temperature in your home remains within a desired range, the furnace or air conditioner remains inactive. When the thermostat detects a temperature that is below the desired range, it sends an electronic message to the furnace and it turns on. The furnace communicates with the thermostat by heating the air in your home. The thermostat monitors the air temperature and when it reaches the desired level, it sends another message telling the furnace to turn off. In this simple system, the furnace and the thermostat work together to keep the temperature in balance. Communication in the form of a simple feedback loop linking the furnace and the thermostat enables the system to operate effectively.

Applying Systems Models to Human Communication

Even simple systems models can be used to represent some forms of human communication. You and a friend can be seen as forming a system in which your friend plays the role of "thermostat." By maintaining communication with him or her, you find out whether your actions are appropriate or inappropriate. Are these the right clothes to wear now? Should you go to a dance of join friends for a movie? When you talk to this friend, you may not be trying to affect her but rather want her to guide you. You want her feedback so you can adjust your actions.

This example also illustrates key limitations of systems models when they are used to represent human communication—the easiest models to create tend to be too simple and too static. Unless you and your friend have a very unusual relationship, you will play many other kinds of roles and communicate with each other across a very broad range of topics. If the only function your friend serves for you is that of a thermostat, you probably need to reexamine your relationship. Assuming that you do have a more complex relationship with your friend, you could probably spend weeks trying to map out a systems model to represent the intricacies of your interrelationship. By the time you finished, you would discover that significant changes have occurred and the model is no longer accurate. Unlike mechanical parts linked by simple forms of communication, both you and your friend can easily alter your roles, your communication links, and the content of your messages. In other words, you regularly and routinely transform the system that links you to others. New feedback loops spring up while old ones vanish. Only recently have systems theorists begun to recognize and try to develop more complex models that allow ongoing transformation of systems.

Adoption of Systems Models by Mass Communication Theorists

Along with other social scientists, mass communication researchers were drawn to systems models. Moderately complex systems models came to be seen as an ideal means of representing communication processes—a big advance over simplistic, linear communication process models that were common prior to 1960. Gradually, systems models replaced the *transmissional model* that was implicit in most of the early effects research. As we've already noted, Harold Lasswell provided a cogent, succinct version of this model when he described the communication process as *Who says What to Whom through what Medium with what Effect*. The transmissional model assumes that a message source dominates the communication process and that the primary outcome of the process is some sort of effect on receivers—usually one intended by the source. Influence moves or flows in a straight line from source to receivers. The possibility that the message receivers might also influence the source is ignored. Attention is focused on whether a source brings about intended effects or whether unintended negative effects occur. Mutual or reciprocal influence is not considered.

Communication theorists proposed new models of communication processes with feedback loops in which receivers could influence sources and mutual influence was possible. The potential for modeling mutual influence was especially attractive for theorists who wanted to understand interpersonal communication. A good example of this type of model was provided by Bruce Westley and Malcolm MacLean (1957). Most conversations involve mutual influence. Participants send out messages, obtain feedback, and then adjust their actions. In everyday life people are constantly adjusting to one another. The overall social environment can be understood as something that is created by ongoing negotiation between actors.

The utility of systems models for representing mass communication processes was less obvious. With most early forms of mass communication, there are few if any *direct* communication links from receivers to sources. Message sources may be unaware of the impact of their messages or find out only after days or

---

Box 11a The Westley-MacLean Model of the Communication Process

The Westley-MacLean Model offers a clear picture of communication as a system.

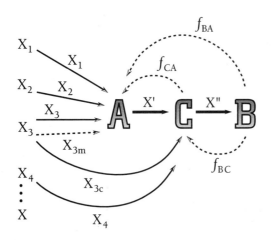

The messages C transmits to B (X") represent his selections from both messages to him from As (X') and C's selections and abstractions from Xs in his own sensory field (X_{3c}, X_4), which may or may not be Xs in A's field. Feedback not only moves from B to A (f_{BA}) and from B to C (f_{BC}), but also from C to A (f_{CA}). Clearly, in the mass communication situation, a large number of Cs receive from a very large number of As and transmit to a vastly larger number of Bs, who simultaneously receive from other Cs.

Source: Reproduced from *Journalism Quarterly*, Vol. 34, No. 1, Winter, 1957, pp. 31–38 with permission of the Association for Education in Journalism and Mass Communication.

---

weeks have elapsed. During the 1960s, however, refinement of media-ratings systems and improved, more scientific public opinion polls allowed indirect communication links to be established between message sources and receivers. Ratings and opinion poll results provided message producers with feedback about audience reaction to their messages. This feedback was quite crude for ratings—either people watch a television show or they don't. If they don't, you change the message without much understanding of what people want. If ratings are high, then you provide more of the same—until people get so tired of the same programming that they finally tune to something else. With opinion polls, the feedback may provide message sources with a bit more information, but not much. Politicians, for example, are constantly experimenting with messages in an effort to alter voter opinions and produce favorable evaluations of themselves.

Closed versus Open Systems

Two fundamentally different types of systems can be differentiated and used to model different forms of communication. Systems can be *closed and homeostatic* or they can be *open and dynamically balanced*. Closed systems are like simple machines that perform a task endlessly. There is limited monitoring of the external environment. The machine works well as long as all the parts interrelate in the same, unchanging manner. If a part becomes so worn that it stops working or a wire that is part of a communication link frays, the system will fail. It has no capacity to adjust to problems. The system can't maintain itself when parts wear out or communication links break down. The role played by communication in these closed systems tends to be highly structured and predictable. The parts of a simple machine don't have much to say to each other. They often communicate in very simple digital messages—turn on and turn off.

Open systems are very different. An open system consists of parts that interrelate in such a way that the overall system can monitor its environment and adjust to both internal and external changes. The parts of open systems can alter their functions so that if one part fails, others can adjust and take over its function. These systems can be capable of growth and change over time. Often, their relationship to the environment can change as well. These systems are said to be dynamically balanced—that is they are able to maintain their integrity and a high level of organization while undergoing significant changes. They are able to combine stability with change.

A classic example of an open system is a biological organism. In your body, the various organs communicate in a variety of ways—using electrical and chemical messages transmitted by the nervous and circulatory systems. As you grow, the relationships between organs changes. Some enlarge and take on more important functions, while others decline. The body can adapt in very complex ways to the failure of some of its parts and to changes in the external environment. Complex adjustments occur—yet the body as a whole maintains its physical integrity—it can grow and change and yet remain highly organized.

In the second half of this chapter, we will review some recent models of mass communication processes that are based on systems notions. Some of these models are complex—they have advanced far beyond simple feedback models. Before examining these models we will review a number of general criticisms that have been offered of systems theories. Then, as we discuss individual theories, we will refer back to relevant criticisms.

The Utility of Systems Models

Critics of systems models fall into two major categories—humanistic scholars who reject the mechanistic analogies inherent in systems models and social scientists who argue that research must stay focused on development of causal explanations and predictions. These two sets of critics have very different concerns.

Humanists who are fundamentally opposed to the use of systems models perceive them to be dehumanizing and overly simplistic. They argue that systems models are often nothing more than elaborate metaphors—sets of descriptive analogies. They are dissatisfied with the ability of systems models to adequately represent complex human or societal interrelationships. After all, people aren't parts of machines. The relationships in a family aren't like the mechanism in an old-fashioned pocket watch. Even complex mechanical systems are simple when compared to the human relationships that are found within a family. Humanists are fearful that in applying mechanistic analogies we demean or trivialize human existence.

Systems theorists defend their models by arguing that though they often begin with simple models, these can be refined based on research findings. They admit to using mechanical models as a starting point but argue that systems models can be refined to represent quite complicated phenomena. New types of models have been created that are based on biological not mechanical systems. Computers now permit the development and application of a new, promising type of model. *Simulation models* of complex social systems can be created in which complicated interrelationships between agents are represented. The operation of the system can be simulated over time in a computer (Simon, 1981).

If you have played the computer game Sim City, then you have seen a simulation model in action. In this game, you make decisions about how parts of the city should be managed and then you watch the consequences over time. An underlying model of how the parts of cities interrelate guides the simulation. You succeed in the game by balancing resources and careful planning of city development. The game provides many warning signs if you make bad decisions about development. You can use this feedback to correct your actions. All communication in this game comes in the form of command and control messages. You issue orders to build roads, utilities, public buildings, and so on. A more complex simulation would permit other forms of communication to be practiced.

After a simulation model is run for a period of time in a computer, its results can be compared to real-world outcomes. If major differences are found, the model can be refined until results are obtained that closely mimic or parallel the operation of actual systems. Can or should these models be used to predict the future? Should they be used as a basis for making changes in systems? Simulation models have already proved useful to control and manage complex machines. Could they work for social systems?

Systems theorists tend to be optimistic about their ability to create ever more useful models. They are careful to temper the claims they make, however, and to specify the limitations of these models. Often, they only model parts of larger systems or model complex systems over brief periods of time. Models of large systems may be useful in predicting the long-term operation of the system as a whole but useless in explaining the operation of specific parts.

Estimating Causality

In the heating and cooling system model, which is the causal agent and which agent is being affected? Does the furnace cause the thermostat to act? Yes. Does the thermostat cause the furnace to act? Yes. So which is dominant in this relationship? Which controls the other? In these models, neither agent is clearly dominant. Each causes the other to change. Thus, in even a very simple process involving feedback, causality can be hard to assess. If you measure the furnace and the thermostat at only one point in time, you are likely to get a completely mistaken impression of their relationship. When these processes become more complicated with the addition of more agents and more feedback loops, you need a schematic diagram to sort out the flow of influence. The effort to assign causality soon becomes a meaningless exercise. For example, given the complexity of the systems we create when we interact with other people, it becomes literally impossible to sort out causality—except for the most simple and narrowly defined systems or parts of systems.

Explanation of causality and identification of powerful causal agents are at the core of the limited effects paradigm and they are what many social researchers still consider to be the essence of the scientific method. It is not surprising, therefore, that some social researchers, our second set of critics, find systems models troublesome because they don't permit development of definitive causal explanations. Systems models permit complex patterns of interrelationships to be traced, but the more complex these patterns, the harder it is to make precise estimates of the causal influence of various agents upon one another.

Should we be concerned about the difficulty of assigning causality in systems models? Is assignment of causality necessary to have a truly scientific theory? Or should we be satisfied if our theories are useful for certain other, more limited purposes? If we could simulate a set of interrelationships that provides insight into people playing certain roles in a particular situation over a limited time span, is that enough? Do we need to be able to say that the person playing role X has .23 causal dominance over the person playing role Y, while the person in role Y has .35 dominance over person X? Just how precise must our understanding of these interrelationships be for the simulation to be of value? Just how precise can we afford to make our simulations given the time and research effort necessary?

Researchers who assert the importance of assigning causality are concerned that if we lower our concern for causality we will create and use systems models that are based upon little more than informed speculation. Although they might allow us to construct fascinating computer games, will they serve any practical purpose? How can the utility of these models be evaluated if we don't use explanation of causal variance as our standard? It may appear that a model fits a particular set of relationships and gives insight into interconnections between parts. But how can we be sure? How can we chose between two competing models that seem to represent a particular set of relationships equally well? These critics are deeply skeptical of the utility of constructing models that contain complex interconnections between agents. They view systems models as unparsimonious — containing too many unnecessary variables and overly complex interrelationships.

A Focus on Structure and Function

Systems models have a third limitation that some critics find troublesome. A status quo bias in systems models can tend to concentrate our attention on observable structures (that is, the parts of a machine) and lead us to assume that the primary function or role of these structures is to maintain and serve the overall system. We are led to ask research questions like, "Is a particular part doing what it should, is it communicating properly, is it maintaining a proper relationship to other parts, is it enabling the system to operate properly?" The value of each part is assessed in terms of its contribution to the whole. When we view systems in this way, we may be concerned about communication, but only in a limited way. We tend to view communication as something that merely serves to interconnect parts in much the same way that our nervous and circulatory systems interconnect the organs in our bodies. Communication is something that primarily serves as a means of command and control, as in the Sim City game. In our body, one organ tells another organ what to do and in the game we order the construction and destruction of public facilities. In such systems, we judge the success of communication by looking at their overall operation. If the system is doing what we think it should, then we conclude that communication must be appropriate. If we think the system is failing, then we look for communication problems. But sometimes systems should fail. Sometimes systems go through necessary transformations in which existing structures breakdown and give way to new structures. In such cases, communication will necessarily play a very different role.

Given their concern for command and control, systems theories with a status quo bias tend to give only superficial attention to the substance of individual messages. If messages are examined, they tend to be quickly categorized according to their function in the overall system — the interconnection that they help maintain or the adaptation that they help manage. Accuracy and clarity of messages is viewed as important since inaccurate or ambiguous messages could lead the system to degrade and fail. Messages are often seen as having no purpose other than interconnection and system regulation. In such systems theories there is little potential for communication to have unanticipated or far-reaching consequences. These theories don't recognize that communication can and should sometimes have transformative power that fundamentally alters the structure or long-term goals of the system.

A more recent form of systems theory, _second-order cybernetic theory_, seeks to overcome status quo biases. It argues that many important systems often or continually undergo fundamental, frequently chaotic, transformations in their structures. These changes are said to be _nonlinear_, that is they can't be predicted by simply examining past behavior of a system. James Gleick (1987, p. 380) put it in these words:

> In our world, complexity flourishes, and those looking to science for a general understanding of nature's habits will be better served by the laws of chaos . . . Nature forms patterns. Some are orderly in space but disorderly in time, others orderly in time but disorderly in space.

Gleick offers the development of ecological systems theory as an example. Simple models assumed the existence of a "natural balance." "Models supposed that equilibriums would exist and that populations of plants and animals would remain close to them" (1987, p. 315). But these models are giving way to more complex ones. According to Gleick, "the traditional models are betrayed by their linear bias. Nature is more complicated . . . Chaos may undermine ecology's most enduring assumptions" (1987, p. 315).

In mechanical or biological systems undergoing profound change, transformative messages can play a central role. They may be necessary if the system is to move through chaotic developmental stages or overcome the limitations of existing structures. On the surface these changes appear to be catastrophic. From the point of view of the older system structure, they are devastating. But for the old structure to be overcome, change may have to be quite radical. New linkages need to be formed and new substructures created, so that a transformed system can emerge. Second-order cybernetic theory focuses on such transformations and seeks to understand rather than fear them or suppress them (Gleick, 1987)

Paul Watzlawick and his colleagues (Watzlawick, et. al., 1974) adapted these ideas to complex systems of human relationships found in families or groups. They argued that second-order cybernetic theory can provide a useful basis for developing psychological therapy strategies. In these strategies, therapists intervene in a system of relationships and intentionally try to disrupt it to provoke useful change. Often these therapy strategies involve changes in communication that induce radical alterations in systems of relationships.

Thus, within simple, dynamically balanced, unchanging systems, the role of communication may be quite limited; we can make many assumptions about this role and our examination of communication can focus on accuracy and clarity. But in complex systems undergoing continual transformations, messages can have many functions. For example, ambiguous messages may be deliberately transmitted because they can serve many different functions simultaneously. Klaus Krippendorf (1986) pointed out that "noise need not be undesirable as in creative pursuits or in political discourse, in which ambiguity may be intentional" (p. 21). He argued that it is possible to develop useful models of systems in which noise is functional rather than inherently disruptive.

Critics charge that too often systems models have restricted concern to a narrow range of communication. Complex problems are reduced to simple questions involving accuracy and channel capacity. But these criticisms have been addressed by second-order cybernetic theorists who argue that we can have systems models that deal with more sophisticated forms of communication.

Most of the models reviewed in the remainder of this chapter focus on command and control functions of communication. They tend to be concerned with accurate, unambiguous transmission of information so that a useful adaptation of the overarching system can take place. Communication researchers are only beginning to develop second order cybernetic theories. Within the next decade we may see the creation of many innovative models of social systems in which communication plays quite different roles.

Quasi-Systems Theories

The theories discussed in this section might best be characterized as *quasi-systems theories*. Each represents an effort to view mass media as a part of a larger system or attempts to trace the use of media content by individuals operating as systems. We use the term quasi-systems theories for three reasons:

1 In these theories, systems are rarely described in complete detail. Researchers are content to sketch out the parameters of a system and then use this as a starting point for an empirical study of system parts.

2 Systems are not studied as integrated wholes. Instead, research proceeds by focusing attention on system parts—generally those related to media. Other parts are ignored.

3 Researchers attempt to draw conclusions about the operation of the system based on observation of a few parts over relatively short time periods. These conclusions often imply a greater ability to make inferences about the larger system than is possible based on the data.

Despite these limitations, quasi-systems theories are interesting and may prove useful in constructing true systems theories. Each represents an important effort to move beyond the transmissional model of the communication process.

The Knowledge Gap Model

During the past two decades, a team of researchers at the University of Minnesota (Tichenor et al., 1970; 1980; Donohue et al., 1986) developed a quasi-systems model of society in which mass media and the use of media messages play a central role. The model focuses on the role played by news media in small cities and towns. These areas are conceptualized as subsystems within larger state and regional social systems. The researchers studied the role played by news media within the subsystems *and* the larger systems. The team began by empirically establishing that news media systematically inform some segments of the population, specifically those in higher socioeconomic groups, better than others. Over periods of several weeks or months the differences between the better informed and the less informed segments tend to grow—the *knowledge gap* between them got larger and larger (Tichenor, Donohue, and Olien, 1970).

But just how should these knowledge gaps be interpreted? Do they pose long-term problems for the subsystem or for the larger system? Could knowledge gaps actually be functional in some way? If we rely on classical democratic theory (see Chapter 5) to answer these questions, these gaps will be troubling. We might be concerned that the people who are less well informed will not be able to act as responsible citizens. If they act at all, they will do so based on ignorance. On the other hand, if we use elite pluralism theory to speculate about the consequences of knowledge gaps, we will be less concerned. After all, there is a strong correlation between political ignorance and political apathy. If the less informed don't vote, then they can't upset the system. As long as there is an active, informed minority of societal leaders, the system should function smoothly—problems should be resolved by this elite based on their superior knowledge.

George Donohue, Phillip Tichenor and Clarice Olien (1980) recognized that documenting the existence of knowledge gaps was only the first step in assessing media's role in social systems at various levels. In the next phase of their research the team explored the long-term implications of knowledge gaps for the operation of local communities by studying the role played by news media when communities confront social conflicts. Would news media enable communities to effectively resolve these conflicts or would the conflicts be exacerbated? What would happen to knowledge gaps?

The researchers studied conflicts in 19 different cities that were debating environmental pollution, wilderness logging, and the construction of high-voltage power lines. These conflicts could have been resolved in several ways. If the elite pluralism perspective was accurate, news media would only inform a politically active minority and this group would take control of the conflict and resolve it. If classical democratic theory was accurate, news media would inform everyone and the conflict would be resolved through negotiation and public debate.

In fact, neither theory was very useful in predicting what happened. A more complicated, systems theory–based perspective proved useful in interpreting the empirical findings. In nearly every case, conflicts were initiated by external agents. Local leaders, including newspaper publishers, were often coopted by powerful regional businesses such as electrical power companies or big manufacturers. The research team found that as conflicts escalated, more and more groups were activated from all segments of a community. Even normally apolitical or apathetic people were eventually drawn into an escalating conflict. News coverage of conflict-related issues increased. As time passed, ordinarily uninformed individuals made better use of news media and gradually became better informed about the specific issues that were directly related to the conflict. Thus, the knowledge gap tended to narrow between those population segments that were initially well informed about these issues and those that were ignorant.

The knowledge gap findings are somewhat reassuring. They imply that all segments of a community will become informed when: (a) the relevancy of that knowledge has been increased by an escalating social conflict and (b) increased news coverage provides better access to information. Closing the knowledge gap should increase the likelihood that a solution will be negotiated based on the best information available. The findings also indicated that news media can help close knowledge gaps. As systems, communities appear to be capable of adapting the roles played by parts (population segments) so that the system as a whole changes its ability to adapt to the environment.

But these optimistic conclusions were tempered by other findings. The researchers also found evidence that within the larger social system, the smaller, rural communities are dominated by large urban centers. They found that most conflicts were not resolved through local negotiations. Rather, solutions were imposed by outside elites who found ways to control local negotiations and direct them toward conclusions favored by urban elites.

The knowledge gap research demonstrates the potential for using systems theory to guide and interpret empirical research. Ultimately, the researchers found it useful to conceptualize a very macroscopic social system, in which local communities were only small parts, to trace out the consequences of knowledge gaps. Resolution of knowledge gaps proved to be less important than might have been hoped. The researchers demonstrated that knowledge gaps decreased when conflicts escalated. This should have facilitated informed, democratic, decision-making at local levels. But this didn't happen because elites from the larger social system intervened. These findings imply that social conflict may be "functional" within smaller social systems because it can improve the flow and use of information. But the escalation of conflict also motivates elites from the larger social system to intervene and they ultimately control the conflict by imposing a solution.

Social-Political Marketing Theory

A quasi-systems theory that has received considerable attention from both communication researchers and media practitioners is *social-political marketing theory*. This theory is not a unified body of thought but rather a collection of middle-range theories concerned with promoting information deemed by elite sources to be socially valuable. Rather than describing each one, we will provide an overarching theoretical framework for them and then discuss some of the important features. Readers interested in a more extended discussion of these theories should consult other sources (Rice and Atkin, 1989; Rogers, 1983).

Social-political marketing theory can be regarded as a logical extension of the persuasion theories outlined in Chapter 7 and of diffusion theory discussed in Chapter 8. It represents an effort to increase the effectiveness of mass media-based information campaigns through greater understanding and manipulation of aspects of macroscopic social systems and microscopic psychological systems. The theory synthesizes the findings of both persuasion and diffusion research. It identifies a variety of social system-level barriers as well as psychological barriers to the flow of influence and information through the mass media. Social-political marketing theory anticipates these and includes strategies for overcoming them. Some strategies are ingenious, others involve the brute force of saturation advertising.

Social-political marketing theories have several key features:

1 Methods for *inducing audience awareness* of campaign topics or candidates. A key first step in promoting ideas or candidates is to make people aware of their existence. The easiest but most costly way to do this is with a saturation television advertising campaign. As social-political marketing theories have gained sophistication, other methods have been developed that are almost as effective but much less costly. These include using news coverage and new media channels to induce awareness. During the 1992 presidential campaign the candidates successfully experimented with many new channels for reaching voters, including radio and television talk shows like "Larry King Live," the MTV cable channel, and late night variety shows like the "Arsenio Hall Show" and "Late Night with David Letterman." H. Ross Perot showed a special talent for using free media and long, paid advertisements to raise voter awareness of his campaign. These efforts permitted the candidates to reach voter segments that can no longer be effectively reached through mainstream media. Young people, for example, no longer read newspapers and have learned to selectively screen out political news stories on television. Thus, new media channels offer a means of overcoming barriers to the flow of information that arise over time.

2   Methods for *targeting messages* at specific audience segments that are most receptive or susceptible to those messages. Limited effects research demonstrated how to identify audience segments that are most vulnerable to specific types of messages. Once these segments are identified, messages can be targeted at them. Targeting is one of several concepts borrowed from product marketing research and converted to the marketing of ideas or political candidates. By identifying the most vulnerable segments and then reaching them with the most efficient channel available, targeting strategies reduce promotional costs while increasing efficiency.

3   Methods for *reinforcing messages* within targeted segments and for encouraging these people to influence others through face-to-face communication. Even vulnerable audience members are likely to forget or fail to act on messages unless they are reinforced by similar messages coming from several channels. A variety of strategies has been developed to make certain that multiple messages are received from several channels. These strategies include visits by change agents, group discussions, messages placed simultaneously in several media, and door-to-door canvassing.

4   Methods for *cultivating images and impressions* of people, products, or services. These methods are most often used when it is difficult to arouse audience interest. If people aren't interested in a topic, it is unlikely that they will seek and learn information about it. Lack of interest forms a barrier against the flow of information. But it is still possible to transmit images. The most prominent method used to cultivate images is image advertising in which easily recognizable, visually compelling images are presented. Relationships are implied between these and objects that are being promoted. For example, a soft drink will be shown being consumed by very attractive people in an interesting setting. To what extent are your impressions of Dr. Pepper or Pepsi shaped by ads that invited you to "Be a Pepper" or a member of the "Pepsi Generation?"

5   Methods for *stimulating interest and inducing information seeking* by audience members. Information seeking occurs when a sufficient level of interest in ideas or candidates can be generated. Numerous techniques have been developed that stimulate interest and induce information seeking. During political campaigns, candidates stage dramatic events designed to call attention to and stimulate interest in their positions on issues (or the positions of their opponents). George Bush was very successful in doing this during the 1988 campaign but much less successful in 1992. In 1988, he took a boat out to observe pollution in the Boston Harbor. News reports of the trip called attention to Michael Dukakis' failure to control pollution and Bush's pledge to do better. Once information seeking is induced, various methods have been developed to give easy access to those forms of information that serve the interest of the campaign planners.

6 Methods for *inducing desired decision-making or positioning*. Once people are aware, informed, or at least have formed strong images or impressions, they are ready to be moved either toward a conscious decision or unconscious prioritization or positioning. Media messages can be transmitted through a variety of channels and used to highlight the value of choosing a specific option or of prioritizing one product/service/candidate relative to others (positioning). Change agents and opinion leaders can also be used, though these are more expensive. This is a critical stage in any communication campaign since it prepares people to take an action desired by campaign planners.

7 Methods for *activating audience segments*, especially those that have been targeted by the campaign. Ideally, these audiences will include people who are properly positioned and have decided to act but have not yet found an opportunity. In other cases, people will have prioritized a product, service, or candidate but need to be confronted with a situation in which they are compelled to make a choice. Many early communication campaigns failed because they didn't have a mechanism for stimulating action by audience members. People were influenced by campaigns but this influence wasn't effectively translated into action. A variety of techniques can be used to activate people including change agents, free merchandise, free and convenient transportation, free services, moderate fear appeals, and broadcast or telephone appeals from high-status sources.

One of the simplest, yet most comprehensive social-political marketing theory is the *hierarchy of effects model* (Rice and Atkin, 1989) which states that it is important to differentiate a large number of persuasion effects—some that are easily induced and others that take more time and effort. This model permits development of a step-by-step persuasion strategy in which the effort begins with easily induced effects, such as awareness, and monitors these effects using survey research. Feedback from that research is used to decide when to transmit messages designed to produce more difficult effects such as decision-making or activation. Thus, the effort begins by creating audience awareness, then cultivates images or induces interest and information seeking, reinforces learning of information or images, aids people in making the "right" decisions, and then activates them. At each step the effectiveness of the campaign until that point is monitored and the messages are changed when the proper results aren't obtained.

The hierarchy of effects model was first developed by product marketers but has now been widely applied to social-political marketing. Critics argue that the assumption that it makes about certain effects necessarily preceding others in time is unwarranted. Some people, for example can be moved to act without ever being informed or even making a decision about an issue or a candidate. Social-political marketers argue that although they can't hope to induce all the desired effects in every targeted person, they have evidence that a well-structured, step-by-step campaign that uses survey data to provide feedback is much more successful than persuasion efforts based on simple linear effects models.

Critics of social-political marketing point to limitations that are very similar to those that we summarized in Chapter 8 in our discussion of information flow and diffusion theories. This is not surprising because social-political marketing theory is an extension of these two earlier theories. Though social-political marketing theory can squeeze some usefulness out of the older source-dominated, linear effects models, it also has many of their limitations. In social-political marketing models, sources use feedback to adjust their actions. This use is generally limited to changes in their messages; however, their long-term persuasion or information goals don't change. If audiences seem resistant, then new messages are tried in an effort to break down the resistance. Little thought is given to whether the audience might be justified or correct in resisting information or influence. If the effort to get out information fails, the audience is blamed for being too apathetic or ignorant—they simply don't know what's good for them.

Thus, the social-political marketing model is tailored to situations where elite sources are able to dominate elements of the larger social system. These powerful sources are able to prevent counter-elites from distributing information or marshaling organized opposition. The theory doesn't allow social conflict and thus can't be applied to situations where conflict has escalated to even moderate levels. It applies best to trivial forms of information and works best when politics is reduced to marketing of competing candidate images or the transmission of innocuous public health messages.

Brenda Dervin (1989) tried to develop an audience-centered, social-political marketing theory that could serve some of the same purposes while overcoming obvious limitations. She argued that campaign planners must conceive of communication as a dialogue between elite sources and various audience segments. There must be a genuine commitment to the flow of information and ideas upward from audiences even at early stages of campaigns. The purpose of campaigns should not be understood as inducing audiences to do things that elite sources want them to do, but rather to help people learn to responsibly reconstruct their lives in ways that will be useful to them. For example, public health campaigns shouldn't scare people into adopting better diets but should encourage people to fundamentally reorient their lives so that better eating habits are formed as one aspect of a larger lifestyle change.

Dervin's model includes many of the systems theory notions we introduced in this chapter. It assumes that mutual interaction between sources and audiences is more effective than a source-dominated communication process. Sources will become better informed about the everyday situations faced by audiences and audiences will gradually learn useful information for restructuring their lives. She argued that elite sources should learn to respect their audiences. If they do, then audiences will be more likely to see the wisdom of some of the things that elite sources want them to do.

Unfortunately, Dervin's model will only work if the many constraints that inhibit or prevent this mutual interaction between elite sources and various audiences—especially lower status or minority group audiences—can be overcome. This will not be easy. Current mass media-based communication systems permit only indirect, usually delayed, often very crude forms of feedback from audiences. This feedback is suitable for redesigning promotional messages but not for gaining deep insight into the life situation and information needs of audience members.

The greater the gap between the life situation of elite sources and that of lower status audiences, the more unlikely it is that useful feedback will be obtained and used. Typically, message sources must be able to pay for sophisticated audience research and then be willing and able to act on it. In her work, Dervin has relied on very large government grants to conduct small-scale pilot projects. The cost of larger-scale efforts could be enormous. Dervin believes that new technologies may significantly reduce the cost of maintaining mutual interaction between sources and audiences. In some of the examples she discusses, newer forms of media, like computerized data bases, are employed.

Information Processing Theory

One advantage of systems theories is that systems can be conceptualized at various levels of analysis. One of the most popular and useful of current systems theories is quite microscopic—a theory that examines how individuals make sense of information. *Information processing theory* uses mechanistic analogies to describe and interpret how each of us takes in and makes sense of the flood of information that we receive from our senses every moment of each day. It envisions individuals as complex computers with certain built-in information handling capacities and strategies.

Each day we are exposed to vast quantities of sensory information; we take in only a small fraction of it, process and use an even smaller fraction, and then we finally store a tiny fraction of this in long-term memory. According to some cognitive theorists, we are not so much information handlers as information avoiders—we have developed sophisticated mechanisms for screening out information. Very little of what goes on around us ever reaches our consciousness and most of this is soon forgotten. Think about it for a moment. As you sit reading this book, consider your surroundings. Unless you are seated in a white, soundproof room with no other people present, there are many sensory stimuli around you. If you have been sitting for some time, your muscles may be getting stiff and your back may have a slight ache. Those around you may be laughing. A radio may be blaring. All of this sensory information is potentially available but if you are good at focusing your attention on reading, then you are routinely screening out most of these external and internal stimuli in favor of the printed words on this page. But just how many of these words are you actually noticing? How many will you remember in ten minutes, or ten hours, or ten days?

Consider what you do when you watch a television program. Unless you have a VCR and can play back scenes in slow motion, you can't pay attention to all of the images and sounds. If you do watch them in slow motion, the experience is totally different from viewing them at normal speed. Viewing television is actually a rather complex task that uses very different information processing skills than does reading a textbook. You are exposed to rapidly changing images and sounds. You must sort these out and pay attention to those that will be most useful to you in achieving whatever purpose you have for your viewing. But if this task is so complex, why does television seem to be such an easy medium to use? Because the task of routinely making sense of television appears to be so similar to the task of routinely making sense of everyday experience. And making sense of that experience is easy, isn't it?

Information processing theory offers fresh insight into our routine handling of information. It challenges some basic assumptions about the way we take in and use sensory data. For example, we assume that we would be better off if we could take in more information and remember it better. But more isn't always better in the case of information. Some people actually experience severe problems because they have trouble routinely screening out irrelevant environmental stimuli. They are overly sensitive to meaningless cues such as background noise or light shifts. Other people remember too much information. You might envy someone with a photographic memory—especially when it comes to taking an exam over textbook material. But total recall of this type can pose problems. Recall of old information can intrude upon one's ability to experience new information. A few cues from the present can trigger vivid recall of past experiences. If you've watched reruns of the same television show several times, "Star Trek: The Next Generation" for example, you probably have found that as you watch one episode it triggers recall of bits and pieces of previous episodes. What if everyday life was like that—the past constantly intruding into the present? Forgetting can have its advantages.

Another useful insight from information processing theory is a recognition of the limitations of conscious awareness. Our culture places high value on conscious thought processes and we tend to be skeptical or suspicious of the utility of mental processes that are only indirectly or not at all subject to conscious control. We associate consciousness with rationality—the ability to make wise decisions based on careful evaluation of all available, relevant information. We associate unconscious mental processes with things like uncontrolled emotions, wild intuition, or even mental illness. No wonder we are reluctant to acknowledge our great dependency upon unconscious mental processes.

According to information processing theory, we can never be conscious of more than a very small fraction of the information present in our environment. As we absorb large quantities of information, we are consciously aware of only a small fraction of it. Our conscious awareness could be compared to a lone engineer in a nuclear power complex. The engineer's primary task is to remain in a master control room and confine his or her activity to reading the output from the equipment that directly monitors the activity of the plant. The engineer rarely observes any of the automated plant operations directly—to do so would be to risk a breakdown in some other part of the plant. The engineer scans the output from the instruments and then records only the most noteworthy information for long-term recall. As long as the plant operates smoothly, the engineer will have little reason to make direct observations or tinker with the equipment.

The point of this analogy is that the overall task of coping with information is much too complex for conscious control to be either efficient or effective. We have to depend upon routinized processing of information and must normally limit conscious efforts to only those instances when intervention is crucial. For example, when there are signs of a breakdown of some kind, when routine processing fails to serve our needs properly, then conscious effort may be required.

One advantage of the information processing perspective is that it provides a more objective perspective on learning. Most of us view learning subjectively. We blame ourselves if we fail to learn something that we think we should have learned or that appears to be easy to learn. We assume that with a little more conscious effort, failure could have been avoided. How often have you chided yourself by saying, "If only I'd paid closer attention," "I should have given it more thought," "I made simple mistakes that could have been easily avoided if only I'd been more careful"? But would a little more attention really have helped all that much? A little more attention to one aspect of information processing might simply have led to a breakdown in some other aspect of processing. Of course, sometimes additional conscious effort can do wonders. But what you may need is some overall revamping of your routine information handling skills and strategies—a transformation of your information processing system. This can take considerable time and effort—not just trying harder in one specific instance.

Information processing theory also provides a more objective assessment of the mistakes we make when processing information. It views these mistakes as routine outcomes from a particular system—not as personal errors due to personal failings. Thus, this theory doesn't blame audience members for making mistakes when they use media content. It links errors to existing structures in the information handling process and implies that there may be ways that input information can be adjusted so that existing structures will process it effectively.

Changing existing structures is necessary only as a last resort since structural change is much harder to bring about than is adjustment in message input. For example, poorly structured news stories will be routinely misinterpreted even if journalists who write them are well intentioned and news consumers try hard to understand them. Rather than retraining people to cope with badly structured stories, it is more efficient to change stories so that more people can use them without making mistakes.

An Information Processing Model

According to information processing theory, what we need is an ability to routinely scan our environment, taking in, identifying and routinely structuring the most useful stimuli and screening out irrelevant stimuli. Then we must be able to process the structured stimuli that we take in, hold these structures in memory long enough so that we can sort out the most useful ones, put the useful ones into the right categories (schemas), and then store them in long-term memory. Described in this way the process may seem simple, but research by cognitive psychologists is finding that the process is quite complex with many different information screening skills and various processing stages.

Processing Television News

Information processing theory has been used most extensively in mass communication research to guide and interpret research on how people decode and learn from television news broadcasts. Numerous studies have been conducted and useful reviews of this literature are now available (Robinson and Levy, 1986; Gunter, 1987; Graber, 1987; Davis and Robinson, 1989; Robinson and Davis, 1990; Davis, 1990). Remarkably similar findings have been gained from very different types of research, including mass audience surveys and small-scale laboratory experiments. A rather clear picture of what people do with television news is emerging.

Though most of us view television as an easy medium to understand and one that can make us eyewitnesses to important events, television is actually a difficult medium to use. Frequently, information is presented on television in ways that inhibit rather than facilitate learning. Part of the problem rests with audience members. Most of us view television primarily as an entertainment medium. We have developed many information processing skills and strategies for television that serve us well in making sense of entertainment content but which interfere with effective interpretation and recall of news. We approach the news passively and rely upon routine activation of *schemas* (more or less highly structured sets of categories or patterns; sets of interrelated conceptual categories). We rarely engage in deep, reflective processing of news content, so most of it is quickly forgotten. Even when we do make a more conscious effort to learn from news, we often lack the schemas necessary to make in-depth interpretations of content or to store these interpretations in long-term memory.

But although we have many failings as an audience, news broadcasters also bear part of the blame. The average newscast is often so hard to make sense of that it can be said to be "biased against understanding." The typical broadcast contains too many stories, each of which tries to condense too much information into too little time. Stories are often complex combinations of visual and verbal content—all too often the visual information is so powerful that it overwhelms the verbal. Viewers are left with striking mental images but little contextual information. Often pictures are used that are totally irrelevant to stories—they distract but don't inform.

Findings presented by Dennis Davis and John Robinson (1989) are typical of this body of research. They interviewed more than four hundred people to assess what viewers learned or failed to learn from three network news broadcasts in June, 1979. They identified numerous story attributes that enhanced or inhibited learning. Stories with complex structure and terminology or powerful but irrelevant visual images were poorly understood. Human interest stories with simple but dramatic storylines were well understood.

The Next Three Chapters

Most of the systems theories reviewed in this chapter and most that make up the limited effects paradigm fall into Lazarsfeld's *administrative research* category. They are best at explaining and controlling the status quo, not in discovering methods for transforming it. For some time now there has been growing opposition to these theories within academia from people dissatisfied with their limitations.

Although the intellectual roots of some opposition to the limited effects paradigm can be traced back to mass society theory, it is highly misleading to suggest that those dissatisfied with limited effects media theories are necessarily voicing a crackpot, long-discredited theory. In the next two chapters we will trace the rise of some opposing theories. Their strengths and limitations will be probed. Then in the final chapter, we will discuss the future of mass communication theory. Can the advocates of current limited effects theories live in harmony with their opposition? What should be the nature of their relationship? Should an integrated paradigm emerge that synthesizes both viewpoints? Or should there be two paradigms that develop side by side with some cross-fertilization? Although we will raise these questions, we cannot answer them. The next generation of media researchers will have to determine the answers.

Summary

The rise of systems theories in the 1950s and 1960s encouraged theorists to move beyond simplistic, linear models of mass communication. Concepts developed by communications engineers were applied to mass media systems. In addition, systems notions from fields as diverse as biology and anthropology have been used. One useful outcome of the development of systems theories has been to direct attention toward more macroscopic levels of analysis. Most limited effects theories were microscopic, concerned with the influence of specific types of messages on specific audience segments. Systems theories can be focused at microscopic levels, as in the case of information processing theory, but most were more macroscopic.

Systems theories have been well suited to conceptualizing the flow of information within systems and developing ways of improving the efficiency and effectiveness of this flow. But improving information flow may not be enough. Newer forms of systems theory such as second-order cybernetic theory overcome this limitation and could prove quite useful.

There is an uneasy relationship between systems theories and the limited effects paradigm. Macroscopic systems theories view effects as taking place within a larger social context that can suppress or enhance effects. Thus, what might appear to be a minor, unimportant effect in a laboratory experiment could be quite significant in a social system where that effect is cultivated and reinforced. Similarly, effects that are easily produced in a laboratory may be effectively suppressed in a social system. Research guided by systems theories sometimes produces findings that don't fit well within the limited effects paradigm.

Information processing theory enables us to answer many important questions concerning people's use of information media. But because it is a microscopic theory, it doesn't address and cannot answer questions about the role of information media in the larger society. Today, there is an increasing gap between our ability to understand ourselves as individual information processors and our understanding of what media can or should do for the society. Though knowledge gap theory addresses some of these larger questions about the media's role, its answers are yet incomplete.

Both information processing theory and knowledge gap theory suggest that significant changes should be made in how information is presented through the media. But these changes may be useless if the social system isn't changed. People today typically have little motivation or ability to learn about the elites who dominate the larger political and social environment. If they do make the effort to learn, this knowledge typically proves useless except in casual conversation with friends. If your friends don't care about politics, then the information is completely meaningless. Of course, this information could be useful in casting an informed vote, but fewer and fewer people value citizenship enough to become informed just for the purpose of voting wisely. By itself, voting can be a rather unsatisfying activity: it is done in private with little sense of its impact upon the overall election outcome. If your candidate wins or loses by millions of votes, what difference does your vote make? Recent sharp declines in voting turnout, despite intensive voter registration efforts, imply that our political system may be slipping into crisis. The 1992 H. Ross Perot third-party campaign for the presidency attracted some of these voters and proved that they could be activated by an atypical candidacy.

Discussion Questions

1 Briefly list and explain the essential elements of a systems model. In what basic way does it differ from a linear effects model?

2 Why was World War II so important in the development of systems notions?

3 Explain some of the criticisms that have been made of systems models. Do you consider these models inherently mechanistic and dehumanizing? Why is it difficult to assess causality in a system?

4 Describe second order cybernetic theory and explain how it differs from other forms of systems theory.

5 What is meant by a knowledge gap? Give an example.

6 Discuss the hierarchy of effects model. How is this model applied in marketing or political campaigns?

7 In this chapter we reviewed theories that provide different insights into management of the flow of information and influence. Which of these perspectives do you find most interesting or useful? Why?

Significant Names

Norbert Wiener

Brenda Dervin

Klaus Krippendorf

John Robinson

Phillip Tichenor

George Donohue

Clarice Olien

Significant Readings

Buckley, Walter (1967). *Sociology and Modern Systems Theory.* Englewood Cliffs, NJ: Prentice Hall.

Gleick, James (1987). *Chaos: Making a New Science.* New York: Viking Penguin.

Graber, Doris (1987). *Processing the News*, second edition. New York: Longman.

Heims, S.P. (1980). *John von Neumann and Norbert Wiener: From Mathematics to the Technologies of Life and Death.* Cambridge, MA: MIT Press.

Krippendorf, Klaus (1986). *Information Theory: Structural Models for Qualitative Data.* Newbury Park, CA: Sage.

Robinson, John P. and Mark Levy with Dennis K. Davis (1986). *The Main Source: Learning from Television News.* Newbury Park, CA: Sage.

Tichenor, Phillip, George A. Donohue and Clarice N. Olien (1970). "Mass Media Flow and Differential Growth of Knowledge." *Public Opinion Quarterly*, 34: 159–170.

Tichenor, Phillip, George A. Donohue and Clarice N. Olien (1980). *Community Conflict and the Press.* Beverly Hills, CA: Sage.

Watzlawick, Paul, John Weakland, and Richard Fisch (1974). *Change: Principles of Problem Formation and Problem Resolution.* New York: Norton.

Wiener, Norbert (1948). *Cybernetics, or Control and Communication in the Animal and Machine.* Cambridge, MA: MIT Press.

Wiener, Norbert (1950). *The Human Use of Human Beings: Cybernetics and Society.* Boston: Houghton Mifflin.

Important Terms

System

Transmissional Model

Cybernetics

Feedback Loops

Interdependence

Self Regulate

Signal

Noise

Channel Capacity

Redundancy

Goal Oriented

Homeostatic

Targeting

Schemas

Knowledge Gap

Dynamically Balanced System

Hierarchy of Effects Model

Information Processing

Simulation Model

Information Theory

Second Order Cybernetic Theory

Social-Political Marketing Theory

SECTION *Five*

The Cultural Turn in Mass Communication Theory: Challenging the Limited Effects Paradigm

1975 ASNE's *Statement of Principles replaces Canons*

1983 Journal of Communication *devotes entire issue to "Ferment in the Field"*

1985 *Meyrowitz's* No Sense of Place

1987 *Chaffee and Berger formalize "communication science"*

1990 *Signorielli and Morgan's* Cultivation Analysis

1991 Boyz N the Hood *banned from many theaters*
Kremlin coup against Premier Gorbachev
Gulf War explodes, CNN emerges as important news source

1992 *ACT disbands; says work is complete*

1993 *Ten years after "Ferment,"* Journal of Communication *tries again with special issue,*
 "The Future of the Field"

Chapter 12

Cultural Analysis

On April 1, 1991, the Associated Press (p. 5A) carried a bizarre story of mistaken identity. A group of Bulgarian journalists and diplomats had entered a supermarket in suburban Minneapolis intent on purchasing some of the bounty of capitalist democracy. Soon they heard a strange announcement from the store's manager over the loud speakers, "Put everything down and leave. We don't want your kind of people in this store." They were stunned. They confronted the manager in person and demanded to know why he was ordering them out of the store. Elena Poptodorova told the manager, "I'm a member of parliament, I have my credentials with me, so would you please explain why you are behaving like that to me?" The manager reported that he replied by saying, "We told them we apologized to them if they weren't gypsies and they are a diplomat [sic] from a foreign country . . . And if they are gypsies, we certainly would like them to get out faster."

What was going on here? It seems the manager had been reading police reports about roving bands of gypsies who entered stores, confused clerks by speaking in a foreign language, and used this diversion as a cover for shoplifting. But State Department interpreter Dana Penoff, who was guiding the group, was incredulous. "These are people who are very educated and very intelligent. These people are well-dressed and well-behaved." She was appalled. "I'm embarrassed as an American. To be in my own country and have one of my own countrymen behave like this is incredible. I will not let this go."

Who was right and who was wrong in this situation? What would you have done had you been the store manager, the interpreter, or a delegation member? The manager was acting on information that led him to expect that gypsies would soon invade and pillage his store. When the group of foreigners appeared, he sized them up and took fast action. Polite behavior and fancy clothes weren't going to fool him. He knew gypsies when he saw them, even though these gypsies were obviously quite sophisticated. They had an accomplice who spoke good English and claimed to be an interpreter. What a scam! Credentials? Anybody knows those can be easily faked. Sure I apologize — but just keep moving out the door.

The store manager was presented with two options — either he could rely on newspaper reports about gypsies or he could trust the "cover story" given him by the Bulgarian group. Which option was more likely to be correct? Before you ridicule his choice, remember that we all are continually and strongly guided by our expectations. Many social situations are highly ambiguous and we must rely on previously developed expectations to make sense of them. The more ambiguous the situation, the more firmly we may cling to our expectations — even when obvious evidence (nice clothes, good manners) appears to contradict them. Like the store manager, we are reluctant to take a risk that might get us in trouble. But in choosing option number one the manager may lose business. More important, he might insult some very nice people and harm international relations.

What would you do in a similar situation? Would you follow the example of the store manager and trust news reports on gypsies to guide your interpretation? Or would you be sensitive to the contradictory cues and be open to changing your expectations? If you decided to trust news reports would they have "caused" you to throw out the diplomats? How much personal responsibility should you take for your own actions? The theories presented in the next two chapters can help you answer these questions.

Overview

In this chapter and the one that follows, we will look at theories that examine the role of media in our culture. These cultural perspectives argue that media can strongly influence how we know ourselves and our environments and how we conduct ourselves in our environments. We'll investigate a number of important dichotomies: British versus American cultural studies, the ritual versus the transmissional perspective, and microscopic versus macroscopic theories.

Some of the most influential ideas that are labeled cultural theories — symbolic interaction, social construction of reality, frame analysis, and cultivation analysis — will be discussed in detail and we'll investigate what they have in common: the presumption that media have influence through the role that they play in shaping everyday life culture.

Be forewarned, though. Many of the theorists whose ideas we will discuss believe in powerful media effects and ask us to accept their view of media influence using logic, argument, and our own powers of observation rather than by presenting us with scientific "proof." Others offer empirical evidence for their belief in powerful media, but they use innovative research methods, and so their work is held in suspicion. Supporters of the limited effects paradigm are troubled by this work and the challenge that it represents to their perspective. They regard cultural theories as too speculative and argue that the empirical research generated from this research has been too loosely structured.

Changing Times

Children begin watching television attentively by the age of three. Before most start school or form close relationships with peers, they have learned the names of countless television characters and are fans of particular programs. By the first day of elementary school, they are already watching nearly three hours a day. By eight years old, they are watching four full hours. By the time they finish high school, average teenagers will have spent more time in front of their television sets than they will have been engaged in any other activity except sleep; this means more time with television than in school. Most children also spend more time with their television set than they do communicating with their friends or family (Liebert, Sprafkin, and Davidson, 1982). If other forms of media like radio, records, movies, video games, magazines, and newspapers are considered, the contrast between the time spent with media and with the "actual" world and "real" people becomes even more striking.

Modern mass media dominate everyday communication. From the time children learn to talk, they are mesmerized by the sounds and moving images of "Sesame Street." During the teen years media supply vital information on peer group culture and most important—the opposite sex. In middle age, as people rear families, people turn to television for convenient entertainment and to magazines for tips on raising teenagers. In old age, as physical mobility declines, people turn to television for companionship and advice.

Media have become a primary means by which many of us experience or learn about many aspects of the world around us. With the advent of mass media, many forms of folk culture fell into sharp decline. Everyday communication was fundamentally altered. Story-telling and music-making ceased to be important within extended families. Instead, nuclear families gathered in front of an enthralling, electronic storyteller. Informal social groups dedicated to cultural enrichment disappeared—along with vaudeville and band concerts. It is no coincidence that our culture's respect for older people and the wisdom they hold has fallen in the age of media. If Joshua Meyrowitz (1985) is right, we are losing touch with locally based cultures and are moving into a media-based, global cultural environment.

Mass society theory (see Chapter 3) viewed these changes with alarm. Mediated culture was assumed to be inferior to elite culture. As mass culture spread, theorists feared it would undermine the social order and bring chaos. People's lives would be ruined. The sudden rise of totalitarian social orders in the 1930s seemed to fulfill these prophecies. In Fascist and Communist nations alike, media were used to propagate new and highly questionable forms of totalitarian culture. But were media ultimately responsible for their creation and promotion? Was the linkage between the new media and their messages so great that the drift into totalitarianism was inevitable? Or could media promote individualism and democracy as easily as collectivism and dictatorship? These are questions that we have struggled with throughout the twentieth century.

The influence of mass society theory declined during the 1960s along with the overt threat of totalitarianism. As we've seen, in the United States most social researchers adopted the limited effects perspective that media rarely produce significant, long-term changes in people's thoughts and actions. Mediated mass culture was no longer assumed to be inherently anti-democratic. American media had become highly effective promoters of capitalism, individualism, and free enterprise. Some critics now argue that newer media technologies, like personal computers and camcorders, are actually biased toward individualism and market economies rather than collectivism and state control. So the role of media in culture seems to be settled—doesn't it? After all, we've won the Cold War. Shouldn't we conclude that media are benign? Can't we safely ignore the warnings in books like *1984* and *Brave New World*?

The Cultural Turn in Media Research

Despite the decline of mass society theory, the reassurance offered by limited effects research, and the end of the Cold War, questions about media's role in culture have resurfaced at the center of contemporary mass media theory. Many new ideas are being developed and old theories are receiving renewed attention. Some explore the potential for media to reshape everyday life in important and innovative ways. Researchers describe these changes and attempt to understand them. They are concerned with providing media consumers with greater insight into the role of media in their own lives. We will use the term *cultural analysis* to refer to this body of thought.

Another set of cultural theories is focused on media use by powerful elite groups to advance and reinforce certain forms of culture. These theories are concerned with understanding how elites use media to propagate *hegemonic culture* as a means of maintaining their dominant position in the social order. Researchers speculate about how alternate forms of culture and innovative media uses are systematically suppressed. These theories challenge the power of elite groups by exposing their media use and criticizing hegemonic culture. We will refer to this as the _critical cultural studies_ perspective. A primary goal of these theories is to cause social change that improves the quality of life for average individuals.

In this chapter we will review cultural analysis approaches and in Chapter 13 we will look at critical cultural studies. Our differentiation and labeling of these theories is somewhat arbitrary. Other authors, James Carey (1989) for example, have labeled these two bodies of theory American cultural studies and British cultural studies. Although this labeling correctly identifies the nations in which each perspective originated, both approaches have moved beyond these geographic boundaries. Differentiation of these theories into two distinct sets is difficult because both share many assumptions about culture and the role of media. Both assume that media can play an important role in shaping culture and that culture itself is of central importance in shaping and transforming the social world. Both have developed innovative ways of exploring and explicating the cultural influence of media. They have developed elaborate theoretical frameworks and pioneered useful methodological developments. Both emphasize the important role played by media in shaping the views that people have of themselves and their social environment. Both assume that media have become a primary means by which people learn about and participate in a larger culture. Both argue that media have had a significant impact on modern social orders.

Despite these shared concerns, there are key differences. Cultural analysis tends to be microscopic and apolitical while critical cultural studies is macroscopic and highly politicized. Cultural analysis has focused on how typical people use media to make sense of themselves and the world around them and explores the consequences of media use for the everyday lives of average individuals. Cultural analysts have not been interested in making or even influencing social policy, and they have tended to remain uncritical. To some extent the followers of cultural analysis have adopted the value-free stance toward research that still dominates American social science. Researchers have been slow to use its insights into everyday life as a basis for criticizing the status quo with the intent of making large-scale social change. Researchers don't regard themselves as constituting a distinctive social movement.

On the other hand, critical cultural studies adopts a more macroscopic perspective. It is centrally concerned with the larger social order and elites' media use and explores the consequences of media use for maintaining elite power. Researchers have focused on media use by powerless groups and assessed whether group members have been duped by media. Critical cultural studies researchers are politically active and make efforts to directly shape social policy. They have made an effort to form their own social movement or serve as leaders within existing movements. Above all, they are critical — they have explicit values that are used to make evaluations of the status quo and to argue for what they perceive to be positive social changes.

Historically, the two approaches were developed by distinct, geographically isolated research communities—one in North America and one in Britain. In North America, sociologists and literary scholars led the development of cultural theory; in Britain, literary scholars and political theorists were primary. During the past decade there has been increasing contact between the two communities. Enclaves of critical cultural studies have been established in the United States, often by importing scholars trained in Britain, and some forms of cultural analysis theory are widely known in Britain. Recently, theories that combine both approaches have been developed (Giddens, 1989; Davis and Puckett, 1991). These attempts at synthesis have aroused criticism from other scholars, however, especially from those who believe that researchers should be politically active. There is concern that an integrated perspective would sacrifice distinctive, essential features of existing approaches.

Cultural analysis and critical cultural studies differ from most of the theories we've discussed in preceding chapters because they do not rely solely, or even primarily, upon quantitative, empirical research to systematically develop or evaluate theory. Instead, a broad range of research methods and theory generation strategies, including some that are unsystematic and selective, are employed. In contrast with the quantitative, empirical research methods described in previous chapters, these techniques are labeled as *qualitative,* that is they highlight essential differences in phenomena. Evaluation of theory tends to be accomplished through debate and discussion involving proponents of contrasting or opposing theoretical positions. Theory is advanced through the formation of schools of thought in which there is consensus about the validity of a specific body of theory. Rival schools of theory emerge that work to undermine opposing theories while defending their own. Proof of a theory's power lies in its ability to attract adherents and be defended against attacks from opponents.

Not surprisingly, researchers who adopt a communication science perspective (see Chapter 14) find cultural theory hard to understand. They are skeptical of theories that are evaluated more through debate than through empirical research. Communication science places far less stress on theory development or criticism. Research methods are used for theory testing rather than as a means of making qualitative differentiations. Communication science argues that if empirical research is conducted according to prevailing standards, findings can be readily accepted throughout the research community. If other researchers doubt the validity of specific findings, they can replicate the research and then report conflicting findings. Actually, these conflicting reports are rare and provoke considerable controversy when they are published. Though there is verbal debate between those who espouse conflicting, empirically based theories, these debates rarely appear in print. When they do, both sides present empirical findings to support their positions. As you'll see in the section of this chapter dealing with cultivation analysis, these arguments often center around methodological disputes rather than the strength of the theoretical propositions — researchers disagree about whether appropriate methods were used, question the application of specific methods, or argue that the data were improperly analyzed. Much less attention is given to the structure and consistency of theoretical propositions.

In Chapter 14 we will return to a discussion of the differences between the cultural theories and the communication science perspective. Both differences and commonalities will be considered. The potential for cooperation and for division are present. Do these two approaches constitute rival paradigms? Can they coexist or must one inevitably displace the other?

Cultural Theories: Transmissional versus Ritual Perspectives

James Carey has been a leading proponent of cultural theories during the past two decades. He contrasted cultural theories with the limited effects paradigm in a series of seminal essays (1989). One essential difference that he found is that limited effects theories focus on the transmission of accurate information from a dominant source to passive receivers while cultural theories are concerned about the everyday rituals that we rely upon to structure and interpret our experiences. Carey argued that the limited effects view is tied to the *transmissional perspective* — the view that mass communication is a "process of transmitting messages at a distance for the purpose of control. The archetypal case . . . then is persuasion, attitude change, behavior modification, socialization through the transmission of information, influence, or conditioning" (Newcomb and Hirsch, 1983, p. 46). In the transmissional perspective, car commercials attempt to persuade us to buy a certain make of automobile, and political campaign messages are simply that, campaign messages designed to cause us to vote one way or another. They may or may not be effective in causing us to act as they intend.

The *ritual perspective*, on the other hand, views mass communication as "not directed toward the extension of messages in space but the maintenance of society in time; not the act of imparting information but the representation of shared beliefs" (Newcomb and Hirsch, 1983, p. 46). Carey (1975a, p. 177) believed, in other words, that "communication is a symbolic process whereby reality is produced, maintained, repaired, and transformed." According to his view, a car commercial sells more than transportation. It is, depending on its actual content, possibly reaffirming the American sense of independence (It's a Chevy, it's your freedom), reinforcing cultural notions of male and female attractiveness (we don't see many homely actors in these ads), or extolling the personal value of consumption, regardless of the product itself (be the first on your block to have one). Similarly, political campaign messages often say much more about our political system and us as a people than they say about the candidates featured in them.

Carey traced the origin of the ritual view to literary criticism. Scholars who study great literary works have long argued that these texts have far-reaching, long-lasting and powerful effects on society. A classic example is the impact that Shakespeare has had on Western culture. By reshaping or transforming culture, these works indirectly influence even those who have never read them or even heard of them. Literary scholars argue that contemporary cultures are analyzed and defined through their arts, including those arts that depend upon media technology. These scholars have not been interested in finding evidence of direct media effects on individuals. They are more concerned with macroscopic questions of cultural evolution—the culture defining itself for itself. Thus, the ritual perspective presumes a grand-scale interaction between the culture, the media used to convey that culture, and the individual content consumers of that culture.

ritual perspective

During the 1970s and 1980s some communication theorists began to move away from more transmissionally-oriented questions like "What effects do media have on society or on individuals?" (for example, persuasion and social learning theories) and "How do people use the media?" (for example, uses and gratifications) toward broader examinations of how cultures organize themselves, how people negotiate common meaning and are bound by it, and how media systems interact with the culture to affect the latter's definition of itself. This, as we'll see, allowed cultural theories to become a base for a variety of people who presumed the operation of powerful mass media, for example advertising and market researchers, neomarxist media critics, and even sophisticated social researchers. The primary issue was no longer do media affect people, but what kind of people are we or have we become in our mass mediated world.

Macroscopic versus Microscopic Theories

Cultural analysis theories are less concerned with the long-term consequences of media for the social order and more concerned with looking at how media affect our individual lives. These theories, as we've seen throughout this book, are said to be micro-level or *microscopic* because they de-emphasize larger issues about the social order in favor of questions involving the everyday life of average people. In Chapter 13, we will consider the *macroscopic* cultural theories, which are less concerned with developing detailed explanations of how individuals are influenced by media and more concerned with how the social order as a whole is affected. Ideally, these theories ought to be complementary. Individual-level explanations of what media do to people should link to societal-level theories. Yet until recently, macroscopic and microscopic cultural theories developed in relative isolation. Theorists were separated by differences in geography, politics, and research objectives. But that is rapidly changing.

Microscopic cultural researchers prefer to understand what is going on in the world immediately around them. For them the social world is an endlessly fascinating place. They are intrigued by the mundane, the seemingly trivial, the routine. They view our experience of everyday life and of reality itself as an artificial construction that we somehow maintain with only occasional, minor breakdowns. They want to know how mass media have been incorporated into the routines of daily life without creating serious disruptions. Perhaps the media have created disruptions that are somehow being compensated for or concealed. If so, how is this being done? Will there be a breakdown eventually — are we being systematically desensitized and trained to be aggressive? Or is everyday life culture being transformed in useful ways — are we somehow becoming kinder and gentler?

Macroscopic researchers are troubled by the narrow focus of microscopic theory. So what if some people experience everyday life in certain ways? Why should we care about things that may affect only a few people? These researchers demand answers to larger questions. How do media affect the way politics is conducted, the way that a national economy operates, or the delivery of vital social services? They want to know if media are intruding into or disrupting large-scale social processes. For example, have media disrupted the conduct of national politics and therefore increased the likelihood that inferior politicians will be elected? Macroscopic researchers believe that such large-scale questions can't be answered if you begin by looking at individuals.

Both types of theory provide interesting and potentially useful insights into contemporary life. In this and the next chapter we will point out how they complement each other and where they conflict. We begin with the microscopic — cultural analysis.

Symbolic Interactionism

Symbolic interactionism was one of the first social science theories to address questions of how we learn and use culture. It developed during the 1920s and 1930s as a reaction to and criticism of stimulus-response theory (see Chapters 4 and 7). It was given a variety of labels until Herbert Blumer coined the term symbolic interactionism. One early name was social behaviorism. Unlike ordinary behaviorists, social behaviorists rejected simplistic conceptualizations of stimulus-response conditioning. They were convinced that attention must be given to the mental processes that mediate learning. Social behaviorists believed that the social environment in which learning takes place must be considered. Behaviorists tended to conduct laboratory experiments in which animals were exposed to certain stimuli and conditioned to behave in specific ways. To social behaviorists, these experiments were absurd. They believed that human existence was far too complex to be understood through conditioning of animal behavior.

George Herbert Mead (1934), a University of Chicago philosopher and social activist, provided a way of understanding social life that differed profoundly from behaviorist notions. Rather than observe rats running through mazes, he proposed that a better way to understand how people learn is to look at how people learn to play baseball (or any team sport). How do we learn to play these games? Surely not by reading textbooks on *The Theory of Playing Second Base*. Not through stimulus-response conditioning. Mead argued that what occurs on a playing field is a sophisticated form of mutual conditioning—the players teach each other how to play the game while they are playing it. Players must learn to structure their actions in very complex ways to cover their positions effectively. But each position must be played differently, so they can't simply mimic one another. According to Mead, each player learns a social role—the pitcher role, the catcher role, or the left fielder role. Each is learned by observing and modeling good players and by interacting with other team members. As they play, team members receive encouragement and friendly criticism from teammates and fans. If they play well, they have the satisfaction of being accepted by others as a productive member of a social unit.

For Mead, a baseball team is (or should be) a microcosm of society. Each of us learns many different social roles through interaction with others. Our actions are being subtly "conditioned" by others while we are affecting their actions. The goal is not to manipulate or dominate each other but rather to create and sustain a productive social unit—a group that provides its members with certain rewards in return for their willingness to take on specific roles. We learn social roles through interaction, through experiences in daily life situations. Over time, we internalize the rules inherent in the situations and structure our actions accordingly. Only in rare cases do we consciously reflect upon and analyze our actions. If asked to explain what we are doing and why we are doing it, we are puzzled— the question seems strange. Why don't you call your mother by her first name? Why do you wear clothes to school? We are doing something because it is commonsense, it's the way everybody does it, it's the normal, the logical, the right way to do things. Once internalized, these roles provide us with a powerful means of controlling our actions. In time, our identity becomes bound up with them—we feel good about ourselves because we play certain roles that are respected by others. And sometimes, like athletes whose physical skills inevitably fail, we experience identity crises because we can't play a role as we or others expect us to play it.

Mead's analogy is insightful and powerful but it has some important limitations common to microscopic theories. Mead assumes that baseball teams operate as a sort of miniature democracy. But where do the teams come from? How do they get established? Who defines the rules of baseball games? Who sells the tickets, pays expenses, and profits from the game? The team members mutually influence each other but often a few older or more experienced players will dominate the others. And what about the team as a whole? They have managers and owners who hire and fire team members.

The baseball team analogy also isn't very helpful for understanding how mass media might affect socialization. Players interact directly with one another. What happens when communication occurs through media? Perhaps a more up-to-date analogy would be a group of people who use computers to engage in an interactive, role-playing game like "Dungeons and Dragons." Unlike baseball players who confront each other physically on the field, these role players meet each other as characters in a complex fantasy-drama. They each sit at their personal computers and are linked to a remote mainframe computer via modems and phone lines. The game can go on endlessly with the computer taking over roles as players drop in and out. Players choose a role as they enter the game and use it to structure their interaction with other players. To take on a role and enjoy the game, players must acquire considerable knowledge about the fantasy world. They could get this knowledge only from playing the game, but this would be inefficient and frustrating—they would literally die a thousand deaths. A more efficient way of learning the game is through media—comic books, books, magazines, and television programs. Once you have found or constructed a role you think you might enjoy playing, you are ready to log on and try it. In this example, there is mutual conditioning but it occurs after use of media and reinforces knowledge gained through media.

Mead offered another important insight into the socialization process. Unlike animals that are conditioned to respond to stimuli in predetermined ways, human socialization permits more or less conscious interpretation of stimuli and planned responses. What is the secret that enables us to do what animals cannot? *Symbols.* Symbols are arbitrary, often quite abstract representations of unseen phenomena. Think of the words you use—all are arbitrary vocalizations that are essentially meaningless except to others who know how to decode them. When we write we cover pages with complicated markings. To read them, someone must be literate in our language. According to Mead, the use of symbols transforms the socialization process—freeing it from the bonds of both space and time. With symbols we can create vivid representations of the past and we can anticipate the future. We can be transported anywhere on the globe or even into the far reaches of space.

In *Mind, Self, and Society*, Mead argued that we use symbols to create our experience of consciousness (Mind), our understanding of ourselves (Self), and our knowledge of the larger social order (Society). In other words, symbols mediate and structure all of our experience because they structure our ability to perceive and interpret what goes on around us. This argument is similar to the one made by information processing theorists (see Chapter 11). In information processing theory, sets of symbols called schemas enable us to routinely make sense of the sensory information we take in. Mead believed that mind, self, and society are internalized as complex sets of symbols. They serve as filtering mechanisms for our experiences. For information processing theorists, schemas perform a similar function.

This may seem to be an extreme argument. Most of us take for granted our ability to look at the world around us and see the things that are obviously there. You may assume that this is an ability you were born with. But think about it. Why do you notice certain things and not others? Unless you are unusually fastidious, you will not notice small amounts of dust and dirt when you enter a room. According to Mead, human perceptual processes are extremely malleable and can be shaped by the sets of symbols we learn so that we will see only what our culture has determined is worth seeing (were you taken in by Charles Stuart's ruse discussed in Chapter 7?). Mead's arguments anticipated information processing research that is beginning to empirically demonstrate much of what he hypothesized.

Thus, symbolic interactionism posits that our actions in response to symbols are mediated (or controlled) largely by those same symbols. Therefore, a person's understanding of and relation to his or her physical or objective reality is mediated by the symbolic environment—the mind, self, and society that we have internalized. Put another way, the meanings we give to signs and symbols define us and the realities that we experience. As we are socialized, culturally agreed-upon meanings assume control over our interactions with our environments.

Consider the meaning that you attach to the sewn red, white and blue cloth that constitutes an American flag. A flag is, in reality (objectively), little more than a piece of colored cloth. That is, it is little more than a piece of cloth until someone attaches symbolic meaning to it. We have decided that a particular array and formulation of colors and shapes should become our flag. Each of us experiences the flag differently yet there is shared meaning as well. To Kuwaiti civilians who saw it fly from the rear of tanks and jeeps in the 1991 Gulf Conflict, the Stars and Stripes signified liberation. To Somalis in 1992, it became associated with food and medical care. To people from some other countries, it might represent oppression. But regardless of the meaning we may attach to our flag, we are not free from its power. When a color guard passes before you at a sporting event, how free are you to remain sitting? At a school function, how free are you to continue chatting with your friends during the pledge of allegiance to that tri-colored piece of fabric?

Although Mead first articulated his ideas in the 1930s, not until the 1970s and 1980s did symbolic interactionism began to be seriously used by mass communication researchers. Given the great emphasis that Mead placed on interpersonal interaction and his disregard for media, it is not surprising that media theorists were slow to see the relevancy of his ideas. Michael Solomon (1983), a consumer researcher, provided a summary of Mead's work that is especially relevant for media research:

1   Cultural symbols are learned through interaction and then mediate that interaction.

2   The "overlap of shared meaning" by people in a culture means that individuals who learn a culture should be able to predict the behaviors of others in that culture.

3   Self-definition is social in nature; the self is defined largely through interaction with the environment.

4   The extent to which a person is committed to a social identity will determine the power of that identity to influence his or her behavior.

Among the most notable efforts by communication scholars to apply this symbolic interactionist thinking to our use of mass media was the book, *Communication and Social Behavior: A Symbolic Interaction Perspective*, written by Don F. Faules and Dennis C. Alexander in 1978. Basing their analysis on their definition of communication as "symbolic behavior which results in various degrees of shared meaning and values between participants," they offered three fundamental propositions on symbolic interaction and communication:

book

1   **People's interpretation and perception of the environment depend on communication.** In other words, what we know of our world is largely a function of our prior communication experiences in that world. This conforms to Solomon's idea of interaction with cultural symbols. As Faules and Alexander wrote, "Communication allows for the reduction of uncertainty without direct sensory experience. The media are a prime source of indirect experience and for that reason have impact on the construction of social reality" (1978, p. 23).

2   **Communication is guided by and guides the concepts of self, role, and situations, and these concepts generate expectations in and of the environment.** Put differently, our use of communication in different settings is related to our understanding of ourselves and others in those situations. This is analogous to Solomon's point about learning a culture and predicting the behavior of others.

3 Communication consists of complex interactions "involving action, interdependence, mutual influence, meaning, relationship, and situational factors" (1978, p. 23). Here we can see not only a communication-oriented restatement of Solomon's precepts three and four, but also a rearticulation of the ritual perspective. Faules and Alexander are clearly reminding us that our understanding of our world and our place in it are created by us in interaction and involvement with media symbols.

Before we get any further into symbolic interaction, however, we must mention some definitional differences between this perspective and its close relative, social construction of reality, discussed in the next section of this chapter. In symbolic interactionist theory, a *sign* is any element in the environment used to represent another element in the environment. Signs can be classified in two ways. One is *natural signs*, those things in nature—like the changing color of leaves—that represent something else in nature—the coming of autumn. The second is *artificial signs*, elements that have been constructed—like the flag—to represent something else in the social world—like patriotism or duty. These artificial signs only work if the people using them agree on their meaning, that is, if they are "interactive," two or more people must agree on their meaning and must further agree to respond to that sign in a relatively consistent fashion.

Another difference is symbolic interaction's distinction between signals and symbols. *Signals* are artificial signs that produce highly predictable responses, like traffic signals. *Symbols*, on the other hand, are artificial signs for which there is less certainty of response, like the flag. As Faules and Alexander explained, (1978, p. 36), "Signals are used to regulate normative behavior in a society, and symbols are used to facilitate communicative behavior in a society."

Social Construction of Reality

What all theories that are classified as cultural analysis theories have in common is the underlying assumption that our experience of reality is an ongoing, social construction, not something that is only sent, delivered, or otherwise transmitted to a docile public by some authority or elite. This assumption contrasts sharply with both mass society theory and the limited effects perspective. Mass society theory envisioned vast populations living in nightmare realities dominated by demagogues. Limited effects research focused on the effective transmission of ideas and information from dominant sources to passive receivers. When the social construction of reality assumption is applied to mass communication it implies what we have already seen termed the *active audience assumption*. Audience members don't just passively take in and store bits of information in mental filing cabinets, they actively process this information, reshape it, and store only what serves culturally defined needs.

Active audience members use the media's symbols to define their environments and the things in it, but those definitions have little value unless they are shared by others. A Porsche, for example, can be as expensive an automobile as a Rolls Royce and both are functionally the same thing—automobiles that transport people from here to there. Yet the "realities" that surround both cars (and the people who drive them) are quite different. Moreover, how these different drivers are treated by other people may also vary, not because any true difference in them as humans, but because the "reality" that is attached to the car of each is used to define them (see, for example, Baran and Blasko, 1984). We'll discuss this more later.

Some early systematic discussions of social construction of reality ideas were provided by a banker whose avocation was sociology, Alfred Schutz (1967, 1970). He was fascinated by what he regarded as the mysteries of everyday existence. Just how do we make sense of the world around us so that we can structure and coordinate our daily actions? How can we do this with such ease that we don't even realize that we are doing it? To answer these questions Schutz used a body of social theory that had been developed in Europe, *Phenomenology*. Relying upon phenomenological notions, he asked his students at the New School for Social Research in New York to *bracket* or set aside their commonsense, taken-for-granted explanations for what they were doing and recognize that everyday life was actually much more complicated than they assumed. Schutz argued that we can conduct our lives with little effort or thought because we have developed *stocks of social knowledge* that we use to quickly make sense of what goes on around us and then structure our actions. One of the most important forms of knowledge that we possess is *typifications*. Typifications enable us to quickly classify objects and actions that we observe and then structure our own actions in response. But typifications operate to some extent like stereotypes—though they make it easy to interpret our experiences, they also distort and bias these experiences.

The concept of typifications is similar to Mead's conception of symbols and the notion of schemas in information processing theory. It differs from these by reminding us of the negative consequences of typifications. When we rely on typifications to routinely structure our experience, we risk making serious mistakes. Remember the store manager who thought he saw gypsies and couldn't be convinced otherwise. He was using a typification to guide his perceptions. It would be interesting to know if he'd ever had any personal experience with gypsies or if this typification had been developed largely from mass media.

Schutz's ideas were elaborated in *The Social Construction of Reality*, written by sociologists Peter Berger and Thomas Luckmann. Published in 1966, the book made virtually no mention of mass communication, but with the explosion of interest in the media that accompanied the dramatic social and cultural changes of that turbulent decade, mass communication theorists (not to mention scholars from numerous other disciplines) quickly found Berger and Luckmann's work and identified its value for developing media theory.

In explaining how reality is socially constructed, the two sociologists assumed first that "there is an ongoing correspondence between *my* meanings and *their* meanings in the world (and) that we share a common sense about its reality" (1966, p. 23). Let's use a common household article as our example. Here are three *symbols* for that article:

1   KNIFE

2

3

A symbol is an object (in these instances, a collection of letters or drawings on paper) that represents some other object—what we commonly refer to as a knife. Here are three other symbols for that same article:

1   MESSER

2   CUCHILLO

3   ⬭⬭

But unless you speak German or Spanish, respectively, or unless you understand what truly horrible artists we are, these symbols have no meaning for you, there is no correspondence between our meaning and yours, we share no common sense about the reality of the object being symbolized.

But who says that KNIFE means what we all know it to mean? And what's wrong with those people in Germany and Mexico? Don't they know that it's KNIFE, not MESSER or CUCHILLO? In English-speaking countries the culture has *agreed* that KNIFE means that sharp thing we use to cut our food, among other things. Just as the folks in German- and Spanish-speaking lands have agreed on something else. There is no inherent truth, value, or meaning in the ordered collection of letters K-N-I-F-E that gives it the reality that we all know it has. We have given it meaning, and because we share that meaning, we can function as a people (at least where the issue is household implements).

But Berger and Luckmann recognized that there is another kind of meaning that we attach to the things in our environments, one that is *subjective* rather than *objective*. They call these signs, objects explicitly designed "to serve as an index of subjective meaning" (1966, p. 35). If you were to wake up tomorrow morning, with your head on your pillow, to find a knife stuck into the headboard inches above your nose, you'd be fairly certain that this was some sort of sign. In other words, people can produce representations of objects that have very specific, very subjective agreed upon meanings. What does the knife in the headboard signify? Says who? What does a Porsche signify? Says who? What do several pieces of cloth—some red, some white, some blue—sewn together in a rectangle in such a way to produce thirteen alternating red and white stripes and a number of stars against a blue field in the upper left hand corner signify? Freedom? Democracy? Food and medicine? The largest car dealer on the strip? Says who?

Remember that symbolic interaction defines signs and symbols in precisely the opposite way that social construction of reality does. This small problem aside, how do people use these signs and symbols to construct a reality that allows a culture to function? Berger and Luckmann developed Schutz's notion of typifications into what they refer to as *typification schemes*, collections of meanings we have assigned to some phenomenon, that come from our social stock of knowledge to pattern our interaction with our environments and the things and people in it. A bit more simply, we, as a people, through interaction with our environment, construct a "natural backdrop" for the development of "typification schemes required for the major routines of everyday life, not only the typification of others . . . but typifications of all sorts of events and experiences, both social and natural" (1966, p. 43).

Of course, what media theorists and practitioners, especially advertisers and marketing professionals, now understand is that whoever has the greatest influence over a culture's definitions of it symbols and signs also controls the construction of the typification schemes that individuals use to pattern their interactions with their various social worlds. Why, for example, is one beer more "sophisticated" than another? Are you less likely to serve generic beer to your house guests than Michelob or Heinekin? Why?

Product Positioning, Social Construction of Reality, and Symbolic Interaction

One common example of the operation of both the social construction of reality and symbolic interaction is advertisers' attempts to "position" their products or, in other words, to attach to them symbolic meanings or realities that will leave consumers little choice but to accept those realities. In Chapter 11, we explained how positioning techniques are used during the latter stages of modern promotional campaigns. Current positioning techniques also derive from William Stephenson's notion of communication play (See Chapter 10).

Advertising executive Robert Pritkin (Haas, 1979) described positioning this way: "Since most products aren't special, most advertising does all that so-called image stuff . . . There's no information about the product, there's only information about the kinds of people who might be inclined to use the product" (p. 46). Sociologist Marcus Felson (1978, p. 57) made a similar observation: "Advertisers, each motivated to exaggerate its own product's quality, collectively confuse the public's ability to distinguish among consumer goods. Moreover, the prosperity of modern society allows enough budgetary leeway so that the average consumer can develop stylistic tastes and idiosyncrasies." Speaking of the positioning of automobiles, for example, he said that this leads people to make "invidious dis-tinctions" among makes of cars, evaluating car owners on some externally cre-ated hierarchy of prestige. In other words, the realities that the advertisers attach to their different automobiles become the realities we attach to them, guiding our judgments of and behaviors toward their owners. Have you ever borrowed a friend's car to go on a date? Why? Have you ever asked "what kind of car does she drive?" when inquiring about a person? When driving, do you ever deny a courtesy to another driver because of the make of car he or she is driving (No way, Mr. Mercedes, I'm not letting you in!).

Stanley Baran, Jinja Mok, Mitchell Land, and Tae Young Kang (1989) made the connection between product positioning and our two symbolic theories when they offered customers at a supermarket different versions of the same shopping list. What these researchers wanted to know (1989, p. 48) was

> how we use our information about various consumer products in making judgments of other people. That is, can an association with products posi-tioned in different ways influence the kinds of judgments people make of one another, even when the products in question have no ostensible rela-tionship to the kinds of judgments asked for? Certain products may be posi-tioned as "upscale" or "chic," for example, but what bearing does or should that have on people's perceptions of another's goodness, charity, or degree of responsibility? . . . Restating the question in Berger and Luckmann's terms, "Is the social stock of knowledge used to typify others in the culture and therefore structure our interaction with them based on advertiser-created or -influenced significations?"

Baran and his colleagues first looked at what advertisers and marketers them-selves thought about the two theories. For example, quoting market theorist Michael Solomon's article entitled "The Role of Products as Social Stimuli: A Symbolic Interactionism Perspective," they showed that advertisers did, indeed, understand their ability to construct realities with their symbols. Solomon (1983, p. 320) saw products as "integral threads in the fabric of social life" and he advised advertisers to place emphasis on the importance of products in "setting the stage" for the multitude of social roles people must play (lover, gourmand, executive, athlete, and so on) . . . Consumers employ product symbolism to define social reality and to ensure that behaviors appropriate to that reality will ensue . . . Product symbolism is often consumed by the social actor for the purpose of defining and clarifying behavior patterns associated with social roles.

Baran and his colleagues used four different hand-printed shopping lists, one with generic names (for example, sun tan lotion and ice cream), one that mixed products positioned as practical and as upscale, and one each that offered only practical (for example, Coppertone and Borden's ice cream) or upscale (for example, Ban de Soleil and Haagen Daaz) products. All four lists also contained non-brand name items like milk, hamburger, and so on.

People who were given the shopping lists were asked to participate in a study of "people's shopping habits." Then they were told that the list belonged to either a man or a woman and asked to answer a few questions about the person who wrote the list. These questions had no obvious relationship with the items on the list:

- If I had a young child, I'd let this person babysit.
- It's likely I'd have this person as a friend.
- This person is probably very popular in his/her social group.
- It's fairly likely that this person is punctual.
- If I were an employer I'd probably hire this person.
- This person is likely to be involved in volunteer social work.
- In social situations this person is probably fairly reserved.

What the researchers discovered surprised them. They wrote, "The results make it clear that variously positioned products do indeed provide a social stock of knowledge that people use in typifying those they meet" (Baran, Mok, Land, and Kang, 1989, p. 52). They had predicted that those people who were buying the more upscale products would be seen as somehow better than those who were buying products positioned as more practical. But what happened was that the gender of the shopper interacted with the brands; that is, men using either of the brand-name shopping lists were seen as the better people, while women who bought generic or practical products were rated lowest.

In explaining this outcome, the researchers wrote, "The results hint at a larger cultural stereotype in the gender roles associated with shopping. Men (who are not typically charged with shopping) who can 'hunt' specifically (by brand name, regardless of positioning) are evaluated as more responsible than women who, presumably, should know the ins and outs of the various products" (Baran, Mok, Land, and Kang, 1989, p. 52).

Framing and Frame Analysis

Remember the situation that opened this chapter, the Bulgarians being tossed out of that Minneapolis supermarket? It may be easy for you to say what you would have done. But imagine walking down a deserted street in any large U.S. city late at night. What would your expectations be concerning a polite and well-dressed foreigner who steps from the shadows? You've seen the television commercials where a woman's battery or antifreeze happens to go bad just as she makes a wrong turn into a ghetto. Those ads never show what happens to her, we just see the look of terror in her eyes as she awaits—what? Those ads don't need to show us what will happen because we all have strongly formed expectations of how such stories end. We get the message without being told. Such "fill-in-the-blank" messages may be even more powerful than explicit arguments because as audience members, we actively participate by providing our own end to the story. These ads avoid being labeled racist or classist because they often don't explicitly show us the lower class, ethnic group members that we all "know" prowl such places after midnight just looking for victims. Ad producers can rely on us to interpret their messages using the racial and class related biases and expectations that we already have. Remember, Charles Stuart realized this all too well.

In 1988, George Bush's Presidential campaign had no need to lecture us on the dangers of releasing the members of certain racial or ethnic groups from jail. Campaign planners had only to give us a symbol or slogan to help us remember what we already feared. Lee Atwater, the Bush campaign chairman, declared his objective was to "scrape the bark off that little bastard [Dukakis] and make Willie Horton his running mate" (*Herald Wire Reports*, 1991, p. 6A)." One media critic (Jamieson, 1989) noted that the Bush campaign ads (showing prisoners coming out of a revolving prison door) featured actors whose physical features were ambiguous. None could be clearly distinguished as belonging to specific racial or ethnic minorities. Yet in focus group interviews, people who watched these spots inevitably remembered seeing black and Hispanic persons. Why? The ad didn't need to tell us what we already knew.

The phenomenon that we have been discussing in these troubling examples has proved very difficult to conceptualize and study. You have probably already encountered many terms in this and other textbooks—stereotypes, attitudes, typification schemes, and racial or ethnic bias. All these concepts emphasize that our expectations: (a) are based on previous experience of some kind, whether derived from a media message or direct personal experience (that is, we aren't born with them); (b) can be quite resistant to change even when they are contradicted by readily available factual information; (c) are often associated with and can arouse strong emotions such as hate, fear, or love; and (d) our conscious control over them may be limited, especially when strong emotions are aroused that interfere with our ability to make sense of new information available in the situation. Developing and using such expectations in this way is a normal and routine part of everyday life. As human beings, we have cognitive skills that allow us to continually scan our environment, make sense of it, and then act upon these interpretations. Our inability to adequately understand these skills in no way prevents them from operating, but it does impede our ability to make sense of our own sense-making. You will always and inevitably make an interpretation of the world around you. Sometimes you will understand what you are doing but more often you won't — typically it doesn't matter whether you do or not. But if you would like to assume more responsibility for your actions, then you should be concerned.

The sociologist Erving Goffman (1974) introduced *frame analysis* to provide a systematic account of how we use expectations to make sense of everyday life situations and the people in them. He was fascinated by the mistakes we make as we go through daily life — including the mistakes we never notice. Like Schutz, Goffman was convinced that daily life is much more complicated than it appears. He studied con artists — people who make their living by inducing the rest of us to make costly mistakes. Goffman argued that we constantly and often radically change the way we define or typify situations, actions, and other people as we move through time and space. In other words, our experience of the world is constantly shifting, sometimes in major ways, yet we usually don't notice these shifts. We can step from one world to another without noticing that a boundary has been crossed. According to Goffman, we don't operate with a limited or fixed set of expectations about social roles, objects, or situations. Rather, we have enormous flexibility in creating and using expectations.

But if our sense-making ability is so great and so flexible, how can we structure it so that we can coordinate our actions with others and experience daily existence as having order and meaning? Life, Goffman argued, operates much like a staged dramatic performance. We step from one social world to another in much the same way that actors move between scenes. Scenes shift, and as they shift we are able to radically alter how we make sense of them. But just how do we know when such shifts are to be made? How do we know when one scene is ending and another beginning? According to Goffman, we are always monitoring the social environment for *social cues* that signal when we are to make a change. For example, when you view a play in a theater, you rely on many conventional cues to determine when a shift in scenes takes place. One of the oldest and most obvious cues involves using a curtain — it rises when a new scene begins and it falls when a scene ends. Other cues are more subtle — shifts in lights and music tempo often signal changes. As lights dim and music becomes ominous, we know that danger threatens. If Goffman was correct, then the same cognitive skills that we use in making sense of plays are also used in daily life. His theory also implies

Box 12a The Framing Process

In a different book (Davis and Baran, 1981), your two authors developed this version of Goffman's theory of framing. Can you explain how it allows for up and downshifting? Can you speculate on how errors in framing can occur?

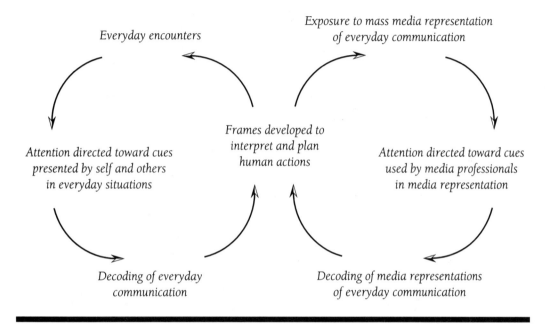

that social cues learned from using media could also be used to mark the boundaries of social worlds in everyday life.

Goffman used the term *frame* to refer to a specific set of expectations that are used to make sense of a social situation at a given point in time. Frames are like the typification schemes described by Berger and Luckmann but they differ in certain important respects. According to Goffman, individual frames are like notes on a musical scale — they spread along a continuum from those that structure our most serious and socially significant actions to those that structure playful, trivial actions. But like the notes on a musical scale, each is different though there is underlying structural continuity. For social action, the continuity is such that we can learn how to frame serious actions by first learning frames for playful actions. Using the musical scale analogy, we can first learn to play simple tunes that use a narrow range of the scale in preparation for playing complex musical scores. For example, many of our games and sports provide useful preparation for more serious forms of action. If we can perform well under the pressures of a big game, we may handle the demands of other situations better. Goffman argued that we are like animal cubs that first play at stalking frogs or butterflies and then are able to transfer these skills to related but more serious situations.

When we move from one set of frames to another, we *downshift* or *upshift*. We reframe situations so that we experience them as being more or less serious. Remember when you were pretending to fight with a friend but one of you got hurt and the fight turned serious. You both downshifted. Suddenly, you no longer pulled punches but tried to make them inflict as much pain as possible. Many of the fighting skills learned during play were used but with a different frame — you were trying to hurt your friend. Perhaps, as you both got tired, one of you told a joke and cued the other that you wanted to upshift and go back to a more playful frame. According to Goffman, daily life involves countless shifts in frames and these shifts are negotiated by using social cues. Some cues are very conventional and universal, like the curtain on a stage; others are very subtle and used by small groups. For example, couples often develop a very complex set of cues to signal when to upshift or downshift their interaction. During the course of a conversation, many upshifts and downshifts can occur. Upshifting and downshifting add a dimension of complexity to everyday interaction that Goffman argued shouldn't be ignored.

So where do media come into this theory? Goffman himself made only limited but heuristic explorations of the way that media might influence our development and use of frames. In *Gender Advertisements* (1979) he presented an insightful argument concerning the affect that advertising could have on our perception of members of the opposite sex. He argued that advertising that uses the sex appeal of women to attract the attention of men inadvertently teaches us social cues that could have serious consequences. He showed how women are presented as less serious and more playful than men in numerous advertisements. They smile, place their bodies in nonserious positions, wear playful clothing, and in various ways signal deference and a willingness to take direction from men. They are not only vulnerable to sexual advances, they signal their desire for them. No wonder these ads attract the attention of men. No wonder they are useful in positioning products. But could these representations of women be teaching social cues that have unexpected consequences?

We may be learning more than product definitions from these ads. We could be learning a vast array of social cues, some blatant but others quite subtle. Once learned, these cues could be used in daily life to make sense of members of the opposite sex and to impose frames upon them, their actions, and the situations in which we encounter them. One possibility is that this advertising leads men to be overly sensitive to playful cues from women and increases the likelihood that they will upshift. Men learn such a vast repertoire of these cues that it may be hard for women to avoid displaying them. Inadvertent actions by women could be routinely misinterpreted by men. Advertising might make it hard for women to maintain a serious frame for their actions. If they smile, bend their elbow in a particular way or bow their head even briefly, men may perceive a cue when none was intended. The more physically attractive the woman, the more likely this problem might arise since most advertising features good-looking women.

Goffman's theory provides an intriguing way of assessing how media can elaborate and reinforce a dominant public culture. Advertisers didn't create sex-role stereotypes but Goffman argued that they have homogenized the way in which women are publicly depicted. He contrasts the variety of ways that women are represented in private photos with their standardized depiction in advertising. Powerful visual imagery is routinely used to associate products with women who explicitly and implicitly signal their willingness to be playful, sexual partners. There are many subtle and not-so-subtle messages in these ads. Consume the product and get the girl is one dominant message. Another is that physically attractive women are sexually active and fun-loving. Ads both teach and reinforce cues. The specific message that each of us gets from the ads will be very different, but their long-term consequence may be similar—dominant myths about women are retold and reinforced.

By comparison to the other theories we have examined in this chapter, Goffman's is the most open-ended and flexible. He was convinced that social life is a constantly evolving and changing phenomenon. And yet we experience social life as having great continuity. Though we have the capacity to constantly reframe our experience from moment to moment, most of us can maintain the impression that our experiences are quite consistent and routine. According to Goffman, we do this by firmly committing ourselves to live in what we experience as the *primary or dominant reality*—a real world in which people and events obey certain conventional and widely accepted rules. We find this world so compelling and desirable that we are constantly reworking and patching up flaws in our experience and we don't notice when rule violations occur. He argued that we work so hard to maintain our sense of continuity in our experience that we inevitably make many framing mistakes. We literally see and hear things that aren't there but that should be there according to the rules we have internalized. For example, most college campuses in America today face the problem of date rape. And ultimately, what is the basic issue in most of these occurrences? Goffman might answer upshifting and downshifting problems between men and women as they attempt to frame the situations (dating) they find themselves in.

From Goffman's viewpoint, we are virtual prisoners of primary reality. We permit ourselves only brief and socially acceptable escapes into clearly demarcated alternative realities that we experience as fantasy worlds. But as the date rape example suggests, when we make framing mistakes in our primary realities, the results can be devastating.

Cultivation Analysis

We conclude this chapter with a consideration of cultivation analysis as developed by George Gerbner. Unlike the other theories in this chapter, cultivation analysis addresses *macroscopic* questions about the role of media in society. But unlike the theories we will examine in Chapter 13, it attempts to use empirical research methods to evaluate its assertions. Also, cultivation researchers were not part of a political movement, though they did try to influence media policy-making. Cultivation analysis represents a hybrid theory that combines aspects of both macroscopic and microscopic cultural theories. Some researchers regard it as a possible prototype for future research while others consider it to be a poor example of how to do research. In our view, this controversy was a pivotal one in the development of mass communication theory. It came when the limited effects paradigm was still strong but had begun to show signs of waning. It came when cultural analysis approaches were beginning to receive more serious attention from humanist scholars. The controversy reveals a great deal about various opposing perspectives, most of which are still widely held.

What percentage of the people arrested for felonies in your state in a given year actually make it to trial? Of those that do get into court, what percentage are actually convicted? Would you be surprised to learn that in California in 1986, there were 109,787 felony arrests and 80 percent of them went to trial. Of those that were tried, convictions were won in 88 percent (Judicial Council, 1986).

You were surprised, weren't you? Because you "just know" that our criminal justice system is in havoc. You "just know" that criminals, with their technicalities and tricky lawyers, can always work deals and avoid trial. And you are "just absolutely certain" that, if these bad guys ever do see the inside of a courthouse, their attorneys can manipulate the law and the jury to win acquittal.

Would you be surprised to learn that, according to one analysis of a sample week of prime-time network television programming, more than 86 percent of the shows that presented the American criminal justice system depicted the bad guys never coming to justice or, when they did, they "beat the system" (Choi, Massey, and Baran, 1988)? But which is real, the perspective represented by official government statistics like the California data or that which appears on television? If you and your fellow citizens' view of the criminal justice system match more closely the one presented on television, then that's the one that's real, because that's the one that you will use when analyzing how your state spends its tax dollars, whether you favor the "law and order" candidate over the "education candidate," and in deciding a host of other issues that relate to crime.

In any given week, what are the chances that you will be involved in some kind of violence, about 1 in 10 or about 1 in 100? In the actual world, about .41 violent crimes occur per 100 Americans, or, less than 1 in 200. In the world of prime-time television, though, more than 64 percent of all characters are involved in violence. Was your answer closer to the actual or to the television world? What percentage of all working males in the United States toil in law enforcement and crime detection? One percent or 5 percent? The U.S. Census says 1 percent, television says 12 percent. What did you say? Finally, of all the crimes that occur in America in any year, what proportion are violent crimes like murder, rape, robbery, and assault? Would you guess 15 or 25 percent? If you hold the television view you chose the higher number. On television, 77 percent of all major characters who commit crimes commit the violent kind. But the *Statistical Abstract of the U.S.* reports that, in actuality, only ten percent of all crime in the country is violent crime.

These last three examples come from the work of Gerbner and his colleagues who founded and popularized *cultivation theory*. But their point was much more complex than simply stating that those who watch more television give answers that are more similar to the "TV answer" than to what official government data would suggest is correct. Their central argument is that television "cultivates" or creates a world view that, although possibly inaccurate, becomes the reality simply because we, as a people, believe it to be the reality and base our judgments about our own, everyday worlds on that "reality."

You'll remember from Chapter 9 that during the 1960s and early 1970s, interest in television as a social force, especially the medium's relationship to increasing individual and societal violence, reached its zenith. You'll also recall that two very important national examinations of the media, again especially television, were undertaken. The first was the National Commission on the Causes and Prevention of Violence, held in 1967 and 1968, and the second was the 1972 Surgeon General's Scientific Advisory Committee on Television and Social Behavior. One of the scientists involved in both efforts was George Gerbner.

His initial task was apparently simple enough: to produce a yearly *Violence Index*, essentially an annual content analysis of a sample week of network television prime-time fare that would demonstrate, from season to season, how much violence was actually present in that programming. The Index, however, was not without critics, and serious controversy developed around it. *TV Guide* magazine even called it the "million dollar mistake."

Debate raged about the definition of violence. How was "television violence" defined? Was verbal aggression really violence? Were two teenagers playfully scuffling violence? Other issues were raised. Why examine only network prime time? After school, early evening, and weekends are particularly heavy viewing times for most children. Why count only violence? Why not racism and sexism? Nonetheless, Gerbner and his associates attempted to meet the demands of their critics and each year refined their definitional and reporting schemes. But regardless of the attacks on their work, one thing did not change: year in, year out, violence still appeared on prime-time television to a degree unmatched in the "real world," and it was violence of a nature unlike that found in that "real world." If television was truly a mirror of society or if that medium did simply reinforce the status quo, this video mirror, the Violence Index seemed to say, was more like one found in a fun house than in a home. In their 1982 analysis of television violence, for example, Gerbner and his colleagues discovered that "crime in prime time is at least 10 times as rampant as in the real world (and) an average of five to six acts of overt physical violence per hour involves over half of all major characters" (Gerbner et al., 1982, p. 106).

But the single most important criticism of the annual Violence Index ("So what?") remained to be answered. Still absent was the demonstration of any causal link between the fluctuating levels of annual televised mayhem and viewer aggressive behavior. The Gerbner team eventually addressed that challenge. As Gerbner and Larry Gross (1976, p. 174) explained, "The study was broadly conceived from the beginning and . . . showed the role and symbolic functions, as well as the extent, of violence in the world of television drama. A conference of research consultants . . . in . . . 1972 recommended that the Violence Index . . . be further broadened to take into account social relationships and viewer conceptions. Implementing that recommendation, we issued the Violence Profile, including violence-victim ratios and eventually viewer responses."

In 1973, moving beyond even the Violence Profile, the group redefined their work as the Cultural Indicators project, in which they conducted regular, periodic examinations of television programming and the "conceptions of social reality that viewing cultivates in child and adult audiences" (Gerbner and Gross, 1976, p. 174). Now they were looking at the "so what" and in doing so, extended their research to issues well beyond violence.

The Cultural Indicators research made five assumptions that were still being questioned in the early 1970s. These were first, that *television is essentially and fundamentally different from other forms of mass media.* Television is in more than 98 percent of all American homes. It does not require literacy, as do newspapers, magazines, and books. Unlike the movies, it's free (if you don't count the cost of advertising added to the products you buy). It combines pictures and sound, unlike radio. It requires no mobility, as do churches, movies, and theaters. Television is the only medium in history with which people can interact at the earliest and latest years of life, not to mention all those years in between.

Because of television's accessibility and availability to everyone, the second assumption of the Cultural Indicators project is that *the medium is the "central cultural arm"* of American society; it is, as Gerbner and his colleagues (1978, p. 178) argued, "the chief creator of synthetic cultural patterns (entertainment and information) for the most heterogeneous mass publics in history, including large groups that have never shared in any common public message systems."

The third assumption flows logically from this shared reality, "the *substance of the consciousness cultivated by TV is not so much specific attitudes and opinions as more basic assumptions about the 'facts' of life and standards of judgment on which conclusions are based*" (Gerbner and Gross, 1976, p. 175).

Because most television stations and networks target the same audiences, and because they depend on relatively generic, formulaic, cyclical, repetitive forms of programs and stories, Cultural Indicators' fourth assumption became *television's major cultural function is to stabilize social patterns, to cultivate resistance to change*; it is a medium of socialization and enculturation. Again, Gerbner and his cohorts said it well (1978, p. 178): "The repetitive pattern of television's mass-produced messages and images forms the mainstream of the common symbolic environment that cultivates the most widely shared conceptions of reality. We live in terms of the stories we tell—stories about what things exist, stories about how things work, and stories about what to do—and television tells them all through news, drama, and advertising to almost everybody most of the time." If you're reading closely, you can hear not only the echoes of social construction of reality and symbolic interaction, but also the call to understand television as a ritual, rather than transmissional medium.

In adopting this more ritualistic view, however, the Cultural Indicators researchers' fifth assumption, that *the observable, measurable, independent contributions of television to the culture are relatively small*, caused additional controversy. In explaining this position, Gerbner used his *ice-age analogy*: "But just as an average temperature shift of a few degrees can lead to an ice age or the outcomes of elections can be determined by slight margins, so too can a relatively small but pervasive influence make a crucial difference. The 'size' of an 'effect' is far less critical than the direction of its steady contribution" (Gerbner et al., 1980, p. 14). Their argument was not that television's impact was inconsequential. Rather, they argued that although television's measurable, observable, independent effect on the culture at any point in time might be small, that impact was, nonetheless, present and significant. Put somewhat differently, television's impact on our collective sense of reality is real and important, even though that effect may be beyond clear cut scientific measurement, may defy easy observation, and may be inextricably bound to other factors in the culture.

The Controversy

Throughout this text, we have introduced you to various controversies, camps, and antagonistic perspectives. The debate (as well as its intensity) that surrounded cultivation analysis, then, should come as no surprise, especially because if nothing else, the Gerbner work attempted to use traditional social scientific research methods to examine very large scale humanistic questions. In other words, Gerbner and his colleagues used tools of inquiry most often identified with the transmissional perspective and limited effects findings to examine questions most often identified with the ritual view. Horace Newcomb (1978, p. 265) wrote, for example, "More than any other research effort in the area of television studies the work of Gerbner and Gross and their associates sits squarely at the juncture of the social sciences and the humanities." This, more than anything, is what fueled so much debate. By asserting effects that were beyond the apparent control of most audience members, the Cultural Indicators project offended those humanists who felt that their turf had been improperly appropriated and misinterpreted. In asserting significant but possibly unmeasurable, unobservable effects, the project challenged the work, if not the belief system of the many social scientists who still adhered to the limited effects paradigm. Actually, the Gerbner group dismissed virtually all existing attitude change research, all television violence research conducted in laboratories, all television research that looked at *change* as the only measure of the medium's effect, and all research that employed an individual program or one particular type of program; in essence, almost all extant television effects research was deemed of small value.

We will let Newcomb speak for the humanists. He claimed that "the question, 'What does it all mean?' is, essentially, a humanistic question" (1978, p. 266). Then he accused Gerbner and his colleagues of misapplying the values of humanism. First, he argued, *television's ideas and the symbols that express them on that medium are not created there.* Those symbols have a history and meaning in the culture that existed long before now and apart from television. Violence, for example, has many meanings and has always had many meanings for Americans.

Second, he argued that the Cultural Indicators project *ignored the wide variety of "organization and expression of these ideas in the world of television."* In other words, violence, for example, is not presented as uniformly on television as Cultural Indicators would have us believe.

Finally, his most serious complaint about the Gerbner research was that it *did not permit the possibility that individual members of the television audience can apply different, individual meanings to what they see on television.* Newcomb summarized his humanist objections this way, "It may be that all the messages of television speak with a single intent and are ruled by a single dominant symbol whose meaning is clear to a mass audience, or to that part of the audience heavily involved with those messages. But I have yet to see evidence sufficient to warrant such a reductive view of human experience in America" (1978, p. 281).

The assumptions of the Cultural Indicators approach are clearly imbedded in Gerbner and Gross' reply (1979). As for Newcomb's first challenge, they argued that those ideas and symbols must be learned *somewhere*, "we are born into and grow up in a symbolic environment of which television is now the mainstream that *cultivates* stable images after some of its own patterns" (p. 228). As to the second humanistic criticism, Gerbner and Gross responded, "we consider most television plays assembly-line drama rather than works of unique craftsmanship. The patterns that the corporate assembly-line imparts to its products becomes the aggregate and repetitive terms of common exposure and usage" (p. 223). And, finally, they asserted that regardless of whether or not individual audience members can apply their own interpretations to what they see on the screen, the

> fact is that heavy viewers overestimate their chances of involvement in violence and their general vulnerability (compared to light viewers in the same social groups) *however defined*. Newcomb's big question, 'what does violence mean to the respondents' is not only irrelevant but distracting. We study what exposure to violence-laden television contributes to their conceptions of the realities of their own lives (p. 227).

But attack also came from social scientists who were as disturbed by Gerbner's research methods as they were by his dismissal of their results. The exchange between Gerbner and Gross and their prime nemesis, Paul Hirsch, is indicative. Hirsch charged the Cultural Indicators group with employing poor definitions of amounts of viewing, of improperly combining groups of viewers in their survey samples, of selectively reporting only results that fit their theory, of failure to employ traditional demographic controls, and of developing explanations after the fact for results that did not match their hypotheses. In addressing these claims, Gerbner and his colleagues (1981a, p. 39) mockingly labeled Hirsch's analysis of their work "a brilliant scholarly surprise attack making mincemeat out of a plodding band of academic poachers," and sarcastically added, his

> masterful "reanalysis" of selected data not only demolishes cumulative results of a decade of fairly massive cooperative research and theory building, along with substantial independent confirmation; it also demonstrates that the research is both worthless and stubbornly wrong-headed. Unlikely as that dramatic coup for pure science might be we intend to demonstrate that Hirsch's analysis is flawed, incomplete, and tendentious.

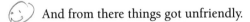 And from there things got unfriendly.

Cultivation analysis pioneers Michael Morgan and Nancy Signorielli (1990, p. 24) remembered the period this way,

> Fierce, prolonged battles (occasionally acrimonious and vaguely ad hominem at times) consumed hundreds of pages of scholarly and research journals; their repercussions were vividly felt at academic conferences and the controversies even spilled over into such popular media as *Time* magazine. The conflicts grew harsher and louder, and the rivers ran red with dead data and mutilated statistical techniques.

Yet Newcomb, called "one of the first" cultivation critics by Morgan and Signorielli, wrote of the Gerbner group (1978, p. 281),

Their foresight to collect data on a systematic, long-term basis, to move out of the laboratory and away from the closed experimental model, will enable other researchers to avoid costly mistakes. Their material holds a wealth of information. The violence topic provides only one of many symbol clusters to be examined. As they move into new areas, and hopefully retrieve more, and more complex information from audiences, we should see whole new sets of questions and answers emerging to aid us in explaining television's role in our culture.

What exactly were the conclusions drawn initially by the Violence Index, then the Violence Profile, and ultimately by Cultural Indicators that generated so much disagreement, that so inflamed what we generally think of as scientific objectivity?

The Products of Cultivation Analysis

To scientifically demonstrate their view of television as a culturally influential medium, cultivation researchers depended on a four-step process. The first they called *message system analysis*, which was detailed content analyses of television programming to assess its most reoccurring and consistent presentations of images, themes, values, and portrayals. The second step is the *formulation of questions about viewers' social realities*. Remember the questions that opened this section, the ones about crime? Those were drawn from a cultivation study. The third step is to *survey the audience*, posing the questions from step two to its members *and* asking them about their amount of television consumption. Finally, step four entails *comparing the social realities of light and heavy viewers*. The product, as stated by Morgan and Signorielli (1990, p. 20), should not be surprising:

> The questions posed to respondents do not mention television, and the respondents' awareness of the source of their information is seen as irrelevant. The resulting relationships . . . between amount of viewing and the tendency to respond to these questions in the terms of the dominant and repetitive facts, values, and ideologies of the world of television . . . illuminate television's contribution to viewers' conceptions of social reality.

What is television's contribution? Cultivation theorists argue that its major contribution is *cultivation*, a cultural process relating "to coherent frameworks or knowledge and to underlying general concepts . . . cultivated by exposure to the total and organically related world of television rather than exposure to individual programs and selections" (Gerbner, 1990, p. 255).

This cultivation occurs in two ways. The first is *mainstreaming*, where, especially for heavier viewers, television's symbols monopolize and dominate other sources of information and ideas about the world. People's internalized social realities eventually move toward the mainstream, not a mainstream in any political sense, but a culturally dominant reality that is more closely aligned with television's reality than with any objective reality. Is the criminal judicial system failing us? It is if we think it is.

The second way cultivation manifests itself is through *resonance*, when viewers see things on television that are most congruent with their own everyday realities. In essence, these people get a "double dose" of cultivation because what they see on the screen resonates with their actual lives. Some city dwellers, for example, may see the violent world of television resonated in their deteriorating neighborhoods.

The Mean World Index

A particularly instructive example of cultivation is the Mean World Index, a series of three questions:

1 Most people are just looking out for themselves?

2 You can't be too careful in dealing with people?

3 Most people would take advantage of you if they got the chance?

Of course, the television answer to these questions is obvious. But would light and heavy viewers give differing responses? Would the amount of television consumed erase individual distinctions like income and education? Gerbner and his colleagues (1980) found the answer to these questions to be "yes." Heavy viewers were much more likely to see the world as a mean place than were light viewers. Better educated, financially better-off viewers in general saw the world as less mean than did those with less education and income, but heavy viewers from the better educated, better-off groups saw the world as just as dangerous as did low income and less educated people. In other words, heavy viewers held a "mainstreamed" perception of the world as a mean place.

A Final Note on Cultivation

 Cultivation analysis has been applied to more than television's portrayals of violence, crime, and the judicial system. Cultivation research has been done on sex roles, marital and family difficulties, physical disability, health, attractiveness, age-role stereotypes, science, educational achievement, politics, and religion. The assumptions of cultivation are supported throughout, though the strength of findings and the quality of the research vary greatly. These consistent results led the theory's creator, George Gerbner, to identify what he called the 3Bs:

1 The *blurring* of traditional distinctions of people's views of their world.

2 The *blending* of their realities into television's cultural mainstream.

3 The *bending* of that mainstream to the institutional interests of television and its sponsors.

He added,

> The historical circumstances in which we find ourselves have taken the magic of human life—living in a universe erected by culture—out of the hands of families and small communities. What has been a richly diverse hand-crafted process has become—for better or worse, or both—a complex manufacturing and mass-distribution enterprise. This has abolished much of the provincialism and parochialism, as well as some of the elitism, of the pretelevision era. It has enriched parochial cultural horizons. It also gave increasingly massive industrial conglomerates the right to conjure up much of what we think about, know, and do in common (1990, p. 261).

Clearly Dr. Gerbner does not seem to think that this is a particularly fair trade-off. You'll see in the next chapter that many critical cultural theorists firmly side with him.

Summary

The ritual perspective of mass communication sees the media as central to the representation of shared beliefs rather than as mere imparters of information. This contrasts with the transmissional perspective which views the media as simple transmitters of information, usually for the purpose of control. As dissatisfaction with limited effects paradigm grew in the 1970s and 1980s, more and more communication theorists, even those with a social science orientation, began to move toward this former perspective.

One such theory is symbolic interaction, which assumes that our experience of reality is a social construction—that when we learn to assign meaning to symbols, we give them power over our experience.

Social construction of reality also assumes that people have a correspondence of meaning when they use symbols (an object that represents some other object) and signs (objects explicitly designed to serve as indices of subjective meaning). These signs and symbols combine into collections of meanings, or typification schemes, that form the social stock of knowledge that patterns people's interactions with their environments.

Goffman's theory of frame analysis took both symbolic interactionism and social construction of reality a step further. He argued that our ability to structure our experience is based upon our ability to continually select appropriate frames to guide our perception and make sense of what we experience. Frames vary along a continuum from nonserious to serious. We constantly use these frames to upshift and downshift — moving from play to work and back again. As we conduct our everyday lives we continually differentiate between the real world or primary reality and various fantasy worlds. Media help us to differentiate these worlds.

Cultivation analysis, a direct outgrowth of the concern with televised violence during the 1960s, is based on five assumptions:

- Television is fundamentally different from other forms of media.
- Television is the central cultural arm of American society.
- Television cultivates a general consciousness on which people's conclusions and judgments are based.
- Television's major cultural influence is to stabilize social patterns.
- The measurable, identifiable contributions of television to the culture at any one time are relatively small.

To reach these conclusions, cultivation analysis requires a four-step methodology of message system analysis, formulation of questions about viewers' social realities, surveying the audience, and comparing the social realities of light and heavy viewers. Cultivation is said to occur in two ways, mainstreaming and resonance, and the theory's founder, George Gerbner, articulated the 3Bs of television's cultural influence: blurring, blending, and bending.

Discussion Questions

1   What is your view of the criminal justice system? What is the basis of your opinion?

2   What examples of failure to share meaning of signs and symbols can you recall from your own experience? What was the outcome of those experiences?

3   Where do you think social construction of reality and symbolic interaction differ? Where are they the same? Which is more useful to you in understanding media?

4   Do you ever make judgments about people based solely on how they look? What kinds of evaluations do you make? Why do you do this?

5   To what extent do you (and others around you) frame your life as a student as "unreal" or less "serious" than life in a "real world" of work? What do you think the consequences of such framing might be?

6   What do you think about Goffman's ideas concerning social cues? Do you think you learn such cues from advertising? Have you had experiences where you framed a situation incorrectly based on a misinterpretation of cues?

Significant Names

James Carey	Horace Newcomb
George Gerbner	Erving Goffman
George Herbert Mead	Larry Gross
Nancy Signorielli	Alfred Schutz
Paul Hirsch	Michael Morgan

Significant Readings

Carey, James (1975). "Culture and Communications." *Communication Research*, 2: 173–191.

Faules, Don F. and Dennis C. Alexander (1978). *Communication and Social Behavior: A Symbolic Interaction Perspective*. Reading, MA: Addison-Wesley.

Goffman, Erving (1974). *Frame Analysis: An Essay on the Organization of Experience*. New York: Harper & Row.

Goffman, Erving (1979). *Gender Advertisements*. New York: Harper & Row.

Signorielli, Nancy and Michael Morgan, eds., (1990). *Cultivation Analysis: New Directions in Media Effects Research*. Newbury Park, CA: Sage.

Gerbner, George and Larry Gross (1972). "Living with Television: the Violence Profile." *Journal of Communication*, 26: 173–199.

Newcomb, Horace M. and Paul M. Hirsch (1983). "Television as a Cultural Forum: Implications for Research." *Quarterly Review of Film*, 8: 45–55.

Important Terms

Cultivation Analysis

Critical Cultural Studies

Cultural Analysis

Transmissional Perspective

Symbols

Ritual Perspective

Macroscopic Theory

Microscopic Theory

Signs

Natural Signs

Artificial Signs

Signals

Phenomenology

Typification

Typification Schemes

Culture

Positioning

Frame Analysis

Social Cues

Downshift

Upshift

Dominant Reality

Message System Analysis

Mainstreaming

Resonance

Mean World Index

Hegemonic Culture

Symbolic Interaction

Chapter 13

Critical Cultural Studies

Remember the last news report you saw or read concerning a natural disaster or major accident such as a plane crash. Most likely, it focused on the factual details of the disaster—how much damage was done, what was destroyed, how many people were hurt. Considerable detail may have been used to describe the emotional reactions of the people involved, especially those whose relatives were killed or who "lost everything." But were there things that the report didn't tell you? Were questions not asked or left unanswered? Could or should the disaster have been prevented? Disasters and major accidents represent important disruptions in the social order. Their occurrence prompts us to wonder, "Are we doing something wrong?" "Should changes be made?" "Are the people running things doing their job?"

Media reports rarely raise these questions. Instead, they offer reassurance. Everyone involved in the disaster is all right. Services are being restored. Your government is working hard to get problems under control. You can relax. One researcher (Gans, 1979) found that 85 percent of the news reports of social disruptions focused on restoration of order by social elites. But why does news give so much attention to the actions of elites and so little attention to factors that cause problems?

Media practitioners have several plausible answers to this question. First, they have little time to do in-depth, investigative reports. When a disaster happens, all their attention must be focused on getting out accurate, factual reports of what took place. By sticking to the facts about a disaster, journalists are able to remain objective at a time when objectivity is crucial. During a crisis there is little time or opportunity to raise questions of blame or determine if changes are needed. In any case, they would argue, it is not the responsibility of journalists to place blame or recommend changes. Highly trained and well-paid experts are expected to do that. By offering reassurance and emphasizing that order is being restored, journalists calm public fears and rumors that might otherwise create even more problems. They say it is socially responsible for news media to calm rather than ignite public fears.

After an air disaster, for example, Federal Aviation Administration officials come to the scene within hours and take control of the crash investigation. Why should journalists second guess them? Isn't it reasonable and responsible to wait a year for the FAA report to be completed? Clearly journalists would be irresponsible to blame the pilot in their early reports only to discover a year later that there had been an equipment failure. Why not tell people that air travel is still safe? Why promote what are likely to be groundless fears about air safety?

To what extent are these defenses offered by journalists justified? How and when should journalists be expected to criticize the status quo and the elites who maintain the existing social order? Clearly, some important constraints will always limit what media practitioners can be expected to do. They are human beings working for fallible social organizations. But not every constraint is as powerful as media practitioners assert. Some constraints could be overcome without great expense or effort. Still others might be countered if industry groups or professional associations chose to address them. Taken as a whole, the U.S. news media are a major industry that commands enormous resources. But they are rarely marshaled in any systematic way to address even the most serious social issues. Instead, these resources are fragmented across hundreds of competing agencies that work against artificially imposed time deadlines.

The media theorists that we will consider in this chapter argue that the obvious failings of news media raise important questions about the motives of media practitioners and their professional norms. Are they really doing everything they can and should to provide us with useful services? Or are they part of the problem? To what extent do their professional norms actually lead them to be socially irresponsible? These questions about the ideal social role of media are much like those discussed in Chapter 5 when we looked at normative theories of mass media. Moreover, these questions imply that the dominant normative theory, social responsibility theory, should be radically changed or replaced.

Overview

The theories in this chapter, *critical cultural studies*, raise questions and provide alternate ways of interpreting the social role of mass media. Most argue that media in general sustain the status quo—even, perhaps especially, when it is under stress or breaking down. Critical theories often provide complex explanations for the media's tendency to consistently support the status quo. For example, some identify constraints on media practitioners that limit their ability to challenge established authority. They charge that few incentives exist to encourage practitioners to overcome those constraints and that media professionals consistently fail to even acknowledge them.

In the preceding chapter, we listed important differences between critical cultural studies and other forms of cultural analysis. First, critical theories assume that social theories should be based on a set of values—ideal purposes or goals for human existence. These form the basis for criticizing social institutions and entire social orders. Second, the goal of critical theory is to guide reformation or transformation of social institutions or social orders so that important values are realized. Third, critical theory often proceeds by examining specific social problems, locating the sources of these problems, and then recommending solutions. Fourth, critical theorists are often members of social movements and as such are dedicated to advancing the goals of their movements. Through these movements they attempt to put their theories into action. Sometimes critical theory is used to guide a movement as it works to make constructive social changes and sometimes it rationalizes a movement's actions.

Critical theories often analyze specific social institutions, probing the extent to which valued objectives are sought and achieved. Mass media and the mass culture they promote have become a focus for critical theory. They have been linked to a variety of social problems. Even when mass media are not seen as the source of specific problems, they are criticized for aggravating or preventing problems from being identified or addressed and solved. For example, a theory may argue that content production practices of media practitioners either cause or perpetuate specific problems. We opened this chapter with an example of such a theory, one that argued that the current strategy for producing news stories about disasters fails to initiate changes that could alleviate future disasters. A common theme in critical theories of media is that content production is so constrained that it inevitably reinforces the status quo and undermines useful efforts for constructive social change.

Consider the last time you read news reports about members of a social movement that strongly challenged the status quo. How were the movement's actions described? How were members and their leaders portrayed? Remember the question we asked you in an earlier chapter? Why were the college students who protested against the Communist Chinese government in Tiananmen Square "heroes of democracy" and those in the American anti-war movement "hippies" and "radicals?"

Like stories about disasters, stories about movements imply problems with the status quo. Movements frequently defy the authority of existing elites and make demands for social change. Journalists are caught in the middle of the confrontation. Movement leaders demand coverage of their complaints and they stage demonstrations designed to draw public attention to their concerns. Elites seek to minimize coverage or to exercise "spin control" so that coverage favors their position. How do journalists handle this? How should they handle it? Existing research indicates that this coverage almost always denigrates movements and supports elites (Tuchman, 1978; Gitlin, 1980).

The Critical Theory Alternative

Despite its long life in American social science, the limited effects paradigm never enjoyed great popularity in Europe. European social research has instead been characterized by what Americans regard as grand social theories—highly ambitious, macroscopic, and speculative theories that attempt to understand and predict important trends in culture and society. In Chapter 3, we presented an early example of a European-style, grand social theory—mass society theory—that illustrated both the strengths and the limitations of grand theory. In Chapter 6, we explained why American social researchers, especially those trained in the Columbia School of empirical social research, preferred middle-range theories.

In Europe, the development of grand social theory remained a central concern in the social sciences. Mass society theory gave way to a succession of alternate ideas. Some were limited to specific nations and others spread across many countries. Some of the most widely accepted have been based on the writings of Karl Marx. *Marxist theory* influenced even the theories that were created in reaction against it. Marxist ideas formed a foundation or touchstone for much post-World War II European social theory and research. Cold War politics colored much of the American response to it. Ironically, in the 1970s and 1980s, at the very time that Marxism failed as a practical guide for politics and economics in Eastern Europe, grand social theories based on Marxist thought were gaining increasing acceptance in Western Europe (Grossberg and Nelson, 1988). We will briefly summarize key arguments in the Marxist perspective and pay particular attention to media. Then we will present some more recent theories that are based on these ideas.

Marxist Theory

Karl Marx developed his theory in the latter part of the nineteenth century during one of the most volatile periods of social change in Europe. In some respects, his is yet another version of mass society theory—but with several very important alterations and additions. Marx was familiar with the grand social theories of his era. He drew on them or constructed his ideas in opposition to them. He identified industrialization and urbanization as problems but argued that these changes were not inherently bad. Instead, he blamed ruthless, robber baron capitalists for exacerbating social problems because they maximized personal profits by exploiting workers. Although mass society theorists demanded restoration of the old order, Marx was a utopian, calling for the creation of an entirely new social order in which all social classes would be abolished. The workers would rise against capitalists and demand an end to exploitation. They would band together to create an egalitarian, democratic social order.

Marx argued that the hierarchical class system was at the root of all social problems and must be ended by a revolution of the workers or proletariat. He believed that elites dominated society primarily through their direct control over the means of production (that is, labor, factories, and land) which he referred to as the *base* of society.

But elites also maintained themselves in power through their control over culture or the *superstructure* of society. One of Marx's most quoted phrases is "religion is the opiate of the masses." He saw culture as something that elites freely manipulated to mislead average people and encourage them to act against their own interest. He used the term *ideology* to refer to these forms of culture. To him, an ideology operated much like a drug. Those who are under its influence fail to see how they are being exploited. In the worst cases, they are so deceived that they actually undermine their own interests and do things that increase the power of elites while making their own lives even worse.

Marx concluded that the only hope for social change was a revolution in which the masses seized control of the base—the means of production. Control over the superstructure—over ideology—would naturally follow. He saw little possibility that reforms in the superstructure could lead to gradual social evolution. Elites would never willingly surrender power. Power must be taken from them. Little purpose would be served by making minor changes in ideology without first dominating the means of production.

Critical Theory and Marxist Theory

Most theories discussed in this chapter can be labeled *neomarxist*. They deviate from classic Marxist theory in at least one important respect—they focus concern on the superstructure issues of ideology and culture rather than on the base. The importance that neomarxists attach to the superstructure has created a fundamental division within Marxism. Many neomarxists assume that useful change can begin with peaceful, ideological reform rather than violent revolution. Some neomarxists have developed critiques of culture that call for radically transforming the superstructure while others call for modest reforms. Tensions have arisen within Marxism over the value of the work being done by the various neomarxist schools.

Textual Analysis and Literary Criticism

Modern critical theories have a second, very different source — humanist criticism of religious and literary texts. Humanists have specialized in analyzing written texts since the Renaissance. One common objective was to identify those texts that had greatest cultural value and to interpret them so that their value would be appreciated and understood by others. Texts were seen as a civilizing force in society (Bloom, 1987). Criticism was used to enhance this force. Humanist scholars ranged from religious humanists who focused on the Bible or the writings of great theologians to secular humanists who worked to identify and preserve what came to be known as the "literary Canon" — a body of the great literature. The literary Canon was part of what was referred to as High Culture, a set of cultural artifacts including music, art, literature, and poetry that humanists judged to have the highest value. By identifying and explicating these important texts, humanist attempted to make them more accessible to more people. Their long-term goal was to preserve and gradually raise the level of culture — to enable even more people to become humane and civilized.

Over the years, many different methods for analyzing written texts have emerged from literary analysis. These methods are now being applied to many other forms of culture, including media content (Littlejohn, 1989, pp. 135–136). They share a common purpose: to criticize old and new cultural practices so that those most deserving of attention can be identified and explicated and the less deserving can be dismissed. This task can be compared to that of movie critics who tell us which films are good or bad and assist us in appreciating or avoiding them. The primary difference is that many movie critics are typically not committed to promoting higher cultural values; they only want to explain which movies we are likely to find entertaining.

As we shall see, the modern critical theory landscape includes both neomarxist and humanist approaches. Hybrid theories combine both. Before examining these, we will look at some of the historically important schools of critical theory that have produced work that is still influential.

The Frankfurt School

One early prominent school of neomarxist theory developed during the 1930s at the University of Frankfurt and became known as the Frankfurt School. Two of the most prominent individuals associated with the school were Max

Horkheimer, its long-time head, and Theodor Adorno, a prolific and cogent theorist. In contrast with most later forms of neomarxism, the Frankfurt School combined Marxist critical theory with humanist literary analysis. Its writings identified and promoted various forms of high culture such as symphony music, great literature, and art. Like most secular humanists, the Frankfurt School viewed high culture as something that had its own integrity, had inherent value, and could not be used by elites to enhance their personal power.

Though high culture was extolled by the Frankfurt School, mass culture was denigrated (Arato and Gebhardt, 1978). Horkheimer and Adorno were openly skeptical that high culture could or should be communicated through media. Adorno argued that radio broadcasts or records couldn't begin to adequately reproduce the sound of a live symphony orchestra. He ridiculed the reproduction of great art in magazines or the reprinting of great novels in condensed, serialized form. He claimed that mass media reproductions of high culture were inferior and diverted people from seeking out (and paying for) the "real thing." If bad substitutes for high culture were readily available, he believed, too many people would settle for them and fail to support better forms of culture.

The Frankfurt School has been criticized along with other forms of traditional humanism for being too elitist and paternalistic. By rejecting the possibility of using media to disseminate high culture, most of the population was effectively denied access to it. Many of the school's criticisms of media paralleled those of mass society theory and had the same limitations that we listed in Chapter 3.

The Frankfurt School eventually had a direct impact upon American social research because the rise of the Nazis forced its Jewish members into exile. Horkheimer, for one, took up residency at the New School for Social Research in New York City. During this period of exile, however, Frankfurt School theorists remained productive. They devoted considerable effort, for example, to the critical analysis of Nazi culture and the way it undermined and perverted high culture. In their view, Nazism was grounded on a phony, artificially constructed folk culture that had been cynically created and manipulated by Hitler and his propagandists. This hodge-podge of folk culture integrated many bits and pieces of culture borrowed from various Germanic peoples. But it did appeal to a people humiliated by war and deeply troubled by a devastating economic depression. It helped them envision the Germany they longed to see—a unified, proud nation with a long history of achievement and a glorious future. As they rose to power, the Nazis replaced high culture with this pseudo-folk culture and discredited important forms of high culture, especially those created by Jews.

Adorno was one of the few members of the Frankfurt School who actively collaborated with American social researchers. His early U.S. contacts included Paul Lazarsfeld, who persuaded the Columbia Broadcasting System (CBS) to finance some of Adorno's research. Adorno's work proved controversial because he wrote devastating criticism of American radio programs and the industry that produced them. He eventually led a research team that studied authoritarian attitudes in the United States and tried to gauge the likelihood that Nazism would spread. Although innovative and ambitious, this research had many serious theoretical and methodological problems. It proved especially difficult to develop unbiased questionnaire items to measure authoritarian attitudes. Adorno's team decided to ask many questions but without computers to assist them, the task of making sense of numerous responses from hundreds of individuals was enormous. Unlike most empirical researchers, Adorno refused to limit his work to those research questions that could be easily addressed using existing empirical methods. He pushed the boundaries of research and insisted on seeking answers to questions that proved unanswerable in his lifetime.

Adorno's example illustrates one of the most common criticisms that critical theorists make of empirical researchers. Critical theorists are disdainful of the limits that empirical researchers seem willing to place upon their work. The former argue that it is irresponsible to ignore important questions just because researchers lack the tools necessary to obtain definitive answers. Empirical researchers respond that it is even more irresponsible to provide overly speculative answers to important questions—especially if theorists fail to adequately qualify these answers and indicate just how tentative they are. Empirical researchers accuse cultural theorists of offering answers based on very limited or selectively chosen evidence.

Contemporary Schools of Neomarxist Theory

Currently, neomarxists are internally divided into several important schools of theory. Two of the most important of these are *British cultural studies* and *political economy theory*. British cultural studies combines Marxist theory with ideas and research methods derived from diverse sources including literary criticism, linguistics, anthropology, and history (Hall, et al., 1980). This theory has attempted to trace historic elite domination over culture, to criticize the social consequences of this domination, and to demonstrate how it continues to be exercised over specific minority groups or subcultures. British cultural studies criticized and contrasted elite notions of culture, including high culture, with popular, everyday forms practiced by minorities. The superiority of all forms of elite culture is challenged and compared to useful, valuable forms of popular culture. Attention has shifted from the study of elite cultural artifacts to the study of minority group "lived culture."

Graham Murdock (1989b) traced the rise of British cultural studies during the 1950s and 1960s. Most of its important theorists came from lower social classes. Their critique of high culture and ideology was an explicit rejection of what they saw as alien forms of culture imposed on minorities. They defended indigenous forms of popular culture as legitimate expressions of minority groups. A dominant early theorist was Raymond Williams, a literary critic who achieved notoriety with his reappraisals of cultural development in England (see Chapter 14 for more details). The first important school of theorists was formed at the University of Birmingham during the 1960s and was led by Stuart Hall.

Hall (1982) was especially influential in directing a number of analyses of mass media that directly challenge limited effects notions and introducing innovative alternatives. He argued that mass media can best be understood as a *public forum* in which various forces struggle to shape popular notions about social reality. In this forum, new concepts of social reality are negotiated and new boundary lines between various social worlds are drawn. Unlike traditional Marxists, he did not argue that elites can maintain complete control over this forum. In his view, elites don't need to have that power to advance their interests. The culture expressed in this forum is not a mere superficial reflection of the superstructure but is instead a dynamic creation of opposing groups. Elites, however, *do* retain many advantages in the struggle to define social reality. Counter-elite groups must work hard to overcome them. Hall acknowledged that heavy-handed efforts by elites to promote their ideology can fail while well-planned efforts to promote alternative perspectives can succeed even against great odds. Nevertheless, the advantages enjoyed by elites enable them to retain a long-term hold on power.

A key strength *and* limitation of British cultural studies theorists is their direct involvement in various radical social movements. Theorists not only study movements, they enlist in them and even lead them. Cultural studies advocates (O'Connor, 1989) argue that a person cannot be a good social theorist unless he or she is personally committed to bringing about change. Cultural studies theorists have been active in a broad range of social movements including feminism, youth groups, racial and ethnic minority groups, and British Labour party factions. But active involvement can make objective analysis of movements and movement culture difficult. Cultural studies theorists usually don't worry about this because they reject the possibility of objectivity anyway and doubt its utility for social research. Their aim is to do research that aids the goals of movements rather than work that serves the traditional aims of scholarship or science.

Cultural studies has produced a variety of research on popular media content and the use that specific social groups make of that content. Many questions have been addressed. Does this content exploit and mislead individuals or does it enable them to construct meaningful identities and experiences? Can people take ambiguous content and interpret it in new ways that fundamentally alters its purpose for them? How can useful social change be achieved through cultural reform rather than social revolution?

In the United States, British cultural studies has influenced much research, particularly the work of feminists (Long, 1989) and those who study popular culture (Grossberg, 1989). Research conducted by Janice Radway (1984) is frequently cited as one of the best examples of work incorporating and expressing cultural studies ideas. Radway initially analyzed the content of popular romance novels. She argued that their characters and plots are derived from patriarchal myths in which a male-dominated social order is assumed to be both natural and just. Men are routinely presented as strong, aggressive, and heroic while women are weak, passive, and dependent. Women must gain their identity through their association with a male character.

After completing an extensive content analysis of romance novels, Radway (1986) decided to interview women who regularly read them. She was surprised to find that many readers used these books as part of a silent rebellion against male domination. They read them as an escape from housework or child rearing. Many of them rejected key assumptions of the patriarchal myths. They expressed strong preferences for male characters who combined traditionally masculine and feminine traits, for example, physical strength combined with gentleness. Similarly, readers preferred strong female characters who controlled their own lives but still retained traditional feminine attributes. Thus, the romance reading could be interpreted as a form of passive resistance against male dominated culture. This resistance nurtured opposition to the patriarchal myths that were at the heart of romance fiction.

Radway's work illustrates an important trend in critical cultural studies. Earlier researchers were often content to study specific media content or texts and draw conclusions about it based on their theories. Recent research, like that of Radway, has begun to combine textual analysis with audience research and has discovered what empirical audience researchers (see especially the uses and gratifications research in Chapter 10) have long recognized—audience interpretations and use of content are typically quite diverse. People don't always perceive content the way that media producers intended or as media critics assume. People often develop highly idiosyncratic uses for it, and groups of fans can nurture these uses (Morley, 1980a; 1980b). Thus, content can have long-term consequences that are very different from those that are predicted based on content analysis.

Critical cultural studies researchers have begun to interpret these oppositional uses of content as evidence that audiences actively resist efforts by media producers to dominate their experience and use of content. For example, Linda Steiner (1988) examined 10 years of the "No Comment" feature of *Ms.* magazine in which readers submit examples of subtle and not so subtle male domination. She argued that readers are routinely engaging in *oppositional decoding* of texts. These texts were intended to be interpreted or "read" in a certain way—the preferred reading (preferred by males who assume their superiority). *Ms.* readers form a community that can act together to construct oppositional readings of these texts. Magazine examples can teach women how to identify these texts and help them make an interpretation that serves their own interests rather than those of a patriarchal elite.

In a series of books that includes *Bad News* (1976) and *More Bad News* (1980), the Glasgow University Media Group (GUMG) used a variety of research techniques to probe news coverage of labor unions in Britain. The group's work provides a good example of an in-depth, long-term mass communication research project that explicitly used a critical cultural studies perspective. As in the United States, the 1970s through the 1980s was a period when labor unions fell into public disfavor in Great Britain. GUMG argued that news coverage was at least partially responsible for this decline. GUMG focused on BBC television news and used a variety of content analysis techniques. The conclusions proved controversial, but are cogent and deserve careful consideration.

GUMG provided a variety of evidence to support its position that news was systematically biased against unions. For example, almost all news stories about unions featured strikes, and the typical story routinely portrayed industrial managers more favorably than union members. Two serious criticisms, however, have been made about the GUMG research: (a) their content analyses were selective—stories that didn't fit their arguments may have been overlooked; and (b) no effort was made to study audiences to see if they actually interpreted the stories in the way that GUMG members did. In other words, GUMG made no effort to assess the extent of oppositional decoding.

Political Economy Theory

Political economy theorists study elite control of economic institutions such as banks and stock markets and then try to show how this control affects many other social institutions, including the mass media (Murdock, 1989). In certain respects, political economists accept the classic Marxist assumption that the base dominates the superstructure. They investigate the means of production by looking at economic institutions, and then they expect to find that these institutions will shape media to suit their interests and purposes. For example, political economists have examined how economic constraints limit or bias the forms of mass culture that are produced and distributed through the media. These economists are less concerned with investigating how mass culture influences specific groups or subcultures and are more concerned with understanding how the processes of content production and distribution are constrained. Why do some forms of culture dominate prime-time television schedules while other forms are absent?

Does audience taste alone explain those differences or are there other, less obvious reasons that can be linked to the interests of economic institutions?

Although the two schools of neomarxist theory appear to be complementary, there has been considerable rivalry between them (Murdock, 1989). Some genuine theoretical differences separate the two, but they also differ in their research methods and the academic disciplines in which they are based. With their focus on economic institutions and their assumption that economic dominance leads to or perpetuates cultural dominance, political economists were slow to acknowledge that cultural changes can affect economic institutions. Nor do they recognize the diversity of popular culture or the variety of ways in which people make sense of cultural content. Murdock suggested that the two schools of neomarxist theory should cooperate rather than compete. For this to happen, however, researchers on both sides will have to give up some of their assumptions and recognize that the superstructure and the base — culture and the media industries — can influence each other. Both types of research are necessary to produce a complete assessment of the role of media.

Marshall McLuhan: The Medium is the Massage

One route by which critical cultural theory reached the United States during the 1960s was via Canada. The exponent was an unlikely source — a literary scholar who had a fascination with media — Marshall McLuhan. McLuhan was highly trained in literary criticism but also read widely in communication theory and history. Although his writings contain few citations to Marx (McLuhan actually castigated Marx for ignoring communication), he based much of his understanding of media's historical role upon the work of Harold Innis, a Canadian economist and neomarxist.

McLuhan is a complex figure and doesn't fit well into a specific theoretical category because his work synthesized so many ideas. We placed him in this chapter because of his links to Innis and his use of critical theories taken from literary analysis. His theory also tends to be macroscopic and somewhat critical of the status quo. McLuhan had no links to any political or social movements, however. He seemed to believe that necessary and worthwhile social change would inevitably occur as a consequence of changes in communication technology. Thus, movements were not needed to bring about change.

Innis was one of the first scholars to systematically speculate about the linkages between communication media and various forms of social structure found at certain points in history. In *Empire and Communications* (1950) and *The Bias of Communication* (1951), he argued that the early empires of Egypt, Greece, and Rome were based upon elite control of the written word. He contrasted these empires with earlier social orders based on the spoken word. Innis maintained that prior to elite discovery of the written word, dialogue was the dominant mode of public discourse and political authority was much more diffuse. Gradually, the written word became the dominant mode of elite communication and its power was magnified enormously by the invention of new writing materials (that is, paper) that made writing portable yet enduring. With paper and pen, small, centrally located elites were able to gain control over and govern vast regions and create empires.

Innis argued that written word-based empires expanded to the limits imposed by communications technology. Thus, expansion was not so much dependent on the skills of military generals as it was on the communication media used to disseminate orders from the capital city. Similarly, the structure of later social orders was also dependent on the media technology available at a certain point in time. For example, the telephone and telegraph permitted even more effective control over larger geographic areas. Thus, the development of media technology has gradually given centralized elites increased power over space and time.

Innis traced the way Canadian elites used various technologies, including the railroad and telegraph, to extend their control across the continent. He harbored a deep suspicion of centralized power and believed that newer forms of communication technology would make even greater centralization inevitable. He referred to this as the inherent *bias of communication*. Because of this bias, the people and the resources of outlying regions that he called "the periphery" are inevitably exploited to serve the interests of elites at "the center."

Although he borrowed freely from Innis, McLuhan didn't dwell upon issues of exploitation or centralized control. He was fascinated by other potentials of new media technology, and he proved successful in communicating this fascination to others. Unlike most media theorists whose work is rarely read outside classrooms, McLuhan's ideas achieved enormous popularity. He became one of the first pop culture gurus of the 1960s. He burst on to the national scene with pronouncements on the first televised presidential debate between Nixon and Kennedy. His ideas continued to receive serious attention through much of the decade, but then fell into disfavor. Why the sudden rise and fall?

Initially, McLuhan's work fit the spirit of the early 1960s — the age of Camelot. In sharp contrast with Innis, he was unabashedly optimistic about the profound but ultimately positive changes that new media technology would make possible. In a series of books so densely written as to be unreadable (the ironically titled *Understanding Media* [1964] is a good example), he claimed to be transcending linear, literacy based thinking and ascending to nonlinear, electronic thought. He proclaimed that *the medium is the message (and the massage)*. In other words, new forms of media transform (massage) our experience of ourselves and our society, and this influence is ultimately more important than the content that is transmitted in its specific messages.

McLuhan used the term *Global Village* to refer to the new form of social organization that would inevitably emerge as instantaneous, electronic media tied the entire world into one great social system. Unlike Innis, McLuhan didn't ask macroscopic questions about elite control over this village or whether village members would be exploited. He was more concerned with microscopic issues, with the impact of media on our senses. He proclaimed media to be "the extensions of man" (sic) and argued that media quite literally extended sight, hearing, and touch through time and space. Electronic media would open up whole new vistas for average people and enable us to be everywhere, instantaneously. But as one media critic (Meyrowitz, 1985) recently noted, to be everywhere is to be nowhere — to have no sense of place. The global village isn't situated in space or time. Is it possible to adjust to living in such an amorphous, ambiguous social structure? Or will the global village merely be a facade used by cynical elites to exploit people? These questions go far beyond the (paeans) to media that McLuhan provided.

Among the most popular of McLuhan's ideas was his conception of *hot* and *cool media*. He argued that during the 1960s the United States was emerging from an era dominated by hot, print media. In the future, the new, cool medium of television would prevail. According to McLuhan, television is cool because it presents us with vague, shadowy images (remember this was 1960, reception was often bad, and sets were black and white). To make sense of these electronic images, we must work hard to fill in missing sensory information, we must literally participate in creating fully formed images for ourselves. McLuhan argued that this gets us involved and so we find the images very compelling and meaningful — this is the secret to the television's ability to attract vast audiences.

Print, on the other hand, is a hot medium. It supplies us with all the information we need to make sense of things. It does the work for us, offering predigested descriptions of the social world. We can't participate in creating meaning. So hot media are out and cool media are in. McLuhan carried this notion a step further and argued that some forms of content are naturally suited to cool media while others are best communicated by hot media. McLuhan's most famous interpretation was that Kennedy had a cool image that was ideally suited to television. Nixon, on the other hand, had a hot image. Thus, the attractiveness of Kennedy's image was greatly enhanced by television while Nixon's hot image was impaired. This assessment was widely accepted by political consultants and became a basis for selecting candidates and molding their public personae.

In the 1960s, McLuhan was the darling of the media industries — their prophet with honor. For a brief period he could command huge fees as a consultant and seminar leader for large companies. His ideas were used to rationalize rapid expansion of electronic media with little concern for their negative consequences. So what if children remain illiterate because they watch too much television? Reading is doomed anyway, why prolong its demise? Eventually, we will all live in a global village where literacy is unnecessary. Why worry about the negative consequences of television when it is obviously so much better than the hot, old media it is replacing? Just think of the limitations that linear thinking imposes on us. If the triumph of electronic media is inevitable, why not get on with it? No need for government regulation of media. No need to worry about media conglomerates. No need to complain about television violence. No need to resist racist or sexist media content. Adopt McLuhan's long-term, global perspective. Think big. Think nonlinearly. Just wait for the future to happen.

But even as his work became more accepted within the media industries, it aroused increasing criticism within academia. Perhaps the most devastating criticism was offered by other literary critics who found his ideas too diverse and inconsistent. They were astounded by his dismissal of literacy as obsolete and found his praise of nonlinear thinking nonsensical or even dangerous. In their view, nonlinear thinking was just another label for logically inconsistent, random thoughts. His books were said to be brainstorms masquerading as scholarship. McLuhan answered by charging that these critics were too pedantic, too concerned with logic and linear thinking. The critics were too dependent upon literacy and print media to be objective about them. Their jobs were dependent upon the survival of literacy. He recommended that they work hard to free their minds from arbitrary limitations. Not surprisingly, few were willing to do so.

Empirical media researchers were also uniformly critical of McLuhan, but for different reasons. Although a few tried to design research to study some of his notions, most found his assumptions about the power of media to be absurd. The limited effects perspective had become dominant. Most empirical researchers were skeptical about the possibility that media could transform people's experience. Even if this was possible, how could research be designed to systematically study it? When early, small-scale empirical studies failed to support McLuhan's assertions, these suspicions were confirmed. McLuhan was just another grand theorist whose ideas were overly speculative and empirically unverifiable.

McLuhan fared even less well with neomarxist theorists. Although they respected Innis, these theorists found McLuhan's theory to be a perversion of Innis' basic ideas. McLuhan was branded a *technological determinist*, someone who believes that all of human history and experience is neatly determined by the constraints imposed by technology. Rather than attempt reform of the superstructure or lead a revolution to take control of the base, McLuhan was content to wait for technology to lead us forward into the global village. Our fate is in the hands of media technology and we are constrained to go where ever it leads, he seemed to say. The neomarxists saw this as a self-fulfilling prophecy, encouraging and sanctioning the development of potentially dangerous new forms of electronic media. These might well lead us to a painful future—a nightmare global village in which we are ruled by remote elites. As long as existing elites remain in power, the neomarxists saw little hope for positive change. They condemned McLuhan for diverting attention from more important work and for perverting the radical notions found in Innis' writing. Some neomarxists even saw McLuhan's ideas as a form of disinformation, deliberately designed to confuse the public so that neomarxist work would be ignored or misinterpreted.

Much in McLuhan's work merits reading even though it is sometimes poorly presented and is generally borrowed from others. Lewis Mumford (1975), for example, claimed that he introduced the global village notion 30 years before McLuhan. In reading McLuhan, you find bits and pieces of many interesting theorists. Although it is advisable to go back and read the original work, McLuhan does provide an introduction to some important thinking—just don't expect that ideas will be presented logically. At his best, he seized the central ideas in other works and expressed them in interesting, cogent ways.

Recent Research on Popular Culture

McLuhan's work did receive favorable attention from one group of literary scholars, people dedicated to the study of what they called popular culture. By 1967, this group had grown large enough to have its own division (Popular Literature Section) within the Modern Language Association of American and to establish its own academic journal, *The Journal of Popular Culture*. Like McLuhan, those in this group have adapted a variety of theories and research methods to study various forms of popular culture. Most have no links to social movements. Much of their attention is focused on television as the premier medium of the electronic era. Many shared McLuhan's optimism about the future and the positive role of popular media.

Some of the best examples of popular culture research have been provided by Horace Newcomb in *TV, The Most Popular Art* (1976) and in an anthology that he edited (1987). These books summarize useful insights produced by popular culture researchers, and one point they emphasize is that popular media content generally, and television programming specifically, is much more complex than they appear on the surface. Multiple levels of meaning are often present, and the content itself is frequently ambiguous. Sophisticated content producers recognize that if they put many different or ambiguous meanings into their content, they will have a better chance of appealing to different audiences. If these audiences are large and loyal, the programs will have high ratings. Though Newcomb wrote long before the advent of "Twin Peaks," "Northern Exposure," or "Wild Palms," these programs illustrate his argument. They make an art of layering one level of meaning on top of another so that fans can watch the same episode over and over to probe its meaning.

A second insight well articulated by Newcomb is that audience interpretations of content are likely to be quite diverse. Some people make interpretations at one level of meaning while others make theirs at other levels. Some interpretations will be highly idiosyncratic and some will be very conventional. Sometimes groups of fans will develop a common interpretation, and sometimes individuals are content to find their own meaning without sharing it.

One person whose work has combined the popular culture approach with neomarxist theory is Larry Grossberg (1983, 1989). Though his synthesis has proved controversial (O'Connor, 1989), it gained wide attention. Part of this popularity stems from his application of contemporary European theories to the study of popular culture. Recently, he has moved more toward neomarxist theory and has coedited two large anthologies of research, *Marxism and the Interpretation of Culture* (Nelson and Grossberg, 1988) and *Cultural Studies* (Grossberg, Nelson, and Treichler, 1992).

Media as Culture Industries

One of the most intriguing and challenging perspectives to emerge from critical cultural studies looks at what happens when culture is mass produced and distributed in direct competition with locally based cultures (Enzensberger, 1974; Jhally, 1987; Hay, 1989). According to this viewpoint, media are industries specializing in the production and distribution of *cultural commodities*. As with other modern industries, they have grown at the expense of small, local producers, and the consequences of this displacement have been and continue to be disruptive to people's lives.

In earlier social orders such as empires, everyday life culture was created and controlled by geographically and socially isolated communities. Though elites might dominate an overall social order and have their own culture, it was often totally separate from and had relatively little influence over the folk cultures structuring the everyday experience of average people. Only in modern social orders have elites begun to develop subversive forms of mass culture that intrude into and disrupt everyday life culture. These new forms can function as very subtle but effective ideologies, leading people to misinterpret their experiences and then act against their own self interest.

Elites are able to disrupt everyday cultures by using a rather insidious and ingenious strategy. They take bits and pieces of folk culture, weave them together to create attractive mass culture content, and then market it as a substitute for everyday forms of folk culture. Thus, not only are elites able to subvert legitimate local cultures but also they earn profits doing it. People actually subsidize the subversion of their everyday culture. As we've seen, one early and particularly tragic example of this was Nazi Germany where a pseudo-folk culture was created and used to transform daily life.

This strategy has been especially successful in the United States where, unlike Nazi Germany, media entrepreneurs have remained relatively independent from political institutions. Mass culture gained steadily in popularity, spawning huge industries that successfully competed for the attention and interest of most Americans. Within the United States, criticism of mass culture was muted. Most Americans accepted the cultural commodities emerging from New York and Hollywood as somehow their own. But these same commodities aroused considerable controversy when U.S. media entrepreneurs exported them to other nations. The power of these commodities to reshape daily life was quite obvious in most Third World nations and even more disruptive.

In *The Media Are American* (1977), Jeremy Tunstall provided a cogent description of how American media entrepreneurs developed their strategy for creating universally attractive cultural commodities. He also traced how it succeeded internationally against strong competition from France and Britain. In the late nineteenth and early twentieth centuries, American entrepreneurs had access to powerful new communications technology but no clear notion of how it could be used to make profits. Most big industrialists regarded media as no more than minor and highly speculative enterprises. Few were willing to invest the money necessary to create viable industries. How could messages broadcast through the air or crude, black and white, moving images on a movie screen be used to earn profits? Would people really pay to see or hear these things? How should industries be organized to manufacture and market cultural products? Most early attempts to answer these questions failed. But through trial and effort, a successful strategy was developed.

According to Tunstall, Tin Pan Alley in New York City provided the model that was later emulated by other U.S. media industries. The authors of popular music specialized in taking melodies from folk music and transforming them into short, attractive songs. These were easily marketed to mass audiences who didn't have the time or the aesthetic training to appreciate longer, more sophisticated forms of music. In its early days, Tin Pan Alley was a musical sweat shop in which song writers were ill-paid and overworked while sheet music and recording company entrepreneurs reaped huge profits. By keeping production and distribution costs quite low, rapid expansion was possible and profits grew accordingly. Inevitably, expansion carried the entrepreneurs beyond the United States. Because many were first generation European immigrants, they knew how to return and gain a foothold in Europe. The Second World War provided an ideal opportunity to subvert European culture. The American military demanded and received permission to import massive quantities of U.S. style popular culture into Europe where it proved popular. American Armed Forces Radio was especially influential in its broadcasts of popular music and entertainment shows.

What are the consequences of lifting bits of everyday life culture out of their context, repackaging and then marketing them back to people? Cultural studies analysts have provided many intriguing answers to this question.

1   **When elements of everyday culture are selected for repackaging, only a very limited range are chosen and important elements are overlooked or consciously ignored.** For example, elements of culture important for structuring the experience of small minority groups are likely to be ignored while culture practiced by large segments of the population will be emphasized. For a good illustration of this, watch some situation comedies from the 1960s like "Father Knows Best" and "Leave It to Beaver." During this era, these programs provided a very homogeneous and idealized picture of American family life. They may make you wonder whether there were any poor people or ethnic groups living in the U.S. in 1965.

2   **The repackaging process involves dramatization of those elements of culture that have been selected.** Certain forms of action are highlighted and their importance is exaggerated while others are ignored. Such dramatization makes the final commodity attractive to as large an audience as possible. Potentially boring, controversial, or offensive elements are removed. Features are added that are known to appeal to large audience segments. Thus, attention-getting and emotion-arousing actions, for example sex and violence, are routinely featured. This is a major reason that car chases, gun fights, and verbal conflict dominate prime-time television while casual conversations between friends are rare (unless they include a joke every fifteen seconds — then you have situation comedy).

3   **The marketing of cultural commodities is done in a way that maximizes the likelihood that they will intrude into and ultimately disrupt everyday life.** The success of the industries depends upon marketing as much content as possible to as many people as possible with no consideration for how this content will actually be used or what its long-term consequences will be. An analogy can be made to pollution of the physical environment caused by food packaging. The packaging adds nothing to the nutritional value of the food but is merely a marketing device — it moves the product off the shelf. Pollution results when we carelessly dispose of this packaging or when there is so much of it that there is no place to put it. Unlike trash, media commodities are less tangible and their packaging is completely integrated into the cultural content. There are no recycling bins for cultural packaging. When we consume the product, we consume the packaging. It intrudes and disrupts.

4   **The elites who operate the cultural industries generally are ignorant of the consequences of their work.** This ignorance is based partly on their alienation from

the people who consume their products. They live in Hollywood or New York City, not in typical neighborhoods. Ignorance is maintained partly through strategic avoidance or denial of evidence about consequences in much the same way that the tobacco industry has resisted research documenting the negative effects of smoking. Media industries have developed formal mechanisms for rationalizing their impact and explaining away consequences. One involves supporting empirical social research and the limited effects findings that it produces. Another involves professionalization. Although this can have positive benefits (see Chapter 5), it can also be used by media practitioners to justify routine production practices while rejecting potentially useful innovations.

5   **Disruption of everyday life takes many forms—some are obviously linked to consumption of especially deleterious content, but other forms of disruption are very subtle and occur over long time periods.** Disruption ranges from propagation of misconceptions about the social world—like those cultivation analysis has examined—to disruption of social institutions. Consequences can be both microscopic and macroscopic and take many different forms. For example, Joshua Meyrowitz (1985) argued that media have deprived us of a sense of place. Neil Postman (1985) believed that media focus too much on entertainment, with serious long-term consequences. And Kathleen Jamieson (1988) lamented the decline of political speechmaking brought about by electronic media.

Following are summaries of research developed by those theorists critical of the media as culture industries, although some is the work of those who would not necessarily call themselves critical cultural theorists.

Advertising: The Ultimate Cultural Commodity

Critical cultural studies researchers have directed their most devastating criticism toward advertising. Advertising is viewed as the ultimate cultural commodity (Jhally, 1987; Hay, 1989). Advertising packages promotional messages so that they will be attended to and acted upon by people who often have little interest in and no real need for most of the advertised products or services. Consumption of specific products is routinely portrayed as the best way to construct a worthwhile personal identity, have fun, make friends and influence people, or solve problems (often ones you never knew you had). Join the Pepsi Generation. You deserve a break today. Just do it.

Compared to other forms of mass media content, advertising comes closest to fitting older Marxist notions of ideology. It is intended to encourage consumption that serves the interest of product manufacturers but may not be in the interest of individual consumers. Advertising is clearly designed to intrude into and disrupt routine buying habits and purchase decisions. For some products, such as cigarettes and alcohol, successful advertising campaigns induce people to engage in self-destructive actions. In most cases, we are simply encouraged to consume things that serve little real purpose for us or serve only the purposes that advertising itself creates. One obvious example is when we buy specific brands of clothing because their advertising has promoted them as status symbols.

News Production Research

During the past two decades a number of studies have been done on the production of news content (Crouse, 1973; Epstein, 1973; Fishman, 1980; Gans, 1979; Gitlin, 1980; Tuchman, 1978). Most of the research we discuss in this section was conducted by British and American sociologists during the 1970s and 1980s. Their purpose was to critically analyze how journalists routinely cover news.

W. Lance Bennett (1988) surveyed the news production literature and summarized four ways in which current production practices distort or bias news content:

1 **Personalized News:** Most people relate better to individuals than to groups or institutions, so most news stories center around people. According to Bennett, "The focus on individual actors who are easy to identify with positively or negatively invites members of the news audience to project their own private feelings and fantasies directly onto public life" (1988, p. 27). Thus, personalization helps people relate to and find relevance in remote events. It does this, however, at a cost—it risks transforming the larger social world into a gigantic soap opera.

2 **Dramatized News:** Like all media commodities, news must be attractively packaged and a primary means of doing this involves dramatization. Edward Jay Epstein (1973) provided the following quotation from a policy memorandum written by a network television news producer:

> Every news story should, without any sacrifice of probity or responsibility, display the attributes of fiction, of drama. It should have structure and conflict, problem and denouement, rising action and falling action, a beginning, a middle, and an end. These are not only the essentials of drama; they are the essentials of narrative (pp. 4–5).

Bennett and Murray Edelman (1985) argued that this type of narrative is very limiting and inherently biased toward supporting the status quo. They have called for development of more innovative narrative structures as one means of reforming the news industry.

3 **Fragmented News:** The typical newspaper and news broadcast is made up of brief, capsulized reports of events—snapshots of the social world. By constructing news in this way, journalists attempt to fulfill their norm of objectivity. Events are treated in isolation with little effort to interconnect them. Connection

requires putting them into a broader context, and this would require making speculative, sometimes controversial linkages. Is there a link between three isolated plane crashes, or between three separate toxic waste spills? By compartmentalizing events, news reports make it difficult for news consumers to make their own connections. Bennett argued that when journalists attempt to do analysis, they create a collage. They assemble evidence and viewpoints from conflicting sources and then juxtapose these pieces in a manner that defies interpretation, especially by news consumers who lack interest or background knowledge. These stories may meet the norm of being "balanced" but they don't assist the reader in making sense of things.

4   **Normalized News**: We opened this chapter with examples of normalized news. Stories about disasters or about social movements tend to "normalize" these potential threats to the status quo. Elite sources are allowed to explain disasters and to challenge movement members. Elites are presented as authoritative, rational, knowledgeable people who are effectively coping with threats. They can be trusted to bring things back to normal. If there is a problem with aircraft technology, it will be repaired. If movements make legitimate demands, they will be satisfied.

Consider how the savings and loan debacle was initially covered: just a few isolated cases — a few bad eggs — not an industry-wide problem; no need for more stringent or effective regulation; trust regulators and the police would take care of it. As the crisis deepened, news stories began to acknowledge the problem but by then it had reached serious proportions. Still, confidence was expressed that existing government agencies could handle the problem. Gradually, the necessity for a new agency, the Resolution Trust Corporation (RTC), was admitted. The operation of the RTC was found acceptable until its own problems escalated. Why were journalists reluctant to engage in early criticism or undertake intensive investigations that might avert such crises? One common excuse is that the public just isn't interested in abstract topics. Even if hard hitting coverage of savings and loans had been written, no one would have read it. Ask yourself how interested you are in HUD, even now that we know that its Reagan-era corruption scandal mirrors that of the S&Ls, if not in amount of money stolen, at least in how the affair unfolded. Ask yourself if you even know what HUD is.

Gaye Tuchman (1978) provided a good example of news production research. She studied how the values held by journalists influence news even when considerable effort is made to guard against that influence. She observed journalists as they covered social movements and concluded that production practices were implicitly biased toward support of the status quo. She found that reporters engaged in *objectivity rituals* — they had set procedures for producing unbiased news stories that actually introduced bias. For example, when leaders of a controversial movement were interviewed, their statements were never allowed to stand alone. Journalists routinely attempted to "balance" these statements by reporting the views of authorities who opposed the movements. Reporters frequently selected the most unusual or controversial statements made by movement leaders and contrasted these with the more conventional views of mainstream group leaders. Reporters made little effort to understand the overall philosophy of the movement. Lacking understanding, they inevitably took statements out of context and misrepresented movement ideals. Thus, though reporters never explicitly expressed negative views about these groups, their lack of understanding, their casual methods for selecting quotes, and their use of elite sources led to stories that were harmful to the movements they covered. Tuchman's arguments have been collaborated by Mark Fishman (1980) and Todd Gitlin (1980).

Corroborated ??

Intrusion of Media into Politics

While news production research was being done by sociologists, political scientists developed another set of studies that critically assessed the role of media. The primary theme of this research has been that media have increasingly intruded into and disrupted American politics. Television news has been the focus of this research. The medium has been blamed for everything from the decline of political parties to low voter turnout in elections. Gradually, a set of arguments has evolved that we will refer to as *media intrusion theory* (Davis, 1990, used this term; Patterson, 1980, articulated many of these arguments but doesn't label them).

Media intrusion theory holds that prior to 1960, American politics were effectively structured by political parties with little interference from media. Parties controlled the nomination of candidates, they organized voter turnout in large cities, and in short, they dominated campaigns. Although this system had some disadvantages, most notably in urban machine politics, it also had important strengths. Party leaders were dedicated, political experts who chose candidates based on ideological commitments, not personality or hair style. Campaigns promoted the parties as much as they promoted candidates. Parties emerged from elections with renewed strength. Strong parties could motivate citizens to vote on the basis of well-established loyalties that persisted from election to election. Voters might occasionally turn against party candidates, but they retained their overall loyalty.

Media intrusion theory can be regarded as a variant of elite pluralism (see Chapter 6). It assumes that politics operate best when they are hierarchically structured, when a political elite mediates between the public and its elected leaders. There is suspicion about trends that might impair the power of this elite.

Box 13a Media Intrusion

Media practitioners, too, are concerned with media intrusion into politics. Carl Bernstein, best known for his coverage of the Watergate scandal, said the following about the American media's contemporary performance and their intrusion into politics.

"The America rendered today in the American media is illusionary and delusionary—disfigured, unreal, disconnected from the true contexts of our lives. In covering real American life the media—weekly, daily, hourly—breaks new ground in getting it wrong. The coverage is distorted by celebrity; by the reduction of news to gossip; by sensationalism, which is always turning away from a society's real condition; and by a political and social discourse that we—the press, the media, the politicians, *and* the people—are turning into a sewer."

He offered this example, "'All right, was it really the best sex you ever had?' Those were the words of Diane Sawyer, in an interview of Marla Maples on Prime Time Live, a broadcast of ABC News (where 'more Americans get their news than any other source'). Those words marked a new low. For more than 15 years we have been moving away from real journalism toward the creation of a sleazoid info-tainment culture in which the lines between Oprah and Geraldo and Diane, between the New York *Post* and *Newsday* are too often indistinguishable. In this new culture of journalistic titillation, we teach readers and viewers that the trivial is significant, that the lurid and the loopy are more important than real news" (Bernstein, 1992, p. 4C).

The theory assumes that there is no good alternative to party control over politics and is skeptical that other ways of structuring politics might be more useful.

The decline of political parties has been well documented as has been the decline in political affiliation and voting. These changes occurred at the same time that television became the dominant medium for news. A linkage between these events is plausible but has proved hard to establish empirically. Media intrusion theorists typically argue that television has subverted politics by undermining political party control over elections. Some even argue that television has replaced parties in the election process. Candidates no longer need party support—some actively avoid it. Instead, candidates hire political consultants to guide their media use. Candidates are often advised to avoid all mention of their political party. Campaigns promote candidates not parties.

The findings of the news production researchers are frequently cited by media intrusion theorists in support of their positions. These theorists claim that political reports are too personalized, too dramatized, and too fragmented. Politics is often reported as a game between opposing teams with the major politicians viewed as star players. Stories focus on big plays, on life and death struggles to score points. These reports don't help news consumers develop useful understandings of politics. Rather, they encourage consumers to become political spectators, content to sit on the sidelines while the stars play the game.

Journalists reject the media intrusion argument by asserting that they have little control over elections. They don't intrude into politics. Instead, their reporting efforts are being disrupted by political consultants. They point out that the political parties chose to give up control over presidential nominations when they decided to permit primary elections to be held across the nation. As the power of political parties has declined and the influence of political consultants has increased, manipulation of media by politicians has increased. Political consultants have developed very effective strategies for obtaining favorable news coverage for their candidates (Davis, 1990). During campaigns, journalists rely upon particular production practices for gathering and generating news stories. Consultants are very knowledgeable about these practices and are skilled at supplying useful information and convenient events. They make it very easy to cover the candidate as the consultant wants and hard for journalists to find material for alternate stories.

For example, one recent news management strategy is to limit what a candidate says each day. By repeating the same terse comment over and over, the candidate hopes to force broadcast reporters to pick up and use the "sound bite of the day." The candidate avoids talking candidly to reporters because statements could be used to construct alternate stories. Since journalists pride themselves on covering, not making news, they find it hard to break out of the limitations imposed by shrewd consultants.

Summary

During the past two decades, critical cultural studies has emerged as an important, alternative perspective on the role of media in society. This approach has its intellectual roots in Marxist theory but has been influenced by and incorporates other perspectives including literary criticism. The theory argues that mass media could and should be used to guide and implement constructive social change. Media are typically thought, however, to support the status quo and to interfere with the efforts of social movements to bring about useful social change.

Unlike most forms of theory and research examined in this textbook, critical cultural theory is more or less explicitly based on a set of social values (see Chapter 14 for a discussion). These values are used to critique existing social institutions and social practices. Institutions and practices that undermine or marginalize important values are criticized. Alternatives to these institutions or practices are offered. In some cases, theory is developed to guide useful social change.

Critical cultural studies views existing mass media as a cultural industry, one concerned with the manufacture and distribution of cultural commodities. This industry is highly constrained in what it does because profits must be earned if the media are to survive and grow. Cultural commodities consist of bits of every-day life culture that are lifted out of context, repackaged, and then marketed as entertainment and news. Repackaging typically involves considerable distortion which in turn fosters many misimpressions about personal identities and the larger social world. Often, these misimpressions provide support for the status quo. Criticism has centered on advertising and political communication. Adver-tising is said to create unnecessary needs while political news intrudes into and disrupts politics. Entertainment content distorts our perspective on ourselves and the social world.

Unlike earlier schools of Marxist theory, most critical cultural theorists reject the view that mass media are totally under the control of well-organized, domi-nant elites who cynically manipulate media content in their own interest. Instead, media are viewed as a public forum in which many people and groups are able to participate. However, elites are seen as enjoying many advantages. Most media content is found to implicitly or explicitly support the status quo. Also, critical theorists reject simplistic notions of audience effects like those found in mass society theory. Even when media content explicitly supports the status quo, audiences may misunderstand or reject this content. Audience members have been found to engage in oppositional decoding of media content, arriving at interpretations that differ markedly from those intended by mes-sage producers.

Current research on media has begun to converge on a common set of themes and issues. These are shared by many qualitative and quantitative researchers (See Chapter 14). Critical cultural studies has played an important role in identifying these themes and prioritizing these issues. Despite the serious questions that have been raised about the value of this approach, it has proved heuristic. This has occurred even though all too often this research is densely written using arcane neomarxist terminology (see Carey and Grossberg, 1988 for examples). Critical cultural theorists make bold assertions and explicitly incor-porate values into their work. They provide a useful challenge to mainstream media theory.

Discussion Questions

1   Discuss the differences between cultural analysis and critical cultural studies as they are presented in Chapters 12 and 13. Do you prefer one approach or the other? Explain.

2   How does critical cultural studies differ from mass society theory as presented in Chapter 3?

3   To what extent do you think media content fosters support for the status quo? Do you agree or disagree with critical cultural studies arguments concerning disaster reporting?

4   Discuss Frankfurt School assertions about mass culture and high culture. Can or should mass media be used to promote high culture? What about the notion of high culture itself? Is this concept inherently elitist?

5   To what extent does the idea of oppositional decoding provide another way of thinking about audience activity? Does it differ fundamentally with conceptions of audience members found in uses and gratifications theory? How? Which do you find more useful?

6   Has your life been affected or disrupted by consumption of cultural commodities, including advertising? Can you think of any examples of misconceptions about yourself or the world that you got from media content? Could you have avoided making these mistakes? To what extent should media practitioners be held responsible for them?

7   Almost everyone agrees that U.S. politics is in need of reform. Do you agree with arguments that place considerable responsibility for this situation on journalists? Could or should national politics and national political campaigns be reported differently?

Significant Names

Janice Radway

Larry Grossberg

Harold Innis

Marshall McLuhan

Stuart Hall

Karl Marx

Significant Readings

Adorno, Theodor and Max Horkheimer (1972). *Dialectic of Enlightenment.* New York: Herder & Herder.

Berman, Art (1988). *From the New Criticism to Deconstruction: the Reception of Structuralism and Post-Structuralism.* Urbana: University of Illinois Press.

Hall, Stuart, Dorothy Hobson, Andrew Lowe, and Paul Willis, eds., (1980). *Culture, Media, Language.* London: Hutchinson.

Innis, Harold A. (1950). *Empire and Communication.* Toronto: Oxford University Press.

Innis, Harold A. (1951). *The Bias of Communication.* Toronto: University of Toronto Press.

Jhally, Sut, ed., (1987). *The Codes of Advertising: Fetishism and the Political Economy of Meaning in the Consumer Society.* London: Frances Pinter.

McLuhan, Marshall (1951). *The Mechanical Bride.* New York: Vanguard Press.

McLuhan, Marshall (1964). *Understanding Media: the Extensions of Man.* New York: McGraw-Hill.

Patterson, Thomas E. (1980). *The Mass Media Election: How Americans Choose Their President.* New York: Praeger.

Radway, Janice (1984). *Reading the Romance: Women, Patriarchy, and Popular Literature.* Chapel Hill: University of North Carolina Press.

Tuchman, Gaye (1978). *Making News: A Study in the Construction of Reality.* New York: Free Press.

Tunstall, Jeremy (1977). *The Media are American: Anglo-American Media in the World.* New York: Columbia University Press.

Important Terms

Base

Superstructure

Neomarxism

Ideology

Frankfurt School

British Cultural Studies

Global Village

Bias of Communication

Hot and Cool Media

Objectivity Rituals

Technological Determinist

Media Intrusion Theory

Cultural Commodity

Oppositional Decoding

Public Forum

Political Economy Theory

Chapter 14

Paradigm Dialogue or Conflict?

In 1987 Wilbur Schramm died and in 1988 Raymond Williams passed away. Their deaths symbolized the passing of an era that saw the full emergence of mass communication as an academic discipline and as a legitimate focus for research. Their lives were affected by the ideas and events we've reviewed in these pages. Both men did much to influence the academic institutions and theories of today. Neither worked alone. Both were part of larger research communities that flourished during their working lives. Both gained international recognition for their research, and both became the focus of sharp criticism from opposing scholars. In many respects, each ideally represented the research community that he led. Each was a talented writer who did much to articulate and advance both theory and research.

Wilbur Schramm was an unlikely developer of a social science-based approach to communication research. Trained as a literary scholar with a Masters Degree from Harvard University and a Ph.D. in English from the University of Iowa, Schramm had little formal training in social science (McAnany, 1988). During the 1930s, when Schramm began his career there, Iowa, along with most midwestern universities, was caught up in the rise of empirical social science. Schramm collaborated with colleagues in education and psychology while helping the Department of English organize the Iowa Writers Workshop.

Schramm's career as a full-time communication researcher began when one of his Iowa mentors, an educational psychologist named George Stoddard, brought him to Washington, D.C. in 1941 to work in the Office of Facts and Figures. Schramm was part of a new generation of wartime scholars determined to use their skills to defeat totalitarianism. He assisted the poet Archibald MacLeish in the drafting of war propaganda, including speeches for President Roosevelt (McAnany, 1988). In this job, Schramm came to know and was influenced by Harold Lasswell, Carl Hovland, and Paul Lazarsfeld as well as by many other people who became prominent social researchers such as Margaret Mead, Ithiel de Sola Pool, and Nathan Maccoby. Schramm reportedly became quite convinced of the persuasive power of both President Roosevelt and of radio.

Schramm later distanced himself from his brief career as a war propagandist. After the publication in 1955 of *Four Working Papers on Propaganda Theory*, his work contains few references to propaganda or his war-related activities. The professional contacts that he made and the perspective on communication that he developed remained with him throughout his career, however. When he organized the Institute for Communications Research at the University of Illinois in 1948, Schramm elicited the support of many of his prominent social science friends.

Like many people who came through the Depression and war years, Schramm believed in progress through the development and application of technology. He was convinced that new communication media could and should be used to overcome worldwide social problems. Properly used, media should educate and inform. Media should prevent rather than stir political unrest. New media could promote economic and political development in Third World nations and thus prevent the spread of Communism (Schramm, 1964). They could revolutionize teaching in both the United States and abroad.

Though Schramm was not himself a creative theorist, he did much to explain, synthesize, and popularize the work of others. A prolific writer, he published numerous books that popularized his perspective. He built important communication research institutes at Illinois, Stanford, and at the East-West Center in Hawaii. Through his textbooks and research, he influenced the first two generations of communication scholars in the United States. Despite his own background in the humanities, Schramm did little to reconcile growing differences between those disciplines and the social sciences. He remained a staunch advocate of systematic, empirically based, and inductive social research. He rejected the notion that values should play any role in scientific inquiry beyond the choice of research questions. Though he accepted criticisms of his views on communication and development (Schramm and Lerner, 1976), he rarely seriously explored or advocated alternative theories. He remained optimistic about the *potential* of mass communication (Schramm, 1988), but less certain about its future role.

The career of Raymond Williams has some surprising parallels to that of Schramm. Though neither Schramm nor Williams came from wealthy families, both attended elite universities. Both excelled as students, and both eventually were trained as literary scholars. But unlike Schramm, Williams was never drawn into the world of practical politics, even when his work inspired and was

Box 14a Recollections of Wilbur Schramm

Dr. Serena Stanford is the Associate Vice President for Graduate Studies and Research at San Jose State University and, as you'll read below, a student of Wilbur Schramm. This is her recollection of him:

It has been nearly 30 years since I walked into the Stanford Press Building to begin my doctoral program in Communication Research. Even then, Wilbur Schramm was something of a legend. I had come across several of his infinitely readable books, and I looked forward to meeting him, expecting someone much different from the man I learned to admire and respect.

It is so interesting to look back into the history of mass communication and dwell on the irony of benefit from international conflict. World War II gave us modern survey research and hastened the development of academic programs whose applied focus could be tolerated in academe. I am always amazed to note how many of those who later established and staffed communications research as social scientists began their careers as journalists. Wilbur was among those pioneers and his unique stamp on the enterprise has affected all who were his students and his colleagues throughout the world.

The world was indeed Wilbur's venue, and he sought to make it better by asking some important questions and attempting to apply social science methods to get answers. Although no one would ever argue that Wilbur was on the cutting edge of methodology, his grounding was more than adequate and his ability to translate the "stuff" of number-crunchers to policy makers and the public was without peer.

It was my pleasure and privilege to work with Wilbur as a research associate in widely varied projects. In each, he defined the scope of work,

then went globe-hopping, properly leaving the mechanics to those of us who needed the experience to learn. He was remarkably folksy in his working relationships but you were never late with material for Wilbur. The workload was formidable because computer applications were still uncertain—neither he nor I could ever grasp computer languages—and SPSS hadn't arrived. So, getting mountains of crosstabs done was a stupendous task, especially with punched cards for as many as 40 different surveys at a time. But it was great experience and instilled courage, if not wisdom, in those of us who left Stanford and headed for independent research opportunities in many different places. And Wilbur was never stingy with author credit.

I am grateful to Wilbur for giving support to a woman at a time when it was still not fashionable for women to think. When I arrived at the Institute for Communication Research, the first greeting I heard (not from Wilbur) was, "You won't make it. Others have tried, but . . ." Two and a half years later I was the first woman Ph.D. in the Stanford program. I am proud of that academic accomplishment. At the same time, it was clear that I had less research experience than others because I had come from a theatre arts background. So Wilbur took personal responsibility for my extended internship; it was a gift that has had infinite value. He gave me opportunities and the rest was up to me. That's all life really offers anyway. I will always remember him with thanks as a mentor and friend.

[handwritten margin note: Schramm vis-a-vis Williams ↓]

espoused by several social movements. Instead, he spent most of his life as an isolated scholar secluded in the small British university community of Cambridge. Whereas Schramm was hailed by his colleagues as a leader and consensus builder, Williams was regarded by many colleagues, including those in his own university, as a loner and an iconoclast. Within his university he gained recognition primarily as a literary historian with a focus on theater. His controversial writing on mass media was ignored. He gathered small groups of highly committed students but rarely made public appearances. In contrast with Schramm, who synthesized and popularized the theories of others, Williams pieced together a highly original perspective based on ideas taken from many sources, including literary theories, linguistics, and neomarxist writing. Schramm built new academic centers dedicated to the study of communication and moved frequently from one university to another; Williams spent his entire career working at Cambridge University in a traditional English Department.

Williams didn't focus his work around mass media to the degree that Schramm did and he was deeply skeptical about mass media's role in modern society. Yet his work inspired a generation of British media scholars, first at the Centre for Contemporary Cultural Studies at the University of Birmingham and then at other universities across England and Europe. Williams was more broadly concerned with issues of cultural change and development as well as elite domination of culture. Committed to certain basic, humanistic values including cultural pluralism and egalitarianism, he lacked Schramm's faith in the march of human progress and the role media might play in it. In contrast with most humanists of his time, Williams rejected the literary Canon as a standard and with it traditional notions of High Culture. On the other hand, he was reluctant to embrace and celebrate folk culture and disdained most forms of popular, mass media culture. If there were to be genuine progress, he felt, it would have to come through significant reform of social institutions. But he did little to lead reform efforts.

Historical circumstances played an important part in shaping the careers of both men. Schramm had the good fortune to be working in a wealthy nation at a time when the size of academic institutions and support for social research grew tremendously. He had access to resources and professional contacts that enabled him to build important new centers for research. As an acknowledged expert on the role of mass media, he became a semi-official representative of the U.S. government, traveling on federal grants and working closely with government officials at home and abroad.

If history provided a global stage for Schramm, it tended to marginalize Williams' career. Through neomarxism enjoyed some following among academics in Western Europe, it was virtually ignored in American universities. Cold War politics precluded serious consideration of theories that were explicitly acknowledged to be based upon the writing of Karl Marx. But Williams wasn't warmly embraced behind the Iron Curtain either. In the U.S.S.R. and Eastern Europe, ideas like those of Williams were often regarded as too unorthodox and revisionist. Within the several schools of neomarxism, Williams enjoyed an uneven reputation, lionized by some and criticized by others.

At the time of the deaths of these two men, the field of communication research had expanded into a global enterprise. Several professional associations had thousands of members around the globe. The media theories popular when Schramm and Williams were born had mostly been abandoned. The paradigms popular during their middle years were being challenged by new perspectives on media's role. In many ways, the field of communications had come of age and the research communities founded or inspired by these two men were instrumental in bringing this about. Firm foundations had been laid for future generations of communication researchers.

Overview

A central objective of this book has been to familiarize you with important historic and contemporary perspectives on media and to provide you with a basic understanding of how researchers regard media and why they hold those views. Keep in mind that our discussions of various theories have been quite brief. If we have stimulated your interest in mass media, you should read the research and the theories that we cite. We hope that you will consider becoming part of a research community dedicated to expanding our understanding of media's role. Without the Cold War to impose artificial restrictions on research communities and bias them toward certain forms of theory, your generation should have greater freedom to explore ideas. The powerful new communication technologies being developed are likely to transform the role of media and open up many new lines of research. These technologies also provide powerful tools for both qualitative and quantitative research. Innovative research communities could be established using their various methods.

In this chapter, we discuss how research communities are likely to develop in the future. In previous chapters, we have surveyed the many new ideas that stimulate and guide current research. But they sometimes appear to lead in contradictory directions. Researchers prefer to study these ideas using many different methods. Can these theories and methods provide a basis for forming coherent and productive research communities? We have argued that such communities can be formed but the task will not be easy even with the aid of new technology.

A number of efforts are currently underway to reconceptualize and restructure the field of communication. During the summer and fall of 1993, one of the leading journals in the field, the *Journal of Communication*, devoted two issues to essays by 48 scholars on the "future of the field." The essays graphically illustrate the wide range of views now held in the discipline. Despite this diversity, most share a commitment to building the field. In general, the essays are optimistic. They reflect the view that as a field, communication has important advantages over more traditional academic disciplines. The ferment of new ideas and our many research methods could be an asset if we avoid divisiveness. The lack of strong disciplinary boundaries could allow us to do more interesting and productive work.

In this chapter we will examine some alternative directions for research. We will compare what is being labeled as the *communication science* approach with the possibilities offered by *cultural theories*. Keep in mind that our views on these two approaches are not definitive. We are offering our conclusions about trends that are very hard to assess. If you are considering a career in this field, we strongly recommend that you read the essays in *Journal of Communication* and develop your own views.

In Chapters 9, 10, and 11, we showed how current empirical research on mass communication has developed, moving away from narrowly conceptualized notions of limited effects and toward exploration of a broad range of new research, some macroscopic and some microscopic, some based on surveys some based on experiments, and still others based on participant observation. This work is bound together by common assumptions and common research methods but not by a well-integrated, overarching theory. Researchers develop middle-range theories and investigate them using empirical, social research methods. Increasingly, these theories and methods are being conceptualized as constituting the communication science approach.

The proponents of communication science (Chaffee and Berger, 1987a) are optimistic about what can be accomplished using their approach. Exciting, innovative work is being done on many topics. We are gaining important insight into the role of media at macroscopic levels (Iyengar and Kinder, 1986; Iyengar, 1991) and are coming to understand the subtle ways that media can intrude into and alter our experience of ourselves and our world. We have empirically demonstrated that media do play a central role in our society even when this role is as an agent that reinforces existing trends. We have come a long way from simplistic theories that postulated direct effects or the equally simplistic views that denied the possibility of important effects.

In Chapters 12 and 13 we examined many different culture-centered studies of mass communication, ranging from neomarxist interpretations of mass culture to symbolic interactionist views of mediated socialization. If you've read these chapters you know something about role models, simulation of social processes, elite domination of the superstructure, cultivation analysis, oppositional decoding, and so forth. This research also has deepened our understanding of media and their importance for us as individuals and for society at large. We argue that the various cultural theories share many assumptions. This could allow an integrated, culture-centered approach to emerge.

To a great extent, the perspectives emerging from culture-centered research *complement* rather than challenge the notions arising form empirical research. Both approaches emphasize that individuals make active use of media, both have identified important social roles for media, both recognize that media operate within an essentially competitive social environment in which the power of media is challenged and constrained by other social institutions, and finally both permit cautious optimism about the ways that media might contribute to improving the quality of our lives in the future. For some time into the future, it is likely that these two approaches will guide much of the scholarship. Neither approach is likely to completely displace the other since each approach serves different purposes.

Finding Continuity within a Diverse Discipline

One reality of mass communication theory that should be evident by now is that it is the product of many different disciplines, many different methodologies, many different world views, many different eras in the development of media, and even many different understandings of the nature of people. Through much of its history, communication has been a "crossroads" discipline that attracted scholars from many fields in the humanities and the social sciences. Communication has benefited from this cross-fertilization, but the field has also been continually disrupted by it. Important new theories in psychology, literary studies, anthropology, sociology, and political science have guided communication research.

Contemporary communication researchers and theorists often express concern about the lack of focus or definition for their field. Most people have a pretty good idea of what psychology is. Same for sociology, even philosophy. But what is "communication?" Is it mass communication? Is it interpersonal communication? Is it the study of communication behaviors, the analysis of texts, the observation of content production, or the description of media industries? This book refers very little to communication between two or a few people (interpersonal communication), but how can we effectively discuss media effects, for example, without taking into account how people manifest those effects in their real worlds—in other words, in their communication with others who share their environments?

And even if we limit our attention to mass communication, can we truly understand it without finding some way to integrate (or at least make compati-

list

ble) social learning theory, persuasion and attitude change theory, uses and gratifications, two-step flow, functional theory, and on and on? But, you'll say, didn't Robert Merton, the originator of middle-range theory, promise us that all these discrete, middle-level theories would eventually be integrated into a broader theory? Why hasn't this happened? Could it still happen? Should it happen?

As communication theory moved toward maturity and respectability, middle-range theories proliferated and they contributed to, rather than reduced disciplinary and intellectual division. As Suzanne Pingree, John Wiemann and Robert Hawkins (1988, p. 7) explained,

names

> Communication's fragmentation is manifest in the many subspecialties that lay claim to the field of communication, and that are distinguished by largely different methods of inquiry, by levels of analysis, by theories that place communication in very different points in the research process (in the simplest distinction, as either antecedent or outcome), and even by differences in what phenomena deserve to be called communication . . . (W)hile such distinctions have value in organizing and focusing academic work, the fragmentation that results can be stifling as well.

Although empirical researchers have been struggling to piece together the discrete findings of thousands of surveys and experiments, qualitative, culture-centered researchers faced even more important divisions. Traditional literary scholars worked to advance high culture and long-standing, humanistic values while neomarxists criticized elite domination of culture and looked for ways to transform the status quo. Humanistic, qualitative scholars in anthropology, history, sociology, psychology, and political science developed contrasting definitions of culture, created very different standards for research, and pioneered many new but unproved methods of data collection and analysis.

Thus, it is not surprising that many people, including many academics, find communication to be an overly ambiguous, perversely ambitious, all too disorderly field of study. For them, it seems much more logical to approach the study of communication from the view of a more "established" discipline. Why risk working with so many different theories? Why draw research methods from such diverse sources? Why force yourself to understand the merits of both quantitative and qualitative research? Though we understand such sentiments, we don't share them. We find diversity challenging. It motivates rather than discourages our work. We readily admit that a half century of communication research seems to have produced far more questions than it has answered. But today's research questions are quite significant. They address fundamental issues about human nature, our cognitive and emotional capacities, our ability to create and share meaning through association with others, and our ability to construct large-scale social orders in which humane values are realized.

Some colleagues may argue that we have exaggerated the disruption caused by theoretical diversity. It is important to recognize that the field contains many well-established research subgroups. Within them, scholars share a body of theory and research methods. They publish their work in a narrow range of journals, and they read each other's books. But the various research subgroups are loosely interrelated. Members of different groups belong to the same academic associations and work as colleagues on the same campuses and even in the same departments. Occasionally, conflicts arise, but on a day-to-day basis they conduct their work in relative isolation. Thus, while students are forced to confront diversity as they are required to learn about the full range of theory and research, scholars can avoid it by confining their work within a particular subgroup. They can be uses and gratifications researchers, agenda-setting researchers, news learning researchers, popular music critics, analysts of certain forms of media content, observers of media organizations, and so forth. They can focus their work on print media while others study television. They can study news while others look at entertainment. Scholarship within many of these research subgroups is as well structured and systematic as work done in other academic disciplines. In fact, these subgroups often look to another academic discipline for new theories and research methods. For example, communication researchers studying how people learn information from television news borrowed theories and research methods from cognitive psychologists.

Why have these research subgroups developed and what are their advantages and disadvantages? One reason for this fragmentation is that almost everything that is studied in the humanities and the social sciences is related in some way to communication. An anthropologist might be interested in Pacific Island tribal masks, which are designed to communicate specific beliefs in native rituals. A literary scholar interested in the plays of Shakespeare may be concerned with what these plays communicated to Renaissance audiences. A psychologist might be interested in spousal abuse; family communication is involved. A political scientist or a political rhetorician surely studies campaigns that are large-scale communication undertakings. And what sociologist interested in how communities operate can ignore the role of communication, what economist can ignore the impact of communication on consumer confidence, what child development expert can remain ignorant of the intrapersonal, interpersonal, and mass communication activity of growing children?

William Paisley (1984, p. 2) summarized this situation for the social sciences when he wrote,

At midcentury, the river of the social sciences flowed through the study of human communication. From the 1930s to the 1950s, communication was a confluence of interest for leading social scientists in the United States. The reading lists of communication students are still dominated by the writings of Carl Hovland, Harold Lasswell, Paul Lazarsfeld, Kurt Lewin—the "founding fathers" of communication research—and their colleagues and students. The disciplines of anthropology, sociology, political science, and economics were all represented.

A second factor that encouraged fragmentation is that the "study of communication" and "communication research" have generally been identified longer and more often with the study of *mass* communication and *mass* communication research. Interpersonal communication was being studied (more or less) by anthropologists, psychologists, and sociologists, but the emergence of mass communication technologies (mass circulation newspapers, motion pictures, radio, and television) seemed to require a newer, more discrete field. So when the discipline of communication began to take shape, it had a definite mass communication orientation and excluded from its membership those who investigated non-mass mediated communication. During the 1960s and 1970s, mass communication programs grew rapidly in size while other areas of communication grew more slowly and traditional speech programs actually declined. Students flocked to mass communication programs because they wanted to be trained for jobs in the media.

The third factor is related: the mass media technologies, especially film and television, appeared during eras of significant cultural and social change in America. This virtually guaranteed that those interested in the process of communication (or those interested in macro-level cultural and social change) would gravitate toward mass communication. This was, as the old saying goes, where the action was. This is what drew neomarxist scholars at the University of Birmingham to the study of contemporary culture just as it attracted the attention of empirical researchers like Lazarsfeld, Hovland, and Schramm during World War II.

Consider, for example, persuasion and attitude change. Persuasion and attitude change—once the realm of rhetoricians and speech teachers, firmly rooted in the writings of Aristotle and focusing on the humanistic arts of argumentation and debate—became a rich area of research and theory in the 1940s, 1950s, and 1960s for people like Lazarsfeld, Hovland, Bernard Berelson, and Joseph Klapper—people interested in how *media* and their content operated to persuade and to change attitudes. What rhetoricians had for centuries called "ethos," for example, now was given the more impressive and scientific-sounding label, "source credibility." The work of these persuasion researchers was soon emulated by media scholars working in journalism schools and radio and television departments. Before long, it was even being read by rhetorical scholars, some of whom followed the example of Wilbur Schramm and deserted the humanities in favor of social science.

Eventually, social scientific study of communication transformed almost every academic program concerned with communication. The disciplines of rhetoric and speech moved from a focus on humanistic and critical research toward more contemporary, objectifiable (scientific) study of interpersonal communication, group communication, and organizational communication. Speech departments were renamed Speech Communication and then simply Communication. In many departments, humanities-based rhetorical scholarship gave way completely to social scientific study of communication processes. In others, the two approaches exist side-by-side.

But even the ascendance of social science-based theories and methods in most communication programs didn't bring about widespread collaboration between all types of communication scholars. Research remained fragmented and focused on bits and pieces of larger communication processes. Each research community had its own set of middle-range theories and its preferred set of research methods to guide its work. Squabbling and side-choosing continued and was often counter-productive. Pingree, Wiemann, and Hawkins (1988) detailed two problems faced by the discipline because of its fragmentation:

1 Narrowly defined specialists tended to lose sight of what others around them were doing. It was difficult to increase understanding of a complex process like communication when focused exclusively on only one small aspect of it.

2 Because divisions in the discipline traditionally had very real historical and political bases like those discussed above, communication theorists tended to find little relevance in the work of "the other side," potentially blinding them to advances that could enrich one another's thinking and research.

But if fragmentation and division had existed throughout communication's life as a discrete discipline, why did the move toward a unifying base not gather force until the 80s? Sadly, much resistance can be blamed on jealousy, suspicion, turf protection, and other very human characteristics of people who have dedicated their careers to study something they see as important. Another factor was the rapid expansion of academic institutions that permitted creation of many different types of communication units. As Pingree and her colleagues suggested, divisions in the field itself helped slow integration.

But events that had begun 20 years before suddenly became especially important in the 1980s. More than anything, they spurred an interest in a more integrated discipline that addressed the full range of communication phenomena. The first was *the development and diffusion of new communication technologies.* Cable television and VCR, especially, helped blur the line between mass and interpersonal communication. These new technologies changed, among other things, the nature of the broadcasting industry, the kind of content that was available on television, how people interacted with the medium, how content was controlled, who controlled it, and how content choices were negotiated. It may now be a cliché that most parents have to ask their children to program the family VCR, but it does suggest that new patterns of relationship and power are developing in homes. The communication surrounding those patterns, by necessity, changes as well.

We'd be remiss if we did not mention personal computers in this vein (de Sola Pool, 1983). Are computer or electronic mail systems mass or interpersonal communication? How has their introduction into the workplace changed communication patterns in those organizations? PCs may be a medium and, when linked to others, could eventually become the core of a mass medium. But what happens to organizational and familial communication when they allow people to work at home? Is family communication strengthened because an otherwise at-work parent is at home more or is it strained because of the pressure on his or her spouse and children created by that constant presence?

A second development that hastened the emergence of more integrated communication perspectives is *the simple ubiquity of mediated communication and our dependence on it in all aspects of our lives.* How can the study of advertising, one of the media's most ubiquitous messages, be separated from an understanding of individual values, people's social mores, and peer or group influence? How can it be separated from an understanding of our contemporary political campaigns, the nature of political discourse in those campaigns, political culture, and our governmental and societal systems?

This leads, then, to the third source of the move to integrated communication perspectives, *the increasing maturity of the discipline itself.* As communication technologies, contexts, and ramifications became more complex and varied, serious communication researchers and theorists became more aware of how limiting their parochialism had become. After years of separation based on different topics of study and different methodologies, a number of theorists realized that they were bound by common sets of assumptions. For example, researchers reached a consensus that "behavior can be both understood and improved through systematic study (and) that improvement must be based upon understanding, which is the primary goal of a science" (Chaffee and Berger, 1987a, p. 99).

A final reason for the recent emergence of new perspectives may be found in *the declining power exercised by the limited effects paradigm.* As long as this paradigm dominated communication research, there seemed to be little need to integrate theory. It provided a unified vision of mass and interpersonal communication processes. In particular, this dominance had a chilling effect on the development of humanistic, culture-centered perspectives because these were seen as overly speculative and unscientific. But the limited effects vision of communication and its social role proved to be superficial and limiting. Although useful as a means of guiding administrative decision-making in the burgeoning media industries, it did little to enhance our understanding of the way we shape ourselves and our social world through communication. When the paradigm lost its hold on researchers' imagination, they suddenly recognized just how fragmented and narrow their work had become. Suddenly, for some at least, the work of humanistic scholars seemed to have potential value.

Defining Communication Science

Communication science, per se, was eventually defined in the late 1980s by researchers who sought to eliminate unfruitful fragmentation and provide a defining core philosophy for the scientific study of all forms of communication. This is an effort to be inclusive rather than exclusive, to reject many of the outdated assumptions of the limited effects paradigm while retaining its strong empirical focus—to unify under a single banner empirical researchers working in all areas of communication.

Charles Berger and Steven Chaffee not only promoted the movement, but also they helped to reify it by entitling their volume, *Handbook of Communication Science* (1987b). In it they offered the following definition and explanation,

> Communication science seeks to understand the production, processing, and effects of symbol and signal systems by developing testable theories, containing lawful generalizations, that explain phenomena associated with production, processing, and effects. This definition is sufficiently general to embrace various communication contexts, including the production, processing, or effects of symbol or signal systems (including nonverbal) in interpersonal, organizational, mass, political, instructional or other contexts (Berger and Chaffee, 1987a, p. 17).

Although this definition is inclusive in certain respects, it also clearly excludes some types of theory and research from its domain. Theory should *explain* phenomena. It should consist of *lawful generalizations* that are *testable* using empirical research methods. These criteria exclude most of the theories and the research that we presented in Chapters 12 and 13. Thus, despite its claims to inclusiveness, communication science adheres to many of the definitions of social research initially formulated by Lazarsfeld and his contemporaries. It attempts to unify one group of scholars while excluding forms of scholarship that don't meet its criteria for scientific research.

Two Views of Communication Science

Chaffee and Berger (1987a) offered a restructuring of the scientific study of communication based not on the usual narrow interest in specific aspects of the communication process as applied in individual circumstances or settings, but one based on the four levels at which communication phenomena occur:

1 **Intraindividual**, the analysis of communication that occurs within the individual

2 **Interpersonal**, the analysis of communication relationships between two or small groups of people

3 **Network or organizational**, the analysis of larger groups of people and the contexts of their continuing relationships

4 **Macroscopic societal**, the analysis of the communication characteristics and activities of large social systems.

Their argument is straightforward: all communication can be best understood, not in isolation, but rather on two or more of these levels. Because all levels are necessarily interconnected, changes at one level must affect other levels. A very simple example should suffice. Investigations of the effects of television violence are generally associated with social learning or modeling theory, usually with mass communication, and usually with researchers trained as psychologists. But what individual factors, self esteem for example, cause a person to favor that form of content (intraindividual level)? How does that person deal with conflict with his or her friends after consuming a steady diet of televised violence (interpersonal level)? What does the presence in our schools, for example, of people socialized by violent television stories imply for how teachers run their classrooms (organizational level)? And what do changes in the operation of our educational system, theoretically linked to alterations in school discipline and authority, mean for us as a society and as a people (macroscopic level)?

Viewing the major distinction in communication theory as between mass communication and interpersonal communication, Pingree, Wiemann, and Hawkins (1988, p. 11) suggested a communication science based on two distinct stages in communication processes: the first, *antecedents of communication*, would involve the study of "situations, personality traits, orientations, abilities, and so on that lead to communication behaviors," resulting in theories "about selection and control mechanisms, and the norms and schemas that bring them into play." The second stage, *consequences of communication*, would involve the study of the results or outcomes of communication and result in theories of the "necessary characteristics of communication, mechanisms of effect, and strength of effects." They believed that this communication science would render the mass versus interpersonal dichotomy obsolete (how, for example, can we understand the effects of televised violence without examining its effects between two or more people?). Thus, it would be obvious to communication scientists that although this antecedent-consequence division is one convenience, it is still artificial and tempts them to continuously integrate the two into better explanations and understandings.

An Example of Communication Science

It is still too early in the life of communication science to determine if it will have the impact on communication (and by extension, mass communication) theory that its proponents foresee. This effort to revitalize empirical research is viewed by some critics as nothing more than an attempt to relabel and restore the limited effects paradigm. Proponents see it as an important effort to integrate existing scholarship, retain and even advance scientific standards, prioritize development of new empirical research methods, and ultimately broaden the scope of empirical research.

Next, we consider an example of communication science that is consciously imbedded in the new approach. We contrast this example with one that doesn't fit the narrow definition of communication science. Is one more "scientific" than the other?

Jennings Bryant and Richard Street (1988) provided an effort to unify, under the antecedents-of-communication umbrella, the discipline's understanding of the *active communicator*. Both mass and interpersonal communication researchers and theorists have examined the idea of active versus passive communicators. Bryant and Street wrote,

> In the mass and interpersonal communication literatures alike, we read statement after statement claiming that today's message receivers have abundant message options and actively select from and act on these messages in such a way as to construct subjective meanings from the manifold symbols available to them . . . (T)he active communicator's choice-making and meaning construction are purposeful, strategic, and goal-directed (p. 162).

They argued, however, that despite the existence of a now-common view of an active communicator, mass and interpersonal communication scholars drew little from each other. This situation developed because of differences in their theoretical focus (receiver-oriented in mass, source-oriented in interpersonal), their different views of the communication process itself (mass communication seeing it as more directional, interpersonal as more interactive), and the outcomes or effects of communication (mass communication accepting receivers' behavior as more changeable, interpersonal communication judging it more stable).

Their implicit message is clear. The limited effects model that for so long dominated mass communication theory might have been less influential had mass communication theorists ignored these distinctions and paid more attention to what they had in common with interpersonal communication scholars: a shared interest in the mechanisms underlying individuals' choices of and exposure to specific messages and a mutual concern for explaining the nature of message perception and how messages are processed.

Bryant and Street (1988, p. 185) concluded,

> Today many of our leading communication scholars seem to recognize that most, but not all, human communicative behavior is purposeful and strategic, and their newer hierarchical models are being equipped with branching arteries designed to accommodate the realities of automatic as well as controlled behavior. Such models would appear to give us the potential to construct theories of communicative behavior as complex and elegant as communication itself. All we need to do is to avoid another wrong turn at this critical junction.

Although Bryant and Street summarized an impressive array of studies spanning mass and interpersonal research, they stopped short of incorporating cultural analysis or critical cultural studies, which would have meant expanding communication science beyond the boundaries of testable theory based on lawful generalizations. As we pointed out in Chapters 12 and 13, cultural research has devoted increasing attention to "audience activity." It recognizes that individuals should not be regarded as social robots doomed to act out cultural scripts or elite ideologies. Instead, people should be understood as relatively autonomous, active seekers of meaning, capable of creating and shaping their experiences using cultural artifacts and practices. When artifacts and practices are too narrowly constrained, as in romance novels, people have the ability to reject simplistic interpretations and to engage in oppositional decoding that transcends the limitations of existing artifacts and practices. This is especially likely if people band together to form groups in which members help one another resist the "dominant reading" inherent in a text and develop an alternate reading.

So just how broad should the definition of communication science be? How much if any interaction should there be between the proponents of communication science and scholars who use theories and research methods based in the humanities? Can both types of research be integrated? We will conclude our discussion of communication science with consideration of a study that defies its current boundaries. Is this study "unscientific" or "prescientific?" Does it represent a potential "wrong turn" for communication research? Or does it provide a useful focus for a communication research community?

Written in 1985, *No Sense of Place* by Joshua Meyrowitz appears to foreshadow many of the concerns of communication science thinking. Meyrowitz provides an integrated (and controversial) perspective on the role of communication in modern life. His thesis is simple: "Electronic media affect social behavior—not through the power of their messages but by reorganizing the social settings in which people interact and by weakening the once strong relationship between physical place and social 'place'" (p. ix). Or, as he further explained, "By bringing many different types of people to the same 'place,' electronic media have fostered a blurring of many formerly distinct social roles. Electronic media affect us, then, not primarily through their content, but by changing the 'situational geography' of social life" (p. 6).

What is not simple, however, is Meyrowitz's convincing presentation of an eclectic body of evidence, including social scientific, humanistic, and anecdotal data, that crosses Chaffee and Berger's four levels of communication analysis. In what he called his investigation of "a common denominator that links the study of face-to-face interactions with the study of media" (1987, p. 4), Meyrowitz offered a revolutionary view of communication and social situations, focusing on alterations in social roles, gender definitions, parental authority, and our political system. Should Meyrowitz's work be ignored because it deviates into consideration of humanistic thought that isn't "testable?" Should it be treated as a primitive theory that must be restructured into a set of testable generalizations before it can be given serious consideration?

Meyrowitz might argue that the primitive testable generalizations typically derived from empirical research are too discrete and narrow and therefore inherently trivial. They must be interpreted within the context of a broader theory like the one he constructed. Though trivial when examined in isolation, these more "scientific" findings acquire greater meaning within Meyrowitz's speculative theory. Should this use of empirical findings be permitted or even encouraged? Or should the boundaries of communication science be drawn in such a way as to prohibit it? Should there be an alternative to communication science which is culture-centered?

Toward a Culture-Centered Paradigm

Along with cultural analysis, critical cultural studies has emerged as the primary alternative to mainstream mass communication theory (or its latest incarnation as communication science). As Chapters 12 and 13 make apparent, these approaches are quite eclectic, combining many diverse ideas and assumptions. Although there is a wealth of new research based on cultural theories, no single, cohesive research community (like mass society or limited effects theorists) has yet emerged. Cultural researchers tend to be even more fragmented by disciplinary boundaries and methodological preferences than their social science colleagues. In addition, some culture-centered research has very explicit political objectives that both traditional humanists and social scientists find objectionable.

The most unified body of culture-centered research has been produced by critical cultural scholars (see Chapter 13). James Carey (1977; 1989) articulated an American alternative (see Chapter 12) to critical cultural studies, but though influential, he has yet to form a large research community around his work. In Britain, critical cultural scholars are already organized as a research community and there is evidence that it has begun to take root in the United States. There is still considerable disagreement over which political agenda an American research community should pursue, however (O'Connor, 1989; Grossberg, 1989).

Dennis Davis and Thomas Puckett (1991) argued that culture-centered researchers share many theoretical assumptions and certain humanistic values. These assumptions and values could form the core of a new paradigm if they are acknowledged and an effort is made to construct a cohesive research community around them. These assumptions and values are listed below and briefly discussed. First, the assumptions:

1   Culture is an essentially arbitrary human construction that structures experience. We must learn a culture (that is, become socialized) to impose order on our experiences (that is, create meaning).

2   No culture is inherently superior to other cultures in its ability to provide a basis for creating meaning. The cultures of elite social groups and working class groups can provide an equally useful basis for structuring the experience of individuals.

3   Experienced from within, culture constitutes an all-encompassing environment, the boundaries of which are difficult to ascertain or to critically assess. A linguist, Ferdinand de Saussure, once asserted that we are spoken by our languages. He meant that language imposes considerable structure upon our experience and may determine much of our action. We are literally the products of language. Yet, we think of ourselves as being in control of language. Culture is far larger than any individual and, like language, will endure long after individuals die.

4   We are highly dependent upon our culture. The more useful it is to us and the more meaningful the experiences that it permits, the harder it is for us to gain a critical understanding of it, to put it into perspective, to distance ourselves from it. As we try to consciously reflect on and understand culture we risk alienation from it—we open the possibility that it might cease to structure our experience effectively.

5   The enveloping nature of culture and our dependency on it means we are likely to be deeply troubled when we confront other cultures. These cultures imply that our own is not necessarily the only or the best way of structuring experience. They imply that there is more than one reality. This is why many people find it hard to accept cultural relativism.

6   A complex relationship exists between culture and the media used to transmit it. Media can amplify certain elements of everyday culture while rendering other

elements invisible or unimportant. Mediated forms of culture can complement or conflict with everyday culture.

7 Media and mediated culture inevitably transform everyday culture by displacing some elements and popularizing new ones. Media can upset delicate balances between various elements of everyday culture, triggering profound changes in the way that we experience and act in the social world. These changes can have both positive and negative consequences. They are not determined by the media technology alone but also by the routinized social practices that structure the way technology is used.

8 Elites are often in a better position to manipulate mediated culture and use it to their advantage. They tend to be cultural conservatives because the existing culture typically assigns superior status to them. They oppose major changes in culture because the consequences are unpredictable. They reinforce existing forms of culture, glorify traditions, exalt familiar rituals, and foster dependency on familiar ways of doing things. Why do most major cities sponsor symphony orchestras, ballets, and operas but not rock 'n roll bands or rap artists? Why does your university or college have a symphonic or jazz but not a hip hop band?

9 The rise of media technology posed (and still poses) serious problems for elites. Although this technology can potentially increase elite control over culture, it is new and has many uses that may not be well understood. Opposition groups could use media technology to subvert elite culture. In Nazi Germany, for example, Hitler demonstrated how a renegade opposition group could use the new media of radio and movies to quickly gain control over and dominate a complex, rather pluralistic social order.

10 In societies with communication freedom, it is useful to view the media system as a public forum—a place where various elites and interest groups can compete to construct the public culture. The product will necessarily be pluralistic and diverse rather than homogeneous and well integrated. Though elites possess advantages that permit them to dominate the forum and thus public culture, other groups can produce significant changes.

11 The boundaries of the future are quite unclear because the future remains to be constructed. This future should not entail the deterministic unfolding of isolated cultures, but rather should allow the interaction of many cultures. This interaction should enrich individual cultures rather than undermine them.

A number of important humanistic values are implicit and explicit in these theoretical assumptions:

1 **Cultural relativism**: No culture is inherently superior; each culture has its advantages and its limitations.

2   **Cultural pluralism:** The ideal social order is one in which many cultures are practiced side by side, where creative interchange between cultures is possible, where cultural diversity is encouraged. In the ideal social order, every individual will be free to practice several cultures and will move between them easily. Individual freedom itself takes on greater meaning in this context because an ability to move between and integrate several cultures provides individuals with more ability to structure their experience in ways that they find personally meaningful.

3   **Radical democracy/anti-elitism:** Political power should be held and exercised as directly as possible by the people being governed; all forms of elite control, even exercised by an elected, representative elite are at best an expedient compromise. New political structures must be developed that produce increasing degrees of democratization.

4   **Community-centered:** The basic unit of society should be the community since communities are the smallest social unit that can create and share culture. New forms of community must be tried. Research must examine the utility of existing models for communities.

5   **Individual choice, responsibility, and freedom:** Individuals should ultimately have the right to responsibly choose the culture they will practice and the communities in which they will participate. Coercion and propaganda should be minimized so that informed choices can be made.

6   **Centrality of individual experience:** Choice of culture should be based upon one's satisfaction with the experiences that this culture structures; it should "feel right" to the people who participate in it. People should be permitted to express themselves and relate to others in ways that they find meaningful. People should be empowered with self understanding and social awareness. Culture should not oppress them with rigid role definitions and stereotypes of others.

7   **Integrity of community and culture:** Communities have the right to maintain the integrity of the cultures they practice, to resist influences that will disrupt their culture, to maintain clear boundaries while coexisting with other communities. Note that this value may well be in conflict with other values. We'll discuss this more later.

8   **Radical egalitarian/anti-hierarchicalism:** As much as possible human relationships should involve coequals rather than superiors and subordinates because individuals can creatively express themselves only in dialogue with peers. This means that hierarchy cannot serve as the basis for social order as it has throughout human history.

Most of these assumptions and values emerged from research that criticizes existing social orders and cultures. They can be regarded as a laundry list of what various researchers find problematic about the status quo. But can they form the center of a new research community?

Critics of these assumptions and values can easily identify what appear to be serious contradictions. These contradictions may prevent critics from offering a coherent focus for future theory and research. How can both the culture of communities and rights of individuals be valued so highly? Doesn't one or the other necessarily have to be the priority? Will individuals actually be able to find personally meaningful cultures and communities or will they simply move from one to another in a vain search for meaning, a sort of culture-of-the-month club? How can communities maintain their integrity if they permit their members so much freedom to choose? If cultures exist in close proximity won't they inevitably meld into a common culture (this is the old American melting pot conception of culture)? Don't communities inevitably maintain the integrity of their cultures through tactics that negatively stereotype outsiders and exalt the goodness of insiders? If so, social conflict and instability are inevitable. Finally, these assumptions and values clearly imply the rejection of bureaucracy as the primary means of organizing social life. But is this practical? How can communities be expected to replace bureaucracy? You may dislike them, but how safe would you be on the streets and how easily could you get from here to there if there were no traffic cops, traffic rules, traffic courts, and, ultimately, the Department of Motor Vehicles? Are these inevitable institutions in a pluralistic society? Laws and the agencies that enforce them use the threat of coercion to compel us to respect certain common rights (for example, the right to cross the street without being run down by someone who ignores a traffic light).

Although most of what cultural theorists have written involves criticism of the status quo, there have been some recent efforts to assess the potential of new technology for community building and culture construction. Considerable optimism exists about the technology emerging around us because it offers so many practical opportunities to decentralize power in social orders yet maintain social stability, to allow for personal creativity while fostering dynamic communities. Are these possibilities real or are they only idealistic hopes? With our modern communications technologies we can link people in an infinite variety of ways.

The Future of Communication Research

A generation ago, with the limited effects paradigm, Lazarsfeld divided social research into two categories that he labeled *administrative* and *critical*. He was personally committed to both types of research and produced important examples of each (Lazarsfeld, 1941). Few people today remember his critical work, including an intriguing diatribe against the U.S. media system (Lazarsfeld and Merton, 1948). His legacy to us is primarily his administrative research and the generation of empirical social researchers that he trained. His administrative research attracted huge grants from the media industries and private foundations and won him international recognition as one of the preeminent social researchers of his day (and of all time).

In previous chapters, we traced the two important reasons why administrative research became predominant in the United States: It was used to resist the subversive influence of totalitarian ideologies and to guide the development of highly profitable media industries and the overall market economy. But with the simultaneous disintegration of totalitarian regimes abroad and the apparent collapse of "Big" media at home, does administrative research appear likely to decline in value?

Most administrative research remains firmly rooted in the old limited effects school. Despite efforts to modernize it using systems theory (see Chapter 11), administrative research is based on theories that are source dominated, linear, mechanistic, and concerned largely with audience attributes and effects. Though university-based researchers have largely moved beyond this paradigm, many industry-based researchers continue to find it useful. For example, the paradigm helps predict the types of changes that sources induce when they mount expensive media campaigns. It can assess the effectiveness of messages in forming impressions. But it is unable to predict or control the major changes now occurring in audience behavior as people adjust their routine media use to take advantage of the many choices available to them from newer forms of media.

As audiences change their media use they, in turn, can force radical restructuring of the media industries. This has already had important consequences for administrative research. The three major commercial television networks have discontinued much of their in-house, social research. Network grants to university researchers have been sharply curtailed. These cost cutting measures may soon extend to audience ratings research. As the advertising industry is "downsized" and shifts its expenditures away from older media, further reductions in traditional forms of advertising research may occur.

Unfortunately for social researchers in general and communication researchers in particular, the decline of administrative research is not likely to provide research funding for other forms of communication research. For some time now there has been growing skepticism among U.S. elites, especially politicians, about the value or utility of all forms of social research.

Most funding for current communication research is provided by universities that allow and in some cases require that faculty conduct research. Professional associations in the field of communication have doubled and redoubled in size over the past two decades. The number of research papers being presented has grown accordingly. New journals have appeared on an almost annual basis to publish this work. But the bulk of this research is done with very modest funding. Only a handful of communication researchers can afford to conduct large-scale social surveys or elaborate experiments. Research has had to be designed that can produce useful results without high costs. Although this research is often suggestive and heuristic, it rarely yields definitive results.

The Future of Communication Theory

Ironically, with the decline of research funding has come a resurgence of interest in communication theory. Without the money to continue old lines of research, scholars have been forced to reconceptualize their work and explore less costly alternatives. As the "tyranny" of the dominant perspective (the limited effects paradigm) has weakened, more imaginative and innovative writing, thinking, and research are "coming out." The challenge of critical, cultural theories has also forced some serious rethinking of mass communication (Dervin, et al., 1989a, 1989b). There is widespread hope is that better theory will provide more useful integration of existing work and ultimately lead to more productive work in the future.

We began this chapter by tracing the careers of Wilbur Schramm and Raymond Williams, two men with very different ideas about the role of media in society. Both were prolific scholars who had important influence over the evolution of media theory. Whose influence will be more enduring? Will both soon be forgotten? Will future research communities be guided by communication science or by culture-centered theories? What factors or forces will shape these communities? There is no easy answer for any of these questions.

It is important to recognize that most ferment and division found in media theory and research can be found throughout the social sciences and the humanities. There are several ways of interpreting this situation. Pessimists are concerned that historically important values, standards and perspectives are being lost. Optimists embrace the diversity but even they find the multiplicity of theories and findings troubling. Consider the following statements.

Commenting on the theory ferment in anthropology, George Marcus and Michael Fischer (1986, p. 10) noted:

> Ours is once again a period rich in experimentation and conceptual risk-taking. Older dominant frameworks are not so much denied—there being nothing so grand to replace them—as suspended. The ideas they embody remain intellectual resources to be used in novel and eclectic ways. The closest such previous period was in the 1920s and 1930s when evolutionary paradigms, laissez-faire liberalism, and revolutionary socialism and marxism all came under energetic critiques . . . The atmosphere was one of uncertainty about the nature of major trends of change and the ability of existing social theories to grasp it holistically . . .

Concluding a recent textbook on the history of psychology, B.R. Hergenhahn (1992, p. 557) wrote:

> Where does this leave the student of psychology? It seems that psychology is not a place for people with low tolerance for ambiguity. The diverse and sometimes conflicting viewpoints that characterize psychology will undoubtedly continue to characterize it in the future. There is growing recognition that psychology must be as diverse as the humans whose behavior it attempts to explain. For those looking for The One Truth, this state of affairs is distressing. For those willing to ponder several truths, psychology is and will continue to be an exciting field.

Concluding a textbook on sociological theory, George Ritzer (1983, p. 429) wrote:

> Greater integrative efforts by *all* sociological theorists would heal many wounds and aid in theoretical development. It is not that theoretical differences should be ignored where they are relevant and important; rather, the tendency to exaggerate differences and minimize similarities for political reasons is a threat to all sociological theory. A healthy regard for both potential points of integration and basic differences should be basic to sociological theory.

With a few revisions these statements would fit the field of communication as well as they do anthropology, psychology, and sociology. As you've seen, communication has many diverse and conflicting viewpoints, most of which are likely to shape the field for years to come. As in anthropology, the theoretical ferment is both exciting and challenging. As in psychology, empirical research is likely to remain central to the discipline but humanistic and critical approaches will become more important. As in sociology, it is crucial that disputes over theory not be politicized and exaggerated.

There is one certainty about media theory. The readers of this book will shape its content and direction well into the next century. Your task will not be easy. But the resources available to you are growing. The new communication technologies are already opening the libraries of the world to anyone with a computer and a modem. Research communities are already quickly forming around electronic journals distributed on diskette or via computer networks. Now, more than ever, the future of media theory is intimately bound up with the future of media technology. Media theory is also inextricably linked to unfolding social change, to the new patterns of communication that are reshaping our communities and altering our experience of ourselves. In conclusion, we offer the following statement by Klaus Krippendorf (1993, pp. 40–41). We hope that it can inspire communication researchers no matter what approach guides their scholarship:

I am suggesting that the strands of scholarship mentioned above could be woven into a radically *new and virtuous synthesis,* seeing humans first as cognitively autonomous beings; second, as reflexive practitioners of communication with others (and this includes social scientists in the process of their inquiries); and third, as morally responsible interveners in, if not creators of, the very social realities in which they end up living. To embrace this new epistemology, let me end this essay by suggesting that communication scholars recognize the social constructibility of reality, with all of its consequences.

Summary

Mass communication theory is the product of many different methodologies, world views, eras in technological development, and understandings of the nature of people. As a result, it and the research that accompanies it have tended to be fragmented and often redundant. This situation developed because mass communication is a discipline that has grown out of several other traditional fields, it has tended to be technology-based, and it has developed in times of significant social change.

This segmentation of the discipline has led scholars to focus on individual, narrow aspects of the communication process and has created suspicion, if not ignorance, of the advances made by their colleagues in related areas of study.

As the 1980s drew to a close, new communication technologies that changed not only people's media habits but their interpersonal communication as well, greater social dependence on media, and a greater understanding of the complexity of the communication process all combined to encourage the development of better integrated, more unified approaches to communication research. We examined two of these approaches. The first involves a proposed restructuring of existing empirical scholarship to create a communication science. The second would create a culture-centered paradigm.

Communication science "seeks to understand the production, processing, and effects of symbol and signal systems by developing testable theories, containing lawful generalizations, that explain phenomena associated with production, processing, and effects" (Berger and Chaffee, 1987a, p. 17). These authors see communication science as the investigation of communication across four levels of analysis: intraindividual, interpersonal, organizational, and macroscopic. Other observers—Pingree, Wiemann and Hawkins, for example—see it as being composed of two levels: antecedents and consequences of communication. In either case, communication science is a way to reduce fragmentation and to get scholars interested in communication better integrated.

Culture-centered theory and research provides an alternative. Scholarship centered around culture remains even more fragmented than that of communication scientists, however. For a research community to emerge there must be more widely acknowledged consensus about theoretical assumptions and values (Davis and Puckett, 1991). Critical cultural studies may provide a viable core for culture-centered research or a more distinctly American school of social theory, such as that advocated by Carey, may emerge.

The future of mass communication theory depends greatly upon people like yourself. Your generation will construct theories based at least in part upon earlier ideas. You are the successors to both Schramm and Williams. We hope that this book has inspired your interest in mass communication theory. If you find yourself intrigued and challenged by it, you too are invited to begin the work of constructing mass communication theory.

Discussion Questions

1 Explain the basic differences between communication science and the culture-centered theories. What do you see as the most important strengths and the limitations of each approach?

2 If you are majoring in another social science or the humanities, to what extent do you think your discipline should concern itself with communication theory and research? Do you agree or disagree with the notion that much of what is studied in the humanities and social sciences involves communication?

3 If you were going to begin a career as a mass communication scholar, what do you think you would choose to study? What theory or theories would you find most useful and which approach to research would you adopt?

4 If you were a mass communication researcher, would you adopt an explicit set of values to guide your work or would you try to set aside values and conduct your work more objectively? Would you want to conduct research that has long-term social value or that guides short-term administrative decision-making?

5 Do you think that a new paradigm will inevitably emerge to dominate media research or has the field moved beyond the need for paradigms? If you think a new paradigm is likely, what form do you think it might take? If you believe a new paradigm is unlikely, explain why.

6 Do you think the construction of media theory should be directly linked to the agenda of a social movement? Recall the example of how feminists have developed theory and used it to critique media content. Among other things, this was intended to provide group members with greater control over their use of media.

Significant Names

Raymond Williams

Ithiel de Sola Pool

Steven Chaffee

Charles Berger

Joshua Meyrowitz

Suzanne Pingree

Robert Hawkins

John Wiemann

Jennings Bryant

Richard L. Street

Significant Readings

Berger, Charles R. and Steven H. Chaffee (1987). "The Study of Communication as a Science." In C.R. Berger and S.H. Chaffee, eds., *Handbook of Communication Science*. Newbury Park, CA: Sage.

Carey, James W. (1989). *Communication as Culture: Essays on Media and Society.* Winchester, MA: Unwin Hyman.

Chaffee, Steven H. and Charles R. Berger (1987). "What Communication Scientists Do." In C.R. Berger and S.H. Chaffee, eds., *Handbook of Communication Science*. Newbury Park, CA: Sage.

Davis, Dennis K. and Thomas F.N. Puckett (1991). "Mass Entertainment and Community: Toward a Culture-Centered Paradigm for Mass Communication Research." In S. Deetz, ed., *Communication Yearbook 15*. Newbury Park, CA: Sage.

Heyer, Paul (1988). *Communications and History: Theories of Media, Knowledge and Civilization.* New York: Greenwood Press.

Meyrowitz, Joshua (1985). *No Sense of Place: the Impact of Electronic Media on Social Behavior.* New York: Oxford University Press.

Important Terms

Communication Science

Cultural Pluralism

Cultural Relativism

Radical Democracy

Community

Radical Egalitarianism

Culture-Centered Theories

Glossary

Active Audience   This bedrock assumption of uses and gratifications theory has many definitions, but all assume some level of activeness or activity by media consumers

Administrative Research   Research that examines audiences to interpret consumer attitudes and behaviors; the use of empirical research to guide administrative decisions

Agenda-Building   A collective process in which media, government, and citizens reciprocally influence one another to determine the important issues of the day

Agenda-Setting   The idea that media don't tell us what to think, but rather what to think about

Aggressive Cues   Information contained in media portrayals of violence that suggests (or cues) the appropriateness of aggression against specific victims

Artificial Signs   In symbolic interaction, elements that have been constructed to represent something else in the social world

Base   Marx's name for a society's means of production

Behavioral Repertoire   In social learning theory, the learned responses available to an individual in a given situation

Behaviorism   The notion that all human action is a conditioned response to external, environmental stimuli

Bias of Communication   Innis' notion that newer forms of communication technology will make even greater centralization of power possible

Big Brother   In Orwell's 1984, the all intrusive, mind controlling government that watches all its citizens from an eye atop their televisions

British Cultural Studies   A hybrid theory that traces historic domination over culture, criticizes that domination, and demonstrates how it continues today

Catharsis   Also called sublimation; the idea that viewing mediated aggression sates, or reduces, people's natural aggressive drives

Causal Relationship   When the manipulation of a particular variable under specific conditions always produces the same effect

Causality   When a given factor influences another, even by way of intervening variables

Change Agent   In diffusion theory, those who directly influence early adopters and opinion leaders

Chicago School   Social researchers at the University of Chicago in the 1940s who envisioned modern cities as "great Communities" made up of hundreds of interrelated small groups

Classic Four Functions   Survey the environment; correlate different aspects of the environment; transmit cultural heritage; entertain

Cognitive Dissonance   Information that is inconsistent with a person's already-held attitudes creates psychological discomfort or dissonance

Communication Science   A means of understanding the production, processing and effects of symbol and signal systems by developing testable theories that explain phenomena associated with that production, processing, and effects

Community   In culture-centered theories, the smallest social unit that can create and share culture

Controlled Variation   Systematic isolation and varying of elements in an experiment

Convergent Selectivity   In play theory, the notion that media serve the important function of providing a host of fads and fashions from which people can choose for personal satisfaction

Critical Cultural Studies   Theories that challenge the power of elite groups by exposing their use of media and hegemonic culture

Cultivation Analysis   A theory that television "cultivates" or creates a world view that, although possibly inaccurate, becomes the reality because people believe it to be so and base their judgments of the real world on it

Cultural Norms   Media, through their selective presentation and emphasis, create the impression of common cultural norms or values

Cultural Pluralism   In culture-centered theories, a social order in which many cultures are practiced side by side, where exchange between cultures is possible, and where diversity is encouraged

Cultural Relativism   In culture-centered theories, the idea that no one culture is inherently superior to another

Cybernetics   The study of regulation and control in complex systems

Developmental Stages   Different intellectual and communication stages in a child's life that influence the nature of media interaction and impact

Diffusion   A theory that explains how innovations are introduced and adopted by various communities

Disinformation   False information spread about the opposition to discredit it

Disinhibitory Effects   In social learning theory, seeing a model rewarded for a prohibited or threatening behavior increases the likelihood that the observer will make that behavior

Dissonance   Psychological discomfort created by information that is inconsistent with pre-existing attitudes and beliefs.

Dominant Reality   In cultivation analysis, the social reality that is created as a result of television's repeated and patterned presentations of social phenomena

Downshift and Upshift   In frame analysis, to move back and forth between serious and less-serious frames

Dynamically Balanced   Open systems in which the parts interrelate so the system can monitor and adjust to its environment

Elaboration Likelihood Model   An approach that sees attitude formation as a function of the directness of information processing

Elite Pluralism   View of the political system that sees the lack of involvement by the uninformed as not necessarily bad; those who are involved will make the best judgments for all

Feedback Loops   In systems, ongoing mutual adjustments

Fourth Estate   Media as an independent social institution that ensures that other institutions serve the public

Fraction of Selection   Schramm's graphic description of how individuals make media and media content choices based on expectation of reward and effort required

Frame Analysis   Goffman's theory of how people use expectations to make sense of everyday life

Frankfurt School   A group of neo-Marxist scholars who worked together in the 1930s at the University of Frankfurt

Freudianism   Freud's notion that human behavior is the product of the conflict between individuals' id, ego, and superego

Functional Analysis   The study of media in terms of their contribution to a society that is a "system in balance;" typically value-neutral

Functional Displacement   When one medium displaces another by performing its functions better or more efficiently and forces the older medium to find new functions

Gate-Keepers   In two-step flow, people who screen media messages and pass on those messages that help others share their views

Gemeinschaft and Gesellschaft   Tonnies' distinction between folk and modern industrial societies, respectively

Global Village   McLuhan's term for the new form of social organization that would emerge as instantaneous electronic media turned the world into one great social system

Goal Oriented   In systems, the effort to serve a specific overall or long-term purpose

Hierarchy of Effects Model   A step-by-step strategy that differentiates a number of persuasive effects

Homeostatic   A closed system; performs the same task endlessly

Hot and Cool Media   McLuhan's distinction between individual media based on the amount of involvement each demands of its consumers

Hypothesis   A testable prediction about some event

Ideology   Marx's term for elite-dominated forms of culture that mislead average people into acting against their own self interest

Identification   A special form of imitation that springs from wanting to be and trying to be like an observed model with regard to some broader characteristics or qualities

Imitation   The mechanical reproduction of observed behavior

Individual Differences   Individuals' different psychological make-up that cause media influence to vary from person to person

Inductive   An approach to theory construction that sees research beginning with empirical observation rather than speculation

Information Flow   Study of how information moves from media to audiences to have specific effects

Information Processing   A theory that uses mechanistic analogies to describe and interpret how people deal with the flood of stimuli they receive

Inhibitory Effects   In social learning theory, seeing a model punished for a behavior is sufficient to reduce the likelihood that the observer will make that behavior

Interdependence   In systems, when a change in one part affects all others

Knowledge Gap   The difference in knowledge between a society's better and less informed segments

Laissez-Faire   The political philosophy that business should be free of governmental oversight

Latent Functions   Unintended and less easily observed consequences of media use; compare manifest functions

Libertarianism   A normative theory that sees people as good and rational and able to judge good ideas from bad

Limited Effects   The idea that media have minimal or limited effects because those effects are mitigated by a variety of mediating or intervening factors

Macroscopic Theory   Attempts to explain effects at the cultural or societal level

Magic Bullet Theory   Media penetrate people's minds and instantly create effects

Mainstreaming   In cultivation analysis, the process, especially for heavy viewers, in which television's symbols dominate and monopolize other sources of information and ideas about the world

Mandatory Access   Rules that require local cable television companies to carry community-based access channels

Manifest Functions   Intended and observed consequences of media use; compare latent functions

Marketplace of Ideas   In Libertarianism, the notion that all ideas should be put before the public, and from that "marketplace" the public will choose the best

Mass Culture   In mass society theory, popular culture that debases higher forms of culture, bringing about a decline in civilization

Mass Society Theory   Not a single theory, but a general label for those theories that see media as all powerful and corrupting and audiences as helpless against this influence

Master Symbols   Symbols that are associated with strong emotions and possess the power to stimulate large-scale, mass action

Mean World Index   In cultivation analysis, a series of questions about the incidence of crime and violence, the answers to which can be used to differentiate heavy and light television viewers

Mechanical and Organic Solidarity   Durkheim's distinction between traditional and modern social orders, respectively

Media Intrusion Theory   The disruption of traditional political processes and practices by the media

Media System Dependency Theory   The more dependent people are on a particular medium, the more important that medium is to them, and therefore, the medium is more influential

Message System Analysis   In cultivation analysis, detailed content analyses of television programming designed to assess its most reoccurring and consistent presentations

Middle Range Theory   Composed of empirical generalizations based on empirical facts

Microscopic Theory   Explains effects at the personal or individual level

Natural Signs   In symbolic interaction, those things in nature that represent something else in nature

Neomarxism   The contemporary incarnation of Marxism that directs its attention at the superstructure

Noise   In systems, information that disrupts the successful operation of the system

Normative Theory   A type of theory that describes an ideal way for media system to be structured and operated

Objectivity Rituals   Sets of procedures used by reporters to produce unbiased stories that actually introduce bias

Observational Learning   In social learning theory, when the observation of a behavior is sufficient to learn that behavior

Opinion Leaders   In two-step flow, those who pass on information from media to opinion followers

Oppositional Decoding   When message consumers "read" texts in ways that oppose the dominant or preferred reading

Paradigm   An organizing theoretical perspective

Paradigm Shift   The displacement of a dominant organizing theoretical perspective

Penny Press   The first mass media; newspapers sold for one cent to increase circulation which was then translated into advertising revenues

Phenomenistic Theory   Klapper's theory that media are rarely the sole cause of effects and are relatively powerless when compared to other social factors; the primary effect of media is reinforcement

Play Theory   Stephenson's theory that media are primarily for unimportant, personal uses

Political Economy Theory   Examines elite control of economic institutions to show how they control other institutions, including media

Positioning Advertisers' efforts to attribute specific realities to products that may or may not bear any relationship to those products

Power Elite Mills' argument that true power in America rests with the small number of leaders in the military-industrial complex

Primacy and Recency In attitude change, the question of the best placement in a persuasive message of information and arguments—at the start or at the end

Propaganda The no-holds-barred use of communication to propagate specific beliefs and expectations

Public Forum Media as a place where various elites and interest groups can compete to construct the public culture

Radical Democracy In culture-centered theories, the idea that political power should be held and exercised as directly as possible by the people governed

Radical Egalitarianism In culture-centered theories, the idea that, as much as possible, human relationships should involve co-equals because people can best express themselves in dialogue with peers

Radical Libertarianism The absolute belief in Libertarianism's faith in a good and rational public and totally free media

Redundancy In systems, the duplication of information to increase accuracy

Reinforcement Theory The same as Phenomenistic Theory

Resonance In cultivation analysis, when viewers see things on television that are congruent with their own everyday lives

Ritual Perspective Views mass communication as the representation of shared belief where reality is produced, maintained, repaired, and transformed

Robber Barons Turn-of-the-century industrialists who created vast monopolies

Schemas In information processing, mental categories used in interpretation

Scientific Method A search for truth through accurate observation and interpretation of fact

Second Order Cybernetics A theory that many systems often or continually undergo fundamental, frequently chaotic transformation

Selective Processes Exposure (Attention), Retention, and Perception; psychological processes designed to reduce dissonance

Self-Righting Principle Milton's idea that in a fair debate, good and truthful arguments will win out over lies and deceit

Signals In symbolic interaction, signs that produce highly predictable responses

Signs   In symbolic interaction, any element in the environment used to represent another element in the environment; in social construction of reality, objects explicitly designed to convey subjective meaning

Social Categories   The idea that members of given groups or aggregates will respond to media stimuli in more or less uniform ways

Social Control   In play theory, when media affect important aspects of an individual's value system; play theory argues that this rarely occurs

Social Learning Theory   Encompasses both imitation and identification to explain how people learn through observation of others in their environments

Social Responsibility Theory   A normative theory that substitutes media industry and public responsibility for Libertarianism's total freedom on one hand and calls for technocratic control on the other

Source Credibility   In attitude change, the question of the believability of a message source

Source-Dominated   Theories that examine the communication process from the point of view of some elite message source

Spiral of Silence   Noelle-Neumann's theory that people holding views contrary to those dominant in the media are moved to keep those views to themselves for fear of rejection

Superstructure   Marx's term for a society's culture

Symbols   In symbolic interaction, artificial signs on which there is less certainty of response; in social construction of reality, objects that represent other objects

System   A phenomenon consisting of a set of parts that are interrelated so that changes in one part induce changes in other parts

Targeting   In social-political marketing theory, directing messages at those audience segments that are most susceptible or receptive

Technocratic Control   Direct regulation of media, most often by government agency or commission

Technological Determinist   Someone who believes that all human history and experience is determined by the constraints of technology

Theory   A conceptual representation or explanation of phenomena

Third-Person Effect   The idea that "media affect others, but not me"

Transmissional Perspective   The view of mass media as mere senders or transmitters of information

Two-Step Flow   The idea that messages pass from the media, through opinion leaders, to opinion followers

Typification Schemes   In social construction of reality, collections of meanings that people have assigned to some phenomenon

Wire Services   Suppliers of information to affiliated news organizations; the first electronically-based media networks

Vicarious Reinforcement   In social learning theory, reinforcement that is observed rather than directly experienced

Viewing Schema   Interpretational skills that aid children (and others) in understanding television content conventions

Yellow Journalism   The irresponsible practices of some of the early mass circulation newspapers

References

Abel, E. (1981). *What's News: the Media in American Society*. San Francisco: Institute for Contemporary Studies.

Adams, W.C. (1978). "Local Public Affairs Content of TV News." *Journalism Quarterly*, 55: 690–695.

Adoni, H. and A.A. Cohen (1978). "Television Economic News and the Social Construction of Economic Reality." *Journal of Communication*, 28: 61–70.

Adoni, H. and S. Mane (1984). "Media and the Social Construction of Reality: Toward an Integration of Theory and Research." *Communication Research*, 11: 323–340.

Adoni, H., A.A. Cohen, and S. Mane (1984). "Social Reality and Television News: Perceptual Dimensions of Social Conflicts in Selected Life Areas." *Journal of Broadcasting*, 28: 33–49.

Adorno, T. (1951). "Freudian Theory and the Pattern of Fascist Propaganda." In A. Arato and E. Gebhardt, eds., (1978). *The Essential Frankfurt School Reader*. New York: Urizen Books.

Adorno, T. and M. Horkheimer (1972). *Dialectic of Enlightenment*. New York: Herder and Herder.

Allport, G.W. (1967). "Attitudes." In M. Fishbein, ed., *Readings in Attitude Theory and Measurement*. New York: John Wiley and Sons.

Allport, G.W. and L.J. Postman (1945). "The Basic Psychology of Rumor." *Transactions of the New York Academy of Sciences*, 8: 61–81.

Altheide, D.L. (1976). *Creating Reality: How TV News Distorts Events*. Beverly Hills, CA: Sage Publications.

Altheide, D.L. and R. P. Snow (1979). *Media Logic*. Newbury Park, CA: Sage Publications.

Altschull, J.H. (1990). *From Milton to McLuhan: The Ideas Behind American Journalism*. New York: Longman.

_____. (1984). *Agents of Power: The Role of News Media in Human Affairs*. New York: Longman.

Anderson, D.R. and E.P. Lorch (1983). "Looking at Television: Action or Reaction?" In J. Bryant and D.R. Anderson, eds., *Children's Understanding of Television: Research on Attention and Comprehension*. New York: Academic Press.

Anderson, J.R. (1981). *Cognitive Skills and Their Acquisition*. Hillsdale, NJ: Lawrence Erlbaum Associates.

Andison, F. S. (1977). "TV Violence and Viewer Aggression: A Culmination of Study Results 1956–1976." *Public Opinion Quarterly*, 41: 314–331.

Arato, A. and E. Gebhardt, eds., (1978). *The Essential Frankfurt School Reader*. New York: Urizen Books.

Associated Press (1991). "Bulgarian Delegation Mistaken for Shoplifters, Thrown Out of Store." Grand Forks *Herald*, April 1, 5A.

Atwood, L.E. (1984). "Perceptions of the Media: A Review of Selected Source Credibility Literature." Paper presented to the Seventh World Media Conference, Tokyo.

Axelrod, R. (1973). "Schema Theory: An Information Processing Model of Perception and Cognition." *American Political Science Review*, 67: 1248–1266.

Bagdikian, B.H. (1983). *The Media Monopoly*. Boston: Beacon Press.

Bailey, K.D. (1982). *Methods of Social Research*. New York: Free Press.

Bailyn, L. (1959). "Mass Media and Children: A Study of Exposure Habits and Cognitive Effects." *Psychological Monographs*, 73, 1–48.

Baker, R.K. and S.J. Ball (1969). *Violence and the Media: A Staff Report to the National Commission on the Causes and Prevention of Violence, Volume 9A*. Washington: U.S. Government.

Bandura, A. (1971). *Psychological Modeling: Conflicting Theories*. Chicago: Aldine Atherton.

_____. (1965). "Influence of Models' Reinforcement Contingencies on the Acquisition of Imitative Responses." *Journal of Personality and Social Psychology*, 1: 589–595.

Bandura, A., D. Ross, and S.A. Ross (1963). "Imitation of Film- Mediated Aggressive Models." *Journal of Abnormal Social Psychology*, 66: 3–11.

Baran, S.J. and V.J. Blasko (1984). "Social Perceptions and the By-Products of Advertising." *Journal of Communication*, 34: 12–20.

Baran, S.J. and T.P. Meyer (1974). "Imitation and Identification: Two Compatible Approaches to Social Learning from the Electronic Media." *AV Communication Review*, 22: 167–179.

Baran, S.J., J.J. Mok, M. Land, and T.Y. Kang (1989). "You Are What You Buy: Mass-Mediated Judgments of People's Worth." *Journal of Communication*, 39: 46–54.

Barber, J.D. (1979). "Not the New York Times: What Network News Should Be." *Washington Monthly*, September, 14–21.

_____., ed. (1978). *Race for the Presidency: The Media and the Nominating Process*. Englewood Cliffs, NJ: Prentice-Hall.

Barnouw, E. (1966). *A History of Broadcasting in the United States: A Tower in Babel*, Volume I. New York: Oxford University Press.

Bauer, R.A. and A.H. Bauer (1960). "America, Mass Society and Mass Media." *Journal of Social Issues*, 10: 3–66.

Becker, L.B., M. McCombs, and J.M. McLeod (1975). "The Development of Political Cognitions." In S.H. Chaffee, ed., *Political Communication: Issues and Strategies for Research*. Beverly Hills, CA: Sage Publications.

Bennett, W.L. (1988). *News: The Politics of Illusion*, 2d Edition. New York: Longman.

Bennett, W.L. and M. Edelman (1985). "Toward a New Political Narrative." *Journal of Communication*, 35: 128–138.

Berelson, B. (1961). "The Great Debate on Cultural Democracy." In D.N. Barrett, ed., *Values in America*. Notre Dame, IN: University of Notre Dame Press.

————. (1959). "The State of Communication Research." *Public Opinion Quarterly*, 23: 1–6.

Berelson, B. (1949). "What 'Missing the Newspaper' Means." In P.F. Lazarsfeld and F.N. Stanton, eds., *Communications Research, 1948–9*. New York: Harper and Brothers.

Berelson, B., P.F. Lazarsfeld, and W.N. McPhee (1954). *Voting: A Study of Opinion Formation in a Presidential Campaign*. Chicago: University of Chicago Press.

Berger, C.R. and S.H. Chaffee (1987a). "The Study of Communication as a Science." In C.R. Berger and S.H. Chaffee, eds., *Handbook of Communication Sciences*. Newbury Park, CA: Sage Publications.

————., eds.. (1987b). *Handbook of Communication Science*. Newbury Park, CA: Sage Publications.

Berger, P.L. and T. Luckmann, (1966). *The Social Construction of Reality: A Treatise in the Sociology of Knowledge*. Garden City, NY: Doubleday and Company.

Berkowitz, L. (1965). "Some Aspects of Observed Aggression." *Journal of Personality and Social Psychology*, 2: 359–369.

Berkowitz, L. and R.G. Geen, (1966). "Film Violence and the Cue Properties of Available Targets." *Journal of Personality and Social Psychology*, 3: 525–530.

Berman, A. (1988). *From the New Criticism to Deconstruction: The Reception of Structuralism and Post-Structuralism*. Urbana: University of Illinois Press.

Bernstein, C. (1992). "Feeding the Idiot Culture." San Jose *Mercury News*, June 21, C1.

Bernstein, R.J. (1979). *The Restructuring of Social and Political Theory*. London: Methuen.

Berry, C. (1983). "Learning from Television News: A Critique of the Research." *Journal of Broadcasting*, 27: 359–370.

Bill, J.A. and R.L. Hardgrave (1973). *Comparative Politics: The Quest for Theory*. Columbus, OH: Charles E. Merrill.

Bloom, A.D. (1987). *The Closing of the American Mind: How Higher Education Has Failed Democracy and Impoverished the Souls of Today's Students*. New York: Simon and Schuster.

Blumer, H. (1969). *Symbolic Interactionism*. Englewood Cliffs, NJ: Prentice-Hall.

————. (1939). "The Mass, the Public and Public Opinion." In A.M. Lee, ed., *New Outlines of the Principles of Sociology*. New York: Barnes and Noble.

Blumer, H. and P.M. Hauser (1933). *Movies, Delinquency, and Crime*. New York: Macmillan.

Blumler, J.G. (1983). "Communication and Democracy: The Crisis Beyond and the Ferment Within." *Journal of Communication*, 33: 166–173.

————. (1979). "The Role of Theory in Uses and Gratifications Studies." *Communication Research*, 6: 9–36.

Blumler, J.G., M. Gurevitch, and E. Katz (1985). "Reaching out: A Future for Gratifications Research." In K.E. Rosengren, L.A. Wenner, and P. Palmgreen, eds., *Media Gratifications Research: Current Perspectives*. Beverly Hills, CA: Sage Publications.

Blumler, J.G. and E. Katz, eds. (1974). *The Uses of Mass Communications: Current Perspectives on Gratifications Research*. Beverly Hills, CA: Sage Publications.

Blumler, J.G., E. Katz, and M. Gurevitch (1974). "Utilization of Mass Communication by the Individual." In J.G. Blumler and E. Katz, eds., *The Uses of Mass Communications: Current Perspectives on Gratifications Research*. Beverly Hills, CA: Sage Publications.

Blumler, J.G. and D. McQuail (1969). *Television in Politics: Its Uses and Influence*. Chicago: University of Chicago Press.

Booth, A. (1970). "The Recall of News Items." *Public Opinion Quarterly*, 34: 604–610.

Bowers, J.W. (1989). "Message Effects: Theory and Research on Mental Models of Messages." In J.J. Bradac, ed., *Message Effects in Communication Science*. Newbury Park, CA: Sage Publications.

Bowers, J.W. and J.A. Courtright (1984). *Communication Research Methods*. Glenview, IL: Scott, Foresman.

Bradac, J.J., ed. (1989). *Message Effects in Communication Science*. Newbury Park, CA: Sage Publications.

Brantlinger, P. (1983). *Bread and Circuses: Theories of Mass Culture as Social Decay*. Ithaca, NY: Cornell University Press.

Bronfenbrenner, U. (1970). *Two Worlds of Childhood: U.S. and U.S.S.R.* New York: Russell Sage Foundation.

Brownell, B.A. (1983). "Interpretations of Twentieth-Century Urban Progressive Reform." In D.R. Colburn and G.E. Pozzetta, eds., *Reform and Reformers in the Progressive Era*. Westport, CT: Greenwood Press.

Bryant, J. and D.R.. Anderson, (1983). *Children's Understanding of Television: Research on Attention and Comprehension*. New York: Academic Press.

Bryant, J. and R.L. Street, (1988). "From Reactivity to Activity and Action: An Evolving Concept and *Weltanschauung* in Mass and Interpersonal Communication." In R.P. Hawkins, J.M. Wiemann and S. Pingree, eds., *Advancing Communication Science: Merging Mass and Interpersonal Processes*. Newbury Park, CA: Sage Publications.

Buckley, W. (1967). *Sociology and Modern Systems Theory*. Englewood Cliffs, NJ: Prentice-Hall.

Budd, R.W., M.S. MacLean, and A.M. Barnes (1966). "Regularities in the Diffusion of Two News Events." *Journalism Quarterly*, 43: 221–230.

Bulmer, M. (1984). *The Chicago School of Sociology: Institutionalization, Diversity, and the Rise of Sociological Research*. Chicago: University of Chicago Press.

Burke, K. (1968). *Language as Symbolic Action: Essays on Life, Literature, and Method*. Berkeley: University of California Press.

————. (1950). *A Rhetoric of Motives*. New York: Prentice-Hall.

————. (1945). *A Grammar of Motives*. New York: Prentice-Hall.

Byars, J. (1987). "Reading Feminine Discourse: Prime-Time Television in the U.S." *Communication*, 9: 289–303.

Cacioppo, J.T. and R.E. Petty (1985). "Central and Peripheral Routes to Persuasion: The Role of Message Repetition." In L.F. Alwitt and A.A. Mitchell, eds., *Psychological Processes and Advertising Effects: Theory, Research and Application*. Hillsdale, NJ: Lawrence Erlbaum Associates.

_____. (1984). "The Elaboration Likelihood Model of Persuasion." In T.C. Kinnear, ed., *Advances in Consumer Research*, Volume 11. Provo, UT: Association for Consumer Research.

Campbell, A., P.W. Converse, W.E. Miller, and D.E. Stokes, (1960). *The American Voter*. New York: Wiley.

Campbell, A., G. Gurin, and W.E. Miller, (1954). *The Voter Decides*. Evanston, IL: Row, Peterson.

Cantor, M.G. (1980). *Prime-Time Television: Content and Control*. Newbury Park, CA: Sage Publications.

Cantril, H., H. Gaudet, and H. Herzog (1940). *Invasion from Mars*. Princeton: Princeton University Press.

Carey, J. (1989). *Communication as Culture: Essays on Media and Society*. Winchester, MA: Unwin Hyman.

_____., ed. (1988). *Media, Myths and Narratives: Television and the Press*. Newbury Park, CA: Sage Publications.

_____. (1977). "Mass Communication Research and Cultural Studies: An American View." In J. Curran, M. Gurevitch, J. Woollacott, J. Marriott, and C. Roberts, eds., *Mass Communication and Society*. London: Open University Press.

_____. (1975a). "Culture and Communications." *Communication Research*, 2: 173–191.

_____. (1975b). *Sociology and Public Affairs: The Chicago School*. Beverly Hills, CA: Sage Publications.

Chaffee, S.H. (1975). "The Diffusion of Political Information." In S.H. Chaffee , ed., *Political Communication*. Beverly Hills, CA: Sage Publications.

Chaffee, S.H. and C.R. Berger (1987). "What Communication Scientists Do." In C.R. Berger and S.H. Chaffee, eds., *Handbook of Communication Sciences*. Newbury Park, CA: Sage Publications.

Chaffee, S.H. and J.L. Hochheimer (1985). "The Beginnings of Political Communication Research in the United States: Origins of the 'Limited Effects' Model." In E.M. Rogers and F. Balle, eds., *The Media Revolution in America and Western Europe*. Norwood, NJ: Ablex Publishing.

Choi, Y.S., K.K. Massey, and S.J. Baran (1988). "Cultivating the Perception of an Unjust World: Media Portrayals of the Criminal Justice System." Paper presented to the Annual Convention of the International Communication Association, San Francisco, CA.

Christensen, F. (1986). "Sexual Callousness Re-Examined." *Journal of Communication*, 36: 174–184.

Christensen, T. (1987). *Reel Politics: American Political Movies from Birth of a Nation to Platoon*. New York: Blackwell.

Clarke, P. and E. Fredin (1978). "Newspapers, Television and Political Reasoning." *Public Opinion Quarterly*, 42: 143–160.

Cohen, B.C. (1963). *The Press and Foreign Policy.* Princeton: Princeton University Press.

Cohen, S. and J. Young, eds. (1973). *The Manufacture of News.* London: Constable.

Collins, W.A. (1982). "Social Scripts and Developmental Patterns in Comprehension of Televised Narratives." *Communication Research,* 9: 380–398.

Commission on Freedom of the Press. (1947). *A Free and Responsible Press.* Chicago: University of Chicago Press.

Compaine, B.M. (1984). *Understanding New Media: Trends and Issues in Electronic Distribution of Information.* Cambridge, MA: Ballinger.

Corner J. and J. Hawthorn, eds. (1983). *Communication Studies.* London: Edward Arnold.

Coser, L.A. (1984). *Refugee Scholars in America: Their Impact and Their Experience.* New Haven: Yale University Press.

Crouse, T. (1973). *The Boys on the Bus.* New York: Random House.

Curran, J., M. Gurevitch, and J. Woollacott (1982). "The Study of the Media: Theoretical Approaches." In M. Gurevitch, T. Bennett, J. Curran, and J. Woollacott, eds., *Culture, Society and the Media.* New York: Methuen.

Czitrom, D.J. (1982). *Media and the American Mind: From Morse to McLuhan.* Chapel Hill: University of North Carolina Press.

Davis, D.K. (1990). "News and Politics." In D.L. Swanson and D. Nimmo, eds., *New Directions in Political Communication.* Newbury Park, CA: Sage Publications.

Davis, D.K. and S.J. Baran (1981). *Mass Communication and Everyday Life: A Perspective on Theory and Effects.* Belmont, CA: Wadsworth.

Davis, D.K. and T. Puckett (1991). "Mass Entertainment and Community: Toward a Culture-Centered Paradigm for Mass Communication Research." In S. Deetz, ed., *Communication Yearbook 15.* Newbury Park, CA: Sage Publications.

Davis, D.K. and J.P. Robinson (1989). "Newsflow and Democratic Society in an Age of Electronic Media." In G. Comstock, ed., *Public Communication and Behavior,* Volume 3. New York: Academic Press.

_____. (1986a). "Theoretical Perspectives." In J.P. Robinson and M. Levy, eds., *The Main Source: Learning from Television News.* Beverly Hills, CA: Sage Publications.

_____. (1986b). "News Story Attributes and Comprehension." In J.P. Robinson and M. Levy, eds., *The Main Source: Learning from Television News.* Beverly Hills, CA: Sage Publications.

Davis, R.E. (1976). *Response to Innovation: A Study of Popular Argument About New Mass Media.* New York: Arno Press.

DeFleur, M.L. (1970). *Theories of Mass Communication.* New York: David McKay.

DeFleur, M.L. and S. Ball-Rokeach (1989). *Theories of Mass Communication,* 5th Edition. New York: David McKay.

_____. (1975). *Theories of Mass Communication,* 3d Edition. New York: David McKay.

DeFleur, M.L. and O.N. Larsen (1958). *The Flow of Information.* New York: Harper & Brothers.

Delia, J. (1987). "Communication Research: A History." In C. Berger and S. Chaffee, eds., *Handbook of Communication Science.* Beverly Hills, CA: Sage Publications.

Dennis, E. (1991). "Introduction." In C. LaMay, M. FitzSimon, and J. Sahadi, eds., *The Media at War: The Press and the Persian Gulf Conflict*. New York: Gannett Foundation.

Dervin, B. (1989). "Changing Conceptions of the Audience." In R.E. Rice and C. Atkin, eds., *Public Communication Campaigns*, 2d Edition. Beverly Hills, CA: Sage Publications.

_____. (1980). "Communication Gaps and Inequities: Moving Toward a Reconceptualization." In B. Dervin and M.J. Voigt, eds., *Progress in Communication Sciences, Volume II*. Norwood, NJ: Ablex Publishing Corporation.

Dervin, B., L. Grossberg, B.J. O'Keefe, and E. Wartella, eds. (1989a). *Rethinking Communication: Volume 1, Paradigm Issues*. Newbury Park, CA: Sage Publications.

_____. eds. (1989b). *Rethinking Communication: Volume 2, Paradigm Exemplars*. Newbury Park, CA: Sage Publications.

de Sola Pool, I. (1983). *Technologies of Freedom*. Cambridge, MA: Belknap Press.

de Sola Pool, I. and H.J. Schiller (1981). "Perspectives on Communication Research: An Exchange." *Journal of Communication*, 31: 15–23.

Deutschmann, P.J. and W.A. Danielson (1960). "Diffusion of Knowledge of the Major News Story." *Journalism Quarterly*, 37: 345–355.

Dewey, J. (1927) *The Public and Its Problems*. New York: Henry Holt and Co.

Dominick, J.R., A. Wurtzel, and G. Lometti (1975). "Television Journalism vs. Show Business: A Content Analysis of Eyewitness News." *Journalism Quarterly*, 52, 213–218.

Donnerstein, E. and L. Berkowitz (1981). "Victim Reactions in Aggressive Erotic Films as a Factor in Violence Against Women." *Journal of Personality and Social Psychology*, 41: 710–724.

Donohew, L. and P. Palmgreen (1981). "Conceptualization and Theory Building." In G. Stemple and B.H. Westley, eds., *Research Methods in Mass Communication*. Englewood Cliffs, NJ: Prentice-Hall.

Donohue, G.A., P.J. Tichenor, and C.N. Olien (1986). "Metro Daily Pullback and Knowledge Gaps, Within and Between Communities." *Communication Research*, 13: 453–471.

Dyer, N. and J.P. Robinson (1980). "News Comprehension Research in Great Britain." Paper presented to the Annual Convention of the International Communication Association, Acapulco, Mexico.

Easton, D. (1965). *A Systems Analysis of Political Life*. New York: Wiley.

Eco, U. (1983). "Towards a Semiotic Inquiry into the Television Message." In J. Corner and J. Hawthorn, eds., *Communication Studies*. London: Edward Arnold.

Edelman, M. (1988). *Constructing the Political Spectacle*. Chicago: University of Chicago Press.

_____. (1972). *The Symbolic Uses of Politics*. Chicago: University of Illinois Press.

_____. (1971). *Politics as Symbolic Action: Mass Arousal and Quiescence*. Chicago: Markham Publishing Company.

Edwards, V.E. (1970). *Journalism in a Free Society*. Dubuque, IA: William C. Brown.

Edwardson, M., D. Grooms, and P. Pringle (1978). "Visualization and TV News Information Gain." *Journal of Broadcasting*, 20: 373–380.

Elder, C.D. and R.W. Cobb (1983). *The Political Uses of Symbols.* New York: Longman.

Elliot, P. (1974). "Uses and Gratifications Research: A Critique and a Sociological Alternative." In J.G. Blumler and E. Katz, eds., *The Uses of Mass Communication.* Beverly Hills, CA: Sage Publications.

Ellis, J.C. (1985). *A History of Film.* Englewood Cliffs, NJ: Prentice-Hall.

Elms, A.C. (1972). *Social Psychology and Social Relevance.* Boston: Little, Brown.

Entman, R.M. (1989). *Democracy Without Citizens: Media and the Decay of American Politics.* New York: Oxford University Press.

Enzensberger, H.M. (1974). *The Consciousness Industry.* New York: Seabury Press.

Epstein, E.J. (1975). *Between Fact and Fiction: The Problems of Journalism.* New York: Vintage Books.

_____. (1973). *News from Nowhere: Television and the News.* New York: Random House.

Erbring, L., E.N. Goldenberg, and A.H. Miller (1980). "Front-Page News and Real-World Cues: A New Look at Agenda-Setting by the Media." *American Journal of Political Science*, 24: 16–49.

Ettema, J.S. and F.G. Kline (1979). "Deficits, Differences and Ceiling: Contingent Conditions for Understanding the Knowledge Gap." *Communication Research*, 4: 179–202.

Faris, R.E.L. (1970). *Chicago Sociology, 1920–1932.* Chicago: University of Chicago Press.

Faules, D.F. and D.C. Alexander (1978). *Communication and Social Behavior: A Symbolic Interaction Perspective.* Reading, MA: Addison-Wesley.

Felson, M. (1978). "Invidious Distinctions Among Cars, Clothes, and Suburbs." *Public Opinion Quarterly*, 42: 49–58.

Feshbach, S. (1961). "The Stimulating Versus Cathartic Effects of a Vicarious Aggressive Activity." *Journal of Abnormal and Social Psychology*, 63: 381–385.

Feshbach, S. and R.D. Singer (1971). *Television and Aggression: An Experimental Field Study.* San Francisco: Jossey-Bass.

Festinger, L. (1962). "Cognitive Dissonance." *Scientific American*, 207: 93.

Findahl, O. and B. Hoijer (1981). "Studying Media Content with Reference to Human Comprehension." In K.E. Rosengren, ed., *Scandinavian Studies in Content Analysis.* London: Sage Publications.

_____. (1976). *Fragments of Reality: An Experiment with News and TV Visuals.* Stockholm: Sveriges Radio.

_____. (1975). "Effects of Additional Verbal Information on Retention of a Radio News Program." *Journalism Quarterly*, 52: 493–498.

_____. (1974). *On Knowledge, Social Privilege and the News.* Stockholm: Sveriges Radio.

_____. (1973). *An Analysis of Errors in the Recollection of a News Program.* Stockholm: Sveriges Radio.

Fishbein, M. (1967). "A Behavior Theory Approach to the Relations Between Beliefs About an Object and the Attitude Toward the Object." In M. Fishbein, ed., *Readings in Attitude Theory and Measurement*. New York: John Wiley.

Fishman, M. (1980). *Manufacturing the News*. Austin: University of Texas Press.

Fiske, J and J. Hartley (1978). *Reading Television*. London: Methuen.

Foucault, M. (1980). *Power/Knowledge*. New York: Pantheon Books.

_____. (1979). *Discipline and Punish*. New York: Vintage Books.

_____. (1978). *The History of Sexuality, Volume. 1*. New York: Random House.

_____. (1972). *The Archaeology of Knowledge*. New York: Random House.

_____. (1970). *The Order of Things: An Archeology of the Human Sciences*. New York: Random House.

Frank, R.S. (1973). *Message Dimensions of Television News*. Lexington, MA: Lexington Books.

Frazier, P.J. and C. Gaziano (1979). *Robert E. Park's Theory of News, Public Opinion and Social Control*. Lexington, KY: Journalism Monographs.

Freedman, L.Z. (1961). "Daydream in a Vacuum Tube: A Psychiatrist's Comment on the Effects of Television." In W. Schramm, J. Lyle, and E.B. Parker, eds., *Television in the Lives of our Children*. Stanford, CA: Stanford University Press.

Friedrich, C.J. (1943). "Principles of Informational Strategy." *Public Opinion Quarterly*, 7: 77–89.

Frost, R. and J. Stauffer (1987). "The Effects of Social Class, Gender, and Personality on Psychological Responses to Filmed Violence." *Journal of Communication*, 37: 29–45.

Fry, V.H., A. Alexander, and D.L. Fry (1990). "Textual Status, the Stigmatized Self, and Media Consumption." In J.A. Anderson, ed., *Communication Yearbook 13*. Newbury Park, CA: Sage Publications.

Funkhouser, G. and M. McCombs (1971). "The Rise and Fall of News Diffusion." *Public Opinion Quarterly*, 50: 107–113.

Gans, H. (1979). *Deciding What's News*. New York: Pantheon Books.

Gantz, W. (1978). "How Uses and Gratifications Affect Recall of Television News." *Journalism Quarterly*, 55: 664–672.

Gaziano, C. (1983). "The Knowledge Gap: An Analytical Review of Effects." *Communication Research*, 10: 447–486.

Gerbner, G. (1990). "Epilogue: Advancing on the Path of Righteousness (Maybe)." In N. Signorielli and M. Morgan, eds., *Cultivation Analysis: New Directions in Media Effects Research*. Newbury Park, CA: Sage Publications.

Gerbner, G. and L. Gross. (1979). "Editorial Response: A Reply to Newcomb's 'Humanistic Critique.'" *Communication Research*, 6, 223–230.

_____. (1972). "Living with Television: The Violence Profile." *Journal of Communication*, 26: 173–199.

Gerbner, G., L. Gross, M. Jackson-Beeck, S. Jeffries-Fox, and N. Signorielli (1978). "Cultural Indicators: Violence Profile No. 9." *Journal of Communication*, 28: 176–206.

Gerbner, G., L. Gross, M. Morgan, and N. Signorielli (1982). "Charting the Mainstream: Television's Contributions to Political Orientations." *Journal of Communication*, 32: 100–127.

_____. (1981a). "A Curious Journey into the Scary World of Paul Hirsch." *Communication Research*, 8: 39–72.

_____. (1981b). "Final Reply to Hirsch." *Communication Research*, 8: 259–280.

_____. (1980). "The 'Mainstreaming' of America: Violence Profile No. 11." *Journal of Communication*, 30: 10–29.

Giddens, A. (1989). "The Orthodox Consensus and the Emerging Synthesis." In B. Dervin, L. Grossberg, B.J. O'Keefe, and E. Wartella, eds., *Rethinking Communication: Volume 1, Paradigm Issues*. Newbury Park, CA: Sage Publications.

_____. (1984). *The Constitution of Society: Outline of the Theory of Structuration.* Cambridge: Polity Press.

_____. (1979). *Central Problems in Social Theory.* London: MacMillan.

Gieber, W. (1964). "News is What Newspapermen Make It." In L.A. Dexter and D.M. White, eds., *People, Society and Mass Communications*. New York: Free Press.

Gitlin, T. (1980). *The Whole World Is Watching: Mass Media in the Making and Unmaking of the New Left*. Berkeley: University of California Press.

_____. (1978). "Media Sociology: The Dominant Paradigm." *Theory and Society*, 6: 205–253.

Glasgow University Media Group, eds. (1980). *More Bad News*. London: Routledge and Kegan Paul.

_____., eds. (1976). *Bad News*. London: Routledge and Kegan Paul.

Glynn, C.J. and J.M. McLeod, (1985). "Implications of the Spiral of Silence Theory for Communication and Public Opinion Research." In K.R. Sanders, L.L. Kaid, and D.D. Nimmo, eds., *Political Communication Yearbook, 1984*. Carbondale: Southern Illinois University Press.

Goffman, E. (1979). *Gender Advertisements*. New York: Harper Colophon Books.

_____. (1974). *Frame Analysis: An Essay on the Organization of Experience*. New York: Harper & Row.

_____. (1963). *Stigma: Notes on the Management of Spoiled Identity*. Englewood Cliffs, NJ: Prentice-Hall.

Goldfield, D.R. and B.A. Brownell (1990). *Urban America: A History*. Boston: Houghton Mifflin.

Golding, P. (1981). "The Missing Dimensions—News Media and the Management of Social Change." In E. Katz and T. Szecsko, eds., *Mass Media and Social Change*. London: Sage Publications.

Golding, P. and P. Elliott (1979). *Making the News*. New York: Longman.

Goodhardt, G.J., A.S.C. Ehrenberg, and M.A. Collins (1975). *The Television Audience: Patterns of Viewing*. London: Saxon House.

Gottlieb, J. (1990). "Subatomic Target-Shoot Hot on Major Discovery." San Jose *Mercury-News*, October 18, 7A.

Gould, J. (1972). "TV Violence Held Unharmful to Youth." New York *Times*, January 11, 27.

Graber, D. (1987). *Processing the News*, 2d Edition. New York: Longman.

Graber, D. and Y.Y. Kim (1978). "Why John Q. Voter Did Not Learn Much from the 1976 Presidential Debates." In B.D. Ruben, ed., *Communication Yearbook Volume 2*. New Brunswick, NJ: Transaction Books.

Greenberg, B.S. (1974). "Gratifications of Television Viewing and Their Correlates for British Children." In J.G. Blumler and E. Katz, eds., *The Uses of Mass Communication: Current Perspectives on Gratifications Research*. Beverly Hills, CA: Sage Publications.

_____. (1964a). "Diffusion of News of the Kennedy Assassination." *Public Opinion Quarterly*, 28: 225–232.

_____. (1964b). "Person to Person Communication in the Diffusion of News Events." *Journalism Quarterly*, 41: 489–494.

Greenberg, B. and Parker, E., eds. (1965). *The Kennedy Assassination and the American Public*. Stanford, CA: Stanford University Press.

Grossberg, L. (1989). "The Circulation of Cultural Studies." *Critical Studies in Mass Communication*, 6: 413–421.

_____. (1983). "Cultural Studies Revisited and Revised." In M.S. Mander, ed., *Communications in Transition*. New York: Praeger.

Grossberg, L. and C. Nelson (1988). "Introduction: The Territory of Marxism." In C. Nelson and L. Grossberg, eds., *Marxism and the Interpretation of Culture*. Urbana: University of Illinois Press.

Grossberg, L., C. Nelson, and P. Treichler (1992). *Cultural Studies*. London: Routledge.

Gunter, B. (1987). *Poor Reception: Misunderstanding and Forgetting Broadcast News*. Hillsdale, NJ: Lawrence Erlbaum Associates.

Haas, C. (1979). "Charlie Haas on Advertising." *New West*, 4: 31– 59.

Habermas, J. (1989). *The Structural Transformation of the Public Sphere*. Cambridge, MA: MIT Press.

Hackett, R.A. (1984). "Decline of a Paradigm?: Bias and Objectivity in News Media Studies." *Critical Studies in Mass Communication*, 1: 229–259.

Hall, P.M. (1972). "A Symbolic Interactionist Analysis of Politics." In S. Effrat, ed., *Perspectives in Political Sociology*. New York: Bobbs-Merrill.

Hall, S. (1982). "The Rediscovery of 'Ideology': Return of the Repressed in Media Studies." In M. Gurevitch, T. Bennett, J. Curran, and J. Woollacott, eds., *Culture, Society and the Media*. New York: Methuen.

_____. (1980a). "Encoding and Decoding in the Television Discourse." In S. Hall, ed., *Culture, Media, Language*. London: Hutchinson.

_____. (1980b). "Cultural Studies: Two Paradigms." *Media, Culture and Society*, 2: 57–72.

Hall, S., D. Hobson, A. Lowe, and P. Willis, eds. (1982). *Culture, Media, Language*. London: Hutchinson.

Halloran, J.D. (1970). *The Effects of Television*. London: Panther Books.

_____. (1964/65). "Television and Violence." *The Twentieth Century*. Winter: 61–72.

Hay, J. (1989). "Advertising as a Cultural Text (Rethinking Message Analysis in a Recombinant Culture)." In B. Dervin, L. Grossberg, B.J. O'Keefe, and E. Wartella, eds., *Rethinking Communication: Volume 2, Paradigm Exemplars*. Newbury Park, CA: Sage Publications.

Hawkins, R.P., J.M. Wiemann, and S. Pingree, eds. (1988). *Advancing Communication Science: Merging Mass and Interpersonal Processes*. Newbury Park, CA: Sage Publications.

Heims, S.P. (1980). *John von Neumann and Norbert Wiener: From Mathematics to the Technologies of Life and Death*. Cambridge, MA: MIT Press.

Herald Wire Reports (1991). "Atwater Sets Aggressive Standard for U.S. Political Campaign." Grand Forks *Herald*, March 30, 6A.

Hergenhahn, B.R. (1992). *An Introduction to the History of Psychology*, 2d Edition. Belmont, CA: Wadsworth.

Herzstein, R.E. (1978). *The War That Hitler Won*. New York: Putnam.

Herzog, H. (1944). "Motivations and Gratifications of Daily Serial Listeners." In P.F. Lazarsfeld and F.N. Stanton, eds., *Radio Research, 1942–1943*. New York: Duell, Sloan and Pearce.

Heyer, P. (1988). *Communications and History: Theories of Media, Knowledge and Civilization*. New York: Greenwood Press.

Hill, R.J. and C.M. Bonjean (1964). "News Diffusion: A Test of the Regularity Hypothesis." *Journalism Quarterly*, 41: 336–342.

Hirsch, P.M. (1981a). "On Not Learning From One's Own Mistakes: A Reanalysis of Gerbner et al.'s Findings on Cultivation Analysis, Part II." *Communication Research*, 8: 3–37.

_____. (1981b). "Distinguishing Good Speculation from Bad Theory: Rejoinder to Gerbner et al." *Communication Research*, 8: 73–95.

_____. (1980). "The 'Scary World' of the Nonviewer and Other Anomalies: A Reanalysis of Gerbner et al.'s Findings on Cultivation Analysis, Part I." *Communication Research*, 7: 403–456.

Hofstetter, C.R. C. Zukin, and T.F. Buss (1978). "Political Imagery and Information in an Age of Television." *Journalism Quarterly*, 55: 562–569.

Hoggart, R. (1976). In Glasgow University Media Group, eds., *Bad News*. London: Routledge and Kegan Paul.

Horkheimer, M. (1941). "The End of Reason." In A. Arato and E. Gebhardt, eds., (1978). *The Essential Frankfurt School Reader*. New York: Urizen Books.

Hovland, C.I., I.L. Janis, and H.H. Kelley (1953). *Communication and Persuasion*. New Haven: Yale University Press.

Hovland, C.I., A.A. Lumsdaine, and F.D. Sheffield (1949). *Experiments on Mass Communication*. Princeton: Princeton University Press.

Hyman, H.H. and P.B. Sheatsley (1947). "Some Reasons Why Information Campaigns Fail." *Public Opinion Quarterly*, 11: 412–423.

Innis, H.A. (1951). *The Bias of Communication*. Toronto: University of Toronto Press.

_____. (1950). *Empire and Communication*. Toronto: University of Toronto Press.

Iyengar, S. (1991). *Is Anyone Responsible? How Television Frames Political Issues.* Chicago: University of Chicago Press.

Iyengar, S. and D.R. Kinder (1987). *News that Matters: Television and American Opinion.* Chicago: University of Chicago Press.

_____. (1986). "More Than Meets the Eye: TV News, Priming, and Public Evaluations of the President." In G. Comstock, ed., *Public Communication and Behavior,* Volume 1. New York: Academic Press.

Iyengar, S., M.D. Peters, and D.R. Kinder (1982). "Experimental Demonstrations of the 'Not-So-Minimal' Consequences of Television News Programs." *American Political Science Review,* 76: 848–858.

Jacoby, J. and W.D. Hoyer (1982). "Viewer Miscomprehension of Televised Communication: Selected Findings." *Journal of Marketing,* 46: 12–26.

Jacoby, J., W.D. Hoyer, and D.A. Sheluga (1980). *Miscomprehension of Televised Communications.* New York: The Educational Foundation of the American Association of Advertising Agencies.

Jamieson, K.H. (1989). "Spotlight on Scholarship: Jamieson, Schudson, and Gitlin on Political Television." Annual Convention of the Speech Communication Association, San Francisco, CA.

_____. (1988). *Eloquence in an Electronic Age: The Transformation of Political Speechmaking.* New York: Oxford University Press.

Janis, I.L. C.I. Hovland, P.B. Field, H. Linton, E. Graham, A.R. Cohen, D. Rife, R.P. Abelson, G.S. Lesser, and B.T. King (1959). *Personality and Persuasibility.* New Haven: Yale University Press.

Jasinski, J. and D.K. Davis (1990). "Political Communication and Politics: A Theory of Public Culture." Paper presented to the Political Communication Division of the American Political Science Association, San Francisco, CA.

Jay, M. (1984). *Adorno.* Cambridge, MA: Harvard University Press.

Jensen, K.B. (1987). "Qualitative Audience Research: Toward an Integrative Approach to Reception." *Critical Studies in Mass Communication,* 4: 21–36.

Jhally, S., ed. (1987). *The Codes of Advertising: Fetishism and the Political Economy of Meaning in the Consumer Society.* New York: St. Martin's Press.

Johnstone, J.W.C., E.J. Slawski, and W.W. Bowman (1976). *The News People: A Sociological Portrait of American Journalists and Their Work.* Urbana: University of Illinois Press.

Journal of Communication. (1983). Special Issue: Ferment in the Field. 33.

Judicial Council of California. (1986). *1986 Annual Report to the Governor and Legislature.* San Francisco: State of California.

Kaplan, A. (1964). *The Conduct of Inquiry.* New York: Harper and Row.

Katz, E. (1983). "Publicity and Pluralistic Ignorance: Notes on 'The Spiral of Silence.'" In E. Wartella and D.C. Whitney, eds., *Mass Communication Review Yearbook 4.* Beverly Hills, CA: Sage Publications.

_____. (1977). *Social Research on Broadcasting: Proposals For Further Development.* London: British Broadcasting Corporation.

_____. (1975). "The Mass Communication of Knowledge." In *Getting the Message Across.* Paris: UNESCO.

_____. (1957). "The Two-Step Flow of Mass Communication." *Public Opinion Quarterly*, 21: 61–78.

Katz, E., H. Adoni, and P. Parness (1977). "Remembering the News: What the Picture Adds to Recall." *Journalism Quarterly*, 54: 231–239.

Katz, E., J.G. Blumler, and M. Gurevitch (1974). "Utilization of Mass Communication by the Individual." In J.G. Blumler and E. Katz, eds., *The Uses of Mass Communications: Current Perspectives on Gratifications Research*. Beverly Hills, CA: Sage Publications.

Katz, E., M. Gurevitch, and H. Haas (1973). "On the Use of the Mass Media for Important Things." *American Sociological Review*, 38: 164–181.

Katz, E. and P.F. Lazarsfeld (1955). *Personal Influence: The Part Played by People in the Flow of Communications*. New York: Free Press.

Kerlinger, F.N. (1964). *Foundations of Behavioral Research*. New York: Holt, Rinehart, and Winston.

Key, V.O. (1961). *Public Opinion and American Democracy*. New York: Alfred A. Knopf.

Kippax, S. and J.P. Murray (1980). "Using the Mass Media: Need Gratification and Perceived Utility." *Communication Research*, 7: 335–360.

Klapper, J.T. (1960). *The Effects of Mass Communication*. New York: Free Press.

_____. (1949). *The Effects of Mass Media*. New York: Columbia University Bureau of Applied Social Research.

Klein, A. (1978). "How Telecast's Organization Affects Viewer Retention." *Journalism Quarterly*, 55: 231–239.

Kornhauser, A. and P.F. Lazarsfeld (1935). "The Technique of Market Research from the Standpoint of a Psychologist." *Institute of Management*, 16: 3–15, 19–21.

Kornhauser, W. (1959). *The Politics of Mass Society*. New York: Free Press.

Kraus, S. (1962). *The Great Debates*. Bloomington: Indiana University Press.

Kraus, S. and D.K. Davis (1976). *The Effects of Mass Communication on Political Behavior*. University Park: Pennsylvania State University Press.

Kreiling, A. (1984). "Television in American Ideological Hopes and Fears." In W.D. Rowland, Jr. and B. Watkins, eds., *Interpreting Television: Current Research Perspectives*. Beverly Hills, CA: Sage Publications.

Krippendorf, K. (1993). "The Past of Communication's Hoped-for Future." *Journal of Communication*, 43: 34–44.

_____. (1986). *Information Theory: Structural Models for Qualitative Data*. Newbury Park, CA: Sage Publications.

Kuhn, T. (1970). *The Structure of Scientific Revolutions*, 2d Edition. Chicago: University of Chicago Press.

LaMay, C., M. FitzSimon and J. Sahadi, eds. (1991). *The Media at War: The Press and the Persian Gulf Conflict*. New York: Gannett Foundation.

Lang, K. (1979). "The Critical Functions of Empirical Communication Research: Observations on German-American influences." *Media, Culture, and Society*, 1: 83–96.

Lang, K. and G.E. Lang (1983). *The Battle For Public Opinion: The President, the Press, and the Polls During Watergate*. New York: Columbia University Press.

_____. (1968). *Politics and Television*. Chicago: Quadrangle Books.

Lanigan, R.L. (1988). *Phenomenology of Communication: Merleau-Ponty's Thematics in Communicology and Semiology*. Pittsburgh, PA: Duquesne University Press.

Larsen, O.N. and R.J. Hill (1954). "Mass Media and Interpersonal Communication in the Diffusion of a News Event." *American Sociological Review*, 19: 426–433.

Lasswell, H.D. (1949). "The Structure and Function of Communication in Society." In W.S. Schramm, ed., *Mass Communication*. Urbana: University of Illinois Press.

_____. (1948). "The Structure and Function of Communication in Society." In L. Bryson, ed., *The Communication of Ideas*. New York: Harper and Brothers.

_____. (1934). *World Politics and Personal Insecurity*. Chicago: University of Chicago Press.

_____. (1927). *Propaganda Technique in the World War*. New York: Alfred A. Knopf.

Lazarsfeld, P.F. (1969). "An Episode in the History of Social Research: A Memoir." In D. Fleming and B. Bailyn, eds., *The Intellectual Migration: Europe and America, 1930–1960*. Cambridge, MA: The Belknap Press of Harvard University.

_____. (1941). "Remarks on Administrative and Critical Communication Research." *Studies in Philosophy and Social Science*, 9: 2–16.

Lazarsfeld, P.F., B. Berelson, and H. Gaudet (1944). *The People's Choice: How the Voter Makes Up His Mind in a Presidential Campaign*. New York: Duell, Sloan and Pearce.

Lazarsfeld, P. and R.K. Merton (1948). "Mass Communication, Popular Taste and Organized Social Action." In L. Bryson, ed., *Communication of Ideas*. New York: Harper & Brothers.

Lazarsfeld, P. and F.N. Stanton, eds. (1942). *Radio Research, 1941*. New York: Duell, Sloan and Pearce.

Leedy, P.D. (1985). *Practical Research: Planning and Design*. New York: Macmillan.

_____. (1981). *How to Read Research and Understand It*. New York: Macmillan.

Lemert, J.B. (1981). *Does Mass Communication Change Public Opinion After All? A New Approach to Effects Analysis*. Chicago: Nelson-Hall.

Lerner, D. (1958). *The Passing of Traditional Society: Modernizing the Middle East*. New York: Free Press.

Levy, M. and S. Windahl (1985). "The Concept of Audience Activity." In K.E. Rosengren, L.A. Wenner, and P. Palmgreen, eds., *Media Gratifications Research: Current Perspectives*. Beverly Hills, CA: Sage Publications.

Liebert, R.M., J.N. Sprafkin, and E.S. Davidson (1982). *The Early Window: Effects of Television on Children and Youth*. New York: Pergamon Press.

Linz, D. and E. Donnerstein (1988). "The Methods and Merits of Pornography Research." *Journal of Communication*, 38: 180–184.

Lippmann, W. (1921). *Public Opinion*. New York: Macmillan.

Littlejohn, S.W. (1989). *Theories of Human Communication*. Belmont, CA: Wadsworth.

Long, E. (1989). "Feminism and Cultural Studies." *Critical Studies in Mass Communication*, 6: 427–435.

Lounsbury, J.W., E. Sundstrom, and R.C.DeVault (1979). "Moderating Effects of Respondent Knowledge in Public Opinion Research." *Journal of Applied Psychology*, 64: 558–563.

Lowenthal, L. and N. Guterman (1949). *Prophets of Deceit*. New York: Harper & Brothers.

Lowery, S.A. and M.L. DeFleur (1988). *Milestones in Mass Communication Research*. White Plains, NY: Longman.

Lund, F.H. (1925). "The Psychology of Belief: IV. The Law of Primacy in Persuasion." *Journal of Abnormal Social Psychology*, 20: 183–191.

Maccoby, E.E. (1954). "Why Do Children Watch Television?" *Public Opinion Quarterly*, 18: 239–244.

MacKuen, M.B. and S.L. Coombs (1981). *More Than News: Media Power in Public Affairs*. Beverly Hills, CA: Sage Publications.

Malamuth, N.M. and E. Donnerstein (1982). "The Effects of Aggressive-Pornographic Mass Media Stimuli." In L. Berkowitz, ed., *Advances in Experimental Social Psychology, v. 15*. New York: Academic Press.

Manheim, J. B. (1976). "Can Democracy Survive Television?" *Journal of Communication*, 26: 84–90.

Marcus, G.E. and M.M. Fischer (1986). *Anthropology as Cultural Critique: An Experimental Movement in the Human Sciences*. Chicago: University of Chicago Press.

Marcuse, H. (1978). *An Essay on Liberation*. Boston, Beacon Press.

————. (1969). *The Aesthetic Dimension*. Boston, Beacon Press.

————. (1941). "Some Social Implications of Modern Technology." In A. Arato and E. Gebhardt, eds., (1978). *The Essential Frankfurt School Reader*. New York: Urizen Books.

Martindale, D. (1960). *The Nature and Types of Sociological Theory*. Boston: Houghton-Mifflin.

Matson, F.M. (1964). *The Broken Image: Man, Science and Society*. New York: George Braziller.

Matthews, D. (1978). "'Winnowing': The News Media and the 1976 Presidential Nomination." In J.D. Barber, ed., *Race for the Presidency: The Media and the Nominating Process*. Englewood Cliffs, NJ: Prentice Hall.

McAnany, E.G. (1988). "Wilbur Schramm, 1907–1987: Roots of the Past, Seeds of the Present." *Journal of Communication*, 38: 109–122.

McCombs, M.E. (1981). "The Agenda-Setting Approach." In D.D. Nimmo and K.R. Sanders, eds., *Handbook of Political Communication*. Beverly Hills, CA: Sage Publications.

McCombs, M.E. and D.L. Shaw (1972). "The Agenda-Setting Function of Mass Media." *Public Opinion Quarterly*, 36: 176–187.

McCombs, M.E. and D.H. Weaver (1985). "Toward a Merger of Gratifications and Agenda-Setting Research." In K.E. Rosengren, L.A. Wenner, and P. Palmgreen, eds., *Media Gratifications Research: Current Perspectives*. Beverly Hills, CA: Sage Publications.

McIntyre, J.S. (1987). "Repositioning a Landmark: The Hutchins Commission and Freedom of the Press." *Critical Studies in Mass Communication*, 4: 95–135.

McLeod, J.M. and L.B. Becker (1981). "The Uses and Gratifications Approach." In D.D. Nimmo and K.R. Sanders, eds., *Handbook of Political Communication*. Beverly Hills, CA: Sage Publications.

McLuhan, M. (1964). *Understanding Media: The Extensions of Man*. New York: McGraw-Hill.

_____. (1951). *The Mechanical Bride*. New York: Vanguard Press.

McQuail, D. (1987). *Mass Communication Theory: An Introduction*. Beverly Hills, CA: Sage Publications.

McQuail, D., J.G. Blumler, and J. Brown (1972). "The Television Audience: A Revised Perspective." In D. McQuail, ed., *Sociology of Mass Communication*. Harmondsworth, England: Penguin.

McQuail, D. and S. Windahl (1982). *Communication Models*. New York: Longman.

Mead, G.H. (1934). *Mind, Self and Society*. Chicago: University of Chicago Press.

Medved, M. (1992). *Hollywood vs. America: Popular Culture and the War on Traditional Values*. New York: HarperCollins.

Melody, W. (1973). *Children's Television: The Economics of Exploitation*. New Haven: Yale University Press.

Mendelsohn, H. (1966). *Mass Entertainment*. New Haven, CT: College and University Press.

Merrill, J.C. (1974). *The Imperative of Freedom*. New York: Hastings House.

Merten, K. (1984). "Some Silence in the Spiral of Silence." In K.R. Sanders, L.L. Kaid, and D.D. Nimmo, eds., *Political Communication Yearbook, 1984*. Carbondale: Southern Illinois University Press.

Merton, R.K. (1967). *On Theoretical Sociology*. New York: Free Press.

_____ (1949). *Social Theory and Social Structure*. Glencoe, IL: Free Press.

Merton, R.K., M. Fisk, and A. Curtis, (1946). *Mass Persuasion: The Social Psychology of a War Bond Drive*. New York: Harper & Brothers.

Meyrowitz, J. (1985). *No Sense of Place: The Impact of Electronic Media on Social Behavior*. New York: Oxford University Press.

Milgram, S. (1963). "Behavioral Study of Obedience." *Journal of Abnormal and Social Psychology*, 67: 371–378.

Miller, G.R. and M. Burgoon (1978). "Persuasion Research: Review and Commentary." In B.D. Ruben, ed., *Communication Yearbook 2*. New Brunswick, NJ: Transaction Books.

Miller, N.E. and J. Dollard (1941). *Social Learning and Imitation*. New Haven: Yale University Press.

Mills, C.W. (1959). *The Sociological Imagination*. New York: Oxford University Press.

_____. (1957). *The Power Elite*. New York: Oxford University Press.

Morgan, M. and N. Signorielli (1990). "Cultivation Analysis: Conceptualization and Methodology." In N. Signorielli and M. Morgan, eds., *Cultivation Analysis: New Directions in Media Effects Research*. Newbury Park, CA: Sage Publications.

Morley, D. (1980a). "Subjects, Readers, Tests." In S. Hall, ed., *Culture, Media, Language*. London: Hutchinson.

————. (1980b). *The "Nationwide" Audience: Structure and Decoding*. London: British Film Institute.

Mosco, V. and A. Herman (1981). "Critical Theory and Electronic Media." *Theory and Society*, 10: 869–896.

Mott, F.L. (1941). *American Journalism*. New York: Macmillan.

Mumford, L. (1975). *Findings and Keepings: Analects for an Autobiography*. New York: Harcourt, Brace, Jovanovich.

Murdock, G. (1989a). "Critical Activity and Audience Activity." In B. Dervin, L. Grossberg, B.J. O'Keefe, and E. Wartella, eds., *Rethinking Communication: Volume 2, Paradigm Exemplars*. Newbury Park, CA: Sage Publications.

————. (1989b). "Critical Studies: Missing Links." *Critical Studies in Mass Communication*, 6: 436–440.

Nelson, C. and L. Grossberg (1988). *Marxism and the Interpretation of Culture*. Chicago: University of Illinois Press.

Neuman, W.R. (1986). *The Paradox of Mass Politics: Knowledge and Opinion in the American Electorate*. Cambridge, MA: Harvard University Press.

————. (1976). "Patterns of Recall Among Television News Viewers." *Public Opinion Quarterly*, 40: 115–123.

Newcomb, H. (1987). *Television: The Critical View*. New York: Oxford University Press.

————. (1984). "On the Dialogic Aspects of Mass Communication." *Critical Studies in Mass Communication*, 1: 34–50.

————. (1978). "Assessing the Violence Profile Studies of Gerbner and Gross: A Humanistic Critique and Suggestion." *Communication Research*, 5: 264–283.

————. (1976). *TV: The Most Popular Art*. New York: Oxford University Press.

Newcomb, H. and P.M. Hirsch (1983). "Television as a Cultural Forum: Implications for Research." *Quarterly Review of Film*, 8: 45–55.

Nie, N.H., S. Verba, and J.R. Petrocik (1976). *The Changing American Voter*. Cambridge, MA: Harvard University Press.

Nimmo, D. and J.E. Coombs (1985). *Nightly Horrors*. Knoxville: University of Tennessee Press.

————. (1983). *Mediated Political Realities*. New York: Longman.

Nimmo, D.D. and K.R. Sanders, eds. (1981). *Handbook of Political Communication*. Beverly Hills, CA: Sage Publications.

Ninety-Second Congress. (1972). *Hearings Before the Subcommittee on Communications on the Surgeon General's Report by the Scientific Advisory Committee on Television and Social Behavior*. Washington, D.C.: U.S. Government.

Noelle-Neumann, E. (1985). "The Spiral of Silence: A Response." In K.R. Sanders, L.L. Kaid, and D.D. Nimmo, eds., *Political Communication Yearbook, 1984*. Carbondale: Southern Illinois University Press.

————. (1984). *The Spiral of Silence: Our Social Skin*. Chicago: University of Chicago Press.

_____. (1974). "The Spiral of Silence: A Theory of Public Opinion." *Journal of Communication*, 24: 43–51.

_____. (1973). "Return to the Concept of the Powerful Mass Media." *Studies of Broadcasting*, 9: 68–105.

Nowak, K. (1977). "From Information Gaps to Communication Potential." In M. Berg, P. Hemanus, J. Ekecrantz, F. Mortensen, and P. Sepstrup, eds., *Current Theories in Scandinavian Mass Communication Research*. Grenaa, Denmark: GMT.

O'Connor, A. (1989). "The Problem of American Cultural Studies." *Critical Studies in Mass Communication*, 6: 405–413.

O'Neill, S. (1992). "Get the Hell Out of Here!" *Columbia Journalism Review*, 31: 23–25.

Ortony, A. (1978). "Remembering, Understanding and Representation." *Cognitive Science*, 2: 53–69.

Orwell, G. (1960). *1984*. New York: Signet Books. (Reprint of Harcourt Brace Jovanovich, 1949).

Paisley, W. (1984). "Communication in the Communication Sciences." In B. Dervin and M.J. Voigt, eds., *Progress in Communication Sciences*, Volume V. Norwood, NJ: Ablex Publishing.

Paivio, A. (1971). *Imagery and Verbal Processes*. New York: Rinehart and Winston.

Palentz, D.L. and R.M. Entman (1981). *Media, Power, Politics*. New York: Free Press.

Palmgreen, P., L.A. Wenner, and J.D. Rayburn (1980). "Relations Between Gratifications Sought and Obtained: A Study of Television News." *Communication Research*, 7: 161–192.

Palmgreen, P., L.A. Wenner, and K.E. Rosengren (1985). "Uses and Gratifications Research: The Past Ten Years." In K.E. Rosengren, L.A. Wenner, and P. Palmgreen, eds., *Media Gratifications Research: Current Perspectives*. Beverly Hills, CA: Sage Publications.

Park, R. (1967). "News as a Form of Knowledge." In R.H. Turner, ed., *On Social Control and Collective behavior*. Chicago: University of Chicago Press. (Reprint of 1940 article in *American Journal of Sociology* 45: 669–686.)

Patterson, T.E. (1982). "Television and Election Strategy." In G. Benjamin, ed., *The Communications Revolution in Politics*. New York: The Academy of Political Science.

_____. (1980). *The Mass Media Election: How Americans Choose Their President*. New York: Praeger.

Patterson, T.E. and R.D. McClure (1976). *The Unseeing Eye: The Myth of Television Power in National Elections*. New York: G.P. Putnam.

Peck, J. (1989). "The Power of Media and the Creation of Meaning: A Survey of Approaches to Media Analysis." In B. Dervin and M.J. Voigt, eds., *Progress in Communication Sciences*, Volume IX. Norwood, NJ: Ablex Publishing.

Peirce, C. (1955). In J. Buchler, ed., *Philosophical Writings of Peirce*. New York: Dover Press.

Peters, J.D. (1989). "Satan and Savior: Mass Communication in Progressive Thought." *Critical Studies in Mass Communication*, 6: 247–263.

Peterson, R.C. and L.L. Thurstone (1933). *Motion Pictures and the Social Attitudes of Children*. New York: Macmillan.

Pine, R.C. (1989). *Science and the Human Prospect*. Belmont, CA: Wadsworth.

Pingree, S., J.M. Wiemann, and R.P. Hawkins (1988). "Editors' Introduction: Toward Conceptual Synthesis." In R.P. Hawkins, J.M. Wiemann, and S. Pingree, eds., *Advancing Communication Science: Merging Mass and Interpersonal Processes*. Newbury Park, CA: Sage Publications.

Postman, N. (1985). *Amusing Ourselves to Death: Public Discourse in the Age of Show Business*. New York: Penguin Books.

Powers, R. (1977a). "Eyewitless News." *Columbia Journalism Review*, 20: 17–23.

————. (1977b). *The Newscasters: The News Business as Show Business*. New York: St. Martin's Press.

Preston, M.I. (1941). "Children's Reactions to Movie Horrors and Radio Crime." *Journal of Pediatrics*, 19: 147–168.

Protess, D.L., F.L. Cook, J.C. Doppelt, J.S. Ettema, M.T. Gordon, D.R. Leff, and P. Miller (1991). *The Journalism of Outrage*. New York: The Guilford Press.

Radway, J. (1986). "Identifying Ideological Seams: Mass Culture, Analytical Method, and Political Practice." *Communication*, 9: 93–123.

————. (1984). *Reading the Romance: Women, Patriarchy, and Popular Literature*. Chapel Hill: University of North Carolina Press.

Rakow, L.F. (1989). "Feminist Studies: The Next Stage." *Critical Studies In Mass Communication*, 6: 209–213.

Real, M.R. (1989). *Super Media: A Cultural Studies Approach*. London: Sage Publications.

————. (1977). *Mass-Mediated Culture*. Englewood Cliffs, NJ: Prentice-Hall.

Rice, R.E. and C. Atkin (1989). *Public Communication Campaigns*, 2d Edition Beverly Hills, CA: Sage Publications.

Ritzer, G. (1983). *Sociological Theory*. New York: Alfred A. Knopf.

Robinson, J.P. (1972). "Mass Communication and Information Diffusion." In F.G. Kline and P.J. Tichenor, eds., *Current Perspectives in Mass Communications Research*. Beverly Hills, CA: Sage Publications.

Robinson, J.P. and D.K. Davis (1990). "Television News and the Informed Public: Not the Main Source." *Journal of Communication*, 40: 106–119.

Robinson, J.P. and M. Levy, with D.K. Davis, eds. (1986). *The Main Source: Learning From Television News*. Newbury Park, CA: Sage Publications.

Robinson, J.P., H. Sahin, and D.K. Davis (1982). "Television Journalists and Their Audiences." In J. Ettema and D.C. Whitney, eds., *Individuals in Mass Media Organizations: Creativity and Constraints*. Beverly Hills, CA: Sage Publications.

Robinson, M.J. (1976). "Public Affairs Television and the Growth of Political Malaise." *American Political Science Review*, 70: 409–432.

Robinson, M.J. and M.A. Sheehan (1983). *Over the Wire and on TV: CBS and UPI in Campaign '80*. New York: Russell Sage Foundation.

Rogers, E.M. (1986). "History of Communication Science." In E.M. Rogers, ed., *Communication Technology: The New Media in Society*. New York: Free Press.

————. (1985). "The Empirical and Critical Schools of Communication Research." In E.M. Rogers and F. Balle, eds., *The Media Revolution in America and Western Europe* Norwood, NJ: Ablex Publishing.

_____. (1983). *Diffusion of Innovations*. New York: Free Press.

_____. (1976). "Communications and Development: The Passing of the Dominant Paradigm." *Communication Research*, 3: 121– 133.

Rogers, E.M., J.W. Dearing, and D. Bergman (1993). "The Anatomy of Agenda-Setting Research" *Journal of Communication*, 43: 68– 84.

Rogow, A.A. (1969). *Politics, Personality, and Social Science in the Twentieth Century: Essays in Honor of Harold D. Lasswell*. Chicago: University of Chicago Press.

Roper, B.W. (1984). *Public Perceptions of Television and Other Mass Media*. New York: Television Information Office.

Roshco, B. (1975). *Newsmaking*. Chicago: University of Chicago Press.

Rosnow, R.L. and E.J. Robinson (1967). *Experiments in Persuasion*. New York: Academic Press.

Rowland, W.D. (1983). *The Politics of TV Violence*. Beverly Hills, CA: Sage Publications.

Rubin, A. (1983). "Television Uses and Gratifications: The Interaction of Viewing Patterns and Motivations." *Journal of Broadcasting*, 27: 37–51.

Rubinstein, E., G. Comstock, and J. Murray, eds., (1972). *Television and Social Behavior*. Washington, D.C.: U.S. Government Printing Office.

Sabato, L.J. (1981). *The Rise of Political Consultants*. New York: Basic Books.

Sahin, H., D.K. Davis, and J.P. Robinson (1982). "Television as a Source of International News: What Gets Across and What Doesn't." In W.C. Adams, ed., *Television Coverage of International Affairs*. Norwood, NJ: Ablex Publishing Corporation.

_____. (1981). "Improving the TV News." *Irish Broadcasting Review*, 11, 50–55.

Salmon, C.T. and F.G. Kline (1985). "The Spiral of Silence Ten Years Later: An Examination and Evaluation." In K.R. Sanders, L.L. Kaid, and D.D. Nimmo, ed., *Political Communication Yearbook, 1984*. Carbondale: Southern Illinois University Press.

Salomon, G. (1979). *Interaction of Media, Cognition, and Learning*. San Francisco: Jossey-Bass.

Schank, R.C. and R.P. Abelson (1977). *Scripts, Plans, Goals and Understanding: An Inquiry Into Human Knowledge Structures*. Hillsdale, NJ: Lawrence Erlbaum Associates.

Schlesinger, P. (1978). *Putting Reality Together*. London: Constable.

Schramm, W. (1988). *The Story of Human Communication: Cave Painting to Microchip*. New York: Harper & Row.

_____. (1964). *Mass Media and National Development: The Role of Information in the Developing Countries*. Paris: UNESCO Press.

_____. (1955). *Four Working Papers on Propaganda Theory*. Urbana: University of Illinois Press.

_____. (1954). *The Process and Effects of Mass Communication*. Urbana: University of Illinois Press.

_____. (1949). *Mass Communications*. Urbana: University of Illinois Press.

Schramm, W. and D. Lerner, eds. (1976). *Communication and Change: The Last Ten Years— and the Next*. Honolulu: University Press of Hawaii.

Schramm, W., J. Lyle, and E. Parker (1961). *Television in the Lives of Our Children*. Stanford, CA: Stanford University Press.

Schroder, K. C. (1987). "Convergence of Antagonistic Traditions? The Case of Audience Research." *European Journal of Communication*, 2: 7–31.

Schudson, M. (1978). *Discovering the News: A Social History of American Newspapers*. New York: Basic Books.

Schutz, A. (1970). *On Phenomenology and Social Relations*. Chicago: University of Chicago Press.

_____. (1967). *The Phenomenology of the Social World*. Evanston, IL: Northwestern University Press.

Schwichtenberg, C. (1989). "Feminist Cultural Studies." *Critical Studies In Mass Communication*, 6: 202–208.

Severin, W.J. and J.W. Tankard (1982). *Communication Theories: Origins, Methods, Uses*. New York: Hastings House.

Shannon, C. and W. Weaver (1949). *The Mathematical Theory of Communication*. Urbana: University of Illinois Press.

Shibutani, T. (1966). *Improvised News: A Sociological Study of Rumor*. New York: Bobbs-Merrill.

Shiller, D. (1981). *Objectivity and the News: The Public and the Rise of Commercial Journalism*. Philadelphia: University of Pennsylvania Press.

Siebert, F.S., T. Peterson, and W. Schramm (1956). *Four Theories of the Press*. Urbana: University of Illinois Press.

Siegel, A.E. (1956). "Film-Mediated Fantasy Aggression and Strength of Aggressive Drive." *Child Development*, 27: 365–378.

Simon, H.A. (1981). *The Sciences of the Artificial*. Cambridge, MA: The MIT Press.

Singer, J.L. and D.G. Singer (1983). "Implications of Childhood Television Viewing for Cognition, Imagination, and Emotion." In J. Bryant and D.R. Anderson , eds., *Children's Understanding of Television: Research on Attention and Comprehension*. New York: Academic Press.

Smillie, D. (1991). "Assessing the Press." In C. LaMay, M. FitzSimon, and J. Sahadi, eds., *The Media at War: The Press and the Persian Gulf Conflict*. New York: Gannett Foundation.

Smith, A. (1973). *The Shadow in the Cave: A Study of the Relationship Between the Broadcaster, His Audience and the State*. London: George Allen and Unwin.

Smith, R.R. (1979). "Mythic Elements in Television News." *Journal of Communication*. 29: 75–84.

Smythe, D.W. and T.V. Dinh (1983). "On Critical and Administrative Research: A New Critical Analysis." *Journal of Communication*, 31: 117–127.

Solomon, M.R. (1983). "The Role of Products as Social Stimuli: A Symbolic Interactionism Perspective." *Journal of Consumer Research*, 10: 319–329.

Sproule, J.M. (1987). "Propaganda Studies in American Social Science: The Rise and Fall of the Critical Paradigm." *Quarterly Journal of Speech*, 73: 60–78.

Stauffer, J., R. Frost, and W. Rybolt (1983). "The Attention Factor in Recalling Network Television News." *Journal of Communication*, 33: 29–37.

————. (1981). "Recall and Learning from Broadcast News: Is Print Better?" *Journal of Broadcasting*, 25: 253–262.

————. (1978). "Literacy, Illiteracy and Learning From Television News." *Communication Research*, 5: 211–232.

Steiner, L. (1988). "Oppositional Decoding as an Act of Resistance." *Critical Studies in Mass Communication*, 5: 1–15.

Stephenson, W. (1967). *Play Theory of Mass Communication*. Chicago: University of Chicago Press.

Sterling, C.H. and J.M. Kittross (1990). *Stay Tuned: A Concise History of American Broadcasting*. Belmont, CA: Wadsworth.

Stouffer, S.A., E.A. Suchman, L.C. DeVinney, S.A. Star, and R.M. Williams (1949). *The American Soldier: Adjustment During Army Life*, Volume I. Princeton: Princeton University Press.

Tannenbaum, P.H. (1954). "Effect of Serial Position on Recall of Radio News Stories." *Journalism Quarterly*, 31: 319–323.

Tichenor, P.J., G.A. Donohue, and C.N. Olien (1980). *Community Conflict and the Press*. Beverly Hills, CA: Sage Publications.

————. (1970). "Mass Media Flow and Differential Growth of Knowledge." *Public Opinion Quarterly*, 34: 159–170.

Trenaman, J.M. (1967). *Communication and Comprehension*. London: Longmans.

Tuchman, G. (1978). *Making News: A Study in the Construction of Reality*. New York: Free Press.

————. (1976). "Telling Stories." *Journal of Communication*, 26: 93–97.

Tunstall, J. (1983). "The Trouble with U.S. Communication Research." *Journal of Communication*, 33: 2–95.

————. (1977). *The Media are American: Anglo-American Media in the World*. New York: Columbia University Press.

Turow, J. (1983). "Local Television: Producing Soft News." *Journal of Communication*, 33: 111–123.

Twitchell, J.B. (1992). *Carnival Culture: The Trashing of Taste in America*. New York: Columbia University Press.

van Dijk, T.A. (1983). "Discourse Analysis: Its Development and Application to the Structure of News." *Journal of Communication*, 33: 20–43.

Vaughn, R. (1972). *Only Victims: A Study of Show Business Blacklisting*. New York: Putnam.

Vincent, R., B. Crow, and D.K. Davis (1989). "When Technology Fails: The Drama of Airline Crashes in Network TV News." *Journalism Monographs*, No. 117.

Wade, S. and W. Schramm (1969). "The Mass Media as Sources of Public Affairs, Science, and Health information." *Public Opinion Quarterly*, 33: 197–209.

Wartella, E. and B. Reeves (1985). "Historical Trends in Research on Children and the Media 1900–1960." *Journal of Communication*, 35: 118–133.

Watzlawick, P., J. Weakland, and R. Fisch (1947). *Change: Principles of Problem Formation and Problem Resolution*. New York: Norton.

Westin, A. (1982). *Newswatch: How TV Decides the News*. New York: Simon and Schuster.

Westley, B.H. and M. MacLean (1957). "A Conceptual Model for Mass Communication Research." *Journalism Quarterly*, 34: 31–38.

on p¹⁹⁷ — White, R.W. (1972). *The Enterprise of Living: Growth and Organization in Personality*. New York: Holt, Rinehart and Winston.

Wiener, N. (1961). *Cybernetics*, 2d Edition Cambridge, MA: The MIT Press.

_____. (1954). *The Human Use of Human Beings: Cybernetics and Society*. Garden City, NY: Doubleday Anchor.

_____. (1948). *Cybernetics, or Control and Communication in the Animal and the Machine*. Cambridge, MA: MIT Press.

Wimmer, R.D. and J.R. Dominick (1983). *Mass Media Research*. Belmont, CA: Wadsworth Publishing Company.

Windhal, S. (1981). "Uses and Gratifications at the Crossroads." In G.C. Wilhoit and H. De Bock, eds., *Mass Communication Review Yearbook*. Beverly Hills, CA: Sage Publications.

Woodall, G. (1986). "Information Processing." In J.P. Robinson and M. Levy, eds., *The Main Source: Learning from Television News*. Beverly Hills, CA: Sage Publications.

Woodall, G., D.K. Davis, and H. Sahin (1983). "From the Boobtube to the Black Box: Television News Comprehension from an Information Processing Perspective." *Journal of Broadcasting*, 27: 1–23.

Wright, C.R. (1986). *Mass Communication: A Sociological Perspective*, 3d Edition. New York: Random House.

_____. (1974). "Functional Analysis and Mass Communication Revisited." In J.G. Blumler and E. Katz, eds., *The Uses of Mass Communications: Current Perspectives on Gratifications Research*. Beverly Hills, CA: Sage Publications.

Wright, J.D. (1976). *The Dissent of the Governed: Alienation and Democracy in America*. New York: Academic Press.

Zajonc, R. (1954). "Some Effects of the 'Space' Serials." *Public Opinion Quarterly*, 18: 367–374.

Zillman, D. and J. Bryant (1986). "Exploring the Entertainment Experience." In J. Bryant and D. Zillman, eds., *Perspectives on Message Effects*. Hillsdale, NJ: Lawrence Erlbaum Associates.

_____. (1982). "Pornography, Sexual Callousness, and the Trivialization of Rape." *Journal of Communication*, 32: 10–21.

Zucker, H.G. (1978). "The Variable Nature of News Media Influence." In B.D. Rubin, ed., *Communication Yearbook 2*. New Brunswick, NJ: Transaction Books.

Zukin, C. (1981). "Mass Communication and Public Opinion." In D.D. Nimmo and K.R. Sanders, eds., *Handbook of Political Communication*. Beverly Hills, CA: Sage Publications.

Index

Name -- description; major points; how it is related to
Scholars associated w/ it   other theories; mjr similarities
strengths → When (begin, grow in popularity, decline)   or differences
wkns   w/ other
        Why (was/is it popular; it is still pop. or has declined)   theories